WASHINGTON, D.C.

Lorette Pierson

Editorial *Series Director:* Claude Morneau; *Project Supervisor:* Pascale Couture; *Editor:* Claude Morneau.

Research and Composition *Author:* Lorette Pierson.

Production *Design:* Patrick Farei (Atoll Direction); *Proofreading:* Tara Salman; *Translation:* Tracy Kendrick, Sarah Kresh, Danielle Gauthier, *Cartography:* André Duchesne, Patrick Thivièrge (Assistant), Marc Rigole, Isabelle Lalonde; *Layout:* Tara Salman, Stéphane G. Marceau.

Illustrations *Cover Photo:* Robert Llewellyn (SuperStock); *Interior Photos:* Lorette Pierson, Bob Burch (Reflexion); *Chapter Headings:* Jennifer McMorran; *Drawings:* Lorette Pierson.

Thanks to Lisa Holland (Convention and Visitors Association, Washington), Oriane Lemaire, Catherine Boivin, Jacqueline Pierson, Juliette et Charlotte, SODEC and the Department of Canadian Heritage for their financial Support.

DISTRIBUTORS

AUSTRALIA: Little Hills Press, 11/37-43 Alexander St., Crows Nest NSW 2065, ☎ (612) 437-6995, Fax: (612) 438-5762

BELGIUM AND LUXEMBOURG: Vander, Vrijwilligerlaan 321, B-1150 Brussel, ☎ (02) 762 98 04, Fax: (02) 762 06 62

CANADA: Ulysses Books & Maps, 4176 Saint-Denis, Montréal, Québec, H2W 2M5 ☎ (514) 843-9882, ext.2232, 800-748-9171, Fax: 514-843-9448, www.ulysses.ca

GERMANY AND AUSTRIA: Brettschneider, Fernreisebedarf, Feldfirchner Strasse 2 D-85551 Heimstetten, München, ☎ 89-99 02 03 30, Fax: 89-99 02 03 31

GREAT BRITAIN AND IRELAND: World Leisure Marketing, Unit 11, Newmarket Court Newmartket Drive, Derby DE24 8NW, ☎ 1 332 57 37 37, Fax: 1 332 57 33 99

ITALY: Centro Cartografico del Riccio, Via di Soffiano 164/A, 50143 Firenze ☎ (055) 71 33 33, Fax: (055) 71 63 50

NETHERLANDS: Nilsson & Lamm, Pampuslaan 212-214, 1380 AD Weesp (NL) ☎ 0294-494949, Fax: 0294-494455, E-mail: nilam@euronet.nl

PORTUGAL: Dinapress, Lg. Dr. Antonio de Sousa de Macedo, 2, Lisboa 1200 ☎ (1) 395 52 70, Fax: (1) 395 03 90

SCANDINAVIA: Scanvik, Esplanaden 8B, 1263 Copenhagen K, DK, ☎ (45) 33.12.77.66, Fax: (45) 33.91.28.82

SPAIN: Altaïr, Balmes 69, E-08007 Barcelona, ☎ 454 29 66, Fax: 451 25 59 altair@globalcom.es

SWITZERLAND: OLF, P.O. Box 1061, CH-1701 Fribourg, ☎ (026) 467.51.11 Fax: (026) 467.54.66

U.S.A.: The Globe Pequot Press, 6 Business Park Road, P.O. Box 833, Old Saybrook, CT 06475, ☎ 1-800-243-0495, Fax: 800-820-2329, sales@globe-pequot.com

Other countries, contact Ulysses Books & Maps (Montréal), Fax: (514) 843-9448 No part of this publication may be reproduced in any form or by any means, including photocopying, without the written permission of the publisher.

Canadian Cataloguing in Publication Data
Pierson, Lorette, 1963-
    Washington, D.C.
    (Ulysses Travel Guide) - Translation of: Washington, D.C. - Includes index.
    ISBN 2-89464-172-9
    1. Washington (D.C.) - Guidebooks. I. Title   II. Series
    F192.3.P5313   1998   917.5304'41   C98-941519-8

© November 1998, Ulysses Travel Publications. All rights reserved
Printed in Canada

«I say to you today, my friends, that in spite of the difficulties and frustrations of the moment, I still have a dream. It is a dream deeply rooted in the American dream... I have a dream that one day every valley shall be exalted, every hill and mountain shall be made low, the rough places will be made plain, and the crooked places will be made straight, and the glory of the Lord shall be revealed, and all flesh shall see it together.»

Martin Luther King, Jr.

TABLE OF CONTENTS

PORTRAIT	9
Geography	10
History	13
Politics	40
Economy	49
Population	50
Cultural life	51
Architecture	55

PRACTICAL INFORMATION	59
Entrance formalities	59
Customs	59
Embassies and consulates	60
Tourist information	62
Guided tours	63
Getting to Washington	64
Time difference	75
Business hours and public holidays	76
Holidays and public holidays	76
Money and banking	76
Mail and telecommunications	78
Climate and clothing	80
Insurance	80
Health	81
Shopping	82
Taxes and tipping	82
Bars and dance clubs	83
Advice for smokers	83
Safety and security	83
Children	84
Handicapped travellers	84
Weights and measures	84
General information	85
Gay and lesbian life	86

EXPLORING	89
Tour A: Capitol Hill	92
Tour B: Downtown	108
Tour C: Around The White House	123
Tour D: The Mall	139
Tour E: Dupont Circle	169
Tour F: Embassy Row And Kalorama	176
Tour G: Foggy Bottom	181

EXPLORING CONT'D	
Tour H: The Banks of The Anacostia River	186
Tour I: Arlington	193
Tour J: Other Washington Attractions	201
Tour K: Georgetown	206
Tour L: The Outskirts Of Washington	218

OUTDOORS	227
Parks	227
Outdoor activities	228

ACCOMMODATIONS	235
Capitol Hill Area	238
Downtown	239
Near The White House	242
Dupont Circle and Adams Morgan	244
Foggy Bottom	250
Embassy Row and Kalorama	253
Georgetown	254

RESTAURANTS	257
Downtown and The Mall	262
Around The White House	267
Dupont Circle	268
Foggy Bottom	273
Adams Morgan	276
Around The Cathedral	279
Waterfront Riverside	279
Georgetown	280

ENTERTAINMENT	283
The Circus	284
Dance	285
Opera and Classical Music	285
Theatre	285
Improv and Comedy	289
Movie Theatres	290
Bars and Nightclubs	292

SHOPPING	303	SHOPPING CONT'D	
Art Galleries	303	Florists	312
The Main Shopping Centres	306	Wine And Spirits	312
		Candy and chocolates	313
Travel Accessories	307	Jewellery	313
Bookshops	308	Sporting goods	314
Clothing Stores	309		
Photo Equipment	310	INDEX	316
Music	311		

WRITE TO US

The information contained in this guide was correct at press time. However, mistakes can slip in, omissions are always possible, places can disappear, etc. The authors and publisher hereby disclaim any liability for loss or damage resulting from omissions or errors.

We value your comments, corrections and suggestions, as they allow us to keep each guide up to date. The best contributions will be rewarded with a free book from Ulysses Travel Publications. All you have to do is write us at the following address and indicate which title you would be interested in receiving (see the list at the end of guide).

Ulysses Travel Publications
4176 Rue Saint-Denis
Montréal, Québec
Canada H2W 2M5
www.ulysses.ca
E-mail: guiduly@ulysse.ca

LIST OF MAPS

District of Columbia Taxi Zones	p 73
Downtown	p 109
National Air and Space Museum	p 145
National Gallery of Art	p 166-167
National Museum of Natural History	p 162
Tour A: Capitol Hill	p 93
Tour B: The Capitol	p 96
Tour C: Around the White House	p 125
Tour D: The Mall	p 141
Tour E: Dupont Circle and Adams Morgan	p 171
Tour F: Embassy Row and Kalorama	p 177
Tour G: Foggy Bottom	p 183
Tour H: The Banks of the Anacostia River	p 187
Tour I: Arlington	p 195
Tour K: Georgetown	p 207
Washington D.C. and surrounding area	p 88
Washington D.C.	p 90-91

SYMBOLS

Symbol	Meaning
🚢	Ulysses' favourite
☎	Telephone number
≖	Fax number
=	Air conditioning
⊗	Ceiling fan
≈	Pool
ℜ	Restaurant
⊛	Whirlpool
ℝ	Refrigerator
K	Kitchenette
△	Sauna
⊙	Exercise room
tv	Colour television
pb	Private bathroom
sb	Shared bathroom
ps	Private shower
bkfst	Breakfast

ATTRACTION CLASSIFICATION

★	Interesting
★★	Worth a visit
★★★	Not to be missed

HOTEL CLASSIFICATION

The prices in the guide are for one room, double occupancy in high season, not including taxes and service charges.

RESTAURANT CLASSIFICATION

$	$10 or less
$$	$10 to $20 US
$$$	$20 to $30 US
$$$$	$30 and more

The prices in the guide are for a meal for one person, not including taxes, drinks and tip.

All prices in this guide are in American dollars.

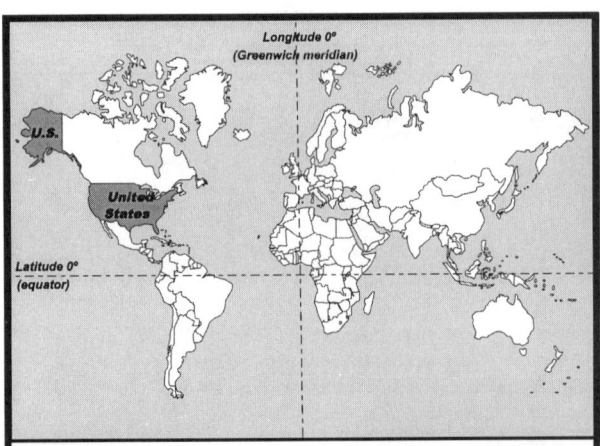

Where is Washington D.C. ?

Washington D.C.	
Population:	1.2 million inhab.
District of Columbia :	700 000 inhab.
Suburbs:	500 000 inhab.
Area:	174 km² (67 mi²)
Currency:	U.S. dollar

© ULYSSES

PORTRAIT

Throughout history, few cities in the world have been destined from their very beginnings to be the seat of power of a nation – a nation itself destined to become an empire. Even fewer have had the privilege of devoting themselves solely to that one role. Washington is one of the chosen few, never serving any other purpose than to be the capital of the United States of America.

Today, people refer to Washington the way people of the past must have spoken about Rome or Versailles. Romulus, who pushed his plough around the seven hills; Le Nôtre, who designed the gardens of Versailles for Louis XIV, and L'Enfant, who drew up the original plans for the American capital, had a great deal in common. They belonged to that select group of people charged with creating an image of grandeur, glorifying political institutions and thus providing the backdrop against which history would unfold. The President has replaced the Emperor and the King; lobbyists have replaced courtesans. Senators are still senators, and many still have the patrician air of their ancient counterparts. And then there are the scores of secretaries, advisers, judges, agency heads and civil servants – all those individuals who are the working mechanisms of government and make the city's pulse beat strongly enough to be felt throughout the country.

All the rest – the monuments, museums, majestic vistas, bustling lawyers and armoured limousines – serves as a reminder that Washington is a city of power, a capital. And it is to feel that power and marvel at the nation's achievements that 20 million tourists, the vast majority American, come here each year. Visitors can roam through the institutions of this great democracy, relive the country's eventful history and see the fruits of human genius. No matter what you do here, though, you will have a little taste of the towering heights of power, a unique sensation that only great capitals can inspire.

GEOGRAPHY

The Atlantic coast of the United States is indented with bays deep enough for ships to safely drop anchor. One of these is the Chesapeake Bay, located just north of Norfolk, Virginia, at the mouth of the Potomac River, the 640-kilometre waterway that marks the border between the mid-Atlantic states of Maryland and Virginia. The Potomac River is a link in the waterway that runs deep into the United States: It flows through the Piedmont Plateau and the Appalachians to the border of western Pennsylvania. Then its only a short portage to Pittsburg and the mouth of the Ohio river, which eventually flows into the Mississippi and the American heartland.

It is not surprising, therefore, that the fledgling American republic decided to found its capital on the banks of the Potomac. The chosen site lies at a latitude of 39° north and a longitude of 77° west, at the confluence of the Anacostia and Potomac rivers, about 120 kilometres from where the Potomac empties into the Chesapeake Bay, and 220 kilometres from the Atlantic Ocean.

This region can be divided into three sections: the coastal plains, the Piedmont plateau and the Appalachians. The abundant swamplands of the wide coastal plains are rich in plant and animal life. The tides play an important role here, particularly in the Chesapeake and Delaware bays. Farther up the Potomac, a stretch of rapids and waterfalls makes it impossible go any farther. This is the beginning of the Piedmont, a plateau that extends east to the Appalachians. Settlers were attracted to the Piedmont because the waterways leading to it not only made it accessible but could also be used to produce hydraulic energy. It was in the middle of all this that Washington was founded. Finally, the Appalachians, which mark the western boundary of the original colonies, split into three subsets at this level – the Blue Ridge Mountains, a valley and the Allegheny Mountains. This entire Appalachian region is a paradise for anyone who enjoys beautiful scenery and hiking.

Washington was originally supposed to occupy a 256 square-kilometre (161 square-mile) piece of land, mostly swampland, around the Potomac, which had been ceded by Virginia and Maryland. This square of land, the District of Columbia, had to give back its southwest side to Virginia in 1846, at the request of the citizens of Alexandria, who were indignant at being absorbed into the District. The remaining land covers an area of 174 square kilometres. The city is flat in the east and near the Potomac, which runs along its entire southwest section. There are a few small hills farther north, but nothing of any significant size. The highest point in the city is only 125 metres above sea level.

Washington was designed by the French architect and urban planner Pierre Charles L'Enfant. He envisioned the city as a sort of checkerboard, with most of the streets running parallel or perpendicular to one another. His stroke of genius was to incorporate 50-metre-wide diagonal avenues into this grid pattern. At the intersection of these avenues, often on a height, he planned a traffic circle with a monument in the middle. L'Enfant thus succeeded in creating spectacular vistas and designing a city that could have several centres of activity.

Finding your way around Washington isn't very hard once you know where you are in relation to the Capitol, which is perched atop a hill and marks the centre of the city. Streets running north-south are numbered; those running east-west are designated by a letter. The avenues are named after states. The city is divided into four quadrants centred around the Capitol dome: northeast (NE), southeast (SE), southwest (SW) and northwest (NW).

The heart of the city is the Mall, a 120-metre-wide rectangular green space that stretches from the Capitol to the Potomac and is surrounded by museums and administrative buildings. This landscaped area is used to commemorate those people and events closest to Americans' hearts. It is here that visitors will find the Lincoln Memorial; the long black wall engraved with the names of all the soldiers who died in Vietnam, and the huge obelisk dedicated to George Washington. Other green spaces have been laid out north and south of the Washington Monument, leading to the Jefferson Memorial and the White House respectively. The White House is linked to the Capitol by Pennsylvania Avenue. Most of the federal departments and agencies are clustered in this area, in a part known as Federal Triangle. The Library of Congress, the Supreme Court and the National Archives are all nearby.

Washington's old residential streets are lined with lovely row houses. The closer you get to the downtown area, the more apartment buildings there are; the farther away you get, the lower the urban density. For more than 30 years now, there has been a continuous effort to keep people from moving out of the city and to preserve the local architecture, which varies distinctly from one neighbourhood to the other.

The stream of urban planners and politicians who have passed through Washington over the past 200 years can take special pride in two achievements. First, they resisted the temptation to build skyscrapers. Unlike all other big American cities, Washington has, literally, kept a low profile, which helps show off its beautiful monuments and lets in lots of sunlight. Their second accomplishment lies in the quality and quantity of green spaces in Washington and its immediate surroundings – more than 80 square metres of park per person in the city proper! The small parks graced with statues, the arboretum, the National Zoo and the other vast stretches of greenery are true oases for weary urban explorers.

Climate

Washington enjoys a temperate continental climate. The dominant winds are from the west, which does not prevent the air from becoming very humid, due to the proximity of Chesapeake Bay and the Atlantic Ocean. The level of precipitation is about the same all year round – between 70 and 105 millimetres per month. Still, there can be heavy down

	Average Temperatures	
	°C	°F
January	-2 to 6	28 to 43
February	2 to 7	36 to 45
March	2 to 12	28 to 54
April	7 to 18	45 to 64
May	13 to 24	55 to 75
June	18 to 28	64 to 82
July	21 to 31	70 to 88
August	20 to 29	68 to 84
September	16 to 26	61 to 79
October	9 to 20	48 to 68
November	4 to 13	39 to 55
December	-1 to 7	30 to 45

pours, especially when a storm is moving up the coast from the West Indies.

The most pleasant seasons are spring and fall, when the temperatures are mild and the city is decked out in blossoming flowers or colourful leaves. Washington summers are so hot and humid that many residents flee to the mountains or the shore. The midday heat can be truly stifling. On the other hand, the nights are balmy. From December to February, it gets cold enough for snow to pile up on occasion. It is even possible to go skiing in the Appalachians.

HISTORY

The banks of the Potomac were first inhabited by nomadic Amerindian tribes. Artifacts dating back over 11,000 years have been found here. Originally hunters and gatherers, these natives gradually evolved into a sedentary society after discovering farming and food preservation methods around 1000 B.C.

When the Europeans arrived, this region, like New England, was inhabited by Algonquins. More precisely, it was the

Piscataway tribe that named the river "Petomeack", meaning "place of trade". Their villages, usually located on a waterway, were made up of wigwams, long, bark-covered dwellings with enough room for an extended family. The Algonquins grew corn, squash, potatoes and beans. Fish played an important role in their diet, and hunting provided them with meat and leather. Like most Native Americans, the Algonquins had an intense spiritual life centred around animism.

The native population was decimated by diseases brought over by the Europeans. Many weakened communities merged with the Iroquois, who had originally settled farther inland. The increasing power of the Iroquois tribes drove the surviving Algonquins to seek the protection of the European settlers.

The Colonial Era

The Potomac River, which natives also designated as "Co-hon-ho-roo-ta", was explored several times by Europeans before the region was colonized. One historian claims that it was discovered as far back as the early 16th century. Be that as it may, the first person officially credited with exploring the river was Spanish admiral Pedro Memendez, governor of the colony of Florida, where he founded St. Augustine in 1565. In 1571, Memendez sailed partway up the river, then known as Espiritu Santo.

In 1607, the first permanent English colony in North America was established in Jamestown, Virginia. The first settlers vowed to rid the New World of Spaniards and Catholicism. Their heads were filled with dreams of gold and silver, and they ignored the warnings of Algonquin chief Powhatan, who advised them to take up farming. Working the land simply did not appeal to the colonists, but after a few lean winters, they finally came around to his way of seeing. In the meantime, they embarked on all sorts of adventures and managed, in the process, to fall out of favour with the Native Americans. In 1608, one of them, a British captain named John Smith, set out to explore the Potomac. He was captured by the Amerindians and would have met his death if Pocahontas, Chief Powhatan's daughter, had not intervened on his behalf.

Virginia founded its first deliberative assembly, the House of Burgesses, in 1619, and became a royal colony in 1624. Its new status did not, however, prevent it from foundering, for it lacked of a viable economic plan. Finally, a colonist named John Rolfe, Pocahontas's husband, came up with a solution. He had noticed that his father-in-law grew, dried and smoked tobacco, and the captains who delivered the colony's supply of rum had told him that tobacco was becoming more and more popular in England and could be sold there at a good price. Furthermore, the native suppliers could no longer meet the demand. Rolfe obtained seeds for the most popular varieties and tried planting them in the fertile local soil. Tobacco ended up making Virginia rich.

In 1629, George Calvert, also known as Lord Baltimore, tried to establish a colony in Virginia but was driven out because he refused to make his colonists take a Protestant oath of allegiance. He obtained a royal grant for the part of Virginia north of the Potomac, where he intended to establish a colony for Catholics fleeing persecution in England. His son, Leonard Calvert, proceeded with the plan, dropping anchor at the mouth of the Potomac, which he renamed the St. Gregory. He sailed up the river with a fur-trader named Henry Fleet, believed to be the first white man to have set foot on the land now occupied by Washington. The colonists' goal was to establish ties with the Piscataways, who controlled the territory. Their mission failed and the colony of Maryland was founded north of the mouth of the river, on Chesapeake Bay. This colony developed into the State of Maryland, whose largest city is named after Lord Baltimore.

The subsequent colonization of Maryland and northern Virginia was hindered only by the excessive taxes imposed by England and territorial disputes, the most famous of which involved the border between Maryland and the more recently founded colony of Pennsylvania, in 1681. England settled the disagreement by appointing two specialists, Mason and Dixon, to survey the boundary, which would later come to be seen as the dividing line between the Northern and Southern United States.

Land grants favoured the creation of big plantations, where the owner, the Lord, built his house and the stores, warehouses and outbuildings necessary for working the land. These self-sufficient estates soon became centres of community life, and villages often grew up around their warehouses.

In 1695, the land then occupied by Washington was incorporated into Prince George's County, whose county seat, Upper Marlborough, was the only sizable town in the region, aside from Annapolis. Georgetown, now part of Washington, was founded in 1751. Two years earlier, on the other side of the river, a small village had developed. Originally known as Hunting Creek Warehouse, it was renamed Belle Haven, then Alexandria.

By the beginning of the 18th century, both banks of the Potomac were occupied by planters, often the cream of society. It was a golden era for plantation owners: tobacco was selling well, and there were slaves to farm it. Gentlemen-planters thus had lots of time to enjoy an active social life. Activities on their schedule included tea with the ladies, card games, picnics, hunting and various competitions. Hospitality reigned, and a stranger with a pleasant face never had to look for a hotel (he would have had a hard time finding one, anyway). Paying a visit to a neighbour who lived a half-day's ride away was considered an act of common courtesy in those days.

However, many other colonists in Maryland and Virginia had to content themselves with contemplating the planters' good fortune from afar. These people were sharecroppers (often German) and small planters with less desirable plots of land, which they farmed themselves, sometimes with the help of a slave or two. Their hard work almost always ended up making the big planters even richer. Better positioned to sell the harvests overseas, the big planters purchased tobacco from their neighbours, who had little choice but to sell. Furthermore, the big planters often opened up a general store next to their warehouse to sell supplies to the small plantations. Farmhands had to work three, four or even five years for a planter who paid their passage to America. After their period of serfdom, they could always settle in the territories opening up to the west.

Nevertheless, lack of sufficient manpower soon became a problem on the plantations, and the big planters turned to slave traders for a solution. At the beginning of the 17th century, a

Dutch merchant, almost by chance, brought about 20 Africans to Virginia, thinking they would be subject to the same conditions as European immigrants. It soon became clear that the Africans were far too different from the whites and Native Americans to succeed in escaping. Furthermore, they had no idea how long they would be slaves. Seeing a golden opportunity to solve their labour problems, the planters took advantage of the africans unfortunate situation. In 1662, slavery was legalized, making it possible to harvest more tobacco. This resulted in a price drop, thus creating a vicious circle: large-scale tobacco farming could no longer be sufficiently profitable without the trade of human flesh.

Captured in Africa, often by other Africans, slaves first had to survive the voyage to the West Indies or America. One in three died. A slave's worth was strictly limited to his market value. His children could be taken from him and he himself could be beaten to death. Slaves could be sexually exploited, and were forbidden to learn how to read. Tens of thousands of African slaves were brought to Maryland and Virginia. In the area now occupied by Washington, they formed the largest segment of the population, the driving force behind the local economy.

The Birth of the United States and the Choice of a Capital

In 1760, Montreal surrendered to British troops, just as Quebec City had the year before. The 13 English colonies in North America had long been trying, with Great Britain's help, to defeat New France, and they finally succeeded. Great Britain planned to recover some of the money it had invested in the conquest by levying taxes on the colonies. The colonists, for their part, felt that they were being poorly thanked for their efforts and had no intention of paying taxes to a government that never negotiated with them. Furthermore, many colonists were fed up with the constraints Britain kept imposing on their economy. England had complete control over the colonies' commercial activities and could tax any imported or exported goods it pleased, without necessarily meeting the colonies' demands. Trouble had been brewing for a long time: in the previous century, a revolt erupted in Virginia, and a planter named Nathaniel Bacon burned Jamestown.

18 Portrait

Tensions mounted and soon people began bracing for an open conflict. In 1775, the American Revolution began when British troops exchanged fire with about 70 Minutemen in Lexington, Massachusetts then were intercepted by the militia shortly after, in Concord. An experienced officer by the name of George Washington was appointed commander-in-chief of the newly formed Continental Army.

The following year, on July 4, 1776, to be precise, the Second Continental Congress, a legislative assembly made up of deputies from the colonies that would later form the United States, formally adopted the Declaration of Independence. The document was written by Thomas Jefferson, a Virginia aristocrat and firm believer in the political philosophy of the Age of Enlightenment.

The British and American armies fought from 1775 to 1781, and a peace treaty wasn't signed until 1783. During this entire period, the Continental Congress had no official meeting place and convened in various cities. At the time, the 13 colonies were still separate states, and not everyone was in favour of establishing a permanent central government. Furthermore, no one had any idea what powers such a governing body should be granted. In 1783, in Philadelphia, soldiers burst into the room where Congress was deliberating and demanded their back pay, prompting Congress to take refuge in Princeton, New Jersey. The place was simply too small, and everyone finally agreed that the fledgling nation needed a capital, a "Federal Town".

The only thing left to decide was where the capital would be located. The Northern and Southern delegates did not trust each other, and each group wanted the Federal Town to be established in their region. It was soon decided that the city should be founded in an area that was not controlled by any one state, so that no state would have an advantage over the others. The delegates finally agreed to have two sites surveyed, both more or less on the dividing line between the North and the South. One was on the Potomac, the other on the Delaware, farther to the north. By 1784, the Delaware site

The Presidents of the United States

1	George Washington (1789-1797)
2	John Adams (1797-1801)
3	Thomas Jefferson (1801-1809)
4	James Madison (1809-1817)
5	James Monroe (1817-1825)
6	John Quincy Adams (1825-1829)
7	Andrew Jackson (1829-1837)
8	Martin Van Buren (1837-1841)
9	William Henry Harrison (1841)
10	John Tyler (1841-1845)
11	James Knox Polk (1845-1849)
12	Zachary Taylor (1849-1850)
13	Millard Fillmore (1850-1853)
14	Franklin Pierce (1853-1857)
15	James Buchanan (1857-1861)
16	Abraham Lincoln (1861-1865)
17	Andrew Johnson (1865-1869)
18	Ulysses Simpson Grant (1869-1877)
19	Rutherford Birchard Hayes (1877-1881)
20	James Abram Garfield (1881)
21	Chester Alan Arthur (1881-1885)
22 and 24	Grover Cleveland (1885-1889 and 1893-1897)
23	Benjamin Harrison (1889-1893)
25	William McKinley (1897-1901)
26	Theodore Roosevelt (1901-1909)
27	William Howard Taft (1909-1913)
28	Thomas Woodrow Wilson (1913-1921)
29	Warren Gamaliel Harding (1921-1923)
30	John Calvin Coolidge (1923-1929)
31	Herbert Clark Hoover (1929-1933)
32	Franklin Delano Roosevelt (1933-1945)
33	Harry S. Truman (1945-1953)
34	Dwight David Eisenhower (1953-1961)
35	John Fitzgerald Kennedy (1961-1963)
36	Lyndon Baines Johnson (1963-1969)
37	Richard Milhous Nixon (1969-1974)
38	Gerald Rudolph Ford (1974-1977)
39	James Earl (Jimmy) Carter (1977-1981)
40	Ronald Wilson Reagan (1981-1989)
41	George Herbert Walker Bush (1989-1993)
42	William Jefferson (Bill) Clinton (1993-present)

seemed to have won out, but the Southern delegates were opposed to the choice. So much bitter debating ensued that the decision was postponed until a later date.

In 1787, the delegates spent four months completing the final draft of the Constitution, a masterpiece of checks and balances. By the following year, it had been ratified by most of the states and immediately went into effect. The Continental Congress gave way to the Congress of the United States of America. In 1789, the country's first president and vice president, George Washington and John Adams, were elected to office. The Senate was divided on the issue of where the capital should be located, so it fell to the president of that legislative body, the Vice President of the United States, to cast the deciding vote. John Adams, a native of Braintree, south of Boston, voted for Germantown, Pennsylvania.

The Southern states rejected this decision and tried to have it overturned in 1790. At the time, a Northern Congressman, Alexander Hamilton, was trying to get the federal government to shoulder debts incurred by all the states. The Northern states were more in debt, however. Hamilton's plan was narrowly rejected, but the fledgling nation was further weakened by the debate. It was at that precise moment that a crucial get-together took place. Thomas Jefferson, a Virginian, was anxious to stabilize the situation. He thus invited Hamilton and two Southern Congressmen to dinner. The food was good and so were the wine and spirits. The tensions eased and an historic compromise was reached: the Southern Congressmen would change their vote to make the federal government take on the states' debts if Hamilton would round up enough support among his Northern colleagues for the capital to be built on the banks of the Potomac. And that's exactly what came to pass.

President Washington was finally able to select the exact site of the Territory of Columbia, named after Christopher Columbus (the word "District" came later). An urban planner named Pierre Charles L'Enfant came to see him and asked to be entrusted with the task of drawing up the plans for the city. A graduate of Paris' Académie Royale de Peinture et de Sculpture, L'Enfant had decided to fight in the American Revolution in 1777. After the war, he had designed Federal Hall in New York, earning

George Washington, the First American Hero

To Americans, the first president of the United States is almost idolized and seen as the model citizen-soldier: courageous in adversity, disciplined and well-educated. Indeed, Washington's first biographer was not satisfied simply with praising him but felt obliged to fabricate the famous tale about young George choosing to admit that he chopped down a cherry tree rather than lie to avoid punishment.

George Washington was born in Virginia in 1732 and grew up to be a man of action and authority. A sportsman, he was an outstanding rider and fit in with plantation society, though he was not an intellectual.

In 1753, Washington became an officer and fought in battles between the French and the English on the Ohio River. As commanding officer, he was forced to surrender to the enemy during his first battle. Later, he joined another expedition to the Ohio River as aide-de-camp to a British general. His unit was ambushed and he almost lost his life.

Meanwhile, George Washington had inherited Mount Vernon plantation, located just 25 km downstream from the site he would later choose for the capital. Soaring tobacco prices and his marriage to a rich widow made him one of the wealthiest men in Virginia. He was elected to the Virginia assembly, where he served for 17 years without distinguishing himself in any particular way. He was also a justice of the peace.

Because of Washington's opposition to Britain's fiscal policy, Virginia sent him to represent the colony at the Continental Congress, which soon appointed him commander of the Continental Army. This was the beginning of a long conflict against a power that was greater in number and better armed, but much farther from its bases. As an aristocrat, Washington shared the same fighting ideals as they did in Europe, that is, without recourse to the guerilla tactics used in America. Instead, his army operated in broad daylight and thereby confirmed more than any other symbol the existence of an American government.

Washington managed to drive out the English from Boston but later suffered a harsh defeat, and lost New York to the enemy. He needed victories to keep up his troops' morale and achieved them by attacking British troops in Trenton and Princeton, where they had ventured too far. In August 1777, England landed a new contingent of soldiers, and Washington was defeated at the Battle of Brandywine. He was forced to retreat and set up winter quarters in Valley Forge, west of Philadelphia. It was a cold and bitter winter for his troops, during which he also had to defend his command before the Continental Congress.

In June 1778, France joined the insurgents in their war against England. A British army retreated to New York and Washington organized his own troops to block them. He was joined by General Rochambeau's army. Over the following two years the American commander more or less maintained his position, but in 1781, he no longer had a choice; he had to win, or his troops would leave him, for they were running out of resources. He wanted to attack New York, but the French had another idea. Their fleet would sail to Virginia, where they could prevent another British contingent from receiving reinforcements by way of the sea. Within five weeks, Washington and Rochambeau managed to move 7,000 French and American soldiers to Virginia in time to set a trap for General Cornwallis at Yorktown. In one full sweep London lost a third of its troops in America. This was the last great confrontation of the war, though the English did not sign a treaty recognizing the independence of the 13 colonies for another two years.

Washington later fought for the creation of a federal government. He chaired the Constitutional Convention of 1787, which allowed him to make himself heard. The people thus elected him President of the United States in 1789, and for a second term in 1792. His candidacy obliged him to organize the federal government. He did so by creating a cabinet to assist him. His administrative style was conciliatory, and he avoided siding with any faction. He did, however, enter into debate once by refusing to form an alliance with the revolutionaries in France. Preferring to bring the country's foreign policy back in line with Great Britain, he used all his political weight to incite Congress to ratify a treaty that would normalize relations between the United States and its former mother country. When he left office in 1797, his farewell speech was a cry for the nation to stay out of foreign conflicts and, above all, to avoid internal dissent.

George Washington passed away at Mount Vernon in December 1799. He was not the most brilliant tactician, nor was he as much of an activist as many other presidents, but he was the right man for the situation when it came to organizing and safeguarding a young republic against enormous odds.

himself something of a reputation as an architect. His ideas impressed Washington, who hired him to design not only the city itself but also its public buildings.

The first thing L'Enfant did was to choose the best site, a hilltop, for the Capitol. Starting from that point, he drew a stately, 120-metre-wide avenue, along which embassies and the city's major museums would be located. This avenue, the Mall, would intersect at right angles with another broad avenue leading to the White House. A diagonal commercial artery would link the Executive Mansion to the Capitol, forming the hypotenuse of a triangle where all the major federal institutions would be located, and around which the city would develop. L'Enfant pictured a huge city with some 800,000 residents and several different hubs of activity.

L'Enfant's plans were magnificent and certainly not lacking in vision. He took on the surveyors and administrators responsible for the city's development, defending each and every detail of his design. Practical considerations were of no importance to him. Unfortunately, he was so inflexible that he was finally replaced. He died, penniless, in 1825. Today, L'Enfant's genius is evident in the city he designed, for his plans were re-adopted in 1899 and have been largely executed. His remains, furthermore, were moved from their original resting place to Arlington National Cemetery.

The Capital Becomes a City

By May 1800, the infrastructures were ready. John Adams was President. George Washington having passed away a year earlier, Congress decided to honour his memory by renaming Federal City after him. The 126 people who worked for the federal government of the United States thus moved to Washington, DC. The entire city had no more than 5,000 inhabitants. At the time, only several official buildings had been erected, and the executive mansion was not ready. Upon his arrival, the Secretary of the Treasury described the place as follows: "There are few houses, most of which are small and miserable shacks which contrast horribly with the public buildings. The people are poor and, from what I can tell, live like fish by feeding on each other. Except for brick ovens and the temporary shacks of labourers, you can look in any direction without seeing so much as a fence on a piece of land the size of New York."

The rusticity of the place did not, however, hinder the flurry of political activity that soon came to characterize life in Washington. Indeed, John Adams hardly got to enjoy the place, for no sooner had he unpacked his bags than he lost the election to Thomas Jefferson. The latter was an unpretentious man with little taste for pomp and circumstance. In his view, the White House was big enough for two emperors, the Pope and the Dalai Lama. Avoiding official receptions, he preferred to invite anyone who wanted to come to celebrate New Year's Eve or the Fourth of July to his home. As for unavoidable social events, the President, a widower, turned to the Secretary of State and his wife, James and Dolly Madison. Madison later became president himself in 1809. In 1801, the House of Representatives moved into a temporary building humorously nicknamed the "The Oven", located where the South Wing of the Capitol, completed in 1807, now stands.

The city of Washington did not grow as rapidly as anticipated, and real-estate developers were unable to sell their projects. Ambassadors were surprised by the pervading sense of desolation, whereas President Madison himself was distressed to find himself in a desert the moment Congress adjourned. There were even murmurings about abandoning the experiment, handing the District of Columbia back to Virginia and Maryland and moving the capital to a real city.

In 1812, matters got worse when the vague expansionist impulse of a large number of American politicians prompted the United States to declare war on Great Britain while it was busy with the Napoleonic Wars. American troops were unable to conquer Canada. The English, on the other hand, managed to land 65 kilometres from Washington in August 1814. They effortlessly drove back the troops defending the capital and on the night of August 24, set all the public buildings on fire, with the exception of the Post Office and the Patent Office. Few private properties were destroyed. As luck would have it, the next day a storm arose, and the British prudently retreated. In the days that followed, an English fleet sailed upriver to Alexandria and replenished their supplies, to the great displeasure of the local residents.

The President and Congress had to move into temporary quarters. The White House was rebuilt by the end of 1817 and a new president, James Monroe, settled in. The original Capitol was completed in 1819. During Monroe's presidency, the cream of Southern society began frequenting the capital. Great attention was paid to elegance and education, and Washington finally began to seem like a real capital.

It was also during Monroe's presidency that the United States resolved to stay away from European conflicts and keep Europeans away from America. The "Monroe Doctrine" declared that the United States would not tolerate any new European colonization efforts in the Americas. This pronouncement was a response to the threat of continental European intervention in Latin America, where many Spanish possessions had revolted. Washington adhered to this policy until the end of the 19th century.

Abolitionism and the Civil War

At the same time, new territories wanted to become part of the United States. This presented a delicate problem. Slavery was illegal in the Northern states, whose economy was based on commerce and industry, but vital to the agrarian, export-based economy of the Southern states. In the South, tobacco had replaced cotton as the leading crop, but Europe was still the best market. Furthermore, Northern states favoured protectionist trade policies, which ensured that the goods they produced would be purchased in the South. Conversely, Southerners were in favour of a free-market economy that would allow them to buy supplies and export their products at the best price.

Proslavers and abolitionists alike feared that the creation of new states might alter the relative balance of power between North and South in Washington. Colonization of the American West had begun, and the progressive ascent of these territories to statehood was imminent. A compromise was reached whereby any new state created in the west (France had sold Louisiana to the United States in 1803) would be a slave state if located below 36° 30′ latitude north, and a free state if located above. States were then admitted two at a time in order to allow both groups to be represented.

Monroe, like John Quincy Adams after him, was politically weakened by mounting opposition lead by Andrew Jackson. This sabotaged his efforts to put a stop to the international slave trade and enforce treaties with Native Americans. Out West, Native American tribes were progressively decimated throughout the 19th century. Few treaties signed with Native Americans were respected, either because the disputed lands were desirable or because a victorious campaign against "hordes of Indian savages" was an ideal springboard for the politically ambitious. It mattered little that Native Americans were few in number, poorly armed and within their rights.

President Andrew Jackson arrived at the White House in 1829. The first president from a working-class background, he was a remarkable demagogue who secured the support of voters by calling his adversaries aristocrats every time they opposed his plans. Many of his projects harmed the nation's economy considerably and lined his friends' pockets in the process. Jackson broke new ground in a number of ways. For one, he vetoed more bills than all his predecessors put together. President Washington had established that Congress' decisions were to be respected, since Senators and Representatives had been delegated by the people, while Jackson challenged that the president's legitimacy was at least equal to that of Congress.

Jackson's reign in Washington also coincided with good news for the capital's economy: a railway would now link Washington, via Baltimore, to a network that was expanding at an exponential rate. The arrival of the railway marked the end of river transportation.

Among Jackson's spiritual sons were President Martin Van Buren, who organized the great coalition of the Democratic Party, and President James K. Polk, who made considerable territorial gains by negotiating an agreement for England to hand over the territory now occupied by the states of Washington and Oregon. Polk went even further, deliberately provoking a war with Mexico. What later became California, Nevada, Utah, Arizona and New Mexico was taken from Mexico by force, as Texas had been earlier.

This expansionist policy made Northern abolitionists fear that Polk was extending the United States' Southern possessions for the purpose of adding slave states. However, in 1850, California joined the Union as an abolitionist state and a provision was made for the Utah and New Mexico territories to choose their status. President Zachary Taylor then announced that he would use military force to oppose any attempt to secede.

Southern states ultimately became a minority in Congress and Northern states increasingly made demands that favoured their economy, often to the detriment of the South. Moreover, abolitionist groups were becoming more and more active. The idea that Kansas and Nebraska had a right to choose their status as new states enraged Northerners. The Republican Party was born out of this anger and nearly won the following election. Neither President Millard Filmore nor his successors Franklin Pierce and James Buchanan could appease the public. Abolitionists viewed slavery as immoral and any compromise as a defeat, even though the Supreme Court of United States had concluded that Congress could not prohibit it.

In 1860, Democrats were divided between North and South. Republicans, although concentrated in the North, had good prospects of having their candidate, Abraham Lincoln, elected. Lincoln's platform included preventing the expansion of slavery and favouring Northern commerce with customs tariffs. Immediately after he was elected, South Carolina announced its secession from the Union, soon to be followed by Mississippi, Florida, Alabama, Georgia, Louisiana and Texas. While taking his oath of office, Lincoln declared that secession was illegal and that he therefore intended to maintain his strongholds within the secessionist states. Among these was Fort Sumter in the port of Charleston, South Carolina. Secessionists demanded its surrender and opened fire on a ship delivering supplies to the garrison. Lincoln issued a call to arms. Tennessee, North Carolina, Virginia and Arkansas joined the new Confederacy, which chose to establish its new capital in Richmond, Virginia, a mere 160 kilometres from Washington.

The Union forces had a clear advantage. Their total population was 22 million inhabitants, and the country's industries, food production, transportation infrastructures and capital were all concentrated there. Furthermore, almost all the large cities in the United States were located in the North. By comparison, the Confederates could count on a population of only nine million people (of which four million were slaves) and a purely agrarian economy based on a few big crops. However, the Confederates had remarkable military officers, such as Robert E. Lee and Stonewall Jackson. Furthermore, their objective was to resist, whereas the Union forces had to attack. Finally, every Confederate soldier knew he could lose everything if he did not fight for it.

The public called for the chief of staff to send troops straight to Richmond, but he convinced Lincoln to set up a naval blockade and take the Mississippi in order to divide the Confederacy by completely isolating the eastern part. During the four years of the Civil War, Lincoln frequently replaced his generals, whom he often found to be too prudent. The North suffered many defeats before he was able to find an officer of the same caliber as the Confederacy's. Ulysses Grant became famous by destroying Confederate fortifications along the Mississippi and strategic positions in Tennessee. In early 1864, he orchestrated an ambitious campaign: by taking the command of the Union army on the Potomac, he intended to head to Richmond while General Sherman attacked Georgia from the strategic positions in Tennessee. Finally, a third Union army would enter the Shenandoah Valley in Virginia to cut Richmond off from any supplies.

General Lee managed to prevent Grant and his army from reaching Richmond. Grant then attacked Petersburg, a rail junction essential for providing Richmond with supplies, and had to besiege it because the town was heavily fortified. On the other hand, Sheridan managed to make it into the Shenandoah Valley, and Sherman drove back the enemy in Georgia, where he captured Atlanta and set it ablaze. Sherman then deployed his army on a front almost 100 kilometres long and advanced toward the ocean, destroying everything that could equip, feed, arm or shelter any Confederate soldier.

In April 1865, Grant conquered Petersburg and Lee had to leave Richmond. He could no longer retreat and surrendered at Appomattox, Virginia.

In the meantime, Sherman's and Sheridan's victories led to President Lincoln's re-election. Throughout the war, Lincoln had been walking a tightrope. The aim of the conflict was to preserve the Union, not to abolish slavery, something his own generals needed to be reminded of from time to time. Had the President appeared too keen on abolishing slavery, he might have risked losing other states to the Confederacy, such as Maryland and Kentucky. He therefore proceeded step by step, doing what was necessary for military success. One law provided for seizing "goods" used by Confederates in the pursuit of war. Seventeen months later, another law emancipated slaves within the former Confederate States. In 1864, he could finally amend the Constitution to abolish slavery.

At the same time, President Lincoln wanted to rebuild the country. His Reconstruction plan allowed for each state to rewrite its constitution and regain its rights within the Union if 10% of its citizens took the oath of allegiance. The plan was generous and Lincoln needed to use all his political weight to convince Congress to accept it.

In 1865, the President announced that he was in favour of granting the African-American population of Louisiana the right to vote, something even many Northerners had not yet contemplated. Lincoln was gunned down shortly thereafter by a pro-Confederate actor named John Wilkes Booth. Abraham Lincoln was a man of principle and a remarkable politician, perhaps the greatest the United States has ever seen.

The Civil War, the first modern war, was nevertheless the worst experience in the country's history: 620,000 men died, and far more were wounded. One Confederate soldier in four and one Union soldier in five died in battle. It was a huge loss to both sides. The federal government of the United States was probably the biggest victor of this war, which enabled it to establish its authority, particularly that of the Executive branch, and affirm its durability. A great number of Civil War battlefields are located near Washington, including Gettysburg, Pennsylvania and Fredericksburg, Petersburg, Richmond, Appomattox and the Shenandoah Valley, in Virginia. Throughout the war, Washington itself became a centre for supplies and care for the wounded. Its population increased from 52,000 in 1850 to over 130,000 in 1870, mostly due to the massive influx of former slaves.

From One War to the Next

Once the war was over, it didn't take the victors long to pass trade laws advantageous to the North, whereas in the South, in Georgia for instance, people were wondering what they could sell now. The slaves had been freed, but Congress had done nothing to facilitate their change in status, to enable them to enjoy true liberty. Lincoln's successor, Andrew Johnson, even gave the land that Lincoln had promised to former slaves back to the people who had owned it before the war. A Southern politician, Johnson then vetoed certain laws aimed at integrating freed slaves. He had gone too far; Congress overrode his veto and passed the Fourteenth Amendment to the Constitution, which provided a broad definition of American citizenship that obviously included blacks, prohibited discriminatory legislation and declared that a state that denied any of its adult male citizens the right to vote would have its representation reduced proportionately. Still, various laws aimed at promoting segregation and keeping former slaves from acquiring any political power whatsoever continued to pop up all over the former Confederate states.

Andrew Johnson was soon succeeded by Ulysses Grant, who was a distinguished soldier but proved ill-equipped for the political arena, a different kind of battleground. It was a difficult time for US presidents. The economy was being modernized. Americans still favoured protectionism, but more and more people were noticing that that policy was having a negative impact on their purchasing power. Inflation, recessions and speculation reared their ugly heads, and the country was poorly prepared to bring them under control. Large and small speculators of dubious moral character invested in industry in search of quick and easy profits. It was now possible to become a millionaire; making one's fortune honestly and without political connections was an entirely different story. Labour movements began to emerge, and the government responded with repression tactics. Finally, there was a population explosion, due to the waves of European immigrants arriving in New York. These newcomers were not only needed to colonize the territory and work in the factories, they were also consumers, and expanded the domestic market considerably.

A newly elected president had to pay off countless political debts by doing favours for his party's supporters. This had always been the case, but the scale had been much smaller before the federal government expanded. Any president lacking in gratitude risked having his own party turn against him and Congress thwart his plans. Worse yet, he might even be killed by an indignant supporter, a fate that befell James A. Garfield in 1881.

As a result, the image of the president became tarnished, and the line between civil servants and political partisans became dangerously blurred. It took a series of strong, determined and upright presidents to reep the bad weeds from the government parties. Rutherford Hayes, Chester A. Arthur and Grover Cleveland all distinguished themselves in this battle.

The year 1871 marked the beginning of another eventful period in the history of the District of Columbia, which was awarded the status of a territory and given permission to elect a local government. Alexander Shepherd launched major construction projects to provide Washington with an infrastructure worthy of a federal capital. Washington ended up much more beautiful than before, but broke. Congress revoked its old territorial status in 1874.

At the turn of the 20th century, President William McKinley succeeded in restoring the business world's confidence in the economy. On the international scene, a change in policy occurred in 1898, when the United States decided to support Cuban revolutionaries in their fight to gain independence from Spain. The war with Spain lasted barely three months. The Spanish suffered a crushing defeat and ceded Puerto Rico and the Philippines to the Americans. It suddenly became clear that the United States was now a world power.

A new era was inaugurated when the next president, Theodore Roosevelt, a war hero who had made a name for himself in Cuba, took office in 1901. Roosevelt was in his early forties, had a talent for public relations, and quickly won public approval by attacking the "trusts", big conglomerates that monopolized entire segments of the economy. When a national coalminers' strike broke out, he stepped in as a mediator rather than send in the troops. Another of his accomplishments was the creation of a number of huge national parks.

On issues of foreign policy, Roosevelt's motto was "Speak softly and carry a big stick". And it worked. His policies kept the Germans away from Venezuela and brought about peace between the Russians and the Japanese. The latter resulted in Roosevelt's becoming the first American to win the Nobel peace prize. At the same time, his "big stick" established the United States as the watchdog of Latin America, enabling the country to gain a foothold around the Panama Canal and take over the completion of the project. Finally, the US Navy was greatly expanded, and its ships sailed around the world, making it clear that American interests were off limits to others.

The capital itself had taken on a new appearance. It had expanded by incorporating Georgetown into the District. Public transportation systems had emerged, along with a ring of suburbs in Maryland and Virginia. At the turn of the century, Congress set up a commission to oversee Washington's development. One of the members' first actions was to unearth Pierre Charles L'Enfant's original plans for the city. Another commission, whom we have to thank for the Jefferson and Lincoln memorials, then took over. In 1910, a height limit was set for buildings in Washington. Finally, an ambitious construction project was launched to build the huge edifices that now grace Federal Triangle.

Off to War and Back Again

President Woodrow Wilson was opposed to US involvement in World War I, even though the American public was very sympathetic to the Allied cause. It was Germany that brought the United States into the war. America was outraged when it learned that the Germans had been trying to persuade Mexico to be their ally in the event of a war with the United States. The country was also appalled when a *Kriegsmarine* U-boat sunk a British ocean liner, the *Lusitania*. When the Germans decided to attack all ships that sailed through English waters, including those flying the American flag, the United States leapt into the fray. It was about time: the Russian Communists had just reached a separate peace agreement, and the entire weight of the war was on the shoulders of the French and the English.

The two million troops that the United States dispatched to the battlegrounds made all the difference, and Germany was forced to surrender on November 11, 1918. Wilson had been ready for this moment for a long time. He had prepared his famous Fourteen Peace Points, designed not only to put an end to the conflict but also to prevent such carnage from ever happening again. It paved the way for the creation of the League of Nations and established the principle of self-determination, according to which a given people in a given territory are masters of their own destiny. Germany agreed to the conditions. France and England could hardly refuse, even though Wilson's plan carved holes in their empires. The Fourteen Points also earned the President the Nobel Prize for peace.

In the end, though, the United States never joined the League of Nations (one of the main reasons for the organization's subsequent failure). Congress refused to ratify the peace treaty proposed by Wilson, and the United States thus adopted a policy of non-intervention. It had become impossible, however, for the Americans to withdraw entirely from European affairs, since they were now its creditors. Fortunately for Wilson, Congress proved much more willing to ratify the bills proposed during his presidency, many of which helped regulate commerce and limit capitalist abuses. The Wilson administration was also responsible for changing the face of the American electorate forever: in 1920, the Nineteenth Amendment gave women the right to vote.

The 1920s were truly the era of the American dream. Everything seemed possible. Industry was booming and liquor flowed freely, despite Prohibition. And then disaster struck in 1929, when the New York stock market crashed. The United States had produced more than it could sell. Factories shut down, some permanently. Within a few years, the number of unemployed had climbed into the millions. This all led to a major drop in consumption, which hurt the factories even more.

Hope in the future was restored by Franklin Delano Roosevelt, who was elected president in 1933. He remained in office until 1945, longer than any other president in American history. Under Roosevelt's "New Deal", the federal government took a more active role in the economy than it ever had before. The United States abandoned the gold standard, on which the value of the US dollar was based. Quotas were established for agricultural production, and major hydroelectric projects were launched, creating jobs and encouraging industrial growth by providing a more efficient infrastructure. The government also devalued the dollar and started exercising tighter control over the stock market. The business community was appalled by various social reforms adopted during this period and brought the issue before the Supreme Court, which declared many of the provisions of the New Deal unconstitutional. Nevertheless, the program did succeed in revitalizing the US economy, and many of the changes Roosevelt introduced would remain part of the American political landscape for many years to come.

World War II broke out in 1939. France fell quickly, as did British positions in the Far East. Soon only England and its colonies were left to fight Hitler's and Hirohito's troops. The American public was not ready to relive the adventure of 1917 and 1918, but was sympathetic enough to the Allied cause for Roosevelt to respond as best as he could to Churchill's calls for help. The Lend-Lease Agreement enabled the United States to loan equipment to England and the USSR, where a second front had opened up. Meanwhile, the United States was rapidly building up its arms supply.

All that remained was a motive to enter the war, and the Japanese provided one in 1941, when they launched a surprise attack on Pearl Harbor, a US naval base in Hawaii. The Pacific fleet's eight battleships were sunk, but luckily all three of its aircraft carriers survived. Exploiting their tactical advantage, the Japanese captured the Solomon Islands and the Philippines. Thanks to its industrial strength and the size of its population, the United States could quickly mobilize 10 million men and convert its factories for wartime.

Roosevelt and Churchill agreed on what strategy the Allies should adopt then reached an understanding with Stalin. Soon after, US troops were sent to North Africa to take Rommel from the rear. They teamed up with British troops in Egypt, and made their way to Sicily, then up mainland Italy. Meanwhile, in England, General Dwight Eisenhower, the supreme commander of the Allied forces in Europe, was preparing Operation Overlord. On June 6, 1944, he gave the signal, and 5000 ships crossed the English Channel to land American, British and Canadian troops on five fortified beaches on the coast of Normandy. This was D-Day, probably the most large-scale military operation of all time. A second landing in Provence backed up the first. The Germans were unable to hold the Allies back and retreated from the Soviet troops, but did not surrender until Germany had been completely destroyed.

On the Pacific front, the war was being fought by the Navy and Marines, with crucial assistance from intelligence services, which had managed to crack the Japanese secret code. The Americans were thus able to learn that a Japanese fleet was targeting the Midway Islands, northwest of Hawaii. Taking a gamble, Admiral Nimitz sent all the aircraft carriers at his disposal to the region, with no other ships to escort them. The aircraft carriers managed to spot the enemy fleet first, and navy pilots succeeded in sinking the Japanese aircraft carriers, suffering heavy losses in the process. The Japanese fleet could not continue without exposing its ships to air strikes. The tide had just turned. Next, General MacArthur's troops recaptured the Japanese-occupied archipelagos one by one. Though short on fuel, pilots and planes, the Japanese put up a fierce fight.

In early 1945, Roosevelt, Churchill and Stalin met in Yalta to decide Europe's fate after the war. The President was ill, which, according to some historians, explains why Stalin was allowed Eastern Europe as a zone of influence. Roosevelt urged his allies to liberalize trade and establish an effective international organization, all to maintain peace. In April 1945, Roosevelt died, leaving Harry Truman to make the hardest decision of the entire war: should the US drop the atomic bomb, which it had been secretly developing for six years, on Japan? Truman considered how many American lives might be lost if the war were to continue and said yes. On August 6, the city of Hiroshima was wiped off the map, followed by Nagasaki on August 9. Hirohito surrendered. By then, the number of war dead had reached 55 million.

Towards American Hegemony

From a domestic point of view, the war had enabled the president to expand the powers of the Executive farther than ever before in US history. He now had so much leeway that he sent troops to Korea without asking Congress. The White House staff grew, and new organizations, such as the National

Security Agency and the Central Intelligence Agency, were established. The government got bigger and the population of the capital soon climbed to 800,000, up from 300,000 at the beginning of the century.

The war had led to the emergence of two great powers, the United States and the USSR. The world didn't seem big enough for both of them; the only thing that induced them to share the planet was their mutual fear of nuclear war. In 1946, the United States joined the United Nations. This time, the Americans were stuck in a corner; they couldn't act as if the rest of the world didn't exist. The problem was that the war hadn't really ended, it had simply grown very cold.

Communism was the enemy, and to keep it as far away as possible, the Americans joined NATO. Never before in its history had the US entered into a military alliance during peacetime. Many American politicians sincerely believed that the Communists wanted to destroy their country. They became fervent propagandists, often incapable of distinguishing between union activists, socialists and Communist revolutionaries. Some people became paranoid, believing that it was too late, that the Communists had already infiltrated the government, the television industry, even Hollywood. Senator Joseph McCarthy presided over the House Committee on Un-American Activities. His investigations ruined people's careers and did absolutely nothing to improve the state of democracy in the United States.

During Dwight Eisenhower's presidency, black Southerners rallied to end segregation. In many states, there were separate bus seats, schools, bathrooms and water fountains for blacks and whites. Worse yet, in some states, registering to vote was a remarkably complicated procedure if you happened to be black. In 1957, the Supreme Court condemned segregation in educational facilities and ordered the states to integrate their schools. Few districts did as they were told, however. The school board of Little Rock, Arkansas, decided to allow five black children to attend Central High School. The state governor declared that he would call in the National Guard to prevent the children from attending classes. President Eisenhower didn't give him the chance: he sent a thousand paratroopers to escort the children to school.

John F. Kennedy continued the process and campaigned actively for legislation that would put an end to institutionalized segregation. The Civil Rights Act, which prohibited discrimination in public facilities, as well as by employers and unions, was passed in 1964, after his assassination.

> ## Demonstrations in Washington
>
> For nearly 50 years, Washington's broad avenues have been the scene of huge demonstrations designed to attract lots of media attention. Unionists, anti-abortionists, pro-choice activists, feminists and all sorts of other special-interest groups take turns invading the Mall.
>
> Two of these demonstrations have gone down in US history. Americans still remember the speech that Reverend Martin Luther King, Jr. delivered at the Lincoln Memorial, before tens of thousands of supporters. "I have a dream", declared the man who envisioned an America in which blacks and whites would finally be equal, de facto and de jure.
>
> Equally impressive was the rally during which hundreds of thousands of youths, many of them students, occupied the Mall for several days to protest American involvement in Vietnam. Heavily covered by the media, this event marked the culmination of public protest against the draft, a bill which sent many young men to fight in Vietnamese rice fields.

The Cold War was in full swing and the Americans and Soviets competed with each other in all sorts of areas. They both courted newly decolonized countries but carefully avoided any direct confrontation that could degenerate into a more serious conflict. The Americans' pride suffered quite a blow when the USSR launched the first satellite in history and then the first manned spacecraft. President Kennedy encouraged schools to develop their science programs and kicked off a race to the moon, which the United States won in 1969, when Neil Armstrong became the first person to set foot on the moon.

The Kennedy administration unwittingly ventured onto a slippery slope by sending 17,000 "military advisers" to South

Vietnam to support a government whose sole virtue was that it wasn't communist.

An even more complex case was that of Cuba, which had been taken over by Communist revolutionaries led by Fidel Castro in 1959. One of the first things Castro did was to nationalize all means of production, including American companies. He also established close ties with the Soviet Union. In 1961, American intelligence agents discovered that Russian missiles were being installed in Cuba, just tens of miles from the coast of the United States. Kennedy had enough. He set up a naval blockade around the island. Tensions rose and Washington issued an ultimatum. The Russians finally agreed to dismantle their installations. Never had a third world war seemed so imminent. The following presidents, until Ronald Reagan, remembered the Cuban Missile Crisis and sought to improve Soviet-American relations. Cuba has been much more isolated since the breakup of the USSR, and the Cuban question still hasn't been resolved in the United States, whose government refuses to lift the economic embargo imposed on that country.

Because of Congress's opposition, Kennedy could only effectuate some of the reforms he had proposed to the nation. Lyndon B. Johnson became president when Kennedy was assassinated, and was reelected. At the time, both the Senate and the House of Representatives were dominated by Democrats, which enabled him to put into effect an impressive legislative program and introduce social reforms aimed at the poor and the elderly. However, that was not enough to win over the American public, for Johnson had let himself be sucked into the maelstrom of the Vietnam War. By the end of 1968, 550,000 American soldiers were stationed in Vietnam. Even at five to one, with top-of-the-line equipment and incredible air support, they could not defeat Ho Chi Minh's troops. And every week, there were heavier losses, increasing the public's condemnation of what had become a dirty war. Young Americans organized protests and tore up their draft cards, and riots broke out on university campuses.

It was Republican president Richard Nixon who made the first move to end the conflict by ordering the gradual withdrawal of American troops. Extremely popular at the time of his reelection, Nixon became the first president to resign from office after the Watergate scandal broke out. Gerald Ford took over during a period of economic and social unrest. The US economy had been hard hit by the oil crisis of 1973, and unemployment and inflation rates were very high. Ford favoured the traditional Republican solution of lowering taxes on the rich to enable them to spend more.

In 1976, Jimmy Carter succeeded Ford. His term in office was marked by one major diplomatic success, the Camp David Agreements, which helped normalize relations between Egypt and Israel. Carter was also responsible for concluding the SALT II accord, aimed at limiting the rate of the nuclear-arms build-up. Paradoxically, relations between the United States and the Soviet Union deteriorated during this period, due to the Russian invasion of Afghanistan. The United States chose to protest the Soviets' action by calling for a boycott on the Olympic Games in Moscow (a favour returned by the Russians during the 1984 Olympics in Los Angeles). A greater failure tainted his presidency and prevented him from being reelected: his inability to help the staff of the US embassy in Teheran, who were taken hostage after the Iranian revolution.

Negotiations with the new Reagan administration led to the hostages' release. Politically speaking, Reagan was a conservative who took the gamble of lowering taxes three years in a row in the hope that the economy would improve, which would increase tax revenues and make it possible to balance the budget. Events proved him wrong, and the US Treasury was left with a huge deficit. Nonetheless, the economy did eventually take off again.

Reagan also supported massive cuts in federal spending, in every area except the military. He favoured taking a hard line with the Soviet Union and was determined to have the means to back up his principles. He went so far as to call the USSR the "evil empire". It took all Mikhail Gorbachev's diplomatic skills to bring his American counterpart around to a slightly less extreme attitude. This enabled the two men to reach an agreement regarding the elimination of medium-range missiles in Europe (the Intermediate Nuclear Forces Treaty, 1987). A major scandal erupted during the Reagan administration, when it was discovered that the White House had authorized illegal weapons sales to Iran and then used the profits to finance rebels in Central America.

George Bush's term in office was dominated by international issues. Anxious to tackle the primary source of crime in the United States, drug use, Bush cracked down on illegal dealing. This also led Washington to overthrow the Panamanian regime of General Manuel Noriega, who was later convicted of drug trafficking.

The Soviet Union's economic collapse and subsequent break-up created a new world order. The Bush administration provided economic support to Eastern European countries to help them make the transition to a market economy.

In the summer of 1990, Iraq was preparing to invade Kuwait, and interpreted the silence of the international community as tacit permission. Saddam Hussein thus proceeded as planned in 1990. Kuwait asked the international community for help. Neighbouring countries feared for their own safety, and Washington was worried that Baghdad wanted to gain control over even more of the region's oil reserves. US troops were thus deployed in Saudi Arabia, where they were joined by contingents from other nations. The subsequent offensive, carried out under the aegis of the United Nations, soon drove the invaders out of Kuwait.

Nevertheless, concern over unemployment and the budget deficit led the American public to choose Bill Clinton over George Bush in the following elections. Clinton arrived at the White House with a whole slew of projects on his agenda – gun control, parental leave, free trade with Canada and Mexico and the liberalization of abortion laws. Since the middle of his first term, however, he has been embroiled in financial and sex scandals, which have been blown all out of proportion by the American media.

POLITICS

The United States of America is made up of 50 states, each of which is a republic, and a few federal territories such as the District of Columbia. Each state has its own constitution, which regulates its internal organization and determines who is eligible to vote. The United States also has a "supreme" constitution regulating the organization of the federal government and determining the division of powers between the United States and the states. If any conflict of law arises, the courts interpret the United States Constitution accordingly.

Scissors, Paper, Rock

The Constitution of the United States of America is regarded as one of the major steps in the history of western political thought. It is the oldest written constitution in the world, having been adopted in 1787 and ratified the following year. It was also the first document to apply the principles of the thinkers of the Enlightenment to a political system. Above all, the Constitution was the achievement of free men who intended to stay that way.

The American constitutional system is founded upon a very strict separation of powers between the Executive, Legislative and Judiciary branches of government. It also provides for a system of checks and balances among these branches. Abuses of power by a president can therefore be thwarted through impeachment by Congress. An act voted by Congress that would violate the Constitution can be invalidated by the Supreme Court. A judiciary interpretation harmful to the smooth running of the United States can bring about either a constitutional amendment or a later revision of the ruling once the composition of Court has changed. Indeed, everything happens much like the game scissors, paper, rock: the paper can cover the rock, the scissors can cut the paper, and the rock can break the scissors.

The Constitution is not a document that is fixed in time. Its interpretation by the courts breathes new life into the ideas behind it. Furthermore, the Constitution can be amended by a majority vote of two-thirds of both Houses of Congress, or by the application of the legislatures of two-thirds of the states, if the proposed amendment is ratified by three-fourths of the states. Moreover, the Constitution was modified immediately after its creation to include fundamental individual rights and liberties. This first series of 10 amendments is known as the Bill of Rights and serves as a charter of rights and liberties. The subsequent amendments pursued equally noble ends, such as the abolition of slavery and women's suffrage. At other times, the Constitution has been amended for pragmatic reasons, for example, by allowing the federal government to collect income taxes or prohibit the sale of alcohol.

Congress

In the 18th century, the government was much less present in the daily life of its citizens than it is today. Legislative power mattered most, and in the United States this power rests in the hands of Congress, which is made up of an upper and a lower House, the Senate and the House of Representatives. The composition of the Senate is equal for every state. There are 100 Senators, two per state. Conversely, the House of Representatives affords each state a representation proportional to its population. For example, of the 435 Representatives who sit in the House, 52 are from California and only one from Vermont. Every two years, on a fixed date, a legislative election renews the entire House of Representatives replaces one-third of the Senators whose six-year term is up.

Only Congress may collect taxes, borrow in the name of the federal government, print money and regulate interstate commerce. Also, only Congress can declare war, raise and support armies and maintain a navy. The support of Congress is essential to the organization and supervision of the workings of the State.

Furthermore, each of the Houses has its own particular prerogatives. Representatives have the initiative regarding taxation issues, and the process of impeachment of a president must begin with a majority vote in the House of Representatives.

The Senate must approve the nomination of federal judges, ambassadors and certain key government figures. If the House of Representatives votes in favour of removing a president from office, the Senate must hear the impeachment procedure and has the sole authority to impeach the president by a two-thirds majority vote. An important element of American foreign policy is that no treaty signed by the president may be brought into effect until it is ratified by a two-thirds Senate majority. Once ratified, a treaty takes precedence over state law under the supremacy clause of the Constitution.

For each vote, Senators and Representatives cast their ballot as they please, there being no such thing as party discipline in the United States. It follows as a matter of course that important votes are often preceded by an intense lobbying campaign during which efforts are made to identify who is on what side of the issue and who needs convincing. There are more than 3,000 accredited professionals in Washington whose job it is to do just that, as well as scores of unaccredited lobbyists.

The President

The president of the United States has far-reaching powers. He is at once Head of State, Prime Minister, Commander-in-Chief of the armed forces and leader of his party. However, his role was perceived as less important when the Constitution was adopted. Two hundred years later, governing the United States has become a very complex task involving three and a half million permanent civil servants and soldiers. American history has also shown that in crisis situations efficient administrations have been those in which the president had lots of leeway – as well as good ideas.

The president and vice president are chosen every four years on a fixed date. A constitutional amendment provides that no president may be elected to office more than twice.

The electoral process is long and quite complex. It requires an intermediary vote between the poll and the winning president. The Constitution requires each presidential candidate to be at least 35 years of age, to have been born in the United States and to have resided there for at least 14 years. A candidate has practically no chance of being elected unless he is part of one of the two great parties that dominate the American political scene. Moreover, a serious electoral campaign costs in the tens of millions of dollars, an absolute fortune. Becoming the presidential candidate for the Democratic or Republican Party requires winning a series of primary elections and then a national convention, which is an achievement in itself.

The Making of a Law

Anybody can promote a bill. But to go through the legislative process, a bill must be filed in either House by one of its members. There are hundreds of bills each session; clearly not all will be considered. Bills are filed according to their aim for House or Senate committees to determine their importance. Once approved by a committee, a bill is generally sent to a sub-committee, which holds public hearings where anybody can argue the necessity of adopting, amending or rejecting it.

The bill may then be the subject of a debate and a vote in the House to which it was submitted. If the bill is adopted, it is sent to the other House for the process to be repeated. It is common for a bill to be filed in both Houses concurrently to save time. If, per chance, the versions adopted by each House differ, a mixed committee is formed to reconcile differences and propose an identical text for the House of Representatives and the Senate to vote on.

A bill that has made it through all these steps must still be submitted to the president. The president may oppose the adoption of any bill within 10 days, in which case Congress can override his veto with a two-thirds majority vote. If the president approves the bill, he signs it into law.

The process is long and complex and calls for the cooperation of representatives and senators in Congress, and the president. Rarely in American history has a president been able to count on a majority of his party in both Houses. The fulfilment of a legislative program can therefore become impossible without serious compromise on all sides.

Each citizen's vote is counted state by state. The candidate with the most votes in a given state gains the support of all the Electors appointed by the legislature in that state. There are as many Electors in a given state as there are Senators and Representatives within that state. A president and his vice president are elected if they win the votes of more than half of the Electoral College (all of the Electors combined). If none of the presidential candidates holds a majority, the House of

Representatives chooses the president by ballot among the three candidates with the most Electoral votes. After the president is chosen, the person with the greatest number of Electoral votes shall be vice president. If there are two or more with an equal number of votes, the Senate chooses the vice president by ballot. Traditional bipartisanship in the United States has made it so that the president is rarely chosen by the House.

Since he is the leading official responsible for national security, the president may deploy troops to protect the United States, but a declaration of war or maintaining armies overseas requires a vote by Congress.

The president has the power to make treaties and appoint senior officers of the United States subject to the advice and consent of the Senate. Each year the president must submit a budget to Congress and report on the State of the Union. If Congress does not approve the budget, a stalemate that can paralyze the entire government ensues.

The principle activities of the American government are divided into 14 Departments: Agriculture, Commerce, Defense, Education, Energy, Health and Human Services, Housing and Urban Development, Interior, Justice, Labor, State, Transportation, Treasury, and, finally, Veteran Affairs. The president appoints a secretary, more or less the equivalent of a minister, to head each of these Departments.

The president also surrounds himself with advisors, assistants, deputies, press secretaries and an entire support staff specially assigned to the White House, the Executive Office. The president's personal ministry has grown enormously since the mid-20th century, and certain advisors – Henry Kissinger, for example – have had more political clout than others.

Finally, the president may seek advice from his personally appointed cabinet, made up of Secretaries of State, the Armed Forces and Foreign Affairs.

Democracy in the Capital of the Democracy

Washington, a relatively new municipal democracy, has only had three mayors since 1973. The first, whose name would seem to have fated him for the job, was Walter Washington, who served from 1975 to 1979. His successor, Marion Barry, Jr., remained in office until 1991, when he had to give up serving as mayor and serve time instead. The entire country saw a tape of him smoking crack in a hotel room, in the company of undercover federal agents.

Marion Barry is a remarkable political animal, however. He was also the first black person to serve as mayor of a major American city. In Washington, that earned him forgiveness and the votes of much of the black population, which forms two-thirds of the city's electorate. He thus succeeded in winning back his title from Sharon Pratt Kelly four years later.

Be it Washington, Barry or Pratt Kelly, however, no one has been able to curb the grave problems faced by the fledgling municipal democracy. The feverish activity of the capital doesn't involve the majority of the city's inhabitants, particularly those in poor black neighbourhoods. There is a lack of new jobs, and the racial divide remains an inescapable reality. Furthermore, the high unemployment rate has repercussions of its own. Crime, especially violent crime and the use of hard drugs, have earned the city a nasty reputation. In the late 1980s, the media even dubbed Washington the "murder capital", hardly a flattering title. It should be noted, however, that this crime epidemic is largely limited to the city's poorer neighbourhoods and does not really affect the tourist areas, which are still very safe.

Mayor Barry was no doubt trying to tackle all these problems head-on when he created a huge municipal government, the largest per capita in the United States. However, all the new jobs did not suffice to bring unemployment under control, no more than all the new police officers were able to wipe out crime. Meanwhile, these efforts plunged the city's finances into the abyss. By 1995, Washington had accumulated over three and a half billion dollars of debt.

Congress thought the situation had gone far enough. The financial hemorrhage that was draining the budget of the fledgling municipal government had to be stopped. The Planning Commission suggested that the situation could be straightened out by injecting federal funds into the economy. Monuments could be erected, museums opened, and government office buildings constructed. It

> was hoped that further enhancing the city's stature as the nation's capital would attract more tourists and private enterprises.
>
> However, President Clinton refused to follow that path because of how expensive it might be for the federal government. Instead, he opted to keep the city under close supervision. Mayor Barry still has all the trappings of a mayor, as well as control over tourism, economic development and recreational services. Meanwhile, a special commission, whose first task is to balance the budget, has been charged with supervising the police, the fire department, social services, education and all other important sectors. In Washington, Mayor Barry and his supporters consider the plan a slap in the face to the city councilors, whose hands are now tied. Many even view it as a racist tactic.

The Supreme Court

The federal judicial apparatus is presided over by a Supreme Court consisting of nine justices. Lower courts include Circuit Courts (appeal courts), District Courts, and specialized tribunals. All federal judges are appointed for life by the president, subject to approval by the Senate. Federal judges possess vast powers since they may invalidate any provision of a law which violates the United States Constitution. This power extends to the invalidation of state law.

This power can be a major agent of change in American society. Indeed, any injured party may petition a Circuit Court to demand that the United States Constitution be respected. This type of appeal has been used to abolish segregation in the southern United States.

The Supreme Court may reverse its earlier decisions so that its opinion on a given topic evolves with the Court's composition. However, if Congress cannot wait for new appointments to modify the rule of law, it can always amend the Constitution.

Citizens Who Don't Vote

For nearly a century, the US Congress administered the city of Washington and the District of Columbia like its private domain. Actually, that's pretty much what the Founding Fathers originally wanted, since they were determined that the capital should be neutral. They also made things this way so that local residents could not vote for their employers. Washingtonians thus paid a dear price for living at the heart of American democracy. In fact, District residents have only been able to vote since 1964, when they participated in a presidential election for the first time.

In 1973, however, things changed. The Home Rule Act allowed the population to elect city councilors and a school board. Congress nonetheless reserved its veto power over municipal administration. Furthermore, municipal budgets are always under the president's control. Finally, the preservation of the capital's heritage and standing has led to the creation of specific regulations and several special commissions that are not within municipal jurisdiction. The mayor's political powers are therefore much more limited than in any other American city.

The Home Rule Act has, among other things, allowed the people of Washington to send a delegate to the House of Representatives. Since 1994, furthermore, this delegate can even vote. A resolution to allow the District of Columbia to ascend to statehood was rejected by Congress in 1993.

Progress or Decay?

A great deal has been written about American political practices since the end of the Second World War. Of course, the integrity of US presidents, like that of all politicians, has always been questioned. However, criticism has become harsher since television came into the picture, exercising a tremendous influence on the average voter.

Americans value moral rectitude above all else. No one has ever made it into the Oval Office without overtly associating his campaign with his family life, his belief in God and his unconditional love of the Stars and Stripes. The presidency and even the vice presidency have always been occupied by white men, preferably married, rich white men who are veterans and good Christians, though not Catholic. The First Lady, for her part, is expected to be a model wife and attentive mother.

However, the mould in which presidents are cast has been battered about quite a bit in the latter half of the 20th century. In 1961, John F. Kennedy became the first Catholic president at the end of a campaign marked by a televised debate. Richard Nixon had to leave office because of the Watergate scandal. Ronald Reagan was subpoena to testify about his role in the Iran-Contra affair, otherwise known as Irangate. More recently, Bill Clinton's reputation has been stained by various scandals related to real-estate dealings, partisan activities and inappropriate sexual conduct (Zippergate). Incidentally, Clinton has become the butt of American sex jokes. For her part Hillary Clinton, the President's long-suffering wife, has deviated from her traditional role by playing an active part in the country's affairs.

It is a sign of the times that Americans are getting tired of muckraking and claim to be more concerned about matters of State than about their leaders' private lives. If Bill Clinton has made a lasting contribution, that just might be it.

ECONOMY

To say that Washington is a capital is not enough; it is a capital and nothing else. Visitors will thus find politicians, civil servants, non-government organizations, diplomats, canvassers, protestors, convention-goers, tourists and all the services and shops necessary to meet everyone's needs. The city has remarkably little industry, aside from some printing and food-processing plants. For that reason, the air here is much cleaner than in other big American cities.

The largest local employer, of course, is the federal government, which provides jobs for 350,000 people, a third of the local workforce. A small number of those employees work for Congress and the Supreme Court, but the civil service is more or less monopolized by federal departments and agencies connected to the Executive branch of government.

The capital also plays host to nearly 150 foreign embassies and every special-interest group, union and charitable organization in the United States. We should also add that Washington is the headquarters of the World Bank, the International Monetary Fund and the Organization of American States, further increasing the amount of diplomatic activity that goes on here.

The service industry accounts for another third of the workforce. Aside from those services aimed at the local population, there are those that cater to the 18 million tourists and convention-goers who come to Washington each year. It is one of the cities with the most hotels in the world.

Like all major urban centres in the United States, Washington is the hub of a complex and efficient transportation network. The city is drained, so to speak, by highways. It is also served by three airports, Washington National, Dulles International and Baltimore-Washington International. Thanks to Union Station, furthermore, visitors can ride right into the city on the train, arriving 800 metres from the Capitol. Finally, of course, there are buses, taxis and a subway system for local travel.

POPULATION

Washington has just over 600,000 inhabitants, making it the nineteenth most populous city in the United States. Like all big cities, the capital, which once had over 800,000 residents, has a hard time keeping the local population within it's city limits. The lure of the suburbs, with their big houses and lawns, is simply too strong for many who can afford to move there.

As a result, the urban area has spread beyond the limits of the city and the District of Columbia. The greater Washington area now extends into five Maryland counties (Calvert, Charles, Prince George's, Montgomery and Frederick) and five Virginia counties (Stafford, Prince William, Arlington, Fairfax and Loudoun). More than four million people have settled in the area, with the help of an extensive public transportation network. These suburbs are now blending into the gigantic urban area that starts around Boston, balloons at New York, then extends to Philadelphia, Baltimore and Washington, stretching some 1000 kilometres in all. This megalopolis covers only 2% of the territory of the United States but is home to 22% of the nation's population – some 50 million people.

The desire to live in the suburbs has had some insidious consequences on the city. Perhaps the worst is the socioeconomic split it has created. Entire neighbourhoods have sunk into poverty after being abandoned by the middle class. This urban phenomenon is clearly one reason why Washington's crime rate soared so high that the city was dubbed the "murder capital". The illegal dealing of hard drugs in poor neighbourhoods has sent police statistics through the roof, and even if the situation is improving, it is best not to wander too far outside the tourist areas.

Seventy percent of Washingtonians are black, but the greater Washington area is two-thirds white. Whites form the majority in the northwest part of the city, which happens to be the most affluent section. Much less cosmopolitan than many other US cities, the capital nonetheless has rapidly growing Hispanic and Asian communities. Various Native American groups, such as the Piscataways, have also managed to preserve their cultural identity.

Most local residents are Christian. Maryland still has a lot of Catholics, though they are now outnumbered by Protestants of various denominations – Presbyterians, Baptists, Episcopalians and Methodists, among others. Virginia, true to its history, is almost 100% Protestant. Jews are still a tiny minority, as are members of the Greek Orthodox Church. It should be noted that black and white Protestants tend to worship God their own way, in their own churches. One positive result of this division has been the emergence of a unique form of music: gospel.

CULTURAL LIFE

Apart from the John F. Kennedy Center for the Performing Arts, many theaters, such as Ford's Theater, the National Theater, Constitution Hall and the Warner Theater, to name but a few, and several cinemas liven up Washington's cultural life.

Once considered a mere testing ground for big New York productions, the capital of the United States, which today boasts no fewer than 20 theatres, refused to play second fiddle. Thanks to the efforts of the Smithsonian Institution and various political authorities, including Presidents Eisenhower and Kennedy, both of whom introduced a project for the construction of a national arts facility, the John F. Kennedy Center, Washington has gradually become a prime destination for large theatrical and musical productions, and for the country's cultural life in general. The more intimate venue of the dinner theatre has also come into its own here, further testifying to the vitality of the performing arts. Their productions are most often comedies (occasionally satirical) or vaudeville. One has only to see the number of reserved tables in these places to understand how popular they are with Washingtonians.

It's a fact that Americans are better than most at making fun of their own institutions, as evidenced by box-office hits like *Forrest Gump*, *Mars Attacks*, or more recently *Wag the Dog*, starring Dustin Hoffman and Robert de Niro. In Hollywood, as in Washington, people know how to find the humour in the unexpected twists and turns of politics. Stand-up comics love tearing this or that political figure to pieces, and are no less merciful to the institutions those individuals represent. Many great American comedians got their start doing stand-up. One example is Ellen de Generes, who has since become famous as the star of the television show *Ellen*.

As for dance, Washington is not lacking. The John F. Kennedy Center for the Performing Arts and the Warner Theater are two of the greatest venues for this branch of the performing arts. The Washington Ballet, which performs regularly at the Kennedy Center, has both classical productions and contemporary choreography in its repertory.

Bel Canto and opera are so prized by Washingtonians that one must reserve a long time ahead to attend a performance by the Washington Opera at the Kennedy Center. The advancement and diffusion of knowledge has always been the Smithsonian's primary objective, and the institution, though better known for its fabulous art collections than its concerts, has not overlooked opera and classical music. Moreover, Washington also has a renowned symphony orchestra, the Washington Civic Symphony, which performs in Constitution Hall.

The city is also rich in libraries. Of course there are private and public university libraries, but the grandest of all is the Library of Congress, located east of the Capitol in an enormous building supplemented by an annex. The Library of Congress is the largest and most important library in the United States with nearly 100 million books, manuscripts and pieces of music preserved within it. It boasts over 5,000 incunabula, including the Gutenberg Bible. Also of particular interest is the Folger Shakespeare Library, dedicated exclusively to the English playwright. With no fewer than 275,000 books and manuscripts, it has one of the world's largest collections of material devoted to Shakespeare's life, work and times. The library also houses a small Elizabethan theatre where pieces by Shakespeare are performed and conferences, public readings and concerts are held.

The Smithsonian Institution

A description of Washington's cultural scene would not be complete without a few paragraphs on the importance and vitality of the Smithsonian Institution. After all, Washington is a museum-goer's paradise.

Art and artifact lovers will be in seventh heaven, especially when they visit the museums that make up the Smithsonian Institution, the largest museum complex in the world and perhaps the only to take an interest all fields of human knowledge.

The Smithsonian Institution is a foundation managed by a board of directors, which by statute includes the Vice President of United States, the Chief Justice of the Supreme Court, three Senators, three members of the House of Representatives and a number of citizens chosen by Congress. It was created in 1846 when Congress followed up on a bequest made by an English chemist and mineralogist named James Smithson. He asked that the money be used to found an institution dedicated to the "increase and diffusion of knowledge". The Smithsonian would become the national museum of the United States.

In 1855, the foundation moved into a brick building on the Mall. Smithson's idea caught on rapidly. The foundation began to receive donations, inherit works of art and make acquisitions. Its present collection has over 100 million catalogued pieces and works, most of which are stored in Maryland in huge warehouses specially built for that purpose. The Smithsonian Institution is devoted to both the sciences and the arts. It also sponsors research and publishes books and magazines.

The original building soon proved too small and poorly suited for its gargantuan collection, so other, more specialized museums were erected. Among these are: the National Air & Space Museum, the National Museum of American Art, the National Museum of American History, the National Museum of Natural History, the National Museum of the American Indian, the National Zoological Park, the Cooper-Hewitt Museum (devoted to the decorative arts), the Freer Gallery of Art (oriental art), and the Hirshhorn Museum and Sculpture Garden (19th- and 20th-century western art). The National Gallery of Art and the John F. Kennedy Center for the Performing Arts, though administered separately, are also connected to the Smithsonian. Finally, the institution has many other smaller museums, archives, specialized research centres and even an astronomical observatory in Boston.

The Smithsonian museums also have one very unusual characteristic: free admission.

ARCHITECTURE

In 1790, when the US Congress legislated in favour of building a national capital to serve as the seat of the federal government, the young republic decided to found its new Rome on the banks of the Potomac River, at the mouth of the Anacostia River. A diamond-shaped site, which originally measured 16 kilometres on each side and straddled the Potomac and Anacostia rivers, was set aside for this purpose. A French architect and urban planner named Pierre Charles L'Enfant was appointed to design what was to be a city-state at the service of American democracy, inspired by the ancient Greek ideal. He imagined a checkerboard pattern, with streets running either parallel or perpendicular to one another and segmented diagonally by large avenues. Traffic circles with monuments in the middle would mark the intersections of major streets and avenues, thereby creating spectacular perspectives that would showcase important government buildings. Grandeur and classicism, which at the time made Charles Dickens laugh when he saw the huge, undeveloped spaces, were the pillars of L'Enfant's vision. It was merely a question of time before the empty spaces between the principal monuments were gradually filled in and the city became a more coherent architectural whole. L'Enfant's genius is palpable in all the city's nooks and crannies, which is all the more extraordinary when you consider that he was dismissed in 1792, barely one year after being appointed, because of his constant insubordination. His plans had nonetheless been filled and served as a source of inspiration for his successors. The city's architecture can be roughly divided into three major phases, all of which bear the stamp of classicism.

The first phase is characterized by Greco-Roman cultural traditions. Whether it be the Georgian or Palladian style of the White House, or the neoclassical style of the Supreme Court and Federal Triangle buildings, all feature pediments, porticos and Doric, Ionic or Corinthian columns. Andrea Palladio, one of the most prominent architects of the Italian Renaissance, took the principal elements of classicism and adapted them to the villas he designed, creating a style that today bears his name. In the 17th century, English architects introduced a modified version of the Palladian style to Britain. This led to the emergence of the Georgian style, which characterizes a large number of opulent private homes in Washington and its surrounding area. The White House is a fine example of a Georgian manor. However, this style was quickly abandoned, since it had been imported by English colonists, and thus became a symbol of colonialism and British oppression. A return to the architectural traditions of ancient Rome and Greece, which conveyed ideals of grandeur, democracy and republicanism, turned out to be a more judicious choice.

The challenges posed by erecting a new capital meant to serve an ambitious, though still unstable, young republic attracted the great talents of the nation and even Europe. Although architects such as William Lovering, William Thornton and Benjamin Henry Latrobe had already established their reputations, a number of amateur architects were assigned ambitious building projects after being chosen through a public bidding process. Such was the case of the doctor and architect James Hoban, who presented plans for a presidential mansion worthy of the greatest despot. Thomas Jefferson put a stop to this extravagance and modified the original design himself. Jefferson, the third president of the United States, was passionately interested in architecture and favoured a style that harked back to the Roman republic. At the time, it seemed that everybody had a plan or some modifications to make, and many people were quick to criticize their competitors or predecessors.

The cornerstone of the White House was laid in 1792. The following year, the Capitol was begun. These two leading monuments of republican power were almost completed when British troops invaded the young capital during the War of 1812 and set fire to it.

The 19th century was dominated by a school of French architecture known as the École des Beaux-Arts, which influenced the city's second phase of construction throughout the 1800s and all the way up until Second World War. Though also characterized by classical forms and symmetrical plans, the Beaux-Arts style may be distinguished from earlier schools by its more elaborate and exuberant use of ornamentation. Pediments and Greek and Roman columns gave way to Mansard roofs, balustrades, terracotta friezes, cornices and huge coffered vaults. The remarkable technical advances of the Industrial Revolution, most notably the use of steel substructures, made it possible to tackle the most daunting architectural challenges, and the resulting structures were light and graceful. The McMillan Commission, which in 1900 was put in charge of supervising the capital's future development by reinterpreting L'Enfant's plans for the city, was greatly inspired by this French school of architecture. The commission is responsible for such magnificent Beaux-Arts style buildings as Union Station, the West Building of the National Gallery of Art and the edifices that make up Federal Triangle. Washington's second architectural phase was also marked by a law enacted by Congress in 1899. Following the construction of the Cairo, a 14-story apartment building on Q Street, Congress passed a law limiting the height of buildings to about 10 floors, so that no building would be higher than the Capitol and obstruct its view. This law, which is still in effect today, has had important economic repercussions on the city. Whereas most large American cities are racing to build skyscrapers because of increasingly high real-estate prices, Washington remains the only city with a low skyline, which highlights its monuments but causes its downtown core to keep expanding. This height limitation posed a quite challenge to architects and urban planners, forcing them to design complex plans that widened government and office buildings, covering entire blocks. The buildings of the Federal Triangle are a good example. The law has also had economic repercussions on the capital's commercial vitality, since pedestrian traffic decreases as the city spreads, which means fewer customers for the local businesses and an overall drop in commercial activity.

The third phase of construction was marked by both the emergence of modernism and political considerations. Early modern architecture was a reaction to the elaborate ornamentation of late 19th-century buildings. The Bauhaus School, founded by Walter Gropius in 1919, rejected the old architectural rules, particularly the Beaux-Arts School, because they promoted a certain image of European aristocracy. When Adolf Hitler came to power, the spread of Nazism lead many members of Bauhaus to emigrate to the United States, where they felt confident that they could advance modern architecture. At the same time, propelled by talented architects like Louis Sullivan and his disciple Frank Lloyd Wright, modernism made a conspicuous entrance into Washington's urban landscape. Among the main achievements of the 1970s were a number of magnificent buildings erected on the Mall, such as the East Wing of the National Gallery of Art (I.M. Pei), the Hirshhorn Museum (Skidmore, Owings and Merrill) and the National Air and Space Museum (Hellmuth, Obata and Kassabaum). However, other projects, such as L'Enfant Plaza (also designed by I.M. Pei), prompted a great deal of skepticism.

Besides the emergence and then supremacy of modernism, the third phase of Washington's architectural evolution was also influenced by political considerations. During John F. Kennedy's inaugural parade up prestigious Pennsylvania Avenue, he couldn't help but notice that this artery, meant to offer the best vista in the city, between the White House and the Capitol, was in pitiful condition. A committee was created to develop and revitalize Pennsylvania Avenue. A large-scale demolition and reconstruction project was almost undertaken but was fortunately dropped at the last minute. Finally, the buildings along the avenue were restored, small businesses that had fallen into ruin because of the lack of economic activity were shut down and new buildings, such as the F.B.I. Headquarters, were erected. In 1965, Congress allocated 435 million dollars for the construction of a subway system in order to offset Washington's steady economic decline. The riots that followed Martin Luther King, Jr.'s assassination in 1968 caused 57 million dollars' worth of damages and made it clear that the downtown area was unsafe and in urgent need of revitalization. Efforts were quickly launched to renovate the neighborhood and make it a more active economic, administrative and commercial centre.

In more recent years, other modern buildings have gone up all over Washington. Among the more noteworthy are the magnificent John F. Kennedy Center for the Performing Arts (Edward Durrell Stone); Washington Harbor (Arthur Cotton Moore); the remarkable Canadian Embassy (Arthur Erickson), located near the Capitol on Pennsylvania Avenue, and several other beautifully designed embassies, including that of Finland (Mikko Heikkiken and Marku Komonen), which, with its series of bronze and glass screens, blends harmoniously into the surrounding landscape (Massachusetts Avenue).

PRACTICAL INFORMATION

nformation in this chapter will help you to better plan your trip, not only well in advance, but once you've arrived in Washington. Important details on entrance formalities and other procedures, as well as general information, have been compiled for visitors from other countries and Americans.

The **area code** for the Washington district is **202**. We have, however, dispensed with the 202 prefix in the current text in order to economize on space. For the numbers requiring a different prefix, such as 703 for the city of Alexandria, we have consistently specified the requisite area code.

ENTRANCE FORMALITIES

CUSTOMS

Foreigners may enter the United States with 200 cigarettes (or 100 cigars) and duty-free purchases not exceeding $400 US, including personal gifts and 1 litre of alcohol (the legal drinking age is 21). There is no limit on the amount of cash you are carrying, though you must fill out a special form if you are carrying the equivalent of more than $10,000 US. Prescription

Practical Information

medication must be placed in containers clearly marked to that effect (you may have to present a prescription or a written statement from your doctor to customs officials). Meat and its by-products, all kinds of food, grains, plants, fruits and narcotics can not be brought into the United States.

For more detailed information, contact:

United States Customs Service
1301 Constitution Avenue Northwest, Washington, DC 20229, ☎(202) 566-8195.

Passports

Travellers from Canada, the majority of western European countries, Australia and New Zealand do not need visas to enter the United States. A valid passport is sufficient for stays of up to three months. A return ticket and proof of sufficient funds to cover your stay may be required. For stays of more than three months, all travellers, except Canadians and citizens of the British Commonwealth, must obtain a visa ($120 US) from the American embassy in their country.

Caution: as medical expenses can be very high in the United States, travel health insurance is highly recommended. For more information, see the section entitled "Health" (p 81).

EMBASSIES AND CONSULATES

United States Embassies and Consulates Abroad

Australia
Embassy: Moonah Place, Canberra, ACT 2600, ☎(6) 214-5600.

Belgium
Embassy: 27 Boulevard du Régent, B-1000 Brussels, ☎(02) 512-2210, ≠ (02) 511-9652.

Canada
Embassy: 2 Wellington Street, Ottawa, Ontario, K1P 5T1, ☎(613) 238-5335, ⇌(613) 238-5720.

Consulate: Place Félix-Martin, 1155 Rue Saint-Alexandre, Montréal, Québec, H2Z 1Z2, ☎(514) 398-9695, ⇌(514) 398-9748.

Consulate: 360 University Avenue, Toronto, Ontario, M5G 1S4, ☎(416) 595-1700, ⇌(416) 595-0051.

Consulate: 1095 West Pender, Vancouver, British Columbia, V6E 2M6, ☎(604) 685-4311.

Denmark
Embassy: Dag Hammarskjölds Allé 24, 2100 Copenhagen Ø, ☎(35) 55 31 44, ⇌(35) 43 02 23.

Germany
Embassy: Clayallee 170, 14195 Berlin, ☎(030) 832-2933, ⇌(030) 8305-1215.

Great Britain
Embassy: 24 Grosvenor Square, London W1A 1AE, ☎(171) 499-9000, ⇌(171) 491-2485.

Italy
Embassy: Via Vittorio Vérito, 11917-121 Roma, ☎467-41, ⇌610-450.

Netherlands
Embassy: Lange Voorhout 102, 2514 EJ, Den Haag, ☎(70) 310-9209, ⇌(70) 361-4688.

Spain
Embassy: C. Serrano 75, Madrid 28001, ☎(1) 577-4000, ⇌(1) 564-1652, Telex (1) 277-63.

Sweden
Embassy: Strandvägen 101, 11589 Stockholm, ☎(08) 783 53 00, ⇌(08) 661 19 64.

Switzerland
Embassy: 93 Jubilam Strasse, 3000 Berne, ☎31-43-70-11.

TOURIST INFORMATION

For all tourist information contact:

Washington Tourism Office
717 14th Street NW, 11th Floor, Washington, DC 20005, ☎(202) 727-4511, ≠(202) 727-3784.

Washington DC Convention and Visitors Association
1212 New York Avenue NW, Suite 600, Washington, DC 20005, ☎(202) 789-7000.

Washington Visitor Information Center
1455 Pennsylvania Avenue NW, Washington, DC 20005, ☎(202) 789-7038.

International Visitors Services *(24 hours a day, ☎939-5566)* provides visitors and new residents from abroad with brochures and information in a variety of languages.

Physically handicapped visitors can obtain information about access for the disabled and a brochure entitled *Access Washington* at the following organization:

Information Protection and Advocacy Center for Handicapped Individuals
4455 Connecticut Avenue NW, Suite B100, Washington, DC 20008, ☎(202) 966-8081.

You can also obtain a wealth of additional tourist-related information on the Internet at the following web sites:

www.Washington.org/
www.washingtonpost.com/wp-srv/local/longterm/tours/guide2.htm
www.rps.gov/rocr/
www.webworqs.com/metrodork/

GUIDED TOURS

If you are short of time but wish to get a good glimpse of the city's most attractive neighbourhoods, you can opt for a guided tour of Washington. A few companies offer worthwhile excursions through the streets of the capital.

Museum Bus Tours *($5 day pass, $15 five-day pass, $25 five-day family pass; everyday 10am to 5pm)* visits 23 museums in the capital as well as the National Zoo.
Information: ☎(202) 588-7470
Ticket purchasing: ☎(202) 842-5387

Tourmobile *(adults $12, children $6; Mon to Sat 9am to 7pm, Sun 9am to 6pm; for information: kiosk at Union Station, Union Station metro, ☎554-5100)* probably offers the most convenient guided tours of Washington, including the main buildings of the Mall and Arlington National Cemetery. Moreover, you can get off at any time to visit one museum or another, without having to pay to get back on board. Departures every 15 minutes.

Old Town Trolley *(adults $20, children $11; departures every 30 min., Mon to Fri 9am to 4pm, Sat and Sun 9am to 4:30pm; ☎832-9800)* offers narrated tours of the city's main tourist attractions. This tour company also allows passengers to disembark and board the next bus at any stop.

For those who may appreciate a more unconventional introduction to the city, **Scandal Tours** *($27; Sat at 1pm; 1100 Pennsylvania Ave. NW, at the Old Post Office pavilion, ☎1-800-758-8687)* organizes an irreverent guided tour of Washington based on all the scandals that have rocked the nation's capital, from Watergate to behind-the-scenes goings-on at the FBI.

GETTING TO WASHINGTON

By Plane

Washington boasts three airports, namely Washington International Airport, which welcomes domestic and Canadian flights; Dulles International Airport, for domestic and international flights; and Baltimore-Washington International Airport, which receives domestic flights as well as a few international flights.

Washington National Airport

Located right by the Potomac, in Arlington County, Virginia, the Washington National Airport *(7 km south of downtown, National Airport metro, ☎703-419-8000)* is the closest one to downtown Washington. Getting there will only take you about fifteen minutes during off-peak hours.

To get there:

● by car: head south along the I-395, then take the southbound George Washington Memorial Parkway and follow the signs to the airport.

● by taxi: the fare runs between $10 and $15.

● by subway: two subway lines, namely the blue and the yellow, lead to the Washington National Airport. National Airport subway station.

● by shuttle: the **Washington Flyer Shuttle** *($8; everyday 6:25am to 9:25pm)* travels between the airport and the downtown area every half-hour. On weekends, departures can be less frequent, namely once an hour.

Dulles International Airport

The Dulles International Airport *(☎703-419-8000)* is located in Virginia, about 40 kilometres from downtown Washington. It is the capital's main airport for international flights.

Getting to Washington

To get there:

- By car: take Constitution Avenue, which runs west along the Mall, then the I-66, which straddles the Potomac across the Theodore Roosevelt Bridge. Approximately 15 kilometres west you will come to the junction of the Dulles Airport Access Road, which leads to the international airport.

- By taxi: this is a rather costly option, because this airport is a fair distance from downtown Washington. Note that it will cost you at least $40, assuming you do not get stuck in traffic.

- By metro: the orange line goes to the West Falls Church metro, where you can take the shuttle *($8; Mon to Fri 6am to 10pm, Sat and Sun 7:30am to 10pm, departures every 30 min.; ☎703-685-1400)* to Dulles Airport.

- By shuttle: the **Washington Flyer Dulles Shuttle** *($16; everyday 5:20am to 10:20pm, Mon to Fri departures every 30 min., Sat and Sun departures every hour; 1517 K St. NW, ☎703-685-1400)* travels to and from the downtown terminal, stopping at Washington's main hotels along the way.

Baltimore-Washington International Airport

The Baltimore-Washington International Airport *(☎301-261-1000)* is situated in Maryland, 45 kilometres north of Washington and 15 kilometres south of Baltimore.

To get there:

- By car: take the eastbound 395 then the northbound 295, which turns into the Baltimore-Washington Parkway, and follow the signs to the airport. It takes about one hour to get there by car.

- By train: the **MARC Train** *($10; ☎1-800-325-7245)* is a commuter rail service that provides transportation to and from Washington's Union Station. The AMTRAK company *(☎1-800-523-8720)* also provides train service to and from Union Station.

• By shuttle: the **SuperShuttle** *($19; everyday 6:10am to 11:10pm, departures every hour; ☎301-369-0009)* and the **Airport Connection Shuttle** *($15; Mon to Fri 7am to 11pm, departures every hour-and-a-half, Sat and Sun 7:30am to 8pm, departures every 2 hours; ☎301-441-2345)* also offer transport to and from the nation's capital.

Airline Companies:

Aeroflot	202-429-4922
Air Canada	800-776-3000
Air France	800-237-2747
Air Jamaica	800-523-5585
All Nippon Airways	800-235-9262
American Airlines	800-433-7300
American Eagle	800-433-7300
America West	800-235-9262
British Airways	800-247-9297
Business Express	800-345-3400
Continental	800-525-0280
Continental Express	703-478-9700
Delta	800-221-1212
Iberia Airlines of Spain	800-775-4642
Icelandair	800-223-5500
Japan Airlines	800-525-3663
Korean Airlines	800-438-5000
KLM Royal Dutch Airlines	800-374-7747
Ladeco	800 825-2332
Lufthansa German	800-645-3880
Northwest	800-225-2525
Sabena Belgian World Airlines	800-873-3900
Saudia	800-472-8342
Southwest Airlines	800-435-9792
SwissAir	800-221-4750
TWA	202-737-7400
United	800-241-6522
USAIR	800-428-4322
Valujet	800-825-8538
Virgin Atlantic Airways	800-862-8621

Getting to Washington 67

By Train

In Washington, the train station is located near the downtown area, a few blocks from the Capitol. The metro stops at Union Station, allowing passengers to reach the city's various districts.

Union Station
50 Massachusetts Avenue NE, ☎484-7540.

To obtain schedules and destinations, contact Amtrak, the main transport company of the American rail network *(toll-free in North America, ☎1-800-872-7245)*. To reach the Washington AMTRAK office, dial ☎202-484-7540. By Internet: www.amtrak.com.

AMTRAK offers various passes that can save you a great deal of money as you travel to Washington and nearby regions. The **North American Rail Pass**, in conjunction with **VIA Rail**, allows you to explore over 900 destinations throughout Canada and the United States for up to 30 consecutive days of travel. In the peak season, this pass costs $645 US ($450 US in the off-peak season). You can also opt for the **Northeastern North America Rail Pass** and, for $400 US ($300 US in the off-peak season), visit the entire northeastern coast of the United States and of Canada, from Detroit, Michigan, in the west, to Newport News, Virginia, in the south, and up to Gaspé in southeastern Quebec. At $195 US ($175 US in the off-peak season), the best-value pass is unquestionably the **Northeast Rail Pass**, which is good for 15 consecutive days of travel along the northeast coast, by way of such places as Virginia Beach, Philadelphia, New York City, Niagara Falls and Montreal. The 30-day pass, for its part, goes for $230 US ($215 US in the off-peak season). The **East Rail Pass** allows travellers to visit the entire east coast of the United States as well as southern Quebec and Ontario. For $250 US ($205 US in the off-peak season), you can travel up the Atlantic coast from Miami to Montreal.

By taking the *Twilight Shoreliner* night train, you can make your way from Boston to Virginia Beach via Williamsburg, Virginia. As of 1999, the **Northeast Corridor High-Speed Train** will run from Boston to New York City every hour, departing twice an hour from New York City to Washington, DC. These trains will be able to reach speeds of up to 240 km/h and transport as many as 301 passengers.

By Bus

Besides by car, the bus is the best way to get from one city to the next in the United States. Efficient and inexpensive, bus service covers most of the country.

For schedules and destinations contact Greyhound (☎402-341-1900 or 1-800-231-2222).

Canadians can buy tickets from Voyageur in Québec (☎514-842-2281 in Montréal) and Greyhound in the rest of the country (☎416-393- 7911 in Toronto).

Smoking is forbidden on most lines. In general children 5 years and under travel for free. Travellers over 60 are eligible for special discounts. Animals are not permitted on board.

The bus station in Washington is located at 1005 1st Street NE at the corner of L Street.

The Ameripass

The Greyhound bus company offers Ameripass, which allows you to travel throughout the United States for $179 (7 days) to $559 (60 days). For further information, contact Greyhound at ☎289-5155 or ☎1-800-231-2222.

By Car

Washington is easily reached from Canada and anywhere in the United States, because it is linked to an excellent network of roads.

The city is located at the intersection of several highways, known as Interstates, which connect various American states.

Getting to Washington

The I-95 (northbound and southbound), the I-66 (eastbound), the US-50 (westbound) and the I-270 (northbound and westbound) lead to an expressway surrounding the capital that is known as the Beltway, or the I-495.

Western European driver's licences are valid in the United States. While Canadian travellers will have no trouble adapting to the American Highway Code, this may not be the case for European visitors. Indeed, the Highway Code is largely different in North America, and motorists from Europe will have to acclimatize themselves accordingly. A few tips for the latter:

There is no priority to the right in North America.

Signs marked "Stop" in white against a red background must always be respected. Some stop signs are accompanied by a small sign indicating "4-way". This means that all vehicles must stop at the intersection. Come to a complete stop even if there is no apparent danger. If two vehicles arrive at the same time, the one to the right has right of way. Otherwise the first car at the intersection has the right of way.

Traffic lights are often located on the opposite side of the intersection, so be careful to stop at the stop line, a white line on the pavement before the intersection.

North American drivers are very respectful of pedestrians and automatically give them the right of way, even in big cities. Pedestrian crosswalks are indicated by a yellow sign. When you see one of these signs, make sure that no one is crossing the road before you proceed.

Turning right on a red light after a full stop is permitted, unless otherwise indicated.

When a school bus (usually yellow) has stopped and has its signals flashing, **you must come to a complete stop, no matter what direction you are travelling in**. Failing to stop at the flashing signals is considered a serious offense, and carries a heavy penalty.

Seat belts must be worn at all times.

There are no tolls on the highways, except on most Interstate highways, indicated by the letter I, followed by a number. Interstate highways are indicated by a blue crest on a white background. The highway number and the state are written on the sign. "Interstate" is written on a red background at the top of the sign.

The speed limit is 55mph (88kph) on most highways. These signs are rectangular with a black border, white background and black writing.

The speed limit on Interstate highways is 65 mph (104 kph).

Red and white triangular signs with the word "Yield" under them indicate that vehicles crossing your path have the right of way.

The speed limit is indicated by square signs with a white background, and "Speed Limit" and the maximum speed underneath are written in black.

A round, yellow sign with a black X and two Rs indicates a railroad crossing.

Because the United States produces its own crude oil, gasoline prices are less expensive than in Europe; gas is also less expensive than in Canada, due to hidden taxes north of the border. Self-serve stations will often ask for payment in advance as a security measure.

Accidents and Emergencies

In case of serious accident, fire or other emergency, dial **911** or **0**.

If you run into trouble on the highway, pull onto the shoulder of the road and turn the hazard lights on. If it is a rental car, contact the rental company as soon as possible. Always file an accident report. If a disagreement arises over who was at fault in an accident, ask for police help.

Getting to Washington 71

Car Rentals

Many travel agencies have agreements with the major car rental companies (Avis, Budget, Hertz, etc.) and offer good deals; contracts often include added bonuses (reduced ticket prices for shows, etc.).

However, like in many other major cities, driving is certainly not the most efficient way, nor the most pleasant, of getting around Washington, particularly since the subway, both modern and altogether safe, runs to the city's major tourist attractions.

If you want to rent a car to visit the capital and its surrounding area, taken note that most car rental companies require that you be at least 25 years old and have a credit card.

Alamo
2780 Jefferson Davis Hwy., Arlington VA, ☎1-800-327-9633.

Avis
Union Station, ☎1-800-331-1212.

Budget
4727 Wisconsin Avenue NW, ☎1-800-527-0700.

Dollar
☎1-800-800-4000.

Enterprise Rent-a-Car
927 North Kansas Street, Arlington VA, ☎1-800-325-8007.

Hertz
901 11th Street NW, ☎1-800-654-3131.

National
Union Station, ☎1-800-328-4567.

Thrifty
☎1-800-367-2277.

When renting a car, find out if the contract includes unlimited mileage and if the insurance offered provides full coverage

Table of Distances (km/mi)
Via the shortest route

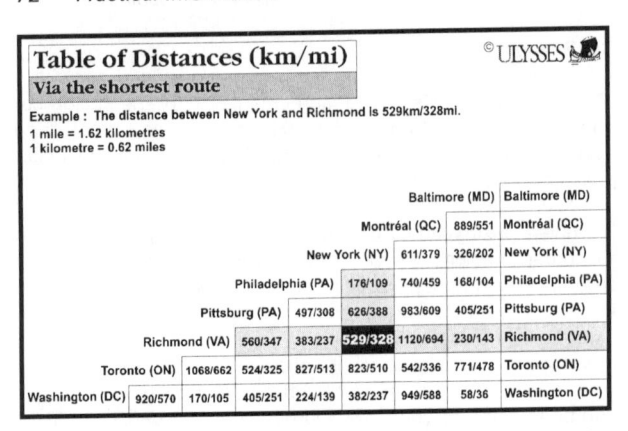

Example: The distance between New York and Richmond is 529km/328mi.
1 mile = 1.62 kilometres
1 kilometre = 0.62 miles

								Baltimore (MD)	Baltimore (MD)
							Montréal (QC)	889/551	Montréal (QC)
						New York (NY)	611/379	326/202	New York (NY)
					Philadelphia (PA)	176/109	740/459	168/104	Philadelphia (PA)
				Pittsburg (PA)	497/308	626/388	983/609	405/251	Pittsburg (PA)
			Richmond (VA)	560/347	383/237	529/328	1120/694	230/143	Richmond (VA)
		Toronto (ON)	1068/662	524/325	827/513	823/510	542/336	771/478	Toronto (ON)
Washington (DC)	920/570	170/105	405/251	224/139	382/237	949/588	58/36	Washington (DC)

(accident, property damage, hospital costs for all passengers, theft).

Certain credit cards, gold cards for example, cover collision and theft insurance. Check this with your credit card company before renting a vehicle.

Most rental cars have an automatic transmission, however you can request a car with a manual shift. Child safety seats cost extra.

By Taxi

Countless taxis work the streets of Washington. Generally, getting a taxi is as easy as lifting your arm to hail one. Nevertheless, here are the phone numbers of a few taxi companies:

Barwood Cab
☎(301) 984-1900.

America Limousine
☎(703) 280-8123.

Capitol Cab
☎(202) 546-2400.

Yellow Cab
☎(202) 544-1212.

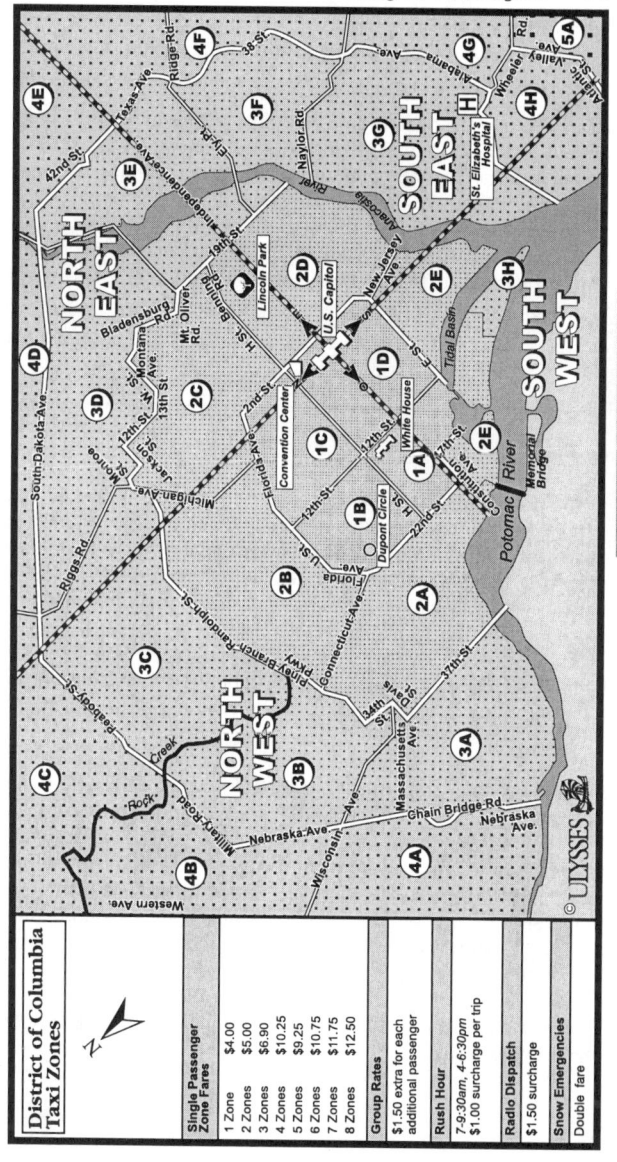

Getting to Washington 73

On Foot

A city is usually best toured on foot, and Washington is no exception to the rule. Walking thus remains the best way to appreciate the capital's architectural wealth, to enjoy its many public squares and parks or to do some window shopping. This guide comprises a dozen tours through Washington's various districts, most of which are to be explored on foot. So, if you're heading to the American capital, don't forget to bring your walking shoes!

Public Transportation

By Bus

The city of Washington is equipped with a good public transit system, known as **Metrobus**. You can reach any destination in downtown Washington by bus. Unfortunately, there is no city map outlining the major bus routes, which sometimes makes it hard to find your way around. Nevertheless, you can easily get more information by calling ☎637-7000.

Note that you must pay with exact change when boarding a bus, and prices vary according to the time of day and destination.

If you have to change buses, ask the driver for a transfer upon boarding.

If you need to transfer from the subway to a bus, get a free transfer at the subway station you first entered. The machines that distribute the transfers are located near the escalators that lead to the subway platforms. Then you only have to give the bus driver 25 cents.

Lastly, note that you cannot obtain a transfer from the bus to the subway.

By Metro (Subway)

Washington can pride itself on having a very good subway system, known as **Metrorail**, which is fast, modern and relatively safe. The network consists of five colour-coded lines: red (from Wheaton station to Shady Grove), orange (from New Carrollton to Vienna), blue (from Addison Road to Van Dorn Street), green (from Anacostia to U Street-Cardozo, and Fort Totten to Greenbelt) and yellow (from Huntington to Van Dorn Street). Metro station entrances are easily identifiable by their tall brown columns marked by the letter *M*. There is a metro map in every station as well as in the trains themselves. The metro runs Monday to Friday from 5:30am to midnight, and on weekends from 8am to midnight.

Farecards can be purchased from the vending machines set up inside every station. These machines accept coins as well as $1 and $5 bills. Some also accept $10 and $20 bills. The basic fare is $1.10, though the ticket price can rise to a maximum of $2.10 during off-peak hours and $3.25 during heavy rush hours, depending on how far you travel. Rush hours extend from Monday to Friday between 5:30am and 9:30am and from 3pm to 8pm.

Fares being relatively high, we advise visitors who plan on mainly getting around by metro to purchase the $5 Metrorail One-Day Pass. This pass allows you to ride the subway as often as you like any weekday from 9:30am to midnight or all day on weekends. These passes can be purchased at the Metro Center station, where the red, blue and orange lines converge.

For further information about Metrorail services, dial ☎637-7000.

TIME DIFFERENCE

Washington, like Montréal, Toronto and New York, is part of the Eastern Time Zone. It is 6 hours behind Europe, 3 hours ahead of Los Angeles and 5 hours ahead of Hawaii, so be sure to check the time before waking someone up too early. The United States also follows Daylight Savings Time.

76   Practical Information

BUSINESS HOURS AND PUBLIC HOLIDAYS

Business Hours

Stores

Generally, stores are open from:

Mon to Sat	10am to 6pm (sometimes 7pm);
Sun	noon to 5pm

Supermarkets and convenience stores are open later, sometimes 24 hours a day.

Holidays and Public Holidays

The following is a list of public holidays in the United-States. Most administrative offices and banks are closed on these days.

New Year's Day (January 1)
Martin Luther King, Jr.'s Birthday (third Monday in January)
President's Day (third Monday in February)
Memorial Day (last Monday in May)
Independence Day (July 4)
Labor Day (first Monday in September)
Columbus Day (second Monday in October)
Veterans' Day (November 11)
Thanksgiving (fourth Thursday in November)
Christmas (December 25)

MONEY AND BANKING

Money

The monetary unit is the dollar ($), which is divided into cents (¢). One dollar = 100 cents.

Bills come in one, five, 10, 20, 50 and 100 dollar denominations; and coins come in one- (penny), five- (nickel), 10- (dime) and 25-cent (quarter) pieces.

Dollar and fifty-cent coins exist, as does a two-dollar bill, but they are very rarely used. Virtually all purchases must be paid in American currency in the United States. Be sure to get your travellers' cheques in American dollars. You can also use any credit card affiliated with an American institution like Visa, MasterCard, American Express, Interbank, Barclay Bank, Diners' Club and Discovery. **Please note that all prices in this guide are in American dollars.**

Banks

Banks are open Monday to Friday from 9am to 3pm.

Banks can be found almost everywhere, and most offer the standard services to tourists. Most automatic teller machines (ATMs) accept foreign bank cards so that you can withdraw directly from your account (check before to make sure you have access) and avoid the potentially high charges of using a real teller. Most machines are open at all times. Cash advances on your credit card are another option, although interest charges accumulate quickly. Money orders are a final alternative for which no commission is charged. This option does, however, take more time. The easiest and safest way to carry your money, however, is with travellers' cheques.

Exchanging Money

Several banks readily exchange foreign currency, but almost all charge a **commission**. There are exchange offices, on the other hand, that do not charge commission, but their rates are sometimes less competitive. These offices often have longer opening hours. It is a good idea to **shop around**.

Thomas Cook Currency Services
1800 K Street NW, ☎(202) 872-1233.
3222 M Street NW, ☎(202) 338-3325.

Exchange Rates

$1 CAN	= $0.64 US	$1 US	= $1.55 CAN
1 £	= $1.64 US	$1 US	= 0.61 £
$1 Aust	= $0.58 US	$1 US	= $1.73 Aust
$1 NZ	= $0.49 US	$1 US	= $2.03 NZ
1 guilder	= $0.49 US	$1 US	= 2.03 guilders
1 SF	= $0.66 US	$1 US	= 1.50 SF
10 BF	= $0.27 US	$1 US	= 37 BF
1 DM	= $0.56 US	$1 US	= 1.80 DM
100 pesetas	= $0.66 US	$1 US	= 152 pesetas
1000 lire	= $0.56 US	$1 US	= 1,774 lire
1 Euro	= $1.10 US	$1 US	= 0.91 Euro

50 Massachusetts Avenue NE, Union Station, ☎(202)371-9219.

Ruesch International Monetary Services
825 14th Street NW, ☎(202) 408-1200.

MAIL AND TELECOMMUNICATIONS

Stamps can be purchased in post offices, of couse, but also from major hotels. Mail is collected daily.

Post Offices

There are numerous post offices scattered throughout Washington. You can call ☎635-5300 to find out where the one nearest you is located. Because the post offices have widely differing business hours, we have listed a number of them below.

Main Office *(Mon to Fri 8am to 10pm, Sat 10am to 6pm, Sun noon to 6pm)* 900 Brentwood Road NE, ☎(202) 635-5300.

North Capital Station *(Mon to Fri 7am to midnight, Sat and Sun 7am to 10pm, Union Station metro)* 2 Massachusetts Avenue NE, ☎(202) 523-2628.

Farragut Station *(Mon to Fri 8am to 6pm)* 1145 19th Street NW, ☎(202) 523-2506.

Martin Luther King Jr. Station *(Mon to Fri 8am to 7pm, Sat 10am to 2pm)* 1400 L Street NW, ☎(202) 523-2000.

Columbia Heights Station *(Mon to Fri 8am to 5:30pm, Sat 8:30am to 3pm)* 1423 Irving Street NW, ☎(202) 523-2397.

Georgetown *(Mon to Fri 8am to 5:30pm, Sat 8:30am to 4pm)* 1215 31st Street NW, ☎(202) 523-2405.

Telephone

The phone system in the U.S. is extremely efficient. Coin-operated pay phones or those that accept credit cards or pre-paid phone cards are easy to find. **The area code for Washington DC is 202**, unless otherwise indicated.

Throughout the guide, you may notice phone numbers preceded by 1-800 or 1-888. These are toll-free numbers, which are generally accessible from all over North America.

To call Washington from elsewhere in North America, dial 1-202 and then the seven-digit number you are trying to reach.

To call Washington from Belgium and Switzerland, dial 00-1-12-202, and then the number you are trying to reach.

To call other places in North America from Washington, dial 1 then the area code then the seven-digit number you are trying to reach.

To call Belgium, dial 011-32, the area code, then the number. To call Switzerland, dial 011-41, the area code and the number.

Moreover, most hotels are equipped with phones in each rooms, as well fax machines (≈). Keep in mind, however, that it can be more expensive to call from your hotel than from a phone booth, even when using your Bell card, wherein your call is billed to your personal account. This option is one of the most costly; as such, we strongly advise you to put your calls through from a pay phone.

CLIMATE AND CLOTHING

The climate in Washington is generally mild, save for the hot and humid summers, when the temperature can rise to above 30°C. Bring light clothing if you plan on travelling during that season. Spring and fall are both very pleasant; it is nevertheless best to bring a jacket, an umbrella and a rain coat.

The temperature in the U.S. is calculated in degrees Fahrenheit. To make the conversion to Celsius, subtract 30, divide that number by 2 and add 2. (For example, when the thermometer reads 80°F, calculate 80 - 30 = 50; 50 x 2 = 25; 25 + 2 = 27°C).

INSURANCE

Cancellation Insurance

Your travel agent will usually offer you cancellation insurance upon purchase of your airline ticket or vacation package. This insurance allows you to be reimbursed for the ticket or package deal if your trip must be cancelled due to serious illness or death. Healthy people are unlikely to need this protection, which is therefore only of relative use.

Theft Insurance

Most residential insurance policies protect some of your goods from theft, even if the theft occurs in a foreign country. To make a claim, you must fill out a police report. It may not be necessary to take out further insurance, depending on the amount covered by your current home policy. As policies vary considerably, you are advised to check with your insurance company. European visitors should take out baggage insurance.

Life Insurance

Several airline companies offer a life insurance plan included in the price of the airplane ticket. However, many travellers already have this type of insurance and do not require additional coverage.

Health Insurance

This is the most useful kind of insurance for travellers, and should be purchased before your departure. Your insurance plan should be as complete as possible because health care costs add up quickly. When buying insurance, make sure it covers all types of medical costs, such as hospitalization, nursing services and doctor's fees. Make sure your limit is high enough, as these expenses can be costly. A repatriation clause is also vital in case the required care is not available on site. Furthermore, since you may have to pay on the spot, check your policy to see what provisions it includes for such situations. To avoid any problems during your vacation, always keep proof of your insurance policy on your person.

HEALTH

Vaccinations are not necessary for people coming from Europe or Canada. On the other hand, it is strongly suggested, particularly for medium or long-term stays, that visitors take out health and accident insurance. There are different types, so it is best to shop around. Bring along all medication, especially prescription medicine. Unless otherwise stated, the water is potable throughout Washington.

For Emergencies, dial ☎ 911

The Québec medicare system reimburses Québec residents for hospital costs, except for medication and doctor's services, and is subject to Québec taxes. It is also recommended that you take out a private insurance to cover any costs not incurred. In case of an accident or sickness, keep all your receipts for compensation from the *Régie de l'assurance-maladie du Québec*.

EMERGENCIES

The ☎**911** emergency number is in operation throughout Washington. If it does not work, dial **0** and tell the operator that you are experiencing an emergency.

SHOPPING

What to Buy

Books and Music: European travellers will be pleased to know that CDs and English-language books are considerably less expensive in the U.S.

Cameras, "walkmans" and portable CD players: these items can also be good bargains for European travellers.

Jeans and sports shoes: also much cheaper than in Europe.

TAXES AND TIPPING

Taxes

The ticket price on items usually **does not include tax**. There is a 6% sales tax on purchases. The hotel tax is 13%, to which there is an additional 1.50 charge for each night you rent a room.

Tipping

Tipping applies to all table services, that is in restaurants or other places in which customers are served at their tables (fast food service is therefore not included in this category). Tipping is also compulsory in bars, nightclubs and taxis.

The tip is usually about 15% of the bill before tax, but varies, of course, depending on the quality of service. The tip is not included in the bill; you must calculate it yourself and leave it on the table for the waiter or waitress.

BARS AND DANCE CLUBS

Some establishments have cover charges, particularly when a show is being held. Tipping the doorperson is not mandatory and thus left at your discretion. Be advised that bartenders and servers expect to be tipped between 50 cents and $1 per drink.

Note that the legal drinking age is 21.

ADVICE FOR SMOKERS

In the United States, cigarette smoking is considered taboo, and is being prohibited in more and more public places:

in most shopping centres;
in buses;
in government offices.

Most public places (restaurants, cafés) have smoking and non-smoking sections. Cigarettes are sold in bars, grocery stores, newspaper and magazine shops.

SAFETY AND SECURITY

A few basic precautions must be taken in Washington, which unfortunately has a dismal crime record. However, if you remain in tourist areas (essentially downtown, Dupont Circle, Adams Morgan, Georgetown and Foggy Bottom), there is not much to worry about in terms of your personal safety. Avoid walking alone in the South-East district come nightfall. If you plan on going there, take a taxi. If you experience any prob-

84 Practical Information

lems, remember that the number to dial for emergencies is **911** or **0**.

CHILDREN

As in the rest of the United States, facilities exist in Washington that make travelling with children quite easy, whether it be for getting around or when enjoying the sights. Generally, children under five travel for free, and those under 12 are eligible for fare reductions. The same applies for various leisure activities and shows. Enquire before you purchase tickets. High chairs and children's menus are available in most restaurants, while a few of the larger stores provide a babysitting service while parents shop.

HANDICAPPED TRAVELLERS

Though considerable efforts have been made to make things more accessible to handicapped individuals, there is still a lot of work to be done.

WEIGHTS AND MEASURES

The United States use the imperial system:

Weights
1 pound (lb) = 454 grams (g)
1 kilogram (kg) = 2.2 pounds (lbs)

Linear Measure
1 inch = 2.2 centimetres (cm)
1 foot (ft) = 30 centimetres (cm)
1 mile = 1.6 kilometres (km)
1 kilometres (km) = 0.63 miles
1 metre (m) = 39.37 inches

Land Measure
1 acre = 0.4 hectare
1 hectare = 2.471 acres

Volume Measure
1 U.S. gallon (gal) = 3.79 litres
1 U.S. gallon (gal) = 0.83 imperial gallon

Temperature
To convert °F into °C: subtract 32, divide by 9, multiply by 5
To convert °C into °F: multiply by 9, divide by 5, add 32

GENERAL INFORMATION

Recreational Drugs: are against the law and not tolerated (even "soft" drugs). Anyone caught with drugs in their possession risks severe consequences.

Electricity: Voltage is 110 volts throughout Canada, the same as in the United States. Electricity plugs have two parallel, flat pins, and adaptors are available here.

Laundromats: are found almost everywhere in urban areas. In most cases, detergent is sold on site. Although change machines are sometimes provided, it is best to bring plenty of quarters (25¢) with you.

Movie Theatres: There are no ushers and therefore no tips.

Museums: Most museums charge admission. Reduced prices are available for people over 60, for children, and for students. Call the museum for further details.

Pharmacies: In addition to the smaller drug stores, there are large pharmacy chains that sell everything from chocolate to laundry detergent, as well as the more traditional items like cough drops and headache medications.

Press: Washington boasts various local newspapers, the biggest and best-known one being *The Washington Post*, which is also one of the best papers in the U.S. The Saturday edition comprises the *Guide to the Lively Arts*, which lists the films and plays currently showing as well as temporary exhibitions. *The Washington Times* is another newspaper published in the capital.

Among Washington's free newspapers, which are a good source of information for visitors, is the *City Paper*, which comes out on Fridays. You can pick it up at several shops in the city as well as in bars and restaurants.

There are several publications catering to the gay and lesbian community. Every issue includes addresses of the city's gay-and-lesbian bars and restaurants. These publications are free and readily available at shops, bars and restaurants. Note that they can also be found on every street corner in Dupont Circle and Adams Morgan. Notable among them are the *Washington Blade*, *MW* and *Woman's Monthly*. The latter is sometimes harder to find, but can always be obtained at a small gay bookshop in Dupont Circle called Lambda Rising *(1625 Connecticut Ave. NW, near R St., Dupont Circle metro, ☎462-6969)*.

Religion: Almost all religions are represented.

Restrooms: Public restrooms can be found in most shopping centres. If you cannot find one, it usually is not a problem to use one in a bar or restaurant.

GAY AND LESBIAN LIFE

In addition to publications catering to the gay and lesbian community, a few titles of which have been mentioned in the "Press" section, Washington boasts a few organizations that may prove useful:

The **Gay and Lesbian Switchboard** *(everyday 7:30am to 10:30pm; for men, ☎628-4667; for women, ☎628-4666)* provides information about gay life in Washington and offers counseling to people experiencing problems and those in distress.

The **Gay and Lesbian Hotline** *(everyday 7am to 11pm; ☎833-3234)* also provides information and counselling.

Gay Information and Assistance *(everyday 24 hours a day; ☎363-3881)* offers the same services as the above-mentioned organizations, but has the advantage of operating around the clock.

The **Gay Men's VD Clinic** *(Tue and Thu 6pm to 7:30pm; 1701 14th St. NW, ☎745-6129)* has initiated a free STD screening service. For men only.

The **Gay and Lesbian Alliance Against Defamation** *(2001 O St. NW, ☎429-9500)* is the place to go if you feel your rights have been infringed on.

Sexual Minority Youth Assistance League *(333 Pennsylvania Ave. SE, Eastern Market or Capitol South metro, ☎546-5940)*. As its name indicates, this organization offers assistance to young homosexuals, lesbians and bisexuals between the ages of 14 and 21.

Gayellow Pages *(PO Box 533, Village Station, New York, NY 10014, ☎212-674-0120, ✺212-420-1136)* publishes an annual directory listing the addresses and phone numbers that may be of interest to gay travellers. It can be found in certain Washington area, notably in Dupont Circle.

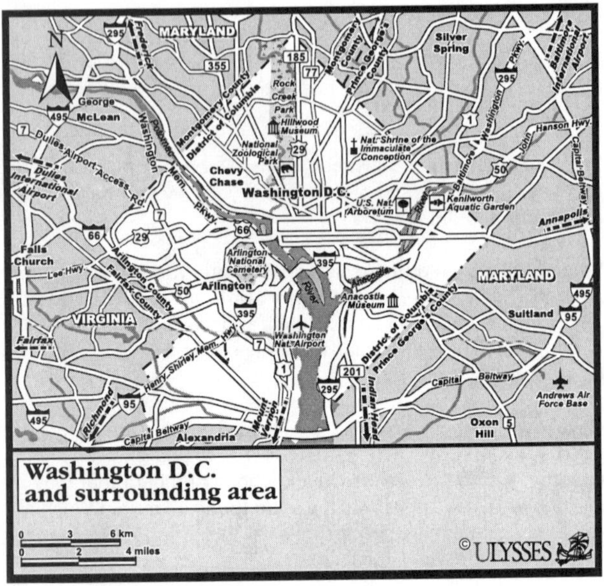

Washington D.C. and surrounding area

EXPLORING

Washington, District of Columbia, the federal capital of the United States, is set on the shores of the Potomac River on an a site that was once nothing but swampland. Downtown Washington was created all at once in 1791 according to the French-style, geometric plans of architect Pierre Charles L'Enfant, which are still apparent in the layout of the city. It is comprised of an east-west avenue called the Mall that runs from the Potomac to Capitol Hill, the seat of Congress, and a perpendicular axis that links the White House to the Jefferson Memorial. Around these intersecting thoroughfares, the city is a grid of parallel and perpendicular streets cut through by diagonal avenues and traffic circles.

Many people think of Washington as nothing more than an administrative centre, and while it is true that the uniqueness of Washington's atmosphere has a lot to do with the business of governing, which drives its economy, this elegant city offers much to discover. Aside from remarkable neoclassical architecture that is exceptional in the United States, the city is also the proud home of first-rate research institutions and world-class cultural centres. Tourism is also booming here. Every year over 20 million visitors stroll the city's grand avenues, parks and many green spaces; admire the magnificent collections of its innumerable museums; visit the White House, the residence of the president of the Untied States, and the Capitol, the home

90 Exploring

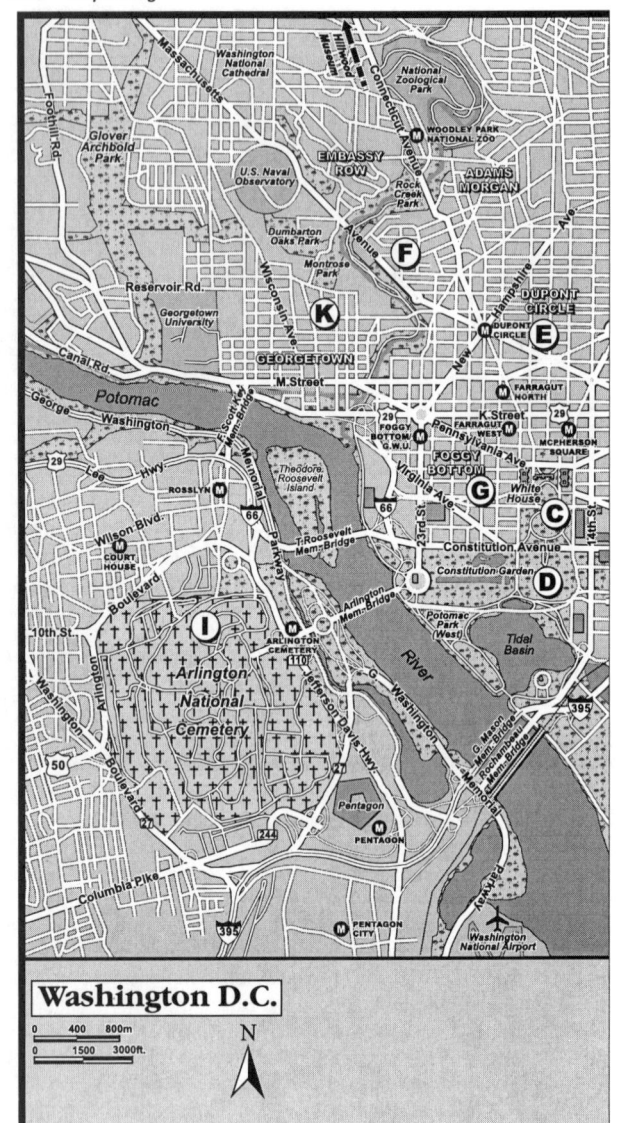

Exploring 91

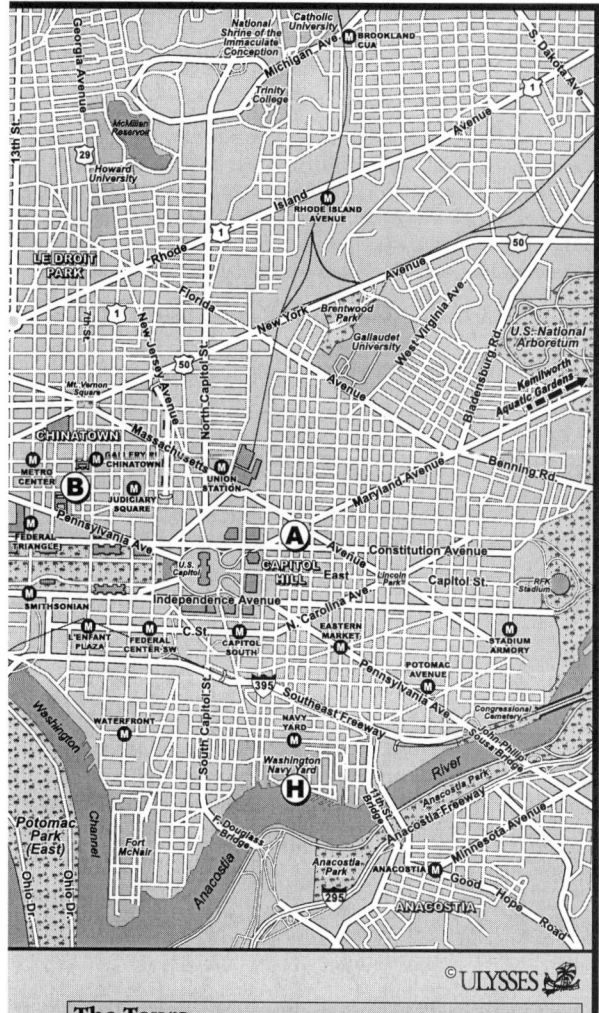

The Tours

- A. Capitol Hill
- B. Downtown
- C. Around the White House
- D. The Mall
- E. Dupont Circle and Adams Morgan
- F. Embassy Row and Kalorama
- G. Foggy Bottom
- H. The Banks of the Anacostia River
- I. Arlington
- K. Georgetown

92 Exploring

of the assemblies of the American Congress; and take in the awesome sight of the Pentagon, the famous symbol of the country's military might.

The tours described here will take you around the various Washington neighbourhoods of interest, so you may appreciate the beauty of the city on a human scale as well as discover the treasures stored in its many museums. From the Mall, a broad esplanade bordered on either side by the city's great museums; to Georgetown, a stylish, popular residential neighbourhood of lovingly restored old red brick houses; by way of Dupont circle and its many restaurants and Adams Morgan, a colourful cultural crossroads, the variety of experiences offered by this ravishing city will suit all tastes and moods.

TOUR A: CAPITOL HILL ★★★

The Capitol Hill area includes the buildings of the Capitol, the Senate and the Supreme Court, as well as the residential streets extending from Union Station in the north to E Street in the south and Lincoln Park to the east.

The hill itself, of a modest height of only 27 metres, was once called Jenkins Hill. Pierre Charles L'Enfant said it resembled "a pedestal waiting for a monument" and decided to make it the centrepiece of his design for the new capital in 1791. While L'Enfant's original plans were not scrupulously followed, the city's nexus remained the Capitol, toward which its large avenues converge forming a star shape. The Capitol, the symbol of American democracy, is also the hub around which the city is divided into quadrants: Northeast (NE), Southeast (SE), Southwest (SW) and Northwest (NW).

Originally, L'Enfant's plans foresaw the development of an entire upper-class residential neighbourhood east of the Capitol, and George Washington himself had two houses built on Capitol Street. With this expected development in mind, William Thornton, the architect entrusted with the construction of the Capitol, oriented the building's main façade toward the east instead of toward the west, and the open vista over the Mall to the Potomac.

Tour A: Capitol Hill 93

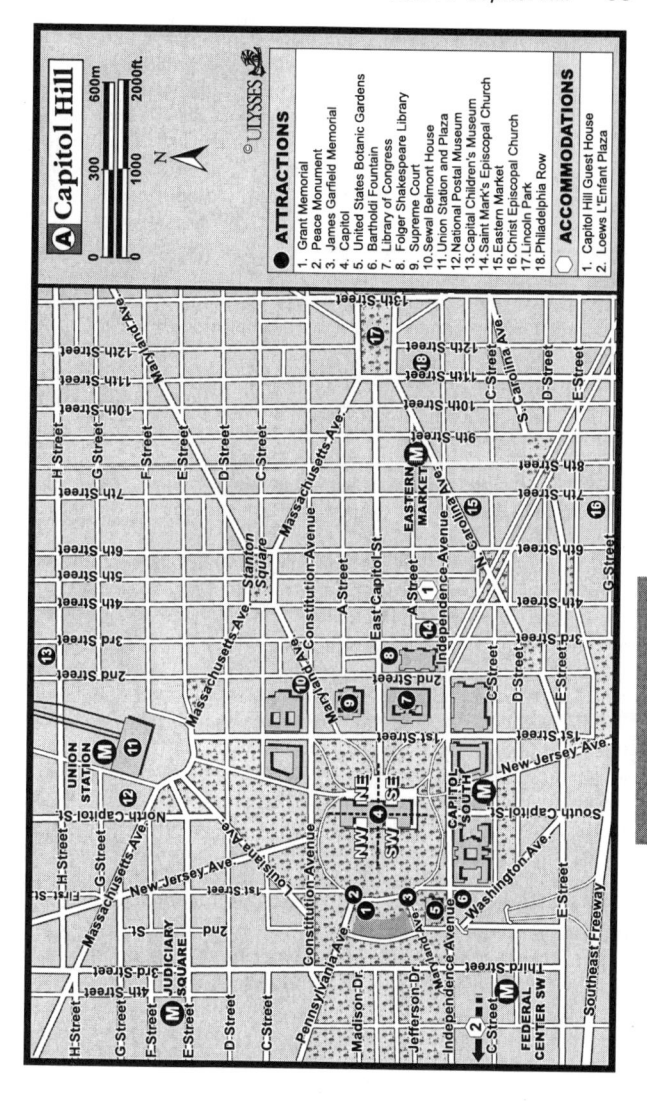

Capitol Hill

ATTRACTIONS
1. Grant Memorial
2. Peace Monument
3. James Garfield Memorial
4. Capitol
5. United States Botanic Gardens
6. Bartholdi Fountain
7. Library of Congress
8. Folger Shakespeare Library
9. Supreme Court
10. Sewal Belmont House
11. Union Station and Plaza
12. National Postal Museum
13. Capital Children's Museum
14. Saint Mark's Episcopal Church
15. Eastern Market
16. Christ Episcopal Church
17. Lincoln Park
18. Philadelphia Row

ACCOMMODATIONS
1. Capitol Hill Guest House
2. Loews L'Enfant Plaza

EXPLORING

94　Exploring

The social makeup of Capitol Hill underwent a transformation over the course of the 20th century, and beginning in the 1950s its relatively wealthy residents began to leave the neighbourhood, making way for a much less fortunate stratum. The mix that resulted from this shift lends an altogether unique character to the neighbourhood today, with poor families living in homes next door to upper-class 19th-century houses.

This tour meanders the streets of Capitol Hill and visits sumptuous beaux-arts buildings from the turn of the century. Many millions of visitors make the annual pilgrimage to the high sphere of the American federal government, so this neighbourhood is one of Washington's major tourist destinations. It is completely safe to explore the area during the day when it is essentially populated by bureaucrats. However, the neighbourhoods east of 11th Street and south of D Street have very high crime rates; let prudence be your guide if you decide to explore these areas, although this tour does not because they have very little to offer in the way of tourist attractions.

The tour begins at the foot of the **Capitol ★★★**, near the **Capitol Reflecting Pool**, across from the Mall, and leads to **Union Station ★** and the **National Postal Museum ★**, northeast of the Capitol.

The Grant Memorial (1) *(corner of First St. and East Mall)* is an imposing equestrian statue of General Ulysses Simpson Grant (1822-1885), commander-in-chief of the Union Army during the American Civil War and 18th President of the United States, which stands behind the Capitol at the end of the Mall. Erected in 1922, it is the work of sculptor Henry M. Schrady and is the largest bronze statue in the world after that of Victor Emmanuel in Rome. The figure of the glorious general sits slightly stooped astride a horse at the centre of a group of several sculptures representing the artillery and cavalry troops under his command. The monument was embellished by the Capitol Reflecting Pool in 1976 following construction of a tunnel for Interstate 395 under this part of the Mall. The underground highway required a sort of large roof that could not be planted with trees because their roots would damage the structure. In addition to satisfying this technical need, the pool creates an aesthetically appealing effect, reflecting the dome of the Capitol in its water.

The Capitol

The **Peace Monument (2)** *(corner First St. and Pennsylvania Ave.)* is another commemorative statue near the Grant Memorial, accredited to Franklin Simmons. This white marble monument represents America in the features of a woman overcome with grief. She pours forth her pain and cries for the dead heroes of the nation on the shoulder of another woman who personifies History, while Neptune, Mars, Victory and Peace, represented by statues surrounding America, console her.

South of the Grant Memorial there is a third commemorative statue, the **James Garfield Memorial (3)** *(corner of First St. and Maryland Ave.)*. In 1881, James Abram Garfield (1831-1881) was elected the 20th President of the United States. Just a few months into his term, on July 2, 1881, Garfield was shot by a lunatic named Charles Guiteau. He died from his wounds on September 19th.

The **Capitol** ★★★ **(4)** *(free; Jun to Aug every day 9am to 8pm, Sep to May every day 9am to 4:30pm; First St., between*

96 Exploring

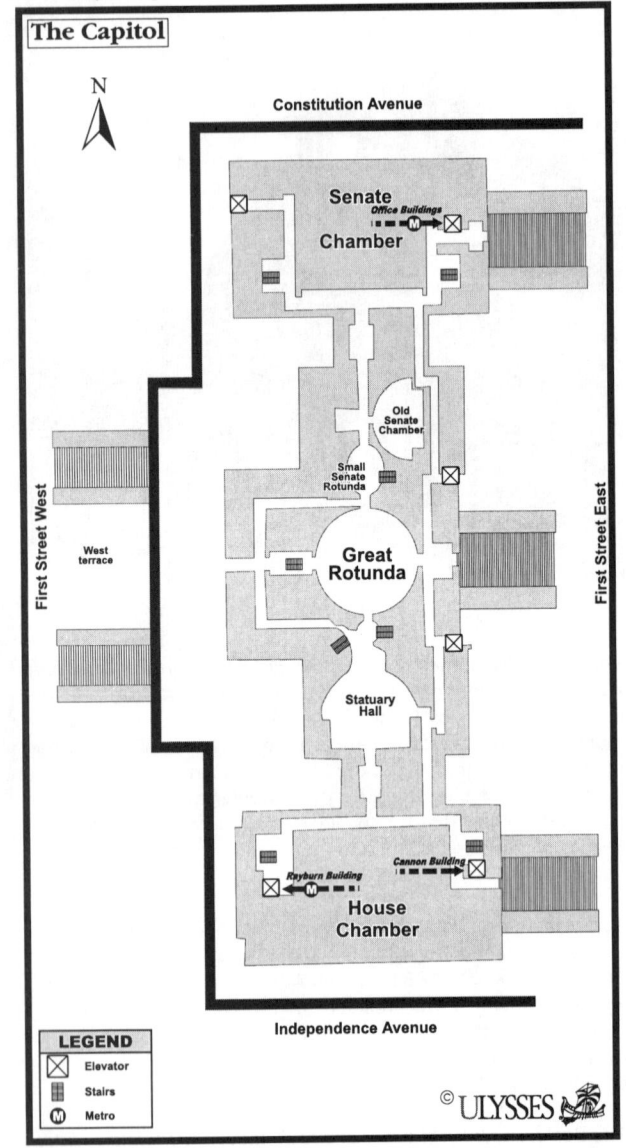

The Capitol

N

Constitution Avenue

Senate Chamber
Office Buildings

Old Senate Chamber

Small Senate Rotunda

Great Rotunda

West terrace

Statuary Hall

First Street West

First Street East

Rayburn Building
Cannon Building

House Chamber

Independence Avenue

LEGEND
- ⊠ Elevator
- ▦ Stairs
- Ⓜ Metro

© ULYSSES

Independence Ave. and Constitution Ave., Capitol South or Union Station Metro station; ☎225-6827), which crowns the top of Jenkins Hill, constitutes one of the most visible landmarks in Washington. Architect Pierre Charles L'Enfant, who was commissioned to plan the city, decided to make the modest 27-metre-high promontory of Jenkins Hill the point of convergence of the entire new capital. The design was implemented so that the broad avenues of the city would meet, forming a star shape, at this central point dominated by the Capitol Building, attracting, literally and figuratively, the entire nation to this institution where the democratic debates that concern it take place. Foreseeing that the city would develop to the east of the Capitol, the building's main façade faces this direction. However, this expectation proved false, and today the Capitol surprisingly turns its back to the main part of the city and to most of the other buildings of the government. For a long time, presidents of the United States were sworn in on the steps of this main entrance, but since the Reagan administration (1981-1989), presidents have declared their oaths of office on the western side of the building, facing the Mall.

From the large terrace on the west side of the Capitol, there is an interesting view down below of the broad esplanade of the Mall, lined by sumptuous buildings, of the obelisk of the Washington Monument, of the Lincoln Memorial and all the way to the shores of the Potomac and the hills of Arlington across the river.

A Construction Spanning over 160 Years

Construction of the Capitol as it appears today was accomplished in four stages. Pierre Charles L'Enfant, who was originally hired to design the plans of the city and the Capitol, was fired in 1792 because of constant dissension and did not have time to complete even the least of his projects. Following his dismissal, President George Washington opened a public contest to choose a plan for the Capitol. The results were not very convincing, and finally the plans of William Thornton, a medical doctor who had an interest in architecture, won the approval of the jury in 1793. Thornton's initial project envisioned a building with three key elements: a central rotunda and two wings, one on the right for the Senate room, and one on the left for the House of Representatives.

The first stone of the first phase of William Thornton's project was laid by President George Washington on September 18, 1793; the silver trowel that Washington used for the event is preserved at the Masonic Museum. First the Senate Chamber was built (the left wing of the original building) from 1793 to 1800, but then incessant rivalries among the many architects who were working on the Capitol provoked Thornton to quit. In 1803, completion of the project was entrusted to architect Henry Latrobe. The House of Representatives was not completed according to Thornton's design until 1807. The two wings were crowned by a small cupola and linked by a wooden gallery until the building's central rotunda was constructed. The United States declared war on the British in 1812 and British troops attacked Jenkins Hill; the Capitol was razed in 1814, with books from the Library of Congress serving as fuel for the fire. The buildings' interiors were completely destroyed and their walls were only saved by a providential hard rain.

Restoration of the two buildings and the second phase of construction had to wait until the end of hostilities between the British and the Americans. On the instigation of a new architect, Charles Bulfinch, a central rotunda toped by 16.8-metre-tall cupola was added between the House and the Senate.

The Capitol acquired the appearance for which it is famous today in the 1850s. The Congress had by then outgrown the building and approved a plan to enlarge it. Thomas Walter was assigned the task of designing new wings on either side of the building to double its length. The House wing was finished in 1857 and the Senate was completed two years later. This expansion work greatly diminished the majesty of Bulfinch's cupola, so in 1863 Walter decided to replace it with an immense dome inspired by St. Peter's Basilica in Rome. Truly a feat of 19th-century engineering, this 4,082-ton dome composed of two superimposed cast-iron shells painted to look like marble, is the very same one that can be admired today. The use of cast iron, which is much lighter that stone but just as strong, was not a new technique; the dome of St. Isaac's Cathedral in St. Petersburg, built in 1842, served as a magnificent prototype.

At the end of the 1950s, Congress decided once again to enlarge the Capitol; this time the eastern wing was modified. The new marble façade was designed as an exact copy, ten metres longer, of the former one.

There are two ways to visit the seat of the American government. You can tour the various rooms that are open to the public on one's own or take advantage of the free guided tours that leave every 20 minutes from the Rotunda. On the tour, visitors are ushered through various rooms, including the Rotunda, the National Statuary Hall, the Chambers of the House of Representatives and the Senate, Brumidi Corridors and the Capitol Crypt.

If you wish to attend a congressional debate, you must contact the offices of a congressional representative directly to obtain a special permit. To find out the dates that Congress is in session, call ☎225-3130 or ☎224-2158, or consult the city's daily newspaper, *The Washington Post*.

Across the threshold of the heavy bronze **Columbus Doors** at the main entrance on the east side of the building is the impressive **Rotunda**, which is 29 metres in diameter and 56-metres high. The walls of this circular room are decorated by eight large oil paintings by John Trumbull, General Washington's aide-de-camp, and these depict some of the epic events of the American Revolution, including the Declaration of Independence. The inside of the dome is adorned with an allegorical fresco signed by Constantino Brumidi. This is *The Apotheosis of Washington*, a symbolic painting depicting the first American President surrounded by Roman gods and goddesses personifying, among others, Liberty, Victory, War, Agriculture, Commerce, Art and Science. Below the fresco, a long greyish frieze painted in trompe-l'œil is signed by the same artist. It represents events that have left their mark on the country from the arrival of Christopher Columbus to the first historic flight of the Wright Brothers at Kitty Hawk, North Carolina, on December 17, 1903. Italian-born Constantino Brumidi worked on the Vatican before emigrating to the United States. His work is so important and so pervasive in this building that he was affectionately nicknamed "The Michelangelo of the Capitol". In 1880, while working on the grey circular frieze that decorates the inside of the Rotunda, he fell from a scaffold and suffered fatal injuries.

The **Small Senate Rotunda**, where the famous columns designed by Latrobe can be seen, is to the north of the main Rotunda. The columns are unique because they are decorated with typical American plants such as corn, tobacco and cotton, instead of the acanthus classically used in the Corinthian style. Past the Small Senate Rotunda, a hallway leads to the **Old Senate Chamber**. The Supreme Court sat in this room from 1860 to 1935, when it was moved to a building across First Street. The new Senate Chamber is at the very end of the north wing of the building.

National Statuary Hall, which originally served as the meeting chamber of the House of Representatives, is south of the Rotunda on the way to the new Chamber of the House of Representatives. A bronze star on the floor of the hall marks the exact spot where President Quincy Adams collapsed, stricken by a heart attack. In 1864 every state in the Union was invited to send two statues of important local men and women to be displayed in this hall of the Capitol. When the statues arrived, the space allotted for them proved insufficient, so today some of these sculptures are exhibited in the **Hall of Columns** on the ground floor and in other corridors.

On the Capitol's ground floor under the Rotunda, there is a circular **Crypt** ornamented with 40 Doric columns that was intended for the tomb of President Washington. The illustrious man's family, however, preferred that he be buried at his ancestral estate in Mount Vernon, Virginia.

It is possible to visit the **Old Supreme Court Chamber**, to the north of the Crypt, which housed the highest court of American justice from 1810 to 1860, when it was moved upstairs to the Old Senate Chamber before being relocated again in 1935 to a separate building facing the Capitol. The chamber's original 19th-century furniture has been preserved. The very modest dimensions of this room and its vaulted ceiling, leather-covered tables and shimmering red carpeting lend the space an intimate, quiet atmosphere.

The famous **Brumidi Corridors** are also on the ground floor, at the northern end of the Capitol. They are two elegant, vaulted hallways ornamented with frescoes by Constantino Brumidi that depict historic scenes and important Americans. Although this artist toiled for over 25 years on the walls of the Capitol, his death left his work incomplete. The spaces left unfilled by Brumidi were painted with historical frescoes commissioned later to 20th-century artists such as Allan Cox, whose work commemorates man's first steps on the moon.

Before leaving the Capitol and venturing out to visit the rest of the neighbourhood, head to the **West Terrace**, which offers a **very beautiful view ★★** of the gardens and green spaces of the Mall and of the Lincoln Memorial and the Potomac off in the distance.

Descend the steps from the West Terrace of the Capitol to the **United States Botanic Gardens (5)** *(every day 9am to 5pm; corner of First St. and Maryland Ave. SW, Federal Center Metro station, ☎225-8333)*. This building encloses greenhouses full of cactuses and ferns, as well as a room dedicated to subtropical plants that is overflowing with orchids. A small patio here, laid out with tables and parasols, is a nice shady place to take a break.

Sculptor Frédéric August Bartholdi did not leave his mark only in New York. Although it is of but modest size compared to the Statue of Liberty, **Bartholdi Fountain (6)** *(corner of First St. and Independence Ave. SW, Federal Center Metro station)* is a very elegant work that was created for the Philadelphia Centennial Exhibition and later purchased by the American government.

Walking east on Independence Avenue, visitors arrive at the largest library in the world, the **Library of Congress ★★★ (7)** *(101 Independence Ave. SE, at First St., Capitol South Metro stop, ☎707-8000)*, whose façade is strangely reminiscent of the Paris Opera. Thomas Jefferson declared one day that a member of Congress ought to be able to consult reference material on any subject at any time. To this end, in 1800 Congress allotted a great sum for the purchase of books and the establishment of a library exclusively for the use of its members. The first volumes were destroyed by the English when they razed the Capitol in 1814, but, to make up for this loss, Jefferson offered to sell his incredible personal library of 6,487 books (largely amassed during his stay in Paris) to the government for $23,950. Unfortunately, another fire destroyed part of the Jefferson collection in 1851. Today, the Library of Congress encompasses within its walls the largest collection in the world with about 90 million books and manuscripts and

8 million musical recordings, stored in 560 kilometres of shelves. As large as the Jefferson Building is, one building could not contain such a treasury. In addition to the library's main building, the Library of Congress occupies two adjacent buildings: the Art-Deco Adams Building, built in 1939, and the post-modern Madison Building, built in 1980. The Library of Congress is to the United States what the British Library is to England, or the Bibliothèque Nationale to France. In addition to its fabulous collection of works of every kind, the Library possesses one of the most lavish interiors in the entire city. If its beaux-arts exterior was subject to criticism in its day, its interior ornamentation, which required the work of no fewer than 22 sculptors and 26 painters, charmed even its most ardent critics.

The **Great Hall** is awe-inspiring, both for its imposing dimensions and the richness of its ornamentation. A large skylight illuminates the hall, accentuating the richly multicoloured mosaics on the vaults of the ceiling and on the floor. A majestic white marble staircase leads to the **Main Reading Room**, a magnificent rotunda 30.5 metres in diameter flanked by Corinthian columns and profusely decorated with sculptures, gilding, frescoes and mosaics. A 49-metre-high dome, entirely covered in frescoes, harmoniously crowns this work. Between the half-moons of the stained-glass windows, eight large stone statues symbolize various vocations, including Commerce, Law, Poetry and Science. Below these, 16 bronze statues are perched on the balustrade, representing some of the great thinkers of Western civilization.

Walking north on Second Street, turn right on East Capitol Street to reach the **Folger Shakespeare Library ★ (8)** *(Mon to Sat 10am to 4pm; 201 East Capitol St. SE, Capitol South Metro station, ☎544-4600)*. This library houses one of the largest collections in the world exclusively dedicated to English poet and playwright William Shakespeare (1564-1616), to his work, to the theatrical presentation of his plays and to his era. A fabulous bequest of 75,000 books that belonged to Henry Clay Folger, a passionate Shakespeare enthusiast and chairman of the board of the Standard Oil Company of New York, established the library, which now preserves almost 275,000 books and manuscripts. Construction of the building began in 1930, but Folger did not survive to see the completion of his dream. The ashes of his body, as well of those of his wife, who actively aided in the foundation of the library, rest on the premises.

The building by architect Paul Cret reveals a classic 1930s Art Deco exterior, while the 16th-century Tudor style of the interior confers on it a much more British atmosphere that perfectly suits its purpose. Visitors can tour the **Great Hall**, which has vaulted ceilings that are reminiscent of the Tudor style, and a reconstruction of an **Elizabethan theatre**, in which conferences, public lectures and concerts are presented. The building's white-marble façade is pierced by nine large rectangular windows adorned with wrought-iron grillwork, underneath which bas-reliefs depict scenes from the Bard's plays, and two entrances surmounted by remarkable masks symbolizing Tragedy and Comedy. Along Second Street there is a marble statue of Puck, the carefree imp who is the demiurge of the adventures of the amorous couples in *A Midsummer Night's Dream* – one of Shakespeare's many masterpieces – engraved with one of his lines denouncing the vanity of human lovers: "Lord, what fools these mortals be".

Those who wish to meander a little bit further east can follow the part of the tour described below, which visits the once very posh residential neighbourhoods between Seward Square and Lincoln Park. From the Folger Shakespeare Library, walk south on Third Street one block to **Saint Mark's Episcopal Church (14)** *(corner of Third St. and A St. SE)*. A parish church in 1869, St. Mark's served as the Episcopal cathedral of the diocese of Washington from 1896 to 1902. The large stained-glass windows of its façade were created in the workshops of Louis Comfort Tiffany.

Walk east on A Street, then turn right on 7th Street and continue south two blocks to **Eastern Market (15)** *(Tue to Sat 7am to 6pm, Sun 9am to 4pm; corner of 7th St. and C St., ☎546-2698)*, which has been in activity since it was built in 1873. This is one of Capitol Hill residents' favourite spots to stop for fruits and vegetables, meat, fish and fresh bread. On weekends, farmers from the city's surroundings come to sell their produce under the cast-iron roof that adjoins the building along 7th Street. On Sundays, craft and antique dealers join in all of this hubbub.

Turn right on C Street to reach Seward Square, then turn left, southward, down 6th Street and continue four blocks to **Christ Episcopal Church (16)** *(620 G St. SE)* at the corner of G Street. This is a charming little church accredited to architect Benjamin Henry Latrobe, the same man who supervised construction of the Capitol from 1803 to 1817. Its congregation has included a few famous men over the years, including Presidents James Monroe, John Quincy Adams and Thomas Jefferson. Construction of the church began in 1805 and was not completed until 1891, during which time many architects succeeded Latrobe and somewhat modified his initial plans. The temple constitutes one of the earliest Gothic-inspired buildings in the area, and one of the most successful. It was restored in the 1950s by Horace Peaslee, who gave it an appearance more in keeping with Latrobe's original design.

Backtrack to Seward Square, then walk east on North Carolina Avenue to **Lincoln Park (17)**. This park is not safe after dark, but during the day it is a very pleasant place to unwind. A commemorative statue that was entirely paid for by freed black slaves was erected here in honour of President Abraham Lincoln. The only commemorative statue in Washington dedicated to a black woman, Mary McLeod Bethune, founder of the National Council of Negro Women, can also be seen here. Turn right on 11th Street, where a string of houses called **Philadelphia Row (18)** *(132-154 11th St. SE)* stretches between numbers 132 and 154. The uniform façades of the houses are regularly interrupted by vaulted doors and windows outlined with white stone sills and lintels. The marble staircases and small, well-kept gardens along the street confer on this group of houses a marked elegance and an altogether charming character.

Come back to the intersection with First Street walking west along East Capitol Street past the Folger Shakespeare Library. Here, across from the Capitol, stands a majestic neoclassical white Vermont marble building that resembles a Roman temple. This is the **Supreme Court ★★ (9)** *(Mon to Fri 9am to 4:30pm; First St., between Maryland Ave. and East Capitol St., Capitol South Metro station, ☎479-3211)*. Built in 1935, this imposing mass certainly evokes the great power of the nation's highest court of law. Made up of nine judges appointed for life by the president of the United States, the court guarantees that the tenets of the American Constitution are upheld. The court's debates on the interpretation of the articles of the Constitution take place in this building. The court can declare that a law or ruling is unconstitutional and its decisions may not be appealed.

The Supreme Court met in the Capitol until 1935 when, because of lack of space, construction of a new building was commissioned to architect Cass Gilbert. On the court's façade, large Corinthian columns support a pediment decorated with bas-reliefs representing Liberty, Law and Order, and historical figures such as William Howard Taft (1857-1930), who served as President of the United States and then Chief Justice of the Supreme Court, dangerously manipulating the executive and judicial powers of the federal government. The frieze under the pediment is inscribed with the motto, "Equal Justice under Law". There are two imposing marble statues sculpted by James Fraser in front of the court, one on either side of the large staircase up to the entrance. On the right is "The Authority of Law", and on the left is "The Contemplation of Justice". Behind the 32 Corinthian columns of the temple's façade, the sculpted panels of the heavy bronze entrance doors, credited to John Donnely Jr., depict the evolution of the legal system through the centuries.

Constitutional law buffs will certainly be delighted to learn that it is possible to attend a session of the Supreme Court, but they must arrive early to get seats. Others might also be interested in the solemnity of all the rituals and traditions that surround the hearings. Two queues are set up for visitors: one for those who would like a quick, three-minute peek at the court proceedings, and another for those who wish to sit and attend an entire hearing. For the Court schedule, call the **Supreme Court Information Line** at ☎479-3030. A 20-minute film that explains the procedures of the Court is presented on the ground floor of the building.

Sewall-Belmont House (10) *(Tue to Fri 10am to 3pm, Sat noon to 4pm; 144 Constitution Ave NE, Union Station or Capitol South metro, ☎546-3989)* is the oldest house on Capitol Hill. Built on a foundation that dates from the 17th century, the brick house that can be seen today was designed in 1800 by Robert Sewall and remained in the Sewall family for over 120 years. It was bought in 1929 by Alva Smith, who successively married two of the richest men in the world, William Vanderbilt and Oliver H. P. Belmont, before spearheading a feminist

Fountain of Union Station

movement for women's suffrage. Her feminist inclinations, however, proved to lend themselves only to politics, because she forced her own daughter, Consuelo, to marry a brutal aristocrat, the ninth Duke of Marlborough. Alva Smith made this residence the headquarters of the National Woman's Party. Today the old house is home to a museum of the American feminist movement.

Backtrack and take First Street northward. Three blocks along is the largest train station in the United States, inaugurated in 1908, **Union Station and Plaza** ★ **(11)** *(40 Massachusetts Ave. NE, Union Station Metro station, ☎289-1908)*. Its name was chosen because it was built to link many smaller stations. In the 1920s and 1930s, during the golden age of the railroad, over 200 trains came through Union Station everyday. Since then, air transport has become predominant in the United States, but this immense station remains very busy with commuter traffic.

In front of the two large arches of the station portico, on the esplanade, there is a monumental fountain by sculptor Lorado Taft that commemorates Christopher Columbus.

The station's portico opens onto a huge hall topped by a giant barrel vault, a beaux-arts version of the Roman baths of Emperor Diocletian, which shelters octagonal coffers embossed in gold leaf. These arcades, colonnades and vaults of unimaginable grandeur, in addition to the 36 statues of Roman legionaries on the balcony, are an unequivocal homage to Burnham, the architect of this grandiose edifice. After a long period of neglect, extensive restoration work was carried out at a cost of 150 million dollars, and the station's doors reopened in 1988. Today, the building houses a crowd of shops and restaurants as well as a nine-screen cinema.

The restored **National Postal Museum ★ (12)** *(every day 10am to 5:30pm; 2 Massachusetts Ave. NE, Union Station Metro station, ☎357-2700)* is located west of Union Station. Graham and Burnham were the architects of this building and its signature façade, which is made up of a line of Ionic columns. The museum has enclosed the Smithsonian's impressive philatelic collection since 1993; until then it had been housed at the Arts and Industry Building on the Mall. Mail airplanes suspended more than 30 metres overhead, mailboxes of all sorts, mail vans, military missives sent between major nations (including, notably, correspondence exchanged during the Gulf War), as well as surprising objects such as the uniform of famous TV postman from *Cheers*, Cliff Claven, and the false mustache of a train bandit are exhibited in this museum in a successful combination of humour and educational value.

The last stop on the tour is the **Capital Children's Museum ★ (13)** *($6, under 2 free; every day 10am to 5pm; 800 Third St. NE, corner of I St., Union Station metro, ☎675-4120)*, behind Union Station, where there are a thousand-and-one wonders to captivate 2- to 12-year-olds and their adult companions. The various exhibits use interactive games to introduce children to the fields of art, science and technology. On the second floor, the formidable advancements in communications technology are explained, from the printing press to the telephone. The **Future Center**, on the third floor, explores the amazing world of computer science. Comic books and a chocolate shop round out the fun.

TOUR B: DOWNTOWN

In keeping with the design of Pierre Charles L'Enfant, one main artery links the Capitol, the seat of the legislative assemblies, to the White House, the presidential residence: Pennsylvania Avenue. It travels through several neighbourhoods that for a long time constituted Washington's commercial centre, and many magnificent 19th-century buildings may be seen along it. Large stores, theatres, luxury hotels, administrative buildings and upper-class homes were happy neighbours in that era, but after the turn of the century, and especially after the Second World War, economic activity in the area decreased dramatically. Pennsylvania Avenue lost its allure and neighbouring streets were practically abandoned. John F. Kennedy (1917-

● ATTRACTIONS

Judiciary Square
1. National Building Museum
2. Chinatown Gateway
3. National Portrait Gallery and National Museum of American Art
4. Ford's Theatre
5. Petersen House
6. J. Edgar Hoover Building (FBI)
7. Navy Memorial
8. Temperance Fountain
9. Canadian Embassy
10. Superior Court of the District of Columbia and the Courthouse of the District of Columbia

Federal Triangle
11. National Archives and Records Administration
12. Justice Department Buildings
13. Internal Revenue Service
14. Old Post Office Pavilion
15. Interstate Commerce Commission
16. Department of the Treasury (Customs Services)
17. Department of Commerce
18. National Aquarium

Around the White House
19. Freedom Plaza
20. District Building
21. Pershing Park
22. Willard Hotel
23. Hotel Washington
24. Colorado Building
25. Church of the Epiphany
26. Crestar Bank
27. Folger Building and Playhouse Theater
28. National Museum of Women in the Arts
29. Central Library

○ ACCOMMODATIONS

1. Best Western Downtown Capitoll Hill
2. Crowne Plaza Washington, DC
3. Days Inn Premier Convention Center Hotel
4. Grand Hyatt Washington
5. Hotel Harrington
6. Red Roof Inns
7. The Madison Hotel
8. Washington International AYH-Hostel
9. Westin Washington, DC City Center Hotel

◇ RESTAURANTS

1. Bertolini's
2. Brasseries Les Halles
3. Café Promenade
4. Capitol City Brewing Company
5. Coco Pazzo
6. Friday's
7. Harry's Restaurant and Saloon
8. Hunan Chinatown
9. John Harvard's Brew House
10. Manhattan Deli
11. Marrakech Restaurant
12. Pizzeria Uno Chicago Bar & Grill
13. Planet Hollywood
14. Porter's
15. Red Sage
16. Restaurant 701
17. Timothy's World Coffee

Tour B: Downtown 109

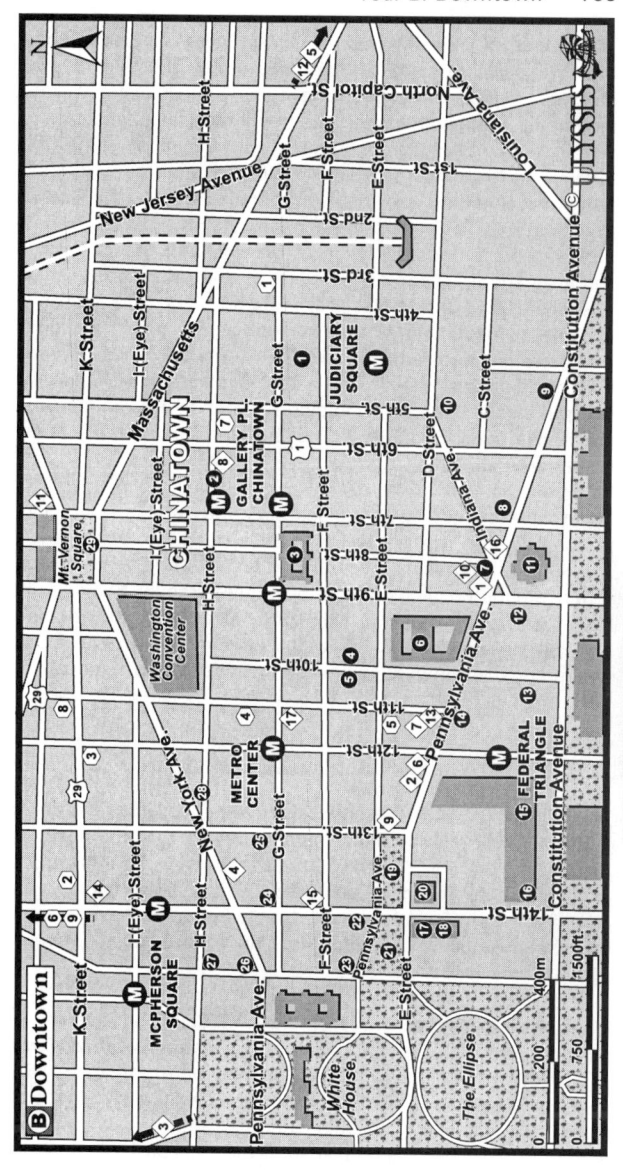

1963), the 35th President of the United States, is credited with the formidable restoration that transformed the avenue. The story goes that while travelling along Pennsylvania Avenue during his inaugural parade, Kennedy was incensed by the dilapidated state of the once-prestigious avenue, so in 1960 he ordered that it be restored and named a committee to oversee the redevelopment of the city's main artery. Downtown Washington's lean years were not over, however. The riots triggered by the assassination of Martin Luther King in 1968 seriously shook up the capital. One of the unfortunate consequences of this unrest was that a great number of downtown businesses moved north of the White House to neighbourhoods that were reputed to be calmer. Today, Pennsylvania Avenue and the adjoining streets shine with the splendour of yesteryear and the area is home to, in addition to architecturally imposing government buildings, many office buildings and tons of hotels, restaurants and small businesses.

This tour explores three main sectors of downtown – Judiciary Square, Federal Triangle and the area around the White House between Pennsylvania Avenue and New York Avenue – and visits famous buildings like the **J. Edgar Hoover Building ★**, headquarters of the FBI, the **National Portrait Gallery and Museum of American Art ★★** and **Ford's Theatre ★**, as well as the administrative buildings along Constitution Avenue.

Judiciary Square ★

The initial plans for the city as envisaged by Pierre Charles L'Enfant and President Washington foresaw the area north of Pennsylvania Avenue as the centre of the new city's municipal administration. The main post office, city hall, a hospital, an administrative tribunal and a prison were all built here, and other, more modest buildings went up in the spaces between these official buildings.

The first stop on this tour is the **National Building Museum (1)** *(Mon to Sat 10am to 4pm, Sun and holidays noon to 4pm; 401 F St., at 4th St., Judiciary Square metro, ☎272-2448)*, also known as the Pension Building. The decision to construct this imposing building, which occupies an entire city block, was made the day after the end of the American Civil War (1861-

1865). It was to house an army of bureaucrats in charge of distributing pensions to the war victims and widows. The project was entrusted to an army engineer, Montgomery C. Meigs, and spanned five years from 1882 to 1887. The building's plans were unabashedly inspired by the Renaissance architecture of the Farnese Palace in Rome, which is in part attributed to Michelangelo. To copy such a masterpiece is no easy feat; but in defence of his own pretension (he wanted to build a bigger, better version of the palace) Meig's can be credited with making use of technological advances that were unknown to the great Italian master in the 16th century, such as a fireproof roof and a very sophisticated ventilation system. It took no fewer than 15.5 million red bricks to complete this monumental building, which did not gain favour with everyone, not by a long shot. General William Tecumseh Sherman summed it up: "The worst of it is, it is fireproof!". Much criticized for its imposing appearance, the building was soon nicknamed "Meigs's Old Red Barn". Today however, everyone agrees that it is one of the brightest successes in the neighbourhood. A terracotta frieze by sculptor Casper Buberl, which runs the length of the building's façade, pays homage to the soldiers who died in the Civil War. Its 35 panels depict Union soldiers from the infantry, cavalry, artillery and marine corps, all marching in step.

The tremendous dimensions of the building's interior are unsurprising in view of its enormous exterior. Meigs simplified the Farnese Palace plans by placing many small offices along the exterior walls, thereby liberating an immense empty space at the heart of the building. The result is particularly impressive. A colonnaded atrium measuring 97 metres in length, 35 metres in width and 49 metres in height is surrounded by four floors of arcades flanked by Doric and Ionic columns that recall the outdoor courts of Renaissance palaces. The whole is crowned by an immense cast-iron-framed skylight supported by eight, 25-metre-tall Corinthian columns painted to imitate Sienna marble (probably the largest "Roman" columns ever built). Light streams in profusely from large upper windows, giving the hall a very pleasant atmosphere. In the cornice above the Corinthian columns, 244 niches are occupied by busts of American artisans and entrepreneurs. Given its dimensions, it is unsurprising that this hall eventually became a favourite locale for sumptuous balls, including the inauguration ceremonies of Presidents Roosevelt, Nixon, Carter, Reagan, Bush and Clinton.

Today, many exhibitions are presented here, and the building also houses a museum dedicated to American architecture, a research centre, offices, a library and conference rooms.

From the National Building Museum, turn left on G Street and stroll up to 7th Street, then walk one block north to the **Chinatown Gateway (2)** *(corner of 7th St. and H St., Judiciary Square metro)*, the entrance to the city's modest Chinese neighbourhood. With its unparalleled span, this is the largest Chinese gate in the world. It was a gift to the city of Washington from the city of Beijing to mark the twinning of the two capitals. Fifteen-metres tall and 19-metres wide, this delicately sculpted arch is reminiscent of the Qing Dynasty.

Chinatown itself is made up of just a few shops and restaurants and is not overly interesting, so the tour backtracks now to F Street. Turn right on F Street to reach the **National Portrait Gallery and National Museum of American Art ★★ (3)** *(every day 10am to 5:30pm; corner of 8th St. and F St., Gallery Place metro, ☎357-2700)*, a Greek-inspired monument in a city where Roman architecture is sometimes favoured to excess. L'Enfant had foreseen this particular site as a "sanctuary for American heroes", and although his wishes were never realized, it could be said that the portrait gallery in some way fulfills the role of a mausoleum. This building served many purposes leading up to its current function: it housed a hospital during the Civil War, then the Office of Indian Affairs and the Patent Office, and finally the Civil Service Commission, and then it was left unused for several years. The building would have been demolished if not for the intervention President Eisenhower, who offered the site to the Smithsonian to be transformed into a portrait gallery and national museum of art.

Construction of this building began in 1836 under architect Robert Mills, who supervised the erection of the right wing. Mills is also accredited with the design of the superb portico flanked by Doric columns, an exact replica of the portico of the Parthenon in Athens. After Mills died in 1855, many different architects oversaw the work of this beautiful architectural ensemble until it was finally completed in 1867.

Exhibition galleries spread over three stories present various works of American art. The Portrait Gallery, which opened its doors in 1968, simply exudes American spirit. In it are dis-

Tour B: Downtown 113

played portraits of men and women who have contributed to the nation's history, including George and Martha Washington. The National Museum of American Art highlights major American art works from the 18th, 19th and 20th centuries, including many popular paintings. The collection features a great number of paintings of Native Americans by George Catlin (1796-1872), a few magnificent intimist, Impressionist canvasses by Mary Cassatt, and portraits by Sargent. The works by Franz Kline, Edward Cooper and Clyfford Still stand out in the collection of contemporary American art. The building's interior court is a peaceful spot embellished by fountains and sculptures, including an imposing work by Alexander Calder entitled *The Spiral*, which is perfect for a relaxing break.

"Sic semper tyrannis" – "thus always to tyrants" – declared John Wilkes Booth after assassinating Abraham Lincoln, 16th President of the United States, on April 14th, 1865. The crime took place in the auditorium of **Ford's Theater (4)** *(every day 9am to 5pm; 511 10th St. NW, Metro Center metro, ☎426-6924)*, where the president and his wife were attending the play *Our American Cousin*. The city was in the throes of preparation for countless festivities because five days earlier General Robert E. Lee had surrendered to General Grant, marking the end of the Civil War. The victorious General Grant was expected at the theatre, and the hall was teeming with people. The balconies had been draped with flags for the occasion, and the evening promised to be beautiful and joyful. In the middle of the third act, Booth discretely edged his way into the presidential box and shot Lincoln in the head, practically at point-blank range. Major Henry Reed Rathbone tried in vain to overpower Booth, who stabbed the Major and managed to escape. Booth jumped over the balustrade, inopportunely became tangled in the hanging flags, and then fell onto the stage, where he delivered his famous diatribe on the fate of tyrants. The audience thought that this apparition was part of the play and was so slow to react that the assassin was able to steal a horse and escape. Once the initial shock had subsided, it was ordered that Lincoln be immediately transported to a nearby home, **Petersen House (5)** *(every day 9am to 5pm; 516 10th St. NW, across from Ford's Theater, Metro Center metro, ☎426-6924)*, where his bloodied body was laid in a ground-floor room. Lincoln was so tall that he had to be placed diagonally across the bed. His wound was particularly grave and proved impervious to the intervention of doctors; the

114   Exploring

president died in the early hours of the morning. You can visit this Victorian-style room, which has been preserved exactly as it appeared when Lincoln lived his last moments here. Even the bloody pillow upon which the President's head rested is still in its place.

The theatre's owner was forced to close down the establishment after Lincoln's assassination and sold the building to the government in 1866, from which time it sat empty for several years. Today, Ford's Theater serves its original purpose as a stage for the performing arts and has recaptured its former prestige. The presidential box has been restored to its appearance on the day of the famous incident, and the theatre also houses a small museum dedicated to the late president.

South of the theatre on 10th Street, there is a massive and austere-looking building: the **J. Edgar Hoover Building** ★ **(6)** *(guided tours only, Mon to Fri 8:45am to 4:15pm; Pennsylvania Ave. between 9th St. and 10th St. NW, Federal Triangle metro, ☎324-3447)*, headquarters of the Federal Bureau of Investigation (FBI). This federal policing agency became the highest crime-fighting institution in the United States (the FBI's battles against organized crime are renowned) essentially due to the efforts of J. Edgar Hoover, its formidable director from 1924 to 1972 who is famous for having assembled files on every public figure in America. The austere and blunt architecture of this concrete edifice is surprising in a city where so much concern for elegance was brought to public buildings. Designed by Stanley Gladych, it is supposed to embody the International Style of French architect Le Corbusier, but its heaviness provokes more controversy than praise.

After submitting to a few security checks, visitors are led by actual FBI agents, walky-talkies in hand, who explain the history and internal procedures of this crime-fighting centre. A panoply of weapons confiscated from legendary criminals such as John Dillinger, as well as photographs and examples of seized drugs, are presented during the course of the tour. Finally, visitors are treated to a sharp-shooting demonstration by an elite marksman who enthusiastically fires on a cardboard replica of a famous gangster.

Take Pennsylvania Avenue southeast to the **Navy Memorial (7)** *(Pennsylvania Ave. NW, between 7th St. and 9th St., Federal*

> ## A Conspiracy Theory
>
> The assassination of President Lincoln was part of an elaborate plot laid out by a band of conspirators led by Booth. He and his accomplices had initially planned a larger-scale action that aimed to assassinate not only the president but also other very high-ranking members of the government. Only Booth was successful in his goal, mortally wounding Abraham Lincoln on the evening of April 14, 1865. Booth was injured when he jumped over the balustrade of the presidential box as he fled. Followed by one of his accomplices, he took refuge at the home of Samuel Mudd, a Maryland doctor who offered him care. His accomplice and he then continued their flight to Virginia, where a detachment of the Cavalry picked up the chase in Port Royal. Booth hid up in a barn and refused to give himself up to the armed forces that had him surrounded. To flush him out of the building, his pursuers set fire to the barn, and it was consumed by flame. Booth was felled by a bullet to the throat. His companion surrendered.

Triangle metro), which stands on the former site of large outdoor market called **Market Square**. This public square once welcomed merchants' stalls on a daily basis, but it changed vocations at the beginning of the century under pressure from a movement called City Beautiful. Today, the semicircular place is flanked by two superb neoclassical buildings from 1990 and shelters a monument to the glory of the Marine Corps on a terrace decorated with masts. A bronze sculpture of a sailor with his gear at his feet mounts guard in front of this monument. The two buildings that border the place are considered a flawless architectural accomplishment, a perfect harmony of neoclassical elegance and simplicity. They house shops, offices, restaurants and a few apartments. The curvature of the buildings creates vistas over two of the most grandiose views in Washington, one down Pennsylvania Avenue with the Capitol in the distance and the other down 8th Street with the National Portrait Gallery as a backdrop.

Temperance Fountain (8) *(corner of 7th St. and Pennsylvania Ave., Federal Triangle metro)*, a small decorative fountain just next to Market Square, is topped by a bronze statue of a heron.

The superb **Canadian Embassy (9)** *(501 Pennsylvania Ave. NW, Judiciary Square metro)*, a white-marble building erected in 1989 by renowned architect Arthur Erickson, is one block further along Pennsylvania Avenue toward the Capitol. Magnificently well situated just a few blocks from the Capitol and across from the National Gallery of Art, this building is an unquestionable aesthetic success that beautifully combines neoclassicism and modernism. The exquisite Rotunda of the Provinces, supported by 12 marble columns, one for each of the provinces and territories of Canada, is especially worth seeing.

Backtrack a little bit to take 6th Street north. At Indiana Avenue, turn right to reach D Street. This route leads past the **Courthouse of the District of Columbia** *(500 Indiana Ave. NW)* to the **Superior Court of the District of Columbia (10)** *(451 Indiana Ave. NW, Judiciary Square metro)*, located in the old city hall, the first municipal building in Washington. A huge funding drive was organized to erect this building, and its construction, which spanned 1820 to 1850, was commissioned to George Hadfield. Its central section is composed of a Greek temple with 12 Ionic columns. As the municipal administration grew, the building was enlarged several times up until 1916.

Federal Triangle ★

Federal Triangle is an administrative complex made up of seven large, neoclassical buildings that were conceived in the 1930s by several different architects. Undoubtedly the best-known of these designers was John Russell Pope (1874-1937), who was also responsible for many other renowned Washington buildings including the National Gallery of Art, the National Archives and, most famous of all, Jefferson Memorial. Tucked between Constitution Avenue, which borders the Mall; Pennsylvania Avenue, which links the Capitol to the White House, and 15th Street, this administrative complex does in effect occupy a space that forms a large triangle, hence its name.

The itinerary presented here aims to familiarize you with this administrative neighbourhood, which is home to some of the main buildings of the federal government including the Interstate Commerce Commission, the Department of Justice and the Department of the Treasury. The tour begins at the **National Archives ★**, where the original Declaration of Independence, Constitution, and Bill of Rights are preserved, and ends at the Department of Commerce, across from the Ellipse, a green space next to the White House. Not all of these buildings are open to the public, but even those that are not can be admired from the outside and appreciated as examples of an architectural style that was very popular at the beginning of this century in Washington. Wide exterior staircases, domes and porticos topped by pediments are typical of John Russell Pope's style.

The **National Archives and Records Administration ★ (11)** *(every day, Apr to Sep 10am to 9pm, Sep to Mar 10am to 5:30, closed Dec 25; Constitution Ave., between 7th St. and 9th St. NW, Archives or Navy Memorial metro, ☎501-5239)*, a magnificent building erected by Russell Pope in 1935, attracts millions of people annually. Of all the buildings that make up Federal Triangle, this is unquestionably the most attractive. The façade of the building, which resembles a real mausoleum, is decorated with Corinthian columns that support a remarkable entrance portico topped by an elegant pediment at the centre of the building. Letters, manuscripts, maps, photographs, newspapers, films, musical scores and recordings of all sorts produced by the government and by famous Americans are preserved here, along with to the original texts that formalized the creation of the United States. These three crucial texts are preciously protected in glass cases in humidity-controlled rooms and, for the sake of utmost safety, the air in these glass cases has been replaced with inert helium to slow the deterioration of this fabulous treasury. When the museum is closed, the documents are stored in a vault. The Declaration of Independence (1776), the Constitution of the United States of America (1787) and the Bill of Rights (1791) have been housed in one building only since 1952. From the Constitution Avenue entrance, a wide staircase leads to a magnificent **Rotunda**, where the three texts are kept. Large mural paintings depict scenes related to these precious parchments. Also on display in the Rotunda is a very rare copy of the British Magna Carta from 1297, on loan to the National Archives from Texas billionaire Ross Perot. The building also houses census records dating back to 1790, to the great pleasure of professional and amateur genealogists alike.

The tour proceeds westward along Constitution Avenue, passing the **Justice Department (12)**, which has an Art-Deco main entrance, and then the **Internal Revenue Service (13)**, which was the first neoclassical building put up in Federal Triangle. There is an amusingly laconic motto engraved above the entrance of the latter: "Taxes are what we pay for a civilized society". Uplifting, isn't it?

Turn right on 12th Street to reach the **Old Post Office Pavilion (14)** *(1100 Pennsylvania Ave. at 12th St. NW, Federal Triangle metro, ☎426-6851)*. Its architecture is a change from the neoclassical austerity of the Federal Triangle buildings, but its rather heavy, fortress-style granite façade and the imposing tower that looms over neighbouring buildings garnered it little praise in its day. In fact, by way of derision it was given the unflattering nickname "Old Tooth". Nonetheless, its interior encloses a vast open hall topped by the one of the first metal structures in the city and an atrium illuminated by an immense skylight. Today, the building houses a small shopping centre with a cafeteria and little stands run by artisans and merchants of all sorts. Observation elevators ride to the top of the clock tower, from which there is a beautiful view of the area. The **Congress Bells** hang near the top of the tower. These bells were cast in London in 1976 and presented by the British government to mark the bicentennial of American independence. They are rung on special occasions and to announce the opening and closing of sessions of Congress.

Back on Constitution Avenue, turn right toward the White House to see two other buildings that embody the purest neoclassical style. Pediments and sculpted friezes, imposing porticos and a profusion of colonnades characterize the **Interstate Commerce Commission (15)** *(corner of 12th St. and Constitution Ave. NW, Federal Triangle metro)*, a gigantic building made up of three sections, designed by architect Arthur Brown in 1935; and the **Department of the Treasury (Customs Services) (16)** *(corner of 14th St. and Constitution Ave. NW, Federal Triangle metro)*, designed by the same architect, also in 1935. Finally, take 15th Street, on the right, to end the tour in front of the **Department of Commerce (17)** *(between 14th St. and 15th St., and E St. and Constitution Ave. NE, Federal Triangle metro)*. With a façade that stretches over 300 metres, this building occupies an entire city block and was the largest office building in the country when it was constructed in 1932. The **National Aquarium (18)** *($2; every day 9am to 5pm, closed Dec 25; in the Department of Commerce Building, 14th St. and Constitution Ave. NW, Federal Triangle metro, ☎482-2826)*, located inside the Commerce Building, was established in 1873 and is apparently the oldest aquarium in the United States. Over 1,500 marine animals are housed here, and on some days the public can witness the feeding of the sharks or of piranhas. A short film about aquatic life is also presented.

Around the White House (from Pennsylvania Avenue to New York Avenue) ★

The buildings that border the east side of the White House, between Pennsylvania Avenue and New York Avenue, form an ensemble that is remarkable for its elegance. For many years, Pennsylvania Avenue was considered "America's Main Street", even if the neighbourhood's state of dilapidation at the beginning of the century cast doubt on the validity of this title. Thanks to the impetus of President John F. Kennedy, a beautification campaign for the avenue and the neighbourhoods around it was undertaken. The results of this project are impressive to everyone who visits the area: the restoration projects and the new buildings, put up in a more contemporary style that melds perfectly with the older buildings, were an unequivocal success.

The tour presented here begins at a small public square called **Freedom Plaza**, at the end of Pennsylvania Avenue, near the White House grounds and the surrounding parkland. It explores the main buildings of this neighbourhood, as well as the **National Museum of Women in the Arts ★**, and then ascends New York Avenue to **Mount Vernon Square**. Among the new public squares in Washington, **Freedom Plaza (19)** *(Pennsylvania Ave., between 11th St. and 14th St. NW, Federal Triangle metro)* certainly offers one of the most appealing views because it is inline with the White House and the Capitol. The square was created by the prestigious architectural firm of Venturi, Rauch and Scott Brown in 1980. A few trees and gardens surround a large terrace of black and white flagstones engraved with an enormous reproduction of L'Enfant's plan of the city. The square is graced on either side by a fountain and an equestrian statue of General Pulaski.

Just across from Freedom Plaza stands a pompous building decorated with Corinthian columns and several statues on an upper-story cornice. This is the **District Building (20)** *(1350 Pennsylvania Ave. NW, at 14th St., Federal Triangle metro)*, which was designed in 1904 by architects Cope and Stewardson. The building's outer shell is made of granite covered with marble slabs.

> ### The Scandal of L'Enfant's Stolen Plans of the City
>
> The design for the city of Washington – a plan that comprised four quarters criss-crossed by broad avenues that converged at the Capitol and the White House – was conceived in 1791 by French Major, Pierre Charles L'Enfant, who had followed the Marquis de Lafayette to the New World as his assistant. Because of his rebellious spirit, his incapacity to take orders, and his tendency to splurge the funds allotted to him for the project, L'Enfant was relieved of his position by President Washington after only one year. Unable to see his project through to its fruition, L'Enfant was surprised some time later to see that one of his old colleagues named Benjamin Banneker, an African-born American surveyor, had shamelessly copied his precious plans from memory. The city was indeed built as L'Enfant had imagined it, but he did not receive the least remuneration. He claimed compensation of $95,000, a considerable sum in that era, which the government refused to pay. He was instead offered $35,000. In the end, Pierre Charles L'Enfant lived out the rest of his life rather modestly and died completely destitute.

A bit further west there is a charming little park with benches and lovely shady trees that is a nice spot for a break. Created in 1981 under the aegis of the Pennsylvania Avenue Development Corporation, **Pershing Park (21)** *(Pennsylvania Ave. between 14th St. and 15th St. NW, Federal Triangle metro)* is a pleasant corner of greenery facing the prestigious Willard Hotel. The park is made even prettier by blossoming azaleas, chrysanthemums and other flowers in warmer months, and in the wintertime a skating rink is maintained here.

The **Willard Hotel (22)** *(corner of 14th St. and Pennsylvania Avenue NW, Federal Triangle metro, ☎628-9100)*, with its characteristic 19th-century style, is without doubt one of the most beautiful hotels in Washington, as much for its interior decoration as for its elegant façade. This particular location was the site of a string of hotels starting in 1816, but it was not until 1901 that Harry Hardenberg drew up the plans for the present building. Opinions vary as to the architect's motivation for sloping the top story of the building. Some believe it was a detour around municipal regulations limiting the height of new constructions, while others see the effect as his desire to re-create the style of other renowned hotels such as the Waldorf-Astoria in New York City. The Willard is considered the most prestigious hotel in the city and has welcomed its share of celebrities. Dr. Martin Luther King Jr.'s famous "I Have a Dream" speech was written in one of its suites. Although it was neglected during the downtown area's lean period, the building was saved from the wrecking ball by the intervention of the Pennsylvania Avenue Development Corporation. Renamed Willard Inter-Continental Hotel, it reopened its doors to a posh clientele in 1986 after major reconstructive surgery. Its interior encloses a superb lobby, completely covered in decorated marble, and a long row of elegant shops that are apparently used as a training ground for FBI agents learning to carry out under-cover operations.

The building adjacent to the Willard is none other than the **Hotel Washington (23)** *(corner of 15th St. and Pennsylvania Ave. NW, Federal Triangle metro, ☎638-5900)*, the oldest hotel in the neighbourhood. It is accredited to architects Carrère and Hastings, the same designers who were behind the New York Public Library on 5th Avenue in New York City. Take note of the decoration of the façade and of the frieze adorned with busts of American presidents.

Another architecturally impressive sight can be seen by taking 15th Street toward the White House, turning right on G Street, and walking one block to the **Colorado Building (24)** *(1341 G St. NW, Federal Triangle metro)*, which is astonishing because of the exuberance of its exterior decoration. Statues of eagles and lions seem to mount guard amid friezes and sculptures in all genres. The lobby presents marble slabs with overlapping motifs, while its ceiling is covered in gilt. An ingenious ventilation system designed at the beginning of the century, which allowed fresh air to circulate on the building's upper floors, was rediscovered during reconstruction work in 1991. Large fans blew over blocks of ice suspended over a ventilation shaft that ran from the roof to the second floor; the shaft was connected to a complex system of ducts, whereby precious cool air circulated throughout the building.

The **Church of the Epiphany (25)** *(1317 G St. NW, Federal Triangle metro)* stands a few steps from the Colorado Building. The sober façade of this Gothic-inspired house of worship has been covered in white stucco. The church's elevated choir houses magnificent organs that are especially appreciated by musicians who occasionally give concerts here.

Backtrack to 15th Street and turn right toward New York Avenue. At the corner of these two streets there is another beautiful example of Washington's architecture, the **Crestar Bank (26)** *(corner of 15th St. and New York Ave. NW, Federal Triangle metro)*. Its red brick façade, rounded corner topped by a small clock, and terracotta decorations creat a pretty overall effect.

The **Folger Building and Playhouse Theater (27)** *(725-727 15th St. NW, Federal Triangle metro)*, which is credited to architect Jules Henri de Sibour, stands just behind the bank. Its elegant beaux-arts-style mansard roof is reminiscent of those of the Willard Hotel and the Renwick and Corcoran Galleries.

The **National Museum of Women in the Arts ★ (28)** *($3; Mon to Sat 10am to 5pm, Sun noon to 5pm; 1250 New York Ave. NW, at 13th St., Metro Center metro, ☎783-5000)*, just a little further east on New York Avenue, is exclusively devoted to the works of women artists. From 1911 to 1980, this building served as Washington's Masonic temple. It underwent major renovations and then a philanthropist couple, Wilhelmina and Wallace Holladay, founded this museum in 1987 by bequeathing their collection of about 200 pieces. Today, about 2,000 works dating from the 16th century to contemporary times are exhibited here, including refined paintings by Frida Kahlo (*Self Portrait*), Camille Claudel (who emerges from Rodin's shadow here), Lila Cabot Perry (*Lady with a Bowl of Violets*), Mary Cassatt (*The Bath*), and Impressionist Berthe Morisot (*The Cage*). Élisabeth Vigée-Lebrun's *Salonière*, which was painted in the court of Marie Antoinette, is also on display here. When Élisabeth Vigée-Lebrun applied for admission to the Académie Royale de Peinture, critics of the day wondered if her paintings were not in fact the work of a man. Long underrepresented in great museums, the artistic work of women has finally been given a place of honour in a large national museum, and Vigée-Lebrun is vindicated!

Further east, New York Avenue opens onto a small public place called **Mount Vernon Square**, which is the location of the **Central Library (29)** *(Mount Vernon Sq., corner of 8th St. and K St. NW, Metro Center metro)*. This imposing beaux-arts marble building donated by Andrew Carnegie served as the District's main library from 1902 until the end of the 1960s. Today the building is part of the **University of the District of Columbia**.

TOUR C: AROUND THE WHITE HOUSE ★★★

For people all over the world, there is no more recognizable symbol of American power than the elegant, whitewashed Georgian manor at 1600 Pennsylvania Avenue. George Washington chose this particular site so that the seats of the executive (the White House) and legislative (the Capitol) branches of the government would be directly linked by Pennsylvania Avenue and thus have an unimpeded view of each other. Later, unfortunately, the Treasury Building, a massive, neoclassical structure, was erected on the east side of the White House, blocking the lovely perspective between the executive mansion and the Capitol. Architect Pierre Charles L'Enfant had envisioned the official home of the American president as an imposing building that would rival the palaces of Europe, but once he was dismissed, his grandiose plans were abandoned in favour of a more modest but nonetheless stately building.

A park originally known as President's Square was laid out immediately north of the White House. Starting with the construction of little St. John's Church in 1815, all sorts of buildings sprang up around the square. In 1818, the first private residence, Decatur House, was erected on the northwest side of the park. Other elegant Victorian homes followed. In 1824, the square was renamed after Marie Joseph de

124   Exploring

Motier, Marquis de Lafayette (1757-1834), the French general who became a hero of the American Revolution; it bears his name to this day.

The Old Executive Office Building (1881), an imposing, French neoclassical edifice made of grey stone, stands on the west side of the White House, at the corner of Pennsylvania Avenue and 17th Street. Originally the headquarters of the State Department, it now houses the offices of the President's adjuncts. Seventeenth Street, which runs along the west side of the White House, is lined with a series of elegant buildings dating from the beginning of the century, including the Corcoran Gallery of Art, the headquarters of the American Red Cross, the headquarters of the Daughters of the American Revolution and the Organization of American States.

South of the executive mansion, a park was laid out adjacent to the Mall. Though square in shape, it is now known as the Ellipse. The Visitor Center, where you can procure tickets to visit the White House, stands in the northeast corner of the Ellipse. The Zero Milestone *(on the north side of the Ellipse, on E Street)*, which is a point for the measurement of distances from Washington on, is the best spot from which to admire the south façade of the executive mansion.

Like his predecessors, Bill Clinton likes having company. Lots of company. Each year, over a million and a half people line up at the doors of the **White House** ★★★ **(1)** *(Tue to Sat 10am to noon; 1600 Pennsylvania Ave. NW, McPherson Sq. or Metro Center metro, ☎456-7041 or 619-7222)*, the world-famous symbol of the United States. When drawing up his plans for the city, French architect Pierre Charles L'Enfant included an imposing mansion that would serve as the official home of the American President. He was relieved of his position, however, and a public competition was held in order to select a design for the executive residence. The winning entry was a three-story Georgian manor designed by James Hoban. Its cornerstone was laid on October 13, 1792, but because of delays in the construction schedule and financial problems, President Washington's acquiesced to a modification of the original design, and the entire third floor was eliminated. The building was not finished during Washington's presidency. His successor, John Adams (1735-1826), became the first president to occupy house in 1800. The next president, Thomas Jefferson

Tour C: Around the White House 125

Around the White House

ATTRACTIONS
1. White House
2. Visitor Center
3. Treasury Building
4. Lafayette Square
5. St. John's Church
6. Decatur House
7. Renwick Gallery of the National Museum of American Art
8. Old Executive Office Building
9. Octagon House
10. Corcoran Gallery of Art
11. American National Red Cross
12. Constitution Hall and the Daughters of the American Revolution (DAR)
13. Organization of American States
14. Lock Keeper's House

ACCOMMODATIONS
1. Hay-Adams Hotel
2. Hotel Washington
3. JW Marriott Hotel
4. The Capital Hilton
5. The Carlton
6. Willard Inter-Continental

RESTAURANTS
1. Café des Artistes
2. Firehook Bakery
3. Starbucks Coffee

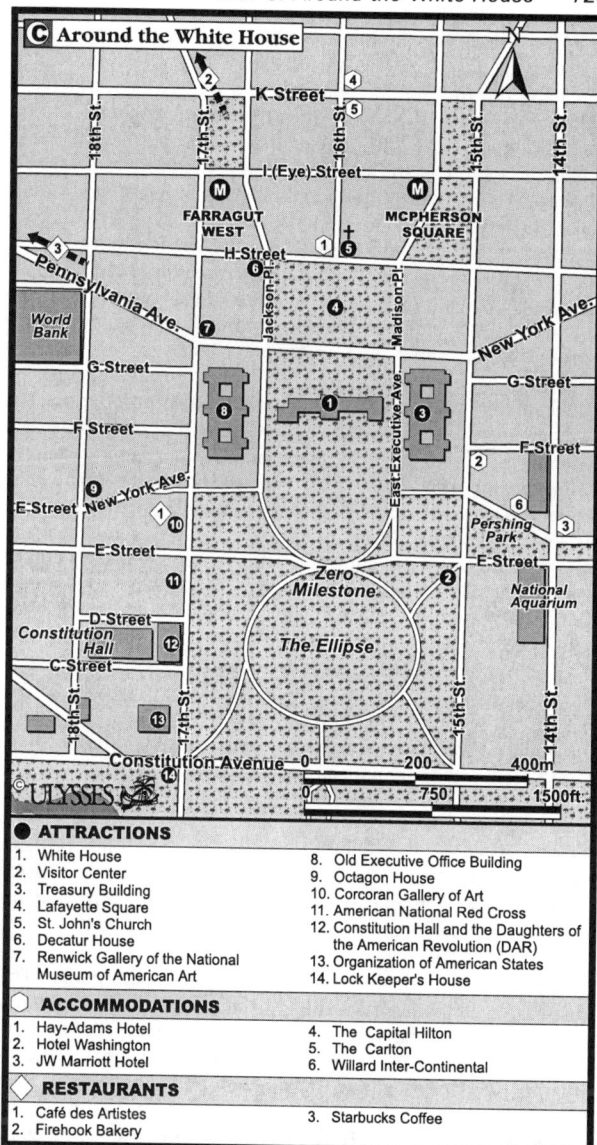

(1743-1826), asked architect Benjamin Latrobe, who was also working on the Capitol, to modify the design somewhat by replacing the roof and adding east and west wings. In August 1814, while the U.S. was at war against England, enemy forces occupied the city of Washington and burned the major buildings, including the Capitol and the White House. Miraculously, these structures were saved from complete destruction by a torrential rain. The supporting walls of the executive mansion had been severely weakened by the fire, however, so the house was torn down and rebuilt on new foundations. The new building went up quickly, and President Monroe was able to move into it in 1824. Visitors can still admire the Empire furniture purchased during his term in office.

The mansion was modified again and again throughout the 19th century. The custom of letting each new president redecorate the house was established, with varying results. Some presidents auctioned off the treasures with which their predecessors had adorned the house. Buchanan, for example, disliked the splendid Bellangé furniture purchased by President Monroe, and thus sold some of it; the remaining pieces can be seen in the Blue Room. Fortunately, Jackie Kennedy, an art lover who put a great deal of effort into redecorating the White House with beautiful furniture and objets d'art, found the sofa in a secondhand shop in Georgetown.

In the 20th century, particularly during Theodore Roosevelt's administration, major modifications and renovations were undertaken. The greenhouses once located on either side of the house were destroyed, and a wing was added to the west side of the building. The East Wing was added in 1942, during Franklin Delano Roosevelt's presidency; the second-floor balcony during Truman's. Thus for nearly 200 years, the White House has been home to every American president and his family, who have each added their own personal touch.

Only a few rooms of this mansion are open to the public. The tour starts on the ground floor of the West Wing. A large portrait of Jacqueline Kennedy Onassis hangs in the **Lobby**. The **Library**, to the right of the corridor, contains nearly 3,000 volumes, while a collection of French and English vermeil from the 17th through the 20th centuries can be found in the **Vermeil Room**, to the left. The **China Room**, decorated with Chinese porcelain, and the **Diplomatic Reception Room**, whose splendid wallpaper depicts American country scenes, may only be visited by U.S. citizens who apply to their congressman for a "Congressional Tour" of the White House several months in advance.

The **East Room**, on the upper floor, is used for concerts and official ceremonies and is thus sparsely furnished. Hanging on the wall is a portrait of George Washington dating from 1797, which was rescued from the great fire of 1814. Upon exiting this room, you'll enter the **Green Room**. Its walls are covered with green silks, whose shades are echoed by the magnificent Turkish carpet on the floor. Porcelain items and mahogany furniture also adorn the room, and a portrait of Benjamin Franklin by David Martin hangs over the mantelpiece. The **Blue Room** is considered the loveliest in the White House. It is here that you will find the gilded Bellangé wing chairs that James Monroe had sent over from Paris. Portraits of the first presidents of the United States hang on the walls. The cozy **Red Room** is decorated with Empire furniture covered with red and gold silk damask. The Empire chandelier, which holds 36 candles, is made of carved wood covered with gold leaf. The small clock on the marble mantelpiece was given to President Truman by his French counterpart, Vincent Auriol, in 1952. The two little gilded porcelain vases on either side of it bear the portraits of the Marquis de Lafayette and General Washington. Above the mantelpiece hangs a portrait of President Van Buren's daughter, Angelica Singleton Van Buren, who is posing in front of a bust of her father – the very same bust you'll see on the wall between the two windows. Finally, the **State Room**, all in gold and white, is decorated in the Queen Anne style. Its long mahogany table is set with a gilded service purchased by President Monroe in 1817 and rococo candelabra acquired during the Hayes presidency. A portrait of a pensive President Lincoln seated in an armchair hangs on the wall. The mantelpiece below is inscribed with these words from a letter written by John Adams after his first night in the White House: "I Pray Heaven to Bestow the Best of Blessings on THIS HOUSE and on All that shall Hereafter Inhabit it. May none but Honest and Wise Men ever rule under this Roof." The tour ends in **Cross Hall**, whose walls are hung with the portraits of the most recent U.S. presidents.

The **Treasury Building (3)** *(guided tours only, Sat 10am 10:20am and 10:40am; appointments must be made one week*

Want to See the President? Good Luck!

The White House is to Washington what the Eiffel Tower is to Paris: a must-see. However, it's a whole lot easier to visit the Eiffel Tower than the White House. Anyone wishing to explore the President's official residence must first purchase same-day tickets at the **White House Visitor Center (2)** *(on the northeast corner of the Ellipse, ☎523-3780)*; get there early – they'll be sold out by 8:00am. Next, arm yourself with patience and take your place in line. After waiting three hours in the blistering summer heat, you will be permitted to cross the hallowed threshold of the White House for a restricted but unguided tour of the premises. If you have any hopes of catching a glimpse of the President, you'd better put them aside: his private quarters are precisely that, private.

---

in advance; 1500 Pennsylvania Ave. NW, at the corner of 15th St., Metro Center metro, ☎622-0896), on the east side of the White House, is the biggest neoclassical building in the city. It is easily recognizable, due to its imposing portico, supported by 30 huge Ionic columns.

The original Treasury Building, completed in 1800, suffered the same fate as the White House and the Capitol when the British occupied the city in 1814. Ravaged by fire, it had to be quickly rebuilt. The task was entrusted to James Hoban, who also designed the White House. Unfortunately, the building was the victim of another fire in 1833. Three years later, architect Robert Mills, whose other credits include the Washington Monument, was commissioned to draw up plans for a new building. The design and location of the Treasury Building, however, did not fit in with L'Enfant's original plans for the city, obstructing the lovely open perspective between the White House and the Capitol, up Pennsylvania Avenue. A whole series of architects became involved in the project, adding a wing here and an inner court there, until the Treasury Building became so gigantic that it now covers two whole blocks. Once it was finished, the last architect to have worked on it, Alfred Mullet, began designing another imposing edifice on the other side of the White House, the Old Executive Office

Whether or not you like aeronautics, a visit to the National Air and Space Museum is an unforgettable experience.
- *Lorette Pierson*

The elegant Georgian-style White House is the most internationally recognized symbol of American power.
- *L. P.*

One of the lovely statues in downtown Washington: General Hancock on his horse. - *L. P.*

Building (see p 131), which Harry Truman called "*the biggest monstrosity in America*".

Opposite the main entrance of the White House lies a pretty public park known as **Lafayette Square (4)** *(between Pennsylvania Ave. and H St., Metro Center metro)*, in the centre of which stands a bronze equestrian statue of a triumphant General Andrew Jackson statue lifting his hat. It is graced with four cannons taken from the English during the War of 1812. Each corner of the park is graced with a statue of a foreign hero who fought for the American cause during the War of Independence: Lafayette (southeast corner, 1891), Jean Baptiste Donatien de Vimeur, Comte de Rochambeau (southwest corner, 1902), Friedrich Wilhelm von Steuben (northwest corner, 1910) and Tadeusz Kosciuszko (northeast corner, 1910).

On the other side of the park, next to the old British embassy, stands an elegant little church that was built after British occupation of the capital. Charming **St. John's Church ★ (5)** *(16th and H streets NW, Farragut North or Farragut West metro)* was designed by the renowned architect Benjamin Latrobe, who was so happy with the end result that he wrote to his son: "I have just completed a Church that made many Washingtonians religious who were not religious before." His original design has been modified somewhat, most notably by the addition of a portico and bell tower in 1822. The building was originally shaped like a Greek cross, but its west transept was extended, so it is now in the form of a Latin cross. The stained-glass windows behind the altar come from France. They were designed by Madame Veuve Lorin, the curator of Notre-Dame Cathedral in Chartres. Pew 54 is reserved for the First Family.

Also facing onto Lafayette Square is a small red-brick house that is considered to be one of architect Henry Latrobe's masterpieces. **Decatur House ★ (6)** *(guided tours Tue to Fri 10am to 3pm; 748 Jackson Pl. NW, Farragut West or Farragut North metro, ☎842-0920)* was built in 1818 for Commodore Stephen Decatur, an American naval hero who only spent a few months under its roof before being killed in a duel. Latrobe died that same year, not by defending his honour with a gun in his hand but from yellow fever. Subsequently, the small, three-story house had a whole series of occupants and owners. Various British, French and Russian diplomats lived here, as did

Van Buren before becoming president. Later, during the Civil War, the house was requisitioned by the government for military purposes. In 1872, adventurer Edward Fitzgerald Beale, a great friend of President Grant's and a frequent guest here, purchased the house and remodeled it. It was Beale who raced back east from San Francisco in 1848 to officially announce that gold had been discovered at Sutter's Mill, thus launching the famous gold rush of 1849. Upon his death, his son took over the house and hosted many diplomatic functions here. Every year, it was the scene of one of the most important social events in Washington such as the dinner following the diplomatic receptions at the White House. Mrs. Beale bequeathed the house to the National Trust for Historic Preservation in 1956. It is now decorated with furniture from Decatur's time, while the second floor is devoted to the Beale era.

The **Renwick Gallery of the National Museum of American Art** ★ **(7)** *(every day 10am to 5:30pm; Pennsylvania Ave. and 17th St. NW, Farragut West or Farragut North metro, ☎357-2700)* is devoted to American crafts. This handsome French Second Empire building was designed by James Renwick, Jr., who was also the architect of the famous Smithsonian Castle, on the Mall.

The building was begun in 1858, but its construction was halted by the outbreak of the Civil War in 1861 and did not resume until 1869. On its west side, there are two niches containing statues by Rubens and Murillo. The Renwick was originally supposed to house a large art collection amassed by financier and co-founder of Riggs Bank, William Wilson Corcoran (1798-1888), whose monogram and profile can be seen above the main entrance, along with the inscription "Dedicated to Art". When it opened in 1874 as the Corcoran Gallery of Art, it was the first museum in Washington. Plaster copies of classical sculptures were displayed in the Main hall. Because of these statues' nudity, there were separate tours for men and women. In 1897, when the Corcoran collection moved to its present quarters farther south on 17th Street, the building was sold to the American government for $300,000. It served as the **U.S. Court of Claims** until 1964. Saved from wrecking ball by President John F. Kennedy, it was renamed after its architect and became part of the Smithsonian Institution in 1965. Today, the Renwick Gallery presents temporary exhibitions on American crafts and decorative arts of today and yesteryear. Its two main galleries, the **Grand Salon** and the **Octagon Room** are among the most elegant rooms in Washington. The former is furnished in the opulent Victorian style of the 1860s and 1870s. The paintings on display are from the permanent collection of the National Museum of American Art. The Octagon Room, for its part, was built around the most remarkable piece in the Corcoran collection, **The Greek Slave**, a female nude by Hiram Powers that can be found at the Corcoran Gallery of Art. The Renwick's permanent collection is made up of a variety of glass, ceramic, wood, fiber and metal objects, exhibited on a rotational basis.

On the west side of the White House, the **Old Executive Office Building ★ (8)** *(Sat 9am to noon, appointments must be made one month in advance; 17th St. and Pennsylvania Ave. NW, Farragut West or Farragut North metro, ☎395-5895)*, which President Truman called "the greatest monstrosity in America", is a big granite building (1871-1888) designed in the Second Empire style. It has a number of distinctive features, most notably its mansard roofs and scores of columns. It took a total of 17 years and four months to build this monumental edifice, which originally housed the Department of State, War and Navy departments. It has housed the offices of the president's adjuncts since 1949. Henry Mullet was the main architect of the building, which stands on the former site of the presidential stables. Copiously decorated with nearly 900 exterior columns and 1,572 windows, it contains over 550 rooms and offices.

Eight U.S. presidents, Herbert Hoover, Richard Nixon, Theodore Roosevelt, William Howard Taft, Franklin Delano Roosevelt, Lyndon B. Johnson, Gerald Ford and George Bush, have all had offices here. On August 21, 1935, the building was listed as a national historic monument. The tour takes visitors through the Executive Office of the President, whose central library has a lovely vaulted ceiling; the **Indian Treaty Room**, whose wrought-iron balcony is decorated with nautical motifs like anchors and shells, and the **Office of the Secretary of the Navy**.

A bit farther to the west stands one of the oldest residences in Washington, the **Octagon House ★ (9)** *(Tue to Fri 10am to 4pm, Sat and Sun noon to 4pm; 1799 New York Ave., Farragut West metro, ☎638-3105)*, which played a central role in the city's early history. Built in 1800 by renowned architect William Thornton (who also worked on the Capitol) for a rich Virginian plantation owner, Colonel John Tayloe III, this house has a strikingly original design. Thornton had to be creative in order to make the most of the triangular lot on which the house was to be built. He came up with a simple but clever design consisting of two rectangular wings laid out on either side of a round central structure. The most influential Washingtonians were guests here. In 1814, during the British occupation, when the city's major buildings went up in smoke, this house was spared thanks to the intervention of a French diplomat named Louis Seurier, who was living here at the time and persuaded the English not to burn down his home. Since the White House was not so lucky, President Madison took refuge at the Octagon from September 1814 to March 1815. It was here, furthermore, that the Treaty of Ghent, which marked the end of the hostilities between England and the United States, was signed on February 17, 1815. Neglected after Mrs. Tayloe's death in 1855, the house was finally purchased by the American Institute of Architects (AIA) in 1902. This prestigious organization restored the building and made it their national headquarters. In 1973, the AIA erected a modern building behind the house, which now contains the institute's administrative offices, as well as a library and a bookstore.

Seventeenth Street, which runs along the west side of the White House, is lined with a string of elegant buildings, including the **Corcoran Gallery of Art** ★★ **(10)** *(Wed to Mon 10am to 5pm, closed Tue; 17th St. and New York Ave. NW, Farragut West metro, ☎638-1439)*, one of the biggest "non-Smithsonian" museums in Washington. Originally intended to house American art, it also has a lovely European collection.

The museum, which originally occupied the handsome Second Empire building now known as the Renwick Gallery, owes its existence to William Wilson Corcoran. An autodidact and philanthropist, Corcoran decided to establish the city's first museum by erecting a building in which to house his own extensive art collection. His project came to a halt in 1861 when the Civil War broke out. A supporter of the Confederate cause, he went into exile in Europe. Upon his return, he picked up where he had left off, and the museum opened its doors to the public in 1874. A few years later, Corcoran donated a large sum of money so that a school of fine arts could be established at the museum. The original building (now the Renwick) proved too small for such a project, so a new museum named after its

Lion of the Corcoran Gallery of Art

generous founder, was erected on 17th Street. Its beautiful atrium, its galleries and its splendid rotunda are the finest possible examples of the Beaux-Arts style.

This magnificent museum was built in two stages. The first part, begun in 1897, was designed by Ernest Flagg, an American architect who studied at the École des Beaux-Arts in Paris. It is topped with a copper roof and has a white marble façade adorned with a frieze bearing the names of various internationally renowned artists. The monogram that can be seen above the main entrance of the Renwick Gallery appears above the entrance of the Corcoran as well, along with the inscription "Dedicated to Art". Today, the Corcoran is considered one of the finest 19th-century buildings in the country. In 1925, Senator William Andrew Clark donated his impressive collection of European paintings, including works by Rembrandt, Turner, Corot and Degas, to name but a few, to the Corcoran, along with $700,000 so that a wing could be added to house the museum's new acquisitions. In 1927, the architect Charles Platt was commissioned to design this addition, which extends southwest of the original building. A few years later, in 1937, the Corcoran's collection grew yet again, thanks to a major bequest from Edward and Mary Walker, which

134   Exploring

included a number of French impressionist paintings. Today, the permanent collection contains nearly 12,000 pieces, many of which are exhibited on a rotational basis. The main entrance is guarded by two magnificent bronze lions sitting on marble pedestals. These were purchased by William Wilson Corcoran himself in 1883 and were restored for the building's hundredth anniversary.

On the ground floor, you'll find a sculpture by Hiram Powers entitled ***The Greek Slave*** (1846), a nude that shocked many puritanical Americans when it was first displayed in the Corcoran's original quarters. It was this statue that prompted the museum to offer separate tours for men and women.

The **Salon Doré** ★★, on the same floor, is a magnificent 18th-century French room from the Hôtel de Clermont, located in the Faubourg Saint-Germain in Paris. This remarkable salon, donated by Senator William A. Clark, is a stunning example of 18th-century French art and interior decorating. Clark purchased it in 1904 and had it installed in one of the rooms of his mansion on Fifth Avenue, in New York. The woodwork and the ceiling were dismantled and transported to New York, then put back together in a slightly larger room, requiring a few minor changes in the original decor. The fresco on the ceiling, by Hugues Taraval (1729-1785), dates from 1773. It shows a sky peopled with putti carrying long garlands of flowers. The fresco is surrounded by allegorical figures representing the Seasons and the Arts, painted to look like stone. Eighteenth-century French furniture was specially designed to match the sculpted, gilded woodwork that extends from floor to ceiling. The Salon Doré is delicately adorned with Corinthian pilasters, garlands and panels carved with emblems representing the military, music, the Arts and Sciences and Peace and Love, while big mirrors reflect the windows and the gilding, making the room seem that much more spacious and opulent. Sitting on the marble mantelpiece is a clock made of Sèvres porcelain and marble, supported by two gilded bronze figurines. This exquisite timepiece, made by Thomire and Robin in 1789, once graced Queen Marie-Antoinette's private sitting room at the Palais des Tuileries in Paris.

The Salon Doré, known as one of the loveliest drawing rooms in Paris, originally graced the house of a great art collector by the name of Gaspard-Marie Grimod, Comte d'Orsay. On the eve of the French Revolution, the Count had to leave his home, the Hôtel de Clermont, and take refuge across the Rhine. During this period, all of his personal belongings and property, including the prestigious mansion on Rue de Varennes, were confiscated by the State. Today, the Hôtel de Clermont houses the offices of a French ministry.

One of the more noteworthy items on display at the Corcoran is a 12th-century **stained-glass window from the Soissons cathedral** ★ (France) depicting the legends of St. Crispin and St. Blaise, both of whom are mentioned in the Old Testament. Right near by, you'll find a gallery devoted entirely to the work of French sculptor **Antoine-Louis Barye** ★ (1796-1875), many of whose bronzes are inspired by mythological scenes such as *Theseus Battling the Minotaur* and *Theseus Battling the Centaur.*

Another gallery, devoted to Italian Renaissance art, displays 16th-century **tapestries** and 15th- and 16th-century **majolica** ★★ (glazed, enameled pottery).

Near the big wooden staircase leading up to the second floor, you will find sculptures and caricatures by **Honoré-Victorin Daumier** (1808-1879), better known in his lifetime as a caricaturist for liberal newspapers like *La Caricature* and *Le Charivari*. Nevertheless, Daumier occupies a very important place in 19th-century French art, for he is recognized as that era's master of social and political irony. The lithographs and busts displayed at the Corcoran are eloquent examples of his satirical style, which reveals the disgust felt by 19th-century French liberals toward the government and its "unjust and criminal" institutions. His works are also highly representative of his era's interest in morphopsychology, the study of the relationship between a person's character and his or her physiognomy.

The second-floor galleries are devoted to American art from the colonial era to the present day. The gallery farthest to the left contains works from the early days of the republic. Most, like those by **Rembrandt Peale** or **Samuel F.B. Morse's** *The Old House of Representatives* (1822), depict historical scenes. The central gallery displays landscape paintings from the mid-19th century, including Frederick Edwin Church's famous painting ***Niagara*** ★, which dates from 1857. Another gallery presents works by 19th- and 20th-century American masters like the portraitist **John Singer Sargent** (*Madame Edouard Pailleron*, 1879) and **Mary Cassatt** (*Susan on a Balcony Holding a Dog*). The two other galleries at the south end of the building, devoted to modern American art, contain remarkable works by Abstract Expressionists like **Mark Rothko** and a few paintings by the uncontested master of Pop Art, **Andy Warhol**.

Another majestic building, the **American National Red Cross (11)** *(Mon to Fri 9am to 4pm; 17th St., between D and E streets NW, Farragut West metro, ☎737-8300)*, stands on the left side of the Corcoran Gallery of Art. Built between 1913 and 1917 by Trowbridge and Livingstone, this edifice was designed as a memorial to the heroines of the Civil War. Its façade, made of white Vermont marble and adorned with Corinthian columns, is easy to identify, thanks to the big red cross on its pediment, which clashes a bit with the elegant architecture. The building boasts three Tiffany windows showing nurses in medieval dress ministering to wounded soldiers.

The neighbouring building, the headquarters of the Daughters of the American Revolution, is a huge complex covering an entire block between C and E and 17th and 18th streets. It houses **Constitution Hall and the DAR Museum (12)** *(guided tours Mon to Fri 10am to 2:30pm, Sun 1pm to 5pm; 17th and D streets, entrance at 1776 D St. NW, Farragut West metro, ☎879-3254)*, which are linked by a large vestibule. The DAR, founded in 1890, is a society of women descended from the American patriots of the War of Independence. Its mission is to "perpetuate the memory and spirit of the men and women who fought for American independence" and to promote "true patriotism and love of country". Today, it has about 200,000 members.

The edifice facing the Ellipse on 17th Street was the first of the three DAR buildings to be erected. When the "Daughters" chose this piece of land as the site of Memorial Continental Hall in 1902, contemporary newspapers poked fun at them because there was an underground spring just below the surface of the land and no one anticipated that the city would expand westward. Ignoring all these warnings, the Daughters, who had hoped that Congress would grant them a piece of land (which indeed it did, on the condition that they wouldn't build anything on it), followed through on their initial plan to purchase a plot right next to the White House. It soon became evident that their idea was far from stupid; shortly after their first building, designed by Edward Pearce Casey, went up, the Pan American Union and American Red Cross were built. When Memorial Continental Hall, a handsome Beaux-Arts building, was finally finished, the *Washington Evening Star* reversed its earlier position, lavishing praise upon the project: "This Valhalla is unique. It is the costliest and most impressive monument of its kind ever built by women in this country or any other... From the artistic standpoint it is one of the finest buildings which the beautiful Capital contains, and from the utilitarian it is destined to become one of the most useful." The entrance, opposite the Ellipse, is a monumental porte-cochère. Its semicircular portico is made up of a terrace with a balustrade supported by 13 columns representing the 13 original colonies. The entrance hall now houses the **Library ★** devoted exclusively to the history of American families. With over 140,000 books and 250,000 files and manuscripts, it is an invaluable resource for genealogical research. The little **DAR Museum** presents an exhibition on decorative arts, featuring antique furniture, silver- and glassware, lovely quilts and old weapons.

A few decades after Memorial Continental Hall was built, another building, designed to house the organization's administrative offices, was erected on D Street. The main entrance of the complex is now in this building, whose address is none other than 1776 (the year of the Declaration of Independence). In need of an auditorium big enough for its annual meetings, the DAR commissioned celebrated architect John Russell Pope, author of a number of nearby buildings, such as the American Pharmaceutical Institute Building (near the Lincoln Memorial), the National Gallery of Art and the National Archives Building (on the Mall) and the Jefferson Memorial, to build a new addition on 18th Street. Completed in 1939, this edifice was named Constitution Hall. The portico is supported by Ionic columns and topped with a large pediment with the name of the building inscribed beneath it. The pediment shows an eagle, the symbol of the United States, flanked by two crucial dates in the country's history: 1776 (the Declaration of Independence) and 1783 (the Treaty of Paris, which marked the end of the war with the English). Below the portico is a series of bas-reliefs flanking three heavy bronze doors (the building has 10 more – five on each of its other façades – for a total of 13, representing the 13 original colonies). Inscribed above the middle door are these words spoken by George Washington at the Constitution Convention in 1787: "Let us raise a standard to which the wise and honest can repair. The event is in the hands of God." This building is unique in that it has three façades, each with its own entrance - on D, 18th and C streets respectively. It is linked by a corridor to the 3800-seat, U-shaped Constitution Hall, which was also built as a venue for concerts and recitals. Its opening night has gone down in history, not because of the recital given on that occasion but because of the scandal that erupted when the Daughters barred opera singer Marian Anderson from performing here because she was black. The incident prompted a general outcry. The First Lady at the time, Eleanor Roosevelt, resigned her DAR membership in protest and organized another concert so that Anderson could sing for some 75,000 people who gathered in front of the Lincoln Memorial on Easter 1939. The incident induced the Daughters to revise their racial policy for future concerts.

Next to the DAR stands the lovely, Spanish colonial-style **Organization of American States Building (13)** *(Mon to Fri 9am to 4pm, guided tours by appointment; call one week in advance; 17th St. and Constitution Ave. NW, Farragut West metro, ☎458-3751)*, often called the "House of the Americas". The OAS, created to promote peace and economic cooperation between the independent nations of North and South America, is the oldest organization of its kind. Founded in 1890, it now has over 35 member States, the newest being Canada, which joined in 1990. When the OAS decided to establish its headquarters in Washington, Congress donated this piece of land, which is now international territory. The architect of the Folger Shakespeare Library, Paul Cret, and Albert Keysley drew up the plans for the building in 1910.

The entrance is made up of three big arches flanked by two allegorical statues. The one on the right, personifying North America is by Gutzon Borglum, best known as the sculptor of Mount Rushmore, while the one on the left, representing South America, is the work of sculptor Isidore Konti. Inside, you'll find a **Tropical Patio** centred around a fountain whose blend of Mayan, Aztec and Zapotec art symbolizes the unity of the Americas. Behind the patio, a small museum exhibits contemporary and traditional sculptures in an Aztec garden. Pieces from the OAS's permanent collection of contemporary Latin

Tour C: Around the White House 139

American and Caribbean art are also on display. The **Hall of the Americas**, on the second floor, contains Tiffany windows and other works of art.

The OAS Building stands on the site formerly occupied by the legendary Van Ness mansion, designed by architect Henry Latrobe in 1816. The house was equipped with hot running water, a luxury at the time, and was reputed to be the most opulent mansion in the country. Unfortunately, this splendid house was torn down in 1907, after falling into a state of serious neglect. All that remains of it are its stables, which can be seen between the bushes and trees at the corner of C and 18th streets.

The **Lock Keeper's House (14)** *(Constitution Ave. and 17th St. NW, Farragut West metro)* was built around 1835. In those days, it stood right beside the canal designed by L'Enfant to facilitate the transportation of heavy merchandise at a time when the city's roads were often inches deep in mud. The canal was opened to boats in 1815, and was later connected to the Chesapeake & Ohio (C&O) Canal, dug between 1828 and 1833. This network of waterways linked the capital to the fertile Ohio valley, opening up the city to trade.

★ TOUR D: THE MALL ★★★

In 1791, when the plans for the city of Washington were finally sketched out by Major Pierre Charles L'Enfant, they included a vast, cruciform esplanade extending from Jenkins Hill to where the Washington Monument now stands, thus creating an elegant, verdant avenue between the White House and the Capitol. However, since the Major was relieved of his duties before the city was even built, the project he had envisaged wasn't realized until 110 years later. For the greater part of the 19th century, this esplanade, known as the Mall, which served as a pasture and a park, was not a stately esplanade surrounded by the loveliest buildings in town, but a sordid, neglected avenue. One of the first buildings to go up on the Mall in the previous century was the **Pennsylvania Railroad** train station, which was relocated northeast and renamed Union Station (see p 106) in the early 20th century. Flanked to the west by swamplands that stretched beyond where the Washington Monument now stands, the Mall was disfigured by a railroad track lined with warehouses and heaps of coal. Veiled by the smoke and ash spewed out by the locomotives, the Mall had none of its present-day majesty. In 1848, workers began constructing the **Washington Monument**, and the **Castle**, the famous building that has become the symbol of the Smithsonian Institution, was begun a year later. At the turn of the century, the Mall was completed by the addition of Potomac Park, a 250-hectare green space on the banks of the Potomac River. In the centre of the park, the Tidal Basin was created in order to supply the Washington Channel with running water; the Jefferson Memorial now looks out onto this body of water.

The Smithsonian Museums

In addition to its many research departments, the Smithsonian Institution has 14 museums and a national zoo.

On the Mall:

The National Air and Space Museum ★★★ (see p 144)
The National Museum of Natural History ★★ (see p 161)
The National Museum of American History ★★ (see p 159)
The Freer Gallery of Art ★★ (see p 151)
The Arthur M. Sackler Gallery ★★ (see p 150)
The National Museum of African Art ★★ (see p 150)
The Arts and Industries Building ★ (see p 147)
The Hirshhorn Museum and Sculpture Garden ★★★ (see p 146)
The National Gallery of Art (East and West Buildings) ★★★ (see p 164)
The National Portrait Gallery ★★ (see p 112)

Off the Mall:

The National Museum of American Art ★ (see p 112)
The Renwick Gallery ★ (see p 130)
The Anacostia Museum (see p 192)
The National Zoological Park ★★ (see p 201)
The Cooper-Hewitt Museum (in New York City)

Tour D: The Mall   141

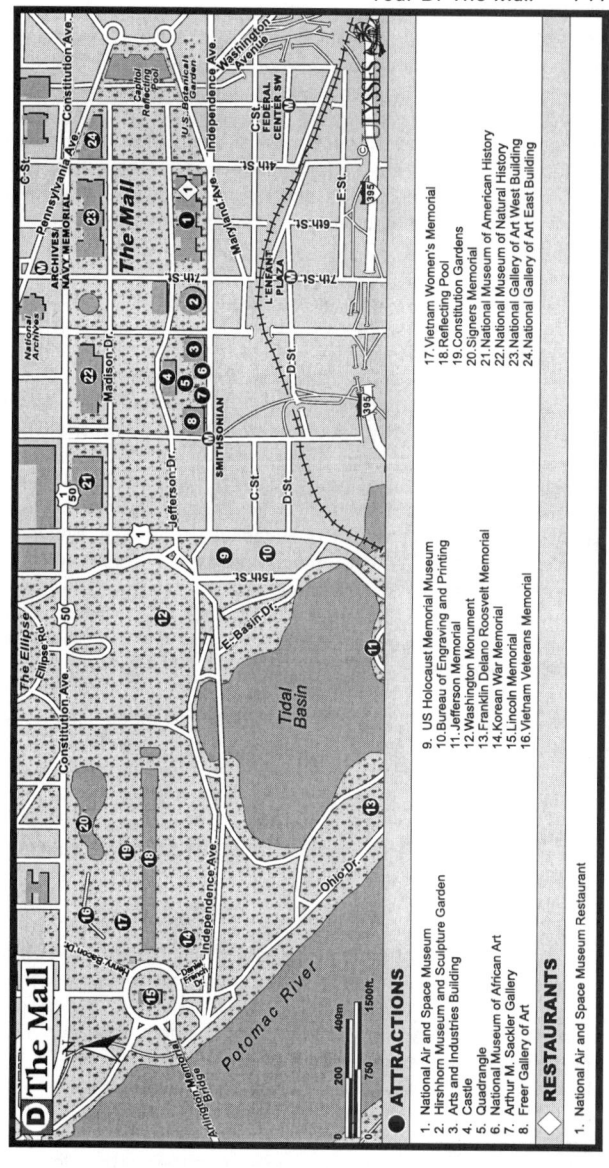

D The Mall

● ATTRACTIONS

1. National Air and Space Museum
2. Hirshhorn Museum and Sculpture Garden
3. Arts and Industries Building
4. Castle
5. Quadrangle
6. National Museum of African Art
7. Arthur M. Sackler Gallery
8. Freer Gallery of Art
9. US Holocaust Memorial Museum
10. Bureau of Engraving and Printing
11. Jefferson Memorial
12. Washington Monument
13. Franklin Delano Roosevelt Memorial
14. Korean War Memorial
15. Lincoln Memorial
16. Vietnam Veterans Memorial
17. Vietnam Women's Memorial
18. Reflecting Pool
19. Constitution Gardens
20. Signers Memorial
21. National Museum of American History
22. National Museum of Natural History
23. National Gallery of Art West Building
24. National Gallery of Art East Building

◇ RESTAURANTS

1. National Air and Space Museum Restaurant

EXPLORING

142 Exploring

In 1902, the McMillan Commission was established in order to develop the city in general, and more specifically to transform the Mall into something more like the lovely, tree-lined promenade L'Enfant had had in mind. The scores of winding trails that snaked their way all over the Mall were thus replaced by straight paths, the train station was relocated, the canals and the marshland were drained and converted into a big park, which is now graced by the **Lincoln Memorial** and the **Jefferson Memorial**.

The Smithsonian Institution's wonderful museums were built, one by one, in the first half of the 20th century, starting with the **Freer Gallery of Art** in 1923, the **National Archives** in 1937 and the **National Gallery of Art** (West Building) in 1941. Other museums, which attract millions of visitors each year, have gone up more recently, such as the **National Museum of American History**, built in 1964, the **Joseph H. Hirshhorn Museum and Sculpture Garden** (1974), the **National Air and Space Museum** (1976), the East Building of the **National Gallery of Art** (1978) and the **U.S. Holocaust Memorial Museum** (1993). In addition, the grounds themselves have been improved, most notably by the addition of pools and artificial lakes, and strewn with new monuments, the **Korean War Memorial**, the **Vietnam Veterans Memorial** and the **Vietnam Women's Memorial**.

The way it appears today, a broad, grassy esplanade flanked by elegant buildings containing some of the finest museum collections in the country, the Mall lends Washington a proud and distinguished air while at the same time providing a green space right in the heart of the city, where local residents come to stroll, jog or relax at the edge of the Tidal Basin, all the while admiring the neoclassical buildings that are the capital's pride and joy.

The tour outlined in the following pages will lead you along the paths of the Mall and into its splendid museums to admire some of the countless treasures contained therein. We'll start off with the National Air and Space Museum, then make our way southwest through the various museums along Jefferson Drive. Near the Tidal Basin, we'll visit the various memorials in the west part of Potomac Park, as well as the Washington Monument, located opposite the White House, before heading back to the Mall to explore the museums on its the north side.

Not to Be Missed in The Huge Air and Space Museum

Gallery 100: "Milestones of Flight":

***Columbia*, Apollo 11 command module and Michael Collins's spacesuit**, from the first moon landing in 1969.

Moon rock taken from the surface of the moon by the Apollo 17 astronauts.

Viking Mars Lander, used to study the surface of Mars.

Gemini 4, in which American astronauts first ventured into space.

The **hot-air balloon** in which French inventors Joseph and Étienne de Montgolfier made the first successful human flight in history in 1783.

The **flying machine** in which the **Wright brothers** made the first successful flight in a heavier-than-air craft in 1903.

The ***Spirit of St. Louis***, in which Charles Lindbergh made the first solo nonstop transatlantic flight in 1927.

Bell XS-1 (X-1), used to make the first manned flight to break the sound barrier.

Gallery 113: Rocketry and Space Flight:
Spacesuits
The ***U.S.S. Enterprise*** model used for the TV show *Star Trek*.

Gallery 114: Space Race
A walk-through replica of ***Skylab***, the first U.S. space station.

A 5-foot-high model of the ***Columbia* space shuttle** on its launching pad.

144   Exploring

> The ***Viking* rocket**, the first American probe designed for scientific purposes.
>
> Gallery 115: Samuel P. Langley Theater *(adults $3.25, children $2; every day 10am to 5pm)*
> **IMAX® films** about aviation shown on a giant, five-by-seven story screen.
>
> Gallery 201: Albert Einstein Planetarium *($3.25 adults, $2 children; every day 10:50am to 4:30pm)* lectures and multimedia shows
>
> Gallery 205: World War II Aviation
> This exhibition enables visitors to compare the technical advantages of fighter planes from five different countries.
>
> Gallery 213: Beyond the Limits: Aerospace and the Computer Age
> Life-sized model of the X-29, a plane with forward-swept wings
> Space station theatre that shows films on flight simulation.

A visit to the **National Air and Space Museum** ★★★ **(1)** *(every day 10am to 5:30pm, closed Dec 25, audiotape tours $5; Independence Ave. and 7th St., SW; entrance on the Mall, on Jefferson Drive, L'Enfant Plaza metro, ☎357-1700)* is a unique and unforgettable experience, whether you're an aeronautics buff or not. This museum displays an impressive collection of airplanes, from the flying machine in which the Wright brothers made the first continuous flight aboard a heavier-than-air craft on December 17, 1903 to the *Spirit of St. Louis*, in which Charles Lindbergh made the first nonstop solo transatlantic flight in 1927 to the Apollo 11 command module, *Columbia*, in which astronauts Neil Armstrong, Buzz Aldrin and Michael Collins returned from their trip to the moon in July 1969. As you make your way through the museum's immense galleries, you will learn about the history of aviation from its very beginnings to the commercial and military flights of the present day. In one section devoted to space exploration, you can examine not only the Apollo 11 space capsule but also a Viking probe, the first space vehicle to land on Mars. Pershing and SS20 missiles are exhibited in the entrance hall. Another gallery

Tour D: The Mall   145

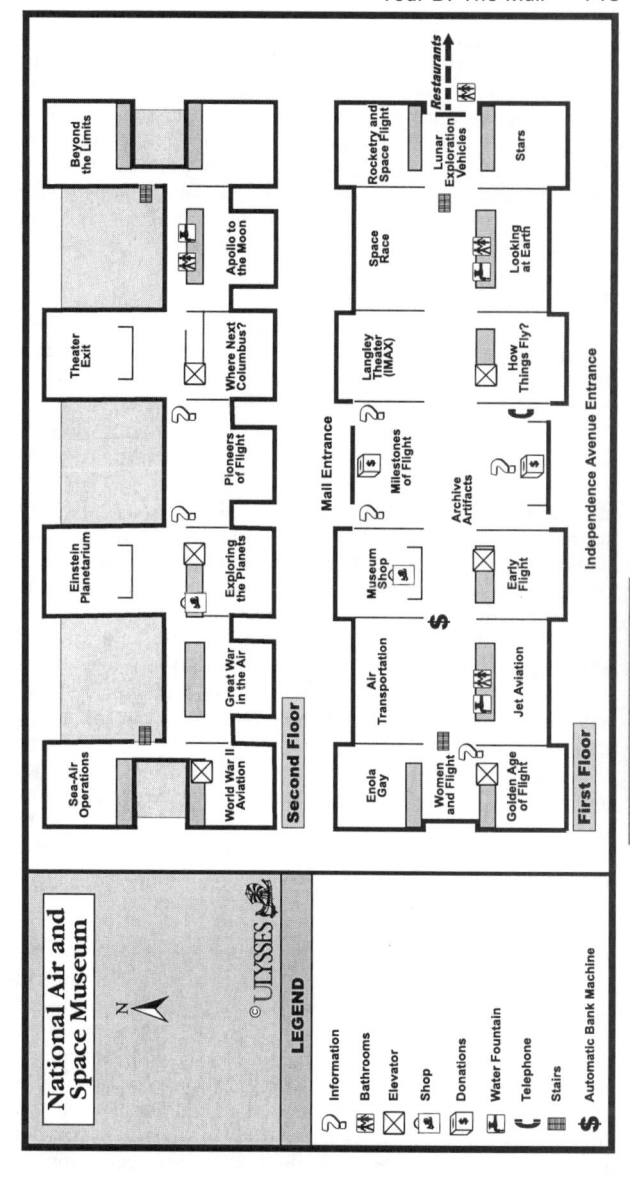

National Air and Space Museum

Second Floor

- Beyond the Limits
- Apollo to the Moon
- Theater Exit
- Where Next Columbus?
- Einstein Planetarium
- Pioneers of Flight
- Exploring the Planets
- Great War in the Air
- Sea-Air Operations
- World War II Aviation

First Floor

- Rocketry and Space Flight
- Lunar Exploration Vehicles → Restaurants
- Stars
- Space Race
- Looking at Earth
- Langley Theater (IMAX)
- How Things Fly?
- Mall Entrance
- Milestones of Flight
- Archive Artifacts
- Museum Shop
- Early Flight
- Air Transportation
- Jet Aviation
- Enola Gay
- Women and Flight
- Golden Age of Flight
- Independence Avenue Entrance

LEGEND

- Information
- Bathrooms
- Elevator
- Shop
- Donations
- Water Fountain
- Telephone
- Stairs
- Automatic Bank Machine

© ULYSSES

EXPLORING

146 Exploring

contains a reconstruction of the bridge of a World War II aircraft carrier. While learning about the amazing history of man's conquest of air (civilian, commercial and military) and space on a self-guided, interactive tour, children and adults alike will gain an understanding of some of the technological marvels developed in this century. Special films on aviation and space exploration are shown on a giant, five-story screen. This enormous exhibition has become the most popular museum attraction in Washington. Except for the planetarium and the audiotape tours, admission is free.

The **Hirshhorn Museum and Sculpture Garden** ★★ (2) *(every day 10am to 5:30pm, closed Dec 25; Independence Ave. and 8th St. SW, L'Enfant Plaza metro, ☎357-2700)*, next to the Air and Space Museum, is easy to identify, thanks to its round, modern architecture. Built by architects Skidmore, Owings & Merrill and Gordon Bunshaft in 1974, it is named after Joseph H. Hirshhorn (1899-1981), an American collector who left over 12,000 works of art from his private collection to the United States. The Hirshhorn's temporary exhibitions offer museum-goers a chance to admire all sorts of treasures of modern art. The walls display modern European and American art from the late 19th century to the present. Ranging from cubism to social realism and from abstract expressionism to pop art and minimalism, this exhibition is made up of an impressive collection of some 5,000 paintings and 3,000 sculptures, including works by Andy Warhol, Matisse, Picasso, Henry Moore and Calder. Outside, on the other side of Jefferson Drive, lies a sculpture garden designed by landscape architect Lester Collins. Monumental works by such renowned artists as Maillol, Rodin, Giacometti, Bourdelle, Picasso and Matisse, to name but a few, are displayed amidst the greenery, around a rectangular pool, creating a calm, serene atmosphere that puts you in just the right mood to contemplate these works.

If you have kids in tow, make sure to pick up a copy of the *Family Guide Hirshhorn Museum and Sculpture Garden*, an excellent brochure distributed free of charge at the information booth at the entrance. It is a collection of cards with colour illustrations of some of the works displayed in the museum and simple, interactive commentaries aimed at young children. This helps pique their interest and gives them an idea of what the artists were trying to convey. The *Family Guide* is by far the best brochure that we found at the Smithsonian museums.

Tour D: The Mall

The **Arts and Industries Building** ★ **(3)** *(every day 10am to 5:30pm, closed Dec 25; Jefferson Dr. and 9th St. SW, L'Enfant Plaza or Smithsonian metro, ☎357-2700)*, designed by Adolph Cuss, is a lovely Victorian edifice made of red brick and Ohio sandstone. Originally known as the American National Museum, it was given its present name several years later, by which time it housed a diverse collection that even included several aircraft. President James Garfield's inaugural ball was held here in March 1881. During the commemoration of the American Bicentennial, the galleries were restored in pure Victorian style. Today, this museum, part of the Smithsonian, displays thousands of pieces of Victorian Americana, many of which were featured at the Centennial Exhibition in Philadelphia in 1876. You'll feel as if you've stepped back in time. A number of technological advances were exhibited on that occasion, including the steam engine (engine 3 of the Santa Cruz Railroad), built in 1876, is displayed in the entrance hall) and a few machines designed to harness electrical energy, the most notable being a 19-ton dynamo. The building, made up of four galleries, is centred around a magnificent rotunda with a charming little fountain adorned with flowers in the middle. The Victorian interior is graced with eagles, flowers, Cupids and other whimsical decorations.

Back outside on the Mall, heading west, you'll see a medieval Renaissance-style building with eight crenellated towers. This is the **Castle (4)** *(every day 9am to 5:30pm, closed Dec 25; Jefferson Dr., between 9th and 12 sts. SW, Smithsonian metro, ☎357-2700)*, the Institution's first building, which now houses the Smithsonian Information Center, the administrative offices and the Woodrow Wilson International Center for Scholars.

The Castle was designed by James Renwick, Jr. (see Renwick Gallery, p 130), whose other credits include St. Patrick's Cathedral in New York City. It was completed in 1855, but the entire upper floor of the main building and the north and south towers were severely damaged by fire just 10 years later. A great many works of art in storage there were also reduced to ashes. It took two years for the building to be restored. From 1880 to 1890, the Castle, which at the time housed the entire Smithsonian Institution (a museum of science, an art gallery, several research laboratories and the administration), was

The Castle

enlarged. The Castle's galleries have recently been restored and some now have Victorian furnishings.

On the ground floor, there is a small theatre that shows a film on the history of the Smithsonian Institution and its various museums in Washington. This is a good way to learn about the National Zoo, the Smithsonian Biopark and the collections housed inside the Institution's 13 museums.

The **Quadrangle (5)**, *(Independence Ave., between 9th and 12th sts. SW, Smithsonian or L'Enfant Plaza metro, ☎357-2700)*, a vast complex that opened in 1987, lies behind the Castle. Stretching 1.7 hectares between the Castle, the Arts and Industries Building and the Freer Gallery of Art, it

What Is the Smithsonian?

Many people incorrectly assume that the Castle is the only building of the Smithsonian, which is actually a huge complex of 14 museums, a zoo and various research facilities. The Institution was born in 1829, when a wealthy Englishman named James Smithson bequeathed a half-million dollars – a huge sum of money in those days – to the American government in order "to found at Washington, under the name of Smithsonian Institution, an Establishment for the increase and diffusion of knowledge". Though he had never even been to the United States, Smithson believed that American democracy, more than British monarchy, was the future of civilization, hence his choice of the U.S. capital. The gift created a certain amount of controversy, since it was feared that accepting it would offend the British Crown. Finally, after eight long years of debate, Congress accepted the donation but decided that the federal authorities were not in a position to administer the funds directly. An organization known as "The Establishment" was thus created to execute Smithson's will, and the renowned architect James Renwick (see Renwick Gallery, p 130) was hired to build the institution's first building, which would house the administration, in the southwest part of the Mall. Today, the Smithsonian is the largest network of museums and art galleries in the world. Supported by the federal government and generous private donations, it possesses over 140 million objects related to all different aspects of human evolution. True to its commitment to increase mankind's knowledge, the Smithsonian also strives to promote research and public education, be it at primary or college level. In addition, it actively supports the performing arts, hosting a wide variety of events, such as concerts, plays and dance performances. It has its own chamber music ensemble and a famous string quartet, both of which give concerts regularly.

houses two museums, the **Arthur M. Sackler Gallery** and the **National Museum of African Art**, as well as the S. Dillon Ripley Center (Ripley ran the Smithsonian from 1964 to 1984), made up of the International Gallery, classrooms, a conference room and two workshops used for public programs.

During his time as director of the prestigious Smithsonian Institution, Ripley was faced with the problem of trying to find room to display Arthur M. Sackler's magnificent collection of Asian and Near Eastern art. At the same time, the Museum of African Art, which was showing its works of art in private homes on Capitol Hill, was also hoping to find a more suitable exhibition space. In order to meet these needs, Congress allocated 36.5 million dollars for the construction of the Quadrangle, much of which lies underground.

Though the Quadrangle's immense galleries are almost entirely underground, glazed sash windows have been cleverly incorporated into the architecture of the complex to let in lots of natural light so that visitors can admire the works of art on display without feeling like they're in a dark, gloomy basement. At ground level, the magnificent **Enid A. Haupt Garden** lies on top of the immense underground structure. Centred around a large Victorian embroidery parterre, it is the perfect place to relax and take a load off your feet. The entrance pavilions of the two museums are easily recognizable, thanks to their roofs – pyramidal in the case of the Sackler and rounded in the case of the National Museum of African Art.

The **National Museum of African Art** ★★ (6) *(every day 10am to 5:30pm, closed Dec 25; 950 Independence Ave. SW, Smithsonian metro, ☎357-2700)* is devoted to the art and culture of African civilizations south of the Sahara. It is the only museum in the United States dedicated exclusively to that subject. Over 900 different cultures are represented here. Portions of the museum's vast collection are displayed during temporary exhibitions, along with works borrowed from other private and public collections. Its collection of cast copper alloy objects from the former kingdom of Benin (now part of Nigeria), made between the 15th and 19th centuries, is particularly remarkable, as is its collection of wooden statues. Visitors will also find masks worn during initiation rites, ritual objects used to communicate with spirits and figurines of women and children symbolizing fecundity and human perfection.

The **Arthur M. Sackler Gallery** ★★ (7) *(every day 10am to 5:30pm; 1050 Independence Ave. SW, Smithsonian metro, ☎357-2700)*, the other museum in the Quadrangle, invites visitors on a journey of discovery of Asian and Near Eastern art from antiquity to the present day. Arthur M. Sackler (1913-

1987), a medical researcher, publisher and art collector, donated over 1,000 remarkable works to the Smithsonian. In addition to displaying this permanent collection, the museum hosts temporary exhibitions of objects on loan from other American and foreign museums. The artistic traditions of Asia (from 3000 BC until today), encompassing regions as far apart as Japan and the Mediterranean, are presented here with extensive written commentary.

Among the works on display are some splendid Chinese scrolls painted by 20th-century artists. The two-thousand-year-old Chinese bronzes and lacquer and jade objects dating from the Neolithic Age to the Qing dynasty (1644-1911) are also among the centerpieces of the collection. Other pieces include a magnificent Japanese palanquin from the Edo period (late 18th and early 19th centuries), made of gold and lacquered wood. The Near East is represented by extraordinary paintings and Islamic and Persian manuscripts, which include examples of nearly all the great classic texts of Persia, such as an exquisite gold and ink watercolour from the 16th-century "Falnama" manuscript, depicting none other than Adam and Eve.

Next to the Sackler, and linked to it by an underground passage, stands a beautiful Florentine Renaissance building made of marble and granite. Designed by architect Charles A. Platt, the **Freer Gallery of Art** ★★ **(8)** *(every day 10am to 5:30pm, closed Dec 25; Jefferson Dr. at 12 St. SW, Smithsonian metro, ☎357-2700)* opened its doors to the public in 1923. This museum owes its existence to Charles Lang Freer (1854-1919), a Detroit businessman with a passion for Asian and contemporary American art. Visitors will thus find two completely different collections – one devoted to Asian art from the Neolithic Age to the early 20th century, the other to late 18th- and early 19th-century American art – under one roof, which would seem to be a rather curious combination. There is an explanation, however: Freer started collecting American art at a very young age and was a patron of James McNeill Whistler, who encouraged him to develop an interest in Asian art, particularly the ancient masterpieces. The Freer thus houses a collection of Asian art, which is separate from the Sackler Gallery, but completes it from a chronological and geographical point of view. Toward the end of his life, Charles Lang Freer donated his collection and a large sum of money to the Smithsonian so that a museum could be built and his works

152 Exploring

of art would be properly looked after. The Freer hosts temporary exhibitions highlighting various segments of its permanent collection, made up of nearly 26,000 pieces.

Particularly noteworthy among the works of Asian art are the Chinese porcelain from the Yuan dynasty (14th century), the decorative objects that once belonged to the Chinese emperors of the Ming (1368-1644) and Qing (1644-1911) dynasties, the bronzes and jade figurines dating from 5000 BC to AD 1000, and the Japanese paintings, sculptures and lacquerwork. Korean ceramics dating from the 10th to the 16th centuries are also on display, as are various works of Indian art and Islamic manuscripts from Iran, Egypt and Syria.

One of the jewels of the Freer's collection of American art is the **Peacock Room** ★, painted between 1876 and 1877 by James McNeill Whistler for a wealthy British merchant named Frederick Leyland. This room is adorned with magnificent gold and oil paintings executed on wood, leather and canvas. This masterly work was originally intended to decorate the walls, shutters and ceiling of Leyland's dining room. Hanging above the mantelpiece is a delicate painting entitled *The Princess from the Land of Porcelain*, also by Whistler. Charles Lang Freer purchased this magnificent room in 1904 and had it moved lock, stock and barrel to his Detroit home before entrusting it to the museum. John Singer Sargent, Abbott Thayer, Metcalf and Thomas Dewing are but a few of the other American artists whose works hang in the Freer.

After the Department of Agriculture, at the corner of Independence Avenue and 14th Street, you'll come to the **United States Holocaust Memorial Museum** ★★ **(9)** *(every day 10am to 5:30pm; 100 Raoul Wallenberg Pl. SW, at the corner of Independence Ave., Smithsonian metro, ☎488-0400)*, which opened in 1993. This institution is a powerful, moving tribute not only to the six million Jews, but also to the Gypsies, disabled persons, homosexuals, Jehovah's Witnesses, communist political prisoners, Soviet POWs and others, who were captured and then exterminated by the German Nazis. The museum's mission is to continue studying the events that took place during this sad and unprecedented chapter of European history in order to keep the memory of those who suffered alive, increase public awareness of this tragedy and encourage the public to ponder the moral and spiritual questions raised by the Holocaust and reflect on our personal responsibilities as citizens of a democracy. The exhibition, which covers three floors, transports visitors back in time by means of explanatory texts, films, photographs, Nazi propaganda, period newspapers and survivors' accounts, all amounting to a painful journey. At the entrance, each person is given the passport of a Polish Jew, Raezel Kisielnicki, which tells the story of her life during this period and describes the horror of the camps. Visitors are then taken by elevator straight to the 4th floor, where the exhibition starts and gradually work their way down to the 2nd floor.

The events of the Holocaust are described in chronological order in three distinct sections. The first gallery, entitled *"The Nazi Assault 1933-1939"*, examines the rise of Nazism in the early 1930s. You'll discover how fundamental rights gradually came to be disregarded, starting with the loss of property rights and ending with the negation of all human dignity. The events that took place on Kristallnacht (November 1938) are described in meticulous detail. Two 15-minute films, one on anti-Semitism and the other on the Nazi regime's ascent to power, are shown continuously in two small theatres. The second gallery, *"The Final Solution: 1940-1944"*, contains victims' personal effects, a reconstruction of a gas chamber and a barracks, as well as one of the railway cars used to transport Polish Jews to Treblinka. Small television screens show scenes of unbearable brutality – mass executions, death marches and the living conditions in the camps. Parental supervision is therefore strongly recommended. In the *Voice of Auschwitz* room, which lies behind a glass wall, visitors can hear the testimonies of various survivors. The third gallery, *"Aftermath 1945 to the Present"*, located on the second floor, concludes this journey back in time with the liberation of the camps by the Allied forces and the Nuremberg trials, as well as the story of those courageous individuals who tried, in all sorts of different ways, to resist the Nazi regime.

At the **Bureau of Engraving and Printing** ★ **(10)** *(Mon to Fri 9am to 2pm, closed federal holidays and between Christmas and New Year's; 14th and C sts. SW, Smithsonian metro, ☎426-6841)*, located next to the United States Holocaust Memorial Museum and in front of the Tidal Basin, visitors can see the presses used to print over 20 billion dollars of bills every year. You'll follow the various steps involved in making

154 Exploring

American money, from printing it to checking it to cutting the sheets of bills. The good old greenback attracts huge crowds, so it is best to arrive early if you don't want to stand in line.

One of the most familiar Washington landmarks is the **Jefferson Memorial** ★★★ **(11)** *(every day 24 hours a day; on the southeast side of the Tidal Basin, at the south end of 15th St. SW, Smithsonian metro, ☎426-6841)*, with its open rotunda surrounded by Ionic columns and topped by a dome. The columns protect a six-metre-high statue of Jefferson (1743-1826), the third president of the United States. Congress passed a resolution authorizing the construction of this memorial in 1934. Designed in 1943 by architect John Russell Pope, the structure pays homage to Jefferson's home, Monticello, which he designed himself. Excerpts from some of Jefferson's best-known writings are engraved on the walls inside, the most famous being the *Declaration of Independence*, the *Virginia Statute of Religious Freedom* and *Notes on Virginia*. The perspective between the Jefferson Memorial and the White House forms a north-south axis that intersects with the east-west axis formed by the Capitol and the Lincoln Memorial, with the Washington Monument grounds as the point of convergence. The steps of the Jefferson Memorial thus offer a lovely view of the Tidal Basin, immediately in front, and the White House in the distance. The pediment shows the five members of the committee responsible for drafting the *Declaration of Independence* – Robert Livingston, Roger Sherman, Thomas Jefferson (standing in the centre), John Adams and Benjamin Franklin (right to left). When John Russell Pope designed the memorial, supposedly an adaptation of the Pantheon in Rome, he clearly drew inspiration from Jefferson's taste for classical architecture. Rudolph Evans' bronze statue of Jefferson stands in the middle of the rotunda. Those visiting toward the end of March and the first few days of April will be able to admire the memorial while the famous cherry blossoms are out – a typical post-card image. These trees, gifts from Japan (1912), were the subject of considerable controversy after the surprise attack on Pearl Harbor in 1941, when the Japanese destroyed a large part of the U.S. Pacific fleet. Many of the cherry trees around the Tidal Basin were destroyed as a sign of protest. A decision was then made to remove those remaining so that the Jefferson Memorial could be built. However, when construction was about to begin, protestors chained themselves to the trees to prevent them from being uprooted. In the end, the memorial

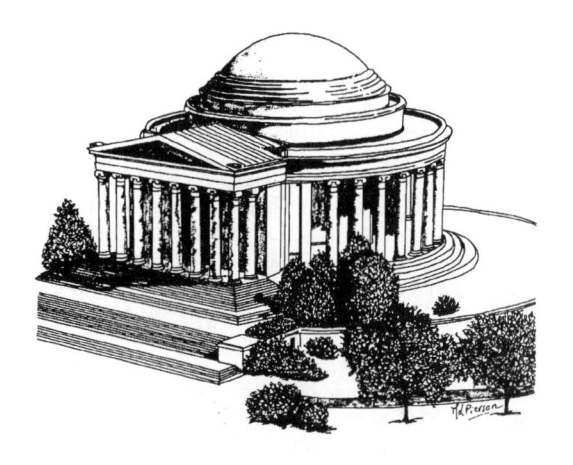

Jefferson Memorial

was built a short distance from where it was originally supposed to be, and the damaged trees were replaced in 1952.

Jefferson, a highly cultivated man of many talents, was a native Virginian. He played an important role in the country's destiny long before he was elected its third president. A lawyer by training with a passion for architecture (he helped draw up the plans for the city of Washington), Jefferson was elected to the House of Burgesses in 1769 and was among those members who revolted against the taxes imposed by England. In 1774, he was sent to the first Continental Congress as a delegate. He quickly became known for his eloquent writing and was thus called upon to draft the Declaration of Independence, signed on July 4, 1776. He was then sent to France as a representative of the fledgling American nation, and became Secretary of State under President George Washington four years later. Under the presidency of John Adams, Jefferson served his country as vice president from 1797 to 1801, before being elected chief executive himself. He held that office from 1801 to 1809, during which time he negotiated the purchase of Louisiana from the French for $15,000,000, among other things. Toward the end of his life, Thomas Jefferson retired to his home in Virginia, Monticello, where he died on July 4, 1826.

156 Exploring

The **Washington Monument** ★★ **(12)** *(Apr to Labor Day 8am to midnight, Sep to Mar 9am to 5pm; in the centre of the Mall, between 17th and 15 sts., Smithsonian metro, ☎426-6840)* is on par with the Capitol and the White House as one of the most famous symbols of Washington. It took nearly 40 years to complete this white marble obelisk, which stands on a small hill opposite the White House, right in the middle of that majestic esplanade known as the Mall. This austere monument, surrounded by American flags, is dedicated to the first president and father of the nation, George Washington. The first stone was laid in 1848, but only a third of the structure had been built when construction was halted because of the Civil War. The obelisk remained untouched until 1876, when new blocks of white marble from the same quarry in Maryland were brought in to finish it. These new stones, however, came from a different stratum, hence the slight variation in colour still visible about a third of the way up the structure. Today, an elevator transports visitors to the top of the monument, where they can take in a sweeping **view** ★★★ of the nation's capital.

The **Franklin Delano Roosevelt Memorial (13)** *(every day 24 hours a day; in West Potomac Park on West Basin Dr., Foggy Bottom metro, ☎619-7222)*, the latest memorial to have been built on the Mall, honours the 32nd president of the United States. A bronze statue shows Roosevelt seated and draped in a long cape, with his loyal Scottish terrier, Fala, at his feet, and behind it is a red granite wall with bas-reliefs depicting scenes from the Great Depression, during which Roosevelt launched the "New Deal". A statue of his wife Eleanor stands near by. This is the only presidential memorial to pay tribute to one of the country's First Ladies. Stricken by polio in 1921, F.D.R. was confined to a wheelchair. Fittingly, on the day the memorial was inaugurated, President Clinton asked Congress to equip it with an access ramp for the disabled.

The **Korean War Memorial** ★ **(4)** *(every day 24 hours a day, at the west end of the Mall, south of the Reflecting Pool, Foggy Bottom metro, ☎619-7222)*, inaugurated in July 1995, is made up of 19 monumental steel statues of 14 foot soldiers, three marines, an Air Force officer and a war doctor, all of whom look frightened and exhausted. The memorial, located near the Lincoln Memorial, south of the Reflecting Pool, is decorated with over 2,000 photographs of scenes from the "forgotten war", in which over 54,000 Americans lost their lives. The images have been etched onto a wall that runs alongside the statues.

Inspired by the Parthenon in Greece, the **Lincoln Memorial ★★★ (15)** *(every day 24 hours a day; at the west end of the mall, at 23rd St., Foggy Bottom metro, ☎426-6841)* plays a key role in Washington's architectural composition. It stands majestically at the west end of the Mall, facing the Capitol. On another axis, it lies between the White House and Arlington Cemetery, and more specifically the tomb of President Kennedy, on the other side of Arlington Memorial Bridge. Shortly after Lincoln was assassinated, there was discussion of erecting a monument in his honour, but it wasn't until 1911 that Congress passed a resolution authorizing the construction of this memorial. Then arose the question of whether the monument should be an obelisk to parallel the Washington Monument, thereby adhering to the Egyptian custom of always building more than one obelisk. How about a pyramid? All sorts of suggestions were considered, but architect Henry Bacon was finally commissioned to draw up the plans for the Lincoln Memorial. At the time, the west part of the mall was still boggy and needed to be drained. Bacon designed a monument based on the Parthenon, but with the entrance facing the Mall and the Capitol rather than the side. He also replaced the pediment of the Greek temple with a recessed roof, lending the structure a somewhat austere air. Its 36 columns represent the number of states in the Union when Lincoln was elected, its 48 festoons the number of states when the memorial was built. The Lincoln Memorial is a very familiar to Americans – after all, it is the façade of this building and the head of the statue inside it that are depicted on the penny.

The interior of the memorial is dominated by a monumental seated statue of President Lincoln. Over five metres high, this marble sculpture was carved by Daniel Chester French. Excerpts from Lincoln's famous Gettysburg Address, which he delivered at the height of the Civil War, on November 20, 1863, are carved into the wall to the left of the statue. The front staircase of the memorial offers a gorgeous **view ★★** of the entire Mall and the magnificent buildings facing onto it. It was from the top of these steps, now a popular place for public demonstrations, that Reverend Martin Luther King, Jr. delivered his famous "I have a dream" speech in 1963. It was also here that black opera singer Marian Anderson, who had not been permitted to perform at Constitution Hall, gave a concert for a huge crowd that had gathered in front of the Reflecting Pool to hear her (see below).

"A rift in the earth a long, polished black stone wall, emerging from and receding into the earth. Take a knife and cut open the earth... and with time the grass will heal it." This is how 21-year-old Maya Ying Lin, a student at Yale University, described her design for the **Vietnam Veterans Memorial ★ (16)** *(every day 24 hours a day; Constitution Ave. and Henry Bacon Dr. NW, at the west end of the Mall, at 22nd St. NW, Foggy Bottom metro, ☎634-1568)*. The names of the 58,132 Americans who lost their lives in the Vietnam War are inscribed on this black granite wall, which bears witness to the fragility of human life. There are books at either end so that visitors can look up the name of their loved one and locate it on the wall. Some people reverently rub a pencil over a piece of tracing paper to reproduce the name of their spouse, companion, son, cousin or someone else they knew. Near by, between the Lincoln Memorial and the wall, stands ***The Faces of Honour***, a bronze statue of three soldiers. Sculptor Frederick Hart described his work as follows: *"They wear it on their uniform and carry the equipment of war; they are young. The contrast between the innocence of their youth and the weapons of war underscores the poignancy of their sacrifice... Their strength and their vulnerability are both evident."*

Also right near by is the **Vietnam Women's Memorial (17)** *(24 hours a day; Constitution Gardens, southeast of the Vietnam Veterans Memorial, Foggy Bottom metro)*, which pays tribute to the more than 265,000 women who served in the Vietnam War. Inaugurated in 1993, this bronze sculpture by Glenna Goodacre represents three women in uniform, two of whom are supporting a wounded soldier.

The long, rectangular **Reflecting Pool (18)** *(24 hours a day, on the west side of the Mall, Foggy Bottom metro)* stretching between the Lincoln Memorial and the Washington Monument was originally supposed to be shaped like a cross, according to the recommendations made by the McMillan Commission in 1902. These plans were thwarted when an ammunition dump was built on Constitution Avenue during World War I. In 1920, Henry Bacon, the architect of the Lincoln Memorial, designed this vast stretch of water, which has lots of ducks paddling around in it. The reflection of the Washington Monument in the sparkling water is sure to delight the photographers among you.

In between the Reflecting Pool and the Lake, lie the charming **Constitution Gardens (19)** *(24 hours a day; on the Mall at 19th St. NW, at the west end of the Mall)*, a popular place for Washingtonians to go jogging or simply kick back and relax. The park was landscaped by architects Skidmore, Owings and Merrill in 1976. As you make your way along the winding paths that run past the Lake, you'll come to the only monument dedicated to the signers of the Declaration of Independence. Of rather modest size, the **Signers Memorial (20)** *(24 hours a day; on the north shore of the Lake, Foggy Bottom metro)*, which stands on a peninsula, is a semicircular structure made of blocks of red marble carved with the signatures that appear at the bottom of the famous document.

The **National Museum of American History** ★★ **(21)** *(every day 10am to 5:30pm, closed Dec 25; Constitution Ave. between 12th and 14th sts. NW, entrance on the Mall, on Madison Dr., Federal Triangle metro, ☏357-2700)* invites visitors to relive the great moments of American history including the evolution of technology and the impact of science on society. The contents and range of this museum's exhibitions will boggle your mind. Consider this: 16 million objects itemized in catalogues. Since it is obviously impossible to display this huge collection in its entirety under one roof, the museum is constantly changing its exhibits. It is therefore advisable to pick up a map at the information counter at the entrance so that you can locate the main points of interest. From the Stars and Stripes to Foucault's Pendulum to a display of gowns worn by First Ladies to General Washington's uniform and tent to a selection of antique cars, this appealing and instructive museum will take you on a veritable trip back in time to earlier periods of American history.

The first floor focusses on the history and social impact of technology. To the left of the Constitution Avenue entrance is an old country store that stood in Headsville, Virginia from 1868 to 1971 and served as the local post office. It may have been moved to the museum, but it's still selling stamps and processing mail! The first exhibit, entitled "Material World" shows the major changes that have occurred in the appearance and texture of our world from the 18th century to the present day. Visitors will discover how the materials in a particular object reveal all sorts of information about the people who made and used it, their surroundings and their values. Another gallery is devoted to farming machinery, from the old wooden ploughs of the colonial era to more recent equipment made of steel. The museum's collection also includes over 40 antique cars. Automobile enthusiasts will be delighted to find that the famous 1913 Ford Model T. Vehicles from earlier eras, such as a horse-drawn chaise dating from 1770, are also on display. An entire gallery is devoted to the railroad, which enabled the United States to enjoy tremendous commercial growth. Visitors can admire the impressive "1401" Pacific-type locomotive, which was built in 1926 for the Southern Railway and weighs 280 tons. You'll also find a whole slew of model trains illustrating the evolution of locomotives and railway cars. When you get to the Electricity Hall, make sure to check out the exhibits on Benjamin Franklin and Thomas Edison. The "American Industrial Revolution" (1790-1860) is explained with the help of a multitude of objects. The exhibition starts with a reconstruction of the Crystal Palace, built for the London Exposition of 1851, and shows how the industrial society and work ethic evolved. Another gallery is dedicated to the physical and medical sciences. From traditional cures and apothecary's remedies to scientific breakthroughs, this exhibition retraces the evolution of medicine in the 18th, 19th and 20th centuries. Finally, another exhibit called "Information Age", which starts with Samuel Morse's telegraph (1830), examines the impact of information technology on our lifestyle. The first telephone, invented by Canadian Alexander Graham Bell, and the ENIAC, an early mainframe computer, are also on view.

The second floor of the museum is devoted to social and political history. The **Star-Spangled Banner**, the true symbol of American patriotism, hangs opposite the Mall entrance. It was this very flag that was flying over Fort McHenry when it was attacked by the English on September 13, 1814, and which, the morning after the American victory over the British navy, inspired Francis Scott Key to write the poem that became the national anthem. Don't miss **Foucault's Pendulum**, invented by a 19th-century French physicist. Suspended from the ceiling of the top floor, a 110-kilogram brass ball swings endlessly back and forth, knocking over, one by one, a series of red markers laid out in a circle around it and thus demonstrating the rotation of the Earth on its axis. The **Ceremonial Court** re-creates the entrance hall of the official home of the President of the United States. Authentic furniture from the White House are on view, as well as personal items that belonged to various presidents. It is here that the most recent First Ladies' gowns are displayed, on wax mannequins, along with pieces of White House china.

The third floor is devoted to the history of the U.S. armed forces, whose evolution is illustrated by uniforms, weapons, flags and model ships. It is here that you will find George Washington's tent and the oldest American warship, the gunboat *Philadelphia*. The exhibit entitled **"A More Perfect Union"** chronicles the history of the 120,000 Japanese-Americans who were sent to detention camps during World War II. Though two-thirds of these individuals were U.S. citizens, the rights and liberties guaranteed them by the Constitution were abruptly suspended because of their race. The exhibit includes a reconstruction of one of the barracks from a detention camp in Topaz, Arkansas, making it easier to imagine the living conditions in the camps. Elsewhere on this floor, you'll find exhibits of stamps, ceramics, musical instruments, photographs and a lovely collection of coins and medals showing the evolution of currency. The **gold room** is a real little gem. There is even a small exhibit on counterfeit bills and coins. In a different vein, visitors with fond memories of the ventriloquist Edgar Bergen will find his famous wooden dummy, Charlie McCarthy, on this floor. Finally, the evolution of printing and graphic arts is illustrated through demonstrations of various techniques.

The **National Museum of Natural History** ★★ (22) *(every day 10am to 5:30pm, closed Dec 25; Constitution Ave. and 10th St. NW, Federal Triangle metro, ☎357-2700)*, designed by Hornblower and Marshall, was the third Smithsonian museum to be built. A neoclassical building composed of a four-story, granite central portion and a portico with Corinthian columns, it has an imperial air perfectly suited to its magnificent collection of over 121 million specimens. The museum specializes in three main scientific fields: biology, anthropology and geology. Upon entering the building, you'll find yourself in an impressive, 38-metre-high rotunda, in front of a giant African bush elephant. This animal stands about four metres high at the shoulder, and it weighed about eight tons when it was killed, making it the largest African elephant slain within the memory

162 Exploring

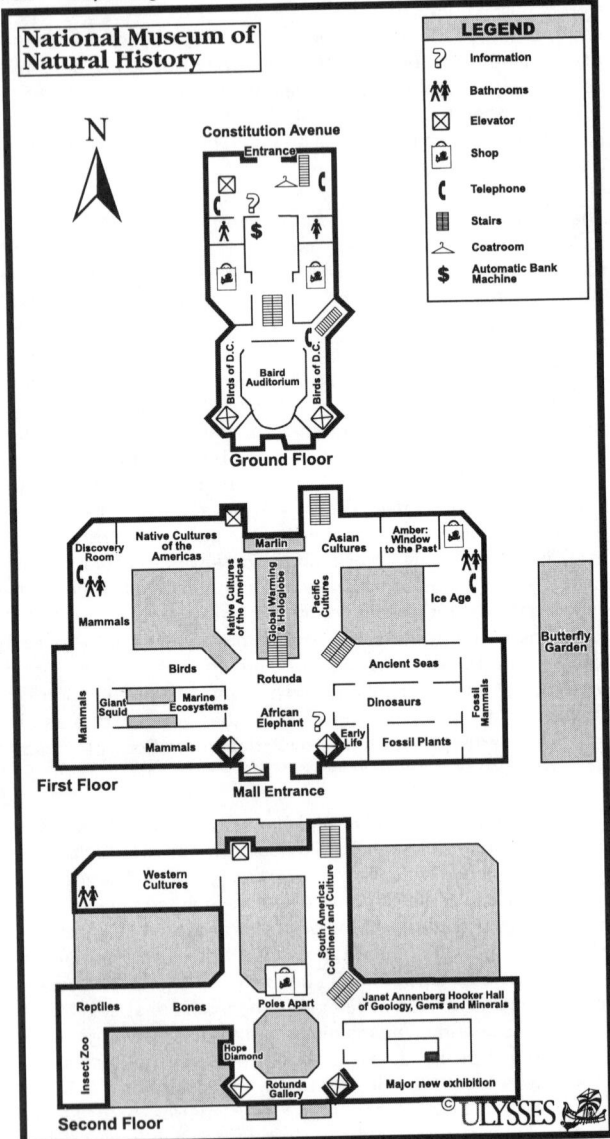

National Museum of Natural History

LEGEND
- ? Information
- 🚻 Bathrooms
- ⊠ Elevator
- 🛍 Shop
- ☏ Telephone
- ▤ Stairs
- ⌒ Coatroom
- $ Automatic Bank Machine

Ground Floor

Constitution Avenue Entrance
Baird Auditorium
Birds of D.C.

First Floor

- Discovery Room
- Native Cultures of the Americas
- Martin
- Asian Cultures
- Amber: Window to the Past
- Mammals
- Global Warming & Hologlobe
- Pacific Cultures
- Ice Age
- Rotunda
- Birds
- Ancient Seas
- Butterfly Garden
- Mammals
- Giant Squid
- Marine Ecosystems
- African Elephant
- Dinosaurs
- Fossil Mammals
- Mammals
- Early Life
- Fossil Plants
- Mall Entrance

Second Floor

- Western Cultures
- South America: Continent and Culture
- Reptiles
- Bones
- Poles Apart
- Janet Annenberg Hooker Hall of Geology, Gems and Minerals
- Insect Zoo
- Hope Diamond
- Rotunda Gallery
- Major new exhibition

© ULYSSES

of man. Multicoloured banners help visitors locate the various galleries on the building's three floors.

The "biology" section displays plant and animal remains that predate human existence. One area is dedicated to fossils, the oldest of which is a conglomerate about the size of a head of lettuce made up of microorganisms some 3.5 billion years old. There is also a remarkable exhibit of marine invertebrate fossils discovered at the Burgess Shale Site in the Canadian Rockies in 1910. The "Life in the Ancient Seas" gallery focusses on prehistoric marine life, with a collection of about 2,000 fossils, including a nearly 15-metre-long skeleton of a Basilosaurus (whale) – a truly impressive sight. From tiny insects preserved in amber to gigantic dinosaur bones (check out the 25-metre-long Diplodocus), visitors can contemplate the transition from life in the oceans to life on land and gain an understanding of how the first animals adapted in order to survive. The next exhibit focusses on the glacial (Pleistocene) epoch and the appearance of man. A short film explains the process of glaciation and shows how these layers of ice transformed the surface of the continents. Skeletons of large mammals from the glacial epoch, including a mammoth and an Irish elk, dominate the gallery. The museum also displays specimens of present-day animals in their "natural" settings – North American creatures like the Canadian elk, the caribou, the grizzly and the puma and other species from the Asian continent. One gallery is devoted entirely to bird specimens from all over the world. The presentation shows their migration patterns, habitats and reproductive and feeding habits. A pair of huge, 12,000-litre aquariums reproduce two different marine environments, the subarctic waters of the Maine coast and the coral reefs of the Caribbean Sea. *Blue Planet*, a 15-minute film explaining these two ecosystems, is shown continuously on a small screen. The largest piece in the museum's collection, a 28-metre-long model of a blue whale, hangs in this gallery. A giant squid, a creature that has captured the imagination of sailors, inspiring many myths and fanciful tales, is also on display. This squid, captured off the coast of the United States, has been kept in the same conditions in which it was caught.

The "anthropology" section has become a museum in its own right, recently named the **National Museum of Man**. It contains skeletons and man-made objects from various cultures and civilizations around the world (African, Asian, Inuit and Amerin-

164 Exploring

dian). Reconstructed settings, large frescoes and slide shows help explain the objects on display in their original context. During the Festival of American Folklife, held in Washington in July, the Smithsonian invites representatives of different American cultures to spend a week acquainting the public with their history, legends, dances, music and way of life.

The "geology" section of the museum is a real treasure trove. Right after the "mineral collection", you'll come to the fabulous **Gem Collection ★★★**, which boasts a number of one-of-a-kind specimens, including a 138-carat ruby, a 157-carat emerald, a 234-carat topaz and an enormous 330-carat sapphire. The centerpiece of the collection, however, is the magnificent Hope Diamond, which, at 49.5 carats, is the largest blue diamond in the world. The "Earth and Meteorites" gallery, also on this floor, contains five rocks brought back from the moon by the Apollo astronauts. The exhibit explains how these moon rocks, which are not as old as the meteorites but older than the Earth, bear witness to cosmic events that altered our solar system. The museum's meteorite collection is the largest of its kind in the world.

The **National Gallery of Art ★★★ (23)** *(West Building: Constitution Ave. and 6th St.; East Building: 4th St., between Constitution Ave. and Madison Dr., Judiciary Square metro, ☎737-4215)* boasts one of the world's finest collections of painting and sculpture from the Middle Ages to the modern era. It occupies two buildings: the West Building houses a permanent collection that includes a large number of works by Flemish (Rubens), Dutch (Franz Hals, Rembrandt, Vermeer), Italian (Botticelli, Raphael, Titian, Leonardo da Vinci), French (Watteau, Nicolas Poussin, Fragonard, Boucher) and English (Turner, Gainsborough) masters, as well as pieces by American artists, while the East Building is used for special exhibitions and also houses the Center for Advanced Study in the Visual Arts, a library and a photographic archive. The two buildings are linked by an underground passageway.

The **East Building** *(Mon to Sat 10am to 5pm, Sun 11am to 6pm, closed Dec 25 to Jan 1; between Constitution Ave. and Madison Dr., at 4th St., Judiciary Square metro, ☎737-4215)* is devoted to contemporary art, and its modern architecture reflects its vocation. This superb, massive marble structure was designed by I.M. Pei. Erected in 1978, it echoes the trapezoidal contours of the site upon which it stands. The building is made up of two isosceles triangles, one containing the collections, the other the administrative offices and research facilities. The impressive atrium is adorned with a magnificent **mobile by Alexander Calder**, made especially for the museum, as well as a sculpture by Jean Dubuffet entitled *Site à l'homme assis*. The lovely **Ailsa Mellon Bruce Collection** of works by French painters such as Degas, Toulouse-Lautrec, Renoir, Vuillard, Bonnard, Corot and Manet can also be found on the ground floor. As you make your way through the museum, you'll be able to admire works by such great 20th-century masters as Alberto Giacometti, Arshile Gorky, Vasily Kandinsky, Henri Matisse, Pablo Picasso, Joan Miró, Max Ernst, Henry Moore and Mark Rothko. Outside, a few sculptures by Picasso, Dubuffet and Calder adorn the grounds.

The **West Building** *(Mon to Sat 10am to 5pm, Sun 11am to 6pm; entrance on Constitution Ave. at 6th St. NW, and on Madison Dr. at 6th St. NW, Judiciary Square metro, ☎737-4215)* houses one of the world's finest collections of European and American painting, sculpture and graphic arts from the 18th century to the present day. An imposing neoclassical building designed by John Russell Pope, the National Gallery owes its existence to Andrew Mellon (1855-1937), one of the great art collectors of his time, who donated his private collection of 17th- and 18th-century paintings (including 21 pieces by Rembrandt, Raphael, Titian and Velasquez from the Hermitage in St. Petersburg) and 15th- and 16th-century Italian sculptures, along with a sizeable sum of money, so that it could be built. Since then, a large number of major donors have entrusted their treasures to the National Gallery, which is part of the Smithsonian Institution but has its own board of directors. The West Building opened its doors to the public in March 1941. Its immense collection includes no fewer than 2,800 paintings, nearly 2,000 sculptures, 550 decorative objects and over 47,000 works on paper. As it would be impossible to mention every piece in this impressive collection, we have limited ourselves to the masters of the various schools of painting represented here.

The Florentine, Venetian and Italian Renaissance Schools (galleries 1-28)
These galleries trace the evolution of icon painting, the prevailing form of art during the period in question. All sorts of

166 Exploring

National Gallery of Art
Main Floor

West Building

Rotunda

West Sculpture Art

West Garden Court

East Garden Court

East Sculpture Art

THE MALL

Micro Gallery

Galleries 1 to 28: Florentine, Venetian and Italian Renaissance Schools

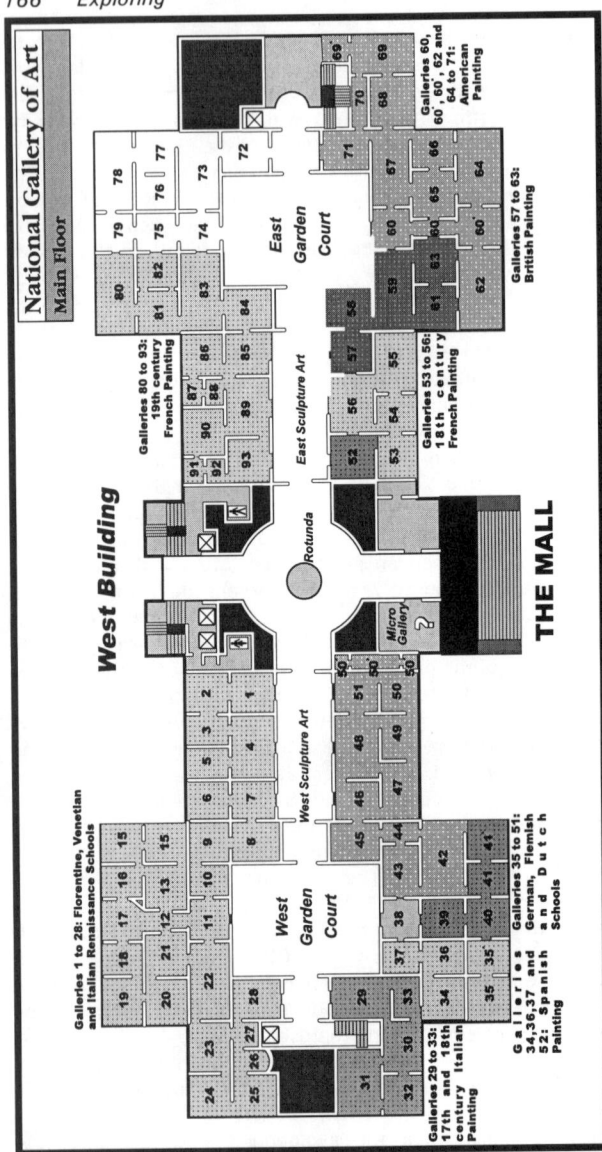

Galleries 29 to 33: 17th and 18th century Italian Painting

Galleries 34, 36, 37 and 52: Spanish Painting

Galleries 35 to 51: German, Flemish and Dutch Schools

Galleries 53 to 56: 18th century French Painting

Galleries 57 to 63: British Painting

Galleries 60, 60, 60, 62 and 64 to 71: American Painting

Galleries 80 to 93: 19th century French Painting

Tour D: The Mall 167

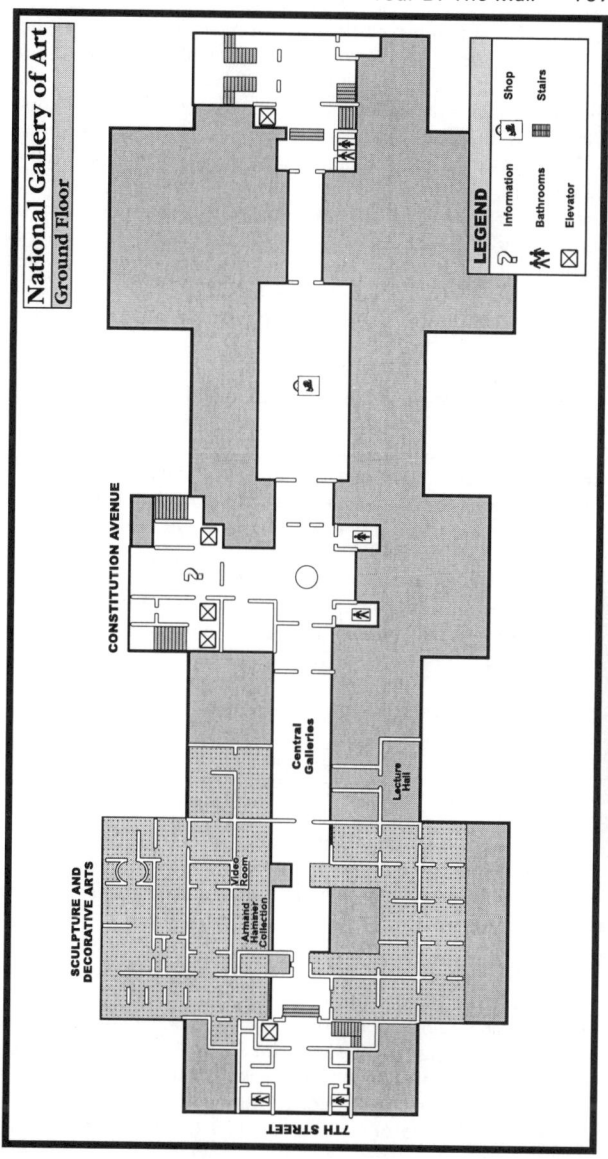

National Gallery of Art
Ground Floor

LEGEND
- Information
- Bathrooms
- Elevator
- Shop
- Stairs

CONSTITUTION AVENUE

Central Galleries

Lecture Hall

SCULPTURE AND DECORATIVE ARTS

Video Room

Armand Hammer Collection

7TH STREET

EXPLORING

168 Exploring

icons, biblical images painted on wooden panels and embellished with gold leaf (icons were originally painted during prayers according to the Orthodox ritual), are displayed. The Sienna School is particularly well-represented in this collection. Visitors will also find works by painters of the quattrocento (15th century), such as Florentine artists like Botticelli and Fra Lippo Lippi, and the cinquecento (early 16th century), such as the prolific masters Raphael (1483-1520) and Leonardo da Vinci (1452-1519), whose *Ginevra de' Benci* is the only painting of his that can be found outside Europe. The last galleries contain works from the Venetian School, such as Titian's (1490-1575) *Venus and Adonis* and various works by Tintoretto (1518-1598).

Italian Painting of the 17th and 18th Centuries
(galleries 29-33)
The frescoes of Giovanni Battista Tiepolo (1696-1770) are a perfect example of refined Baroque art. These galleries also contain works by two French artists, Nicolas Poussin and Claude Lorrain (born Claude Gellée), who lived in Rome.

Spanish Painting (galleries 34, 36, 37 and 52)
This section features portraits by Velasquez (1599-1660) and Goya (1746-1828), as well as biblical paintings by El Greco (1540-1614).

The German, Flemish and Dutch Schools
(galleries 35 to 51)
The walls of these galleries are lined with remarkable paintings by such luminaries as the Flemish artists Peter Paul Rubens (1577-1640), Sir Anthony Van Dyke (1539-1641) and Jan van Eyck (1390-1441), the German artist Albrecht Dürer (1471-1528) and the Dutch artists Rembrandt van Rijn (1606-1669), Frans Hals (1580-1666) and Jan Vermeer (1632-1675), a true master of light.

French Painting of the 18th and 19th Centuries
(galleries 53 to 56 and 80 to 93)
At the beginning of the 18th century, Paris became the cultural centre of Europe. A great number of illustrious painters emerged during this period. The National Gallery's collection of French paintings of the 18th and 19th centuries is quite simply dazzling. It includes one of the world's largest collections of impressionist art. Visitors can admire masterpieces by Watteau

(1684-1721), who depicted the pompous behaviour of 18th-century French society with the utmost delicacy; Boucher (1703-1770); Fragonard (1732-1806); David (1748-1825), court painter under Napoleon I, and Ingres (1780-1867). Next come the works of an entirely different group of uncontested masters, who rejected the classical school of painting: Delacroix (1798-1863), Corot (1796-1875), Courbet (1819-1877), Daumier (1808-1879), the famous caricaturist for the periodical *Charivari*, whose physiognomical studies and satire of the 19th-century bourgeoisie helped launch a new style of art, and finally Manet (1832-1883). The impressionist school, as mentioned above, is also well-represented here by its foremost masters. Magnificent paintings by Monet (1840-1926), Renoir (1841-1919), Degas (1834-1917) and Toulouse-Lautrec (1864-1903), whose work depicts the frivolity of Parisian life, particularly in his famous *Moulin-Rouge*. This collection would not be complete if it didn't also include works by Cézanne (1839-1906), Van Gogh (1853-1890) and Gauguin (1848-1903), who fell in love with the South Sea Islands.

British Painting (galleries 57 to 63)
In these galleries, you will find magnificent portraits of English aristocrats by Thomas Gainsborough (1727-1788), as well as masterpieces by Turner (1775-1851) and Constable (1776-1837).

American Painting
(galleries 60-60A-60B, 62 and 64 to 71)
Though the National Gallery of Art is located in the United States, its collection of American painting seems quite modest when compared to its vast collection of European works. Be that as it may, the museum does possess pieces by the great American portraitists of the 18th and 19th centuries, when it was popular to paint the nation's statesmen. Next came the dominant school of landscape painters, represented by Thomas Cole and Frederick Church. Works by Whistler and Sargent, who were more influenced by European movements, particularly impressionism, can also be admired in these galleries.

TOUR E: DUPONT CIRCLE ★

Back when Washington was first founded, the Dupont Circle area, then known as Slashes because of its swampy terrain, was bordered in by two waterways, Rock Creek and Slash Run. Finally, in the 1870s, a man named Alexander "Boss" Shepherd launched a project to channel Slash Run underground and drain the neighbouring land. While this major undertaking was being carried out, Shepherd, bearing in mind L'Enfant's original plans, designed a new neighbourhood that was destined to become one of the most desirable addresses in Washington for wealthy Americans.

The opulent lifestyle enjoyed by these fabulously rich families was curbed somewhat by the stock market crash of 1929 and the Second World War. Little by little, the neighbourhood took on a new character, and by the 1950s, many elegant homes had become private clubs, businesses and boarding houses. Then, in the 1960s, students and hippies took over the area, which became the centre of the counterculture in Washington. In 1969, tax reforms led to the demolition of many old houses. However, thanks to local residents' tireless efforts, the neighbourhood was finally recognized as an historic district and has thus managed to retain its character.

● ATTRACTIONS

1. Dupont Circle
2. Historical Society of Washington, DC
3. Washington Club
4. B'nai B'rith Klutznick National Jewish Museum
5. Cairo
6. Belmont House
7. Blaine Mansion
8. Indonesian Embassy
9. Society of Cincinnati
10. Phillips Collection

○ ACCOMMODATIONS

1. Adams Inn
2. Best Western New Hampshire Suites
3. Brenton
4. Doubletree Hotel Park Terrace
5. Dupont Plaza Hotel
6. Embassy Row Hilton Hotel
7. Embassy Suites Hotel Downtown
8. Embassy Inn
9. Embassy Square, A Summerfield Suites Hotel
10. Governor's House Hotel
11. Hampshire Hotel
12. Holiday Inn Central Washington, DC
13. Quality Hotel Downtown
14. Renaissance Mayflower Hotel
15. Travelodge Hotel
16. Washington International Student Center
17. Washington Marriott
18. Windsor Inn

◇ RESTAURANTS

1. Anna Maria's
2. Annie's Paramount Steak House
3. Bua Restaurant & Bar
4. Café Luna
5. Firehook
6. Gusti's
7. Il Radicchio
8. Java House
9. Kramerbooks Café & Grill
10. La Tomate
11. Maracas Bay Café
12. Mudd House
13. Raku
14. Sign of the Whale
15. Skewers
16. Sol
17. Starbucks Coffee
18. Tout Va Bien
19. Trio Restaurant
20. Trumpets Restaurant & Loundge
21. Café Lautrec
22. Felix
23. Franklyn's
24. Isola Verde
25. Kalorama Café
26. La Fourchette
27. Little Fountain Café
28. Perry's
29. Peyote Café
30. Roxane
31. Star of Siam

Tour E: Dupont Circle 171

172   Exploring

Today, Dupont Circle and its surrounding area have once again come into favour with a relatively affluent segment of the population, and its scores of cafés, restaurants, shops and art galleries make it very popular with visitors.

Elegant streets and avenues lined with sumptuous-looking houses radiate outward from **Dupont Circle (1)** *(19th St. and Massachusetts Ave. NW, Dupont Circle metro)*, formerly known as Pacific Circle. In 1882, the U.S. Congress decided to pay homage to Admiral Samuel Francis Dupont (1803-1865), a Civil War hero, by renaming Pacific Circle after him. A small bronze statue of the admiral was supposed to stand in the centre of the circle, but Dupont's family found the project far too modest and managed to circumvent the federal government by taking matters into their own hands and commissioned architect Henry Bacon, who designed the Lincoln Memorial, and sculptor Daniel Chester French, who created the statue of Lincoln inside it, to build a more imposing memorial. The result was what you see now: a landscaped circle with a large marble fountain in the middle.

The **Historical Society of Washington DC** ★★ **(2)** *($3, guided tour Wed to Sat noon to 4pm; 1307 New Hampshire Ave. NW, at the corner of 20th St., Dupont Circle metro, ☎785-2068)* occupies the old Heurich House, a fine example of a Romanesque Revival mansion, with its gargoyles, brick façade, columned porch, archways and tower. This imposing building, erected in 1892 for Christian Heurich, a rich industrialist who owned a brewery that once stood on the site now occupied by the Kennedy Center for the Performing Arts (see p 182), is one of the best-preserved houses in the area and one of the first fireproof structures. Now home to the city's historical society, it contains over 10,000 manuscripts, maps and photographs related to Washington.

The first and second floors, richly adorned with carved oak and mahogany, paintings and stencilled decorations, have been converted into a small museum, while the third and fourth floors display the Historical Society's extensive collection. The Breakfast Room, which looks like a German tavern, shows what a bon vivant Heurich was. The slogan of his brewery was "Drinking beer is strongly recommended by physicians". The walls of the room are covered with scenes depicting the virtues of beer, interspersed with such sayings as *"Raum ist in der kleinsten Kammer für den grossten Katzenjammer"* (There is space in the smallest room for the biggest hangovers).

The former home of newspaper magnate Robert Wilson Patterson, publisher of the *Chicago Tribune*, is now the **Washington Club (3)** *(15 Dupont Circle NW, Dupont Circle metro)*. Though it is not open to the public, this magnificent terracotta and white marble house, reminiscent of an Italian Renaissance palace, is definitely worth a look. Built at the beginning of the century by architect Stanford White, it had its heyday back in the 1930s, when Patterson's daughter Cissy (a publisher in her own right, of the *Washington Times-Herald*) threw lavish parties attended by the cream of Washington society. Many distinguished guests stayed here, including Charles Lindbergh, who was cheered by a crowd that gathered on Dupont Circle after his transatlantic flight, and President Coolidge and his wife when the White House was undergoing major renovations in 1927.

The **B'nai B'rith Klutznick National Jewish Museum (4)** *(donations welcomed; Sun to Fri 10am to 5pm; 1640 Rhode Island Ave. NW, at the corner of 17th St., Dupont Circle metro, ☎857-6583)* is the only museum in Washington devoted to Jewish history from antiquity to the present day. This small museum is essentially made up of three galleries dedicated respectively to art, history and Jewish ethnography, as well as a small inner court containing a few sculptures. The B'nai B'rith Museum is of interest mainly for its permanent collection of Judaica. It also hosts temporary exhibitions of paintings, lithographs, photographs and works by contemporary Jewish artists.

Upon exiting the museum, head north on 17th Street to Q Street, then turn right. You'll come to a strange-looking building called the **Cairo (5)** *(1615 Q St. NW, Dupont Circle metro)*, which dates from 1894. Its construction created quite a fuss among Washington residents. In fact, it was the tallest building in town at the time, which prompted Congress to introduce an ordinance limiting the height of future structures. The Cairo was also one of the first steel-framed apartment buildings to go up in the city. Its promotional brochures described it as the biggest and most luxurious apartment complex in town.

174 Exploring

A stroll down Q Street offers a chance to admire a quiet, trim residential neighbourhood. Retrace your steps and continue west on Q Street to New Hampshire Avenue to see the **Belmont House (6)** *(1618 New Hampshire Ave. NW, Dupont Circle metro)*, another opulent residence that is not open to the public. It was erected in 1908 by Étienne Sansom and Horace Trumbauer, who truly made the most of the triangular space they had to work. This unusual yet elegant house, which has a façade reminiscent of the Louis XIV style, cost diplomat Perry Belmont a mere million and a half dollars (in those days!).

Near Dupont Circle itself stands the imposing **Blaine Mansion (7)** *(2000 Massachusetts Ave. NW, at the corner of 20th St., Dupont Circle metro)*. This austere brick building, which is not open to the public, is the oldest mansion in the neighbourhood. It was built in 1881 by architect John Fraser for James G. Blaine (1830-1893), an American politician who co-founded the Republican Party. It now contains offices.

The **Indonesian Embassy ★ (8)** *(Mon to Fri 9am to 4pm, tours by appointment; call two weeks ahead; 2020 Massachusetts Ave. NW, Dupont Circle metro, ☎775-5306)* occupies the former home of the fabulously wealthy Walsh-McLean family. Thomas Walsh, born to a poor Scottish family, emigrated to the United States in 1869, at the age of 19. Any ambitions he might have had were more than fulfilled when he made his first fortune in the gold rush in the Black Hills. His lucky streak continued afterward, and he got his hands on Camp Bird Mine in Colorado, which turned out to be the biggest gold mine in the world. Having made his fortune and tired of the mining business, he sold his gold mine for 45 million dollars and a percentage of future profits. He then took up residence in Washington, where, in 1903, he built himself an incredible 60-room house, which cost him over three million dollars, making it the most expensive mansion in the city. To show the source of his wealth, he had a stone studded with gold nuggets inlaid into the front porch. During Theodore Roosevelt's presidency, the Walshes entertained the cream of Washington society in their magnificent home and hosted lavish, memorable parties. Upon their death, their daughter Evalyn Walsh-McLean inherited the house. Accustomed to an opulent lifestyle, she squandered most of her father's fortune, which totalled over 100 million dollars. She was the last private owner of the famous Hope Diamond, now displayed at the National Museum of American

Tour E: Dupont Circle 175

History. In 1951, she sold the mansion to the Indonesian government for $350,000 – a tenth of what her father paid to have it built.

The architect employed several different styles when designing the house, whose distinguishing features include a terrace with a balustrade, a second-story loggia with limestone ornamentation, a façade with rounded corners and corrugated walls, and a mansard roof. Inside, an enormous art-nouveau staircase with mahogany railing winds its way from one floor to the next. The walls of the Louis-XVI sitting room are covered with damask and adorned with gilded pilasters, and mouldings frame a fresco on the ceiling.

A few steps from the Indonesian embassy stands a mansion once owned by Belgian diplomat Larz Anderson, now occupied by the **Society of Cincinnati (9)** *(Tue to Sat 1pm to 4pm; 2118 Massachusetts Ave. NW, Dupont Circle metro, ☎785-2040)*, a patriotic organization founded by officers who served under General George Washington. A large collection of objects dating from the American Revolution is displayed inside.

This Italian-style mansion was built by architects Little and Brown between 1902 and 1905. Art lovers and collectors, Larz Anderson and his wife meticullously decorated their magnificent home with pieces that they had acquired in the course of their many trips around the world. The house was maintained in its original state after being donated to the Society of Cincinnati, to which Anderson belonged. Among other things, visitors will find a bust of Washington by Thomas Crawford (whose other credits include the Statue of Freedom that stands atop Capitol dome), 18th- and 19th-century portraits of American military men, and other objects related to military history. On the second floor, jade objects dating from the Ching dynasty, 16th-century Chinese porcelain, oriental antiques and Italian and English paintings are displayed. The dining room is adorned with magnificent 17th-century Belgian tapestries. The gardens give onto a pond and an 18th-century Japanese statue of Buddha.

The **Phillips Collection** ★★ **(10)** *($6.50; Tue to Sat 10am to 5pm; 1600 21st St. NW, at the corner of Q St., Dupont Circle metro, ☎387-2151)* was the first museum in the United States devoted to modern art. It opened in 1921, eight years before the Museum of Modern Art in New York, in the home of Duncan Phillips (1886-1966), a passionate art collector. The collection includes impressionist masterpieces by Renoir, Van Gogh, Monet, Degas and Cézanne, as well as paintings by Picasso, Matisse, Klee, Mondrian and Bonnard. Modern American art is also well represented by pieces by Homer, Eakins, O'Keeffe, Rothko, Jacob Lawrence, Tack and Diebenkorn.

★ TOUR F: EMBASSY ROW AND KALORAMA ★

At the end of the 19th century, the American elite built some hundred marvelous Beaux-Arts-style mansions around Dupont Circle and along Connecticut and Massachusetts avenues, which quickly began to rival New York City's prestigious Fifth Avenue. What is now known as "Embassy Row", the section of Massachusetts Avenue between Sheridan Circle and Observatory Circle, was once Washington's poshest artery. At the turn of the century, the richest of the American rich built magnificent mansions here, veritable Beaux-Arts palaces that flaunted their owners' wealth. However, in the wake of the 1929 Wall Street stock market crash, the Great Depression ushered in a change in lifestyle for these affluent American families, who were no longer able to maintain such sumptuous houses. The British and Japanese embassies relocated to this prestigious avenue, signalling the advent of a new order in the area. They were followed nearly 50 other embassies and all sorts of private businesses, which set up shop in the luxurious mansions of Massachusetts Avenue and Kalorama (which is Greek for "the magnificent view"), an adjacent residential neighborhood bordering Rock Creek Park, between Massachusetts and Connecticut avenues.

Our tour starts at **Sheridan Circle (1)** *(Sheridan Circle and Massachusetts Ave., Dupont Circle metro)*, a small circle formerly named Decatur Circle in honour of Stephen Decatur, an American naval hero. In 1890, it was renamed after General Philip H. Sheridan, who distinguished himself during the Civil War, notably at the Battle of Shenandoah in 1864, and during several particularly vicious conflicts with Native Americans. He is said to have coined the gruesome saying: "The only good Indian is a dead Indian". The bronze equestrian statue showing

Tour F: Embassy Row and Kalorama

Embassy Row and Kalorama

● **ATTRACTIONS**
1. Sheridan Circle
2. Turkish Embassy
3. Embassy of Haiti
4. Embassy of Pakistan
5. Embassy of the Republic of Cameroon
6. Woodrow Wilson House
7. Textile Museum
8. Islamic Center
9. British Embassy
10. Embassy of Finland

○ **ACCOMMODATIONS**
1. Connecticut-Woodley Guest House
2. Days Inn Uptown on Connecticut Avenue
3. Kalorama Guest House
4. Sheraton Washington

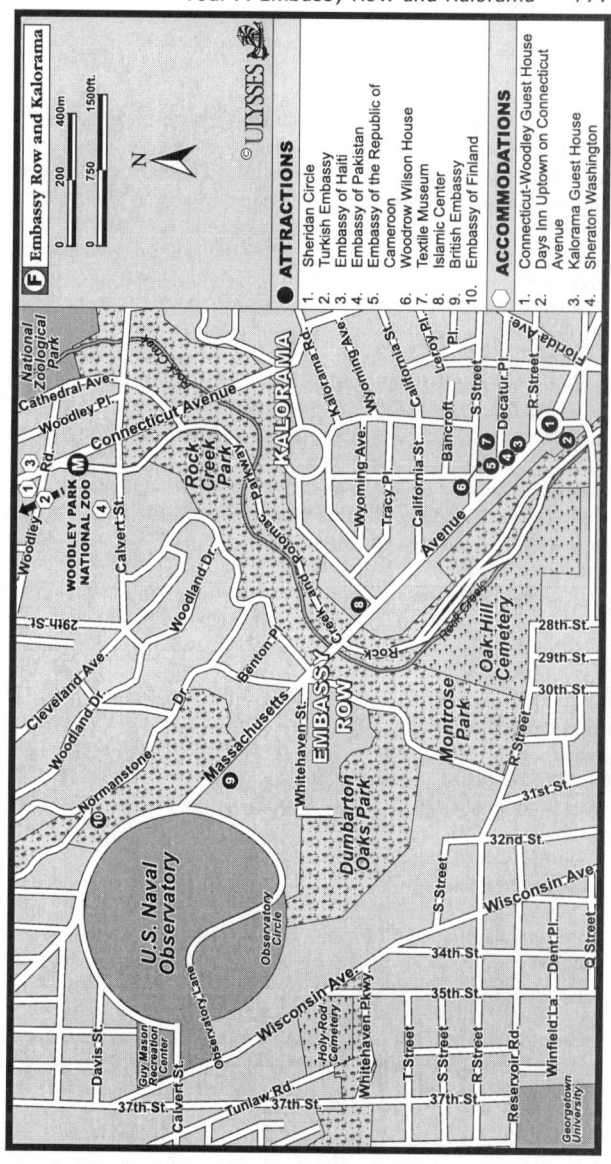

EXPLORING

178   Exploring

him as a proud and energetic man was sculpted by Gutzon Borglum in 1908.

Near Sheridan Circle, you can admire the **Turkish Embassy ★ (2)** *(1606 23rd St. NW, Dupont Circle metro)*, one of the prettiest in the area. It was once the home of Edward Hamlin Everett, an American millionaire who made his fortune in such varied domains as mining, oil and gas and breweries, as well as collecting substantial licensing fees for a bottle cap invention. This mansion, built in 1914 by architect George Oakley Totten, Jr., soon became known the most sumptuous on Embassy Row. Its most notable features are a glass and wrought-iron portico supported by marble columns and a balustraded roof, which lend the structure a neoclassical style of both French and Italian inspiration. The ornate interior, decorated with carved woodwork, includes a sumptuous ballroom covered in gold-embroidered damask, where Mrs. Everett, a former opera singer, liked to host concerts, inviting the world's greatest opera singers to perform. Finely gilded door handles, a superb basement swimming pool and the sheer opulence of the interior decoration all helped earn this sumptuous mansion the nickname "San Simeon on the Potomac" (in reference to William R. Hearst's chateau in San Simeon, California).

On the other side of Sheridan Circle is the **Embassy of Haiti (3)** *(2315 Massachusetts Ave. NW)*, a more modest mansion whose architecture, inspired by the 18th-century French style, is nonetheless remarkable. Built at the turn of the century by the architect Nathan C. Wyeth for Gibson Fahnestock, a financier, it has a Beaux-Arts facade decorated with finely sculpted Corinthian pilasters and topped by a large, steeply sloping mansard roof.

George Oakley Totten, Jr., architect of the sumptuous Turkish Embassy, also designed the no less magnificent mansion that now houses the **Embassy of Pakistan ★ (4)** *(2315 Massachusetts Ave. NW, Dupont Circle metro)*. Located at west end of one of Washington's poshest blocks (home also to the Embassy of Haiti), lined with old mansions built in the purest Beaux-Arts style, which together form a perfectly harmonious whole, the Embassy of Pakistan stands majestically at the corner of Massachusetts Avenue and Decatur Place. Its distinguishing features include a mansard roof, cornices, pilasters, bas-reliefs

Tour F: Embassy Row and Kalorama   179

and cartouches. The rounded roof tower adorned with terracotta mouldings and a small stone balcony at the north end of the building, facing Decatur Place, seems to punctuate the end of one of the most opulent blocks in the city.

On the other side of Decatur Place, beyond the Austrian Embassy, stands a tremendous chateau-style home which used to belong to an extremely wealthy Norwegian diplomat by the name of Christian Hauge. This mansion now houses the **Embassy of the Republic of Cameroon ★ (5)** *(2349 Massachusetts Ave. NW, Dupont Circle metro)*, built by none other than George Oakley Totten, Jr., the same architect who designed the Pakistani and Turkish embassies. This mansion marks the end of the series of Beaux-Arts-style residences sprinkled along Massachusetts Avenue between 17th Street to S Street. Intended to be the Hauge family residence and also to house the Norwegian diplomatic delegation, this magnificent building, inspired by Azay-le-Rideau, a 16th-century chateau in France's Loire Valley, was, like the Everett home (the current Turkish Embassy), the scene of many society events until 1927. The building was sold to the Republic of Cameroon in 1972 after belonging to Czechoslovakia for almost 40 years.

Turn right onto S Street and you will reach President Woodrow Wilson's former residence, now a museum dedicated to his memory. As 29th President of the United States, he lead the nation through the First World War and was the instigator of the League of Nations, for which he was awarded the Nobel Peace Prize in 1920. In 1921, at the end of his term in office, he moved into a charming, modest home to spend his final days peacefully: the **Woodrow Wilson House (6)** *(4$; Tue to Sun 10am to 4pm; 2340 S St. NW, Dupont Circle metro, ☎387-4062)*. He only lived there a few years before passing away in 1924. Wilson's presidency was marked by several democratic reforms, such as the creation of a federal income tax (1913), the election of senators by universal suffrage (1913) and women's suffrage (1920). His widow continued residing in the house until 1961. Preserved in its original state, the building now houses a small museum illustrating the middle-class lifestyle of the 1920s, as well as many personal objects dating from Wilson's time at the White House and gifts he received during that period.

180 Exploring

The **Textile Museum ★ (7)** *(Mon to Sat 10am to 5pm, Sun 1pm to 5pm; 2320 S St. NW, Dupont Circle metro, ☎667-0441)*, a small museum founded by George Hewitt Myers in 1925, displays an incredible collection of 15,000 woven pieces and 1,800 oriental rugs. This museum not only emphasizes the beauty of the works on display but also offers visitors insight into the historical and cultural context within which they were made. Along with a very beautiful pre-Columbian collection from Peru, the museum also exhibits textiles from the Middle East, Asia and Africa, and others created by Native Americans. The museum occupies two residences listed as historical monuments, one of which was built by Waddy B. Wood, the architect who designed the Woodrow Wilson House; it also includes a library devoted to rugs and the textile industry (open to the public).

Return to Massachusetts Avenue.

Two blocks West of S Street stands the **Islamic Center (8)** *(Mon to Thu and Sat to Sun 10am to 5pm; guided tours by appointment one week in advance; 2551 Massachusetts Ave. NW, 30-minute walk from Dupont Circle metro, ☎332-8343)*. Note that visitors must be properly dressed, completely covering arms and legs, and leave their shoes at the entrance in order to enter the mosque. Women must also cover their heads with a scarf. This institution is funded by Islamic countries in order to serve the needs of the 70,000 Muslims living in the Washington area and as a centre for Islamic studies. Erected in the 1950s, this building is typical of Islamic architecture, with horseshoe arches, a crenelated roof and a minaret; of course, it also faces Mecca. Persian silk rugs donated by the late Shah of Iran cover the floor of the mosque, where the faithful can come say their five daily prayers. The ebony pulpit is inlaid with ivory, and the verses of the *Koran* are represented by magnificent mosaics all around the entrance. At the center of the mosque hangs an immense copper chandelier weighing almost two tons, a gift from the Egyptian government.

The **British Embassy (9)** *(3100 Massachusetts Ave. NW, a half-hour walk from Dupont Circle metro)* was one of the first embassies built north of Sheridan circle. Great Britain commissioned one of its most prestigious architects, Sir Edwin Lutyens, to draw up the plans. Construction lasted from 1927

Tour F: Embassy Row and Kalorama 181

to 1931. The U-shaped building, topped by high chimneys and facing Massachusetts Avenue, houses the office of the chancery, while the ambassador's residence is located in back and is therefore not visible from the park gates nor from the huge main gate.

Beyond the British embassy, Massachusetts Avenue climbs uphill alongside Normanstone Park, skirting round the U.S. Naval Observatory and the residence of the Vice-President of the United States of America. Though you can always take one of the many buses that run up the avenue towards the Washington National Cathedral (see p 203), it can be pleasant to stroll through so much greenery. Many embassies with modern architecture are located here. Among these, the **Embassy of Finland (10)** *(3301 Massachusetts Ave. NW)*, built in 1994, is particularly noteworthy, since it has a very original design and blends beautifully in with its natural surroundings. The building has a partitioned façade and several transparent panels that highlight the surrounding vegetation. The first panel consists of a bronze wire mesh structure that serves as a support for climbing plants. The second panel forms the embassy's central core, where the offices and conference rooms are located. The stairs and footbridge echo the design of the first partition. Finally, a third panel, a glass wall, reinforces the impression of being in the middle of nature.

TOUR G: FOGGY BOTTOM ★

Foggy Bottom, the westernmost section of downtown Washington, is centred around Washington Circle. It is roughly bounded to the east by 17th Street NW; to the west by the mouth of Rock Creek, which empties into the Potomac River; to the south by the Mall and to the north by M Street. It was thus nicknamed because of the fumes from the gasworks and breweries located here up to the turn of the century. Before the federal capital of the United States was even founded, a small German community built a little village called Hamburg here. The area only really began to develop in the 19th century, however, when glassworks, breweries and cement works set up shop here. In 1856, the city's gasworks were built here, attracting a mainly Irish labour force to the area. Before long, M Street had become the dividing line between the posh Dupont Circle area and the working-class neighbourhoods to

182   Exploring

the south. George Washington University, founded in 1912 near Washington Circle, south of Pennsylvania Avenue, changed the face of the neighbourhood, lending it a university atmosphere. Then, in the middle of the century, government departments and company headquarters gradually began replacing the factories and gasworks. In 1947, the State Department moved into its present quarters, a huge, austere building at the corner of 23rd and D streets. Today, the local population consists of a mixture of professionals, workers, civil servants and students.

In the following pages, we will explore this part of Washington between the White House and the Potomac River, home to the John F. Kennedy Center for the Performing Arts, the notorious Watergate complex, the Diplomatic Reception Rooms, which now house one of the country's largest collections of decorative arts, and the Department of the Interior Museum.

The **John F. Kennedy Center for the Performing Arts** ★★ *(Mon to Fri 10am to midnight, Sat and Sun noon to midnight; guided tours every day 10am to 1pm; at the corner of New Hampshire Ave. and the Rock Creek and Potomac Pkwy., Foggy Bottom metro, ☎467-4600)* was built in 1971 on the site once occupied by Christian Heurich's brewery (see Dupont Circle Tour, p 172). Though its architecture and location have been harshly criticized, the Kennedy Center has helped provide the city with an internationally renowned cultural scene. Whatever its original detractors thought, today everyone agrees that the Kennedy Center's five theatres boast outstanding acoustics. Furthermore, the building does have its share of attractive features, such as its magnificent, willow-lined terrace looking out onto the Potomac and its marble façade.

The idea of establishing a national cultural centre first emerged in 1958. President Eisenhower proposed the project, which was in turn supported by John F. Kennedy himself. Then, in 1964, after the tragic events that took place in Dallas the year before, which sent the entire nation into mourning, Congress decreed that a memorial akin to those for Lincoln and Jefferson would be built in Kennedy's honour and allocated a sum of 23 million dollars for the construction of this cultural centre bearing his name. Gifts from over 40 countries flooded in from all over the world. The crystal chandeliers in the **Grand Foyer** were donated by Sweden, the Matisse tapestries that hang outside the Opera

Foggy Bottom

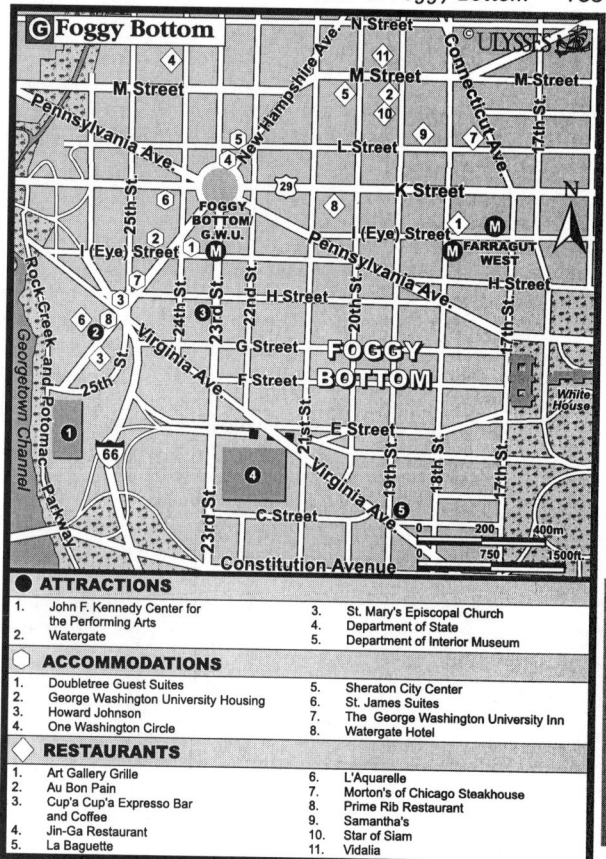

ATTRACTIONS
1. John F. Kennedy Center for the Performing Arts
2. Watergate
3. St. Mary's Episcopal Church
4. Department of State
5. Department of Interior Museum

ACCOMMODATIONS
1. Doubletree Guest Suites
2. George Washington University Housing
3. Howard Johnson
4. One Washington Circle
5. Sheraton City Center
6. St. James Suites
7. The George Washington University Inn
8. Watergate Hotel

RESTAURANTS
1. Art Gallery Grille
2. Au Bon Pain
3. Cup'a Cup'a Expresso Bar and Coffee
4. Jin-Ga Restaurant
5. La Baguette
6. L'Aquarelle
7. Morton's of Chicago Steakhouse
8. Prime Rib Restaurant
9. Samantha's
10. Star of Siam
11. Vidalia

House by France, the silk curtain in the Opera House by Japan, the mirrors by Belgium. Italy sent 3,700 tons of Carrara marble, which adorns both the interior and exterior of the building. The flags of the various countries with which the United States maintains diplomatic relations hang in the **Hall of Nations**. A huge bronze bust of J.F.K., sculpted by Robert Berks, dominates the Grand Foyer. In addition to its three main theatres – the 2,318-seat **Opera House**, the 2,759-seat **Concert Hall** and

The Watergate Scandal

Watergate, one of the greatest scandals in U.S. history and the cause of President Richard Nixon's downfall, has been the subject of numerous articles and books, as well as several films.

On June 17, 1972, on the sixth floor of the Watergate complex at 2600 Virginia Avenue, a small group of professional burglars hired by the Committee to Reelect the President (CREEP), broke into the headquarters of the Democratic National Committee in search of documents that would discredit Richard Nixon's Democratic opponent, Senator George McGovern. This wasn't the first time that Gordon Liddy, the general counsel of CREEP, had done this. The offices had already been searched on May 27, 1972, but nothing incriminating had been discovered. One of the dominant themes of Nixon's campaign was illegal contributions made by big companies to political parties. Former Attorney General John Mitchell, ordered Liddy to return to the premises to find a cheque for $25,000 that the Democratic National Committee had supposedly received. Liddy thus orchestrated another break-in at the Watergate complex on that fateful night of June 17, 1972. To prevent the door from locking behind them, the burglars put a piece of tape on the bolt. Liddy and a few henchmen supervised the operation from a room at the Howard Johnson's Hotel across the street. Unfortunately for them, a security guard making his rounds saw some tape sticking out from the door. Suspecting a robbery was underway, he alerted the police, who caught the burglars red-handed, with sophisticated spying equipment and a large sum of money in small bills in their possession. Nixon and his entourage tried to pressure the FBI into halting their investigation, so the public wouldn't find out about the incident right away. Nixon put up a fight, but finally had to provide authorities with tapes of his June 23, 1972 conversations at the White House. These recordings clearly implicated the President in the scheme, and he resigned soon after.

the 1,142-seat **Eisenhower Theater**, the John F. Kennedy Center for the Performing Arts houses the **American Film Institute Theater**; the **Terrace Theater**, a smaller venue used for chamber music concerts, recitals and plays, and the **Theater Lab**. The world's greatest artists have performed here – Placido Domingo, Duke Ellington, Ella Fitzgerald, Rudolf Nureyev, Frank Sinatra, Elizabeth Taylor and Arthur Rubinstein to name but a few. The **Performing Arts Library**, open to the public, is a mine of information for anyone interested in the subject.

Opposite the Kennedy Center stands a building complex with distinctive, curvilinear architecture. This is the **Watergate** *(2500-2700 Virginia Ave. NW, Foggy Bottom metro)*, which became world-famous following the events that took place there on the night of June 17, 1972 and the resulting scandal that led to President Richard Nixon's resignation.

Upon exiting the Watergate, take H Street to 23rd Street, where you'll find **St. Mary's Episcopal Church** *(730 23rd St. NW, Foggy Bottom metro)*, built for the local black population. Originally named St. Mary's Chapel for Colored People, it was the first black Episcopal church in Washington and thus occupies an important place in African-American ecclesiastical history. Erected in 1887, the church boasts lovely stained-glass windows made in France, which show St. Cyprian and St. Simon the Cyrenaic.

Inside the **Department of State**, where U.S. foreign policy is determined, visitors will find the **Diplomatic Reception Rooms ★** *(guided tours only, by appointment 2 months in advance; Mon to Fri 9:30am, 10:30am and 2:30pm; 23rd St., between C and D sts. NW, Foggy Bottom metro, ☎647-3241)*, which now contain one of the country's largest collections of decorative arts. The rooms are lavishly decorated with Chippendale and Queen Anne furniture, oriental rugs, Chinese porcelain, etc. Also on display is the desk used for the signing of the Treaty of Paris, which put an end to the American Revolution.

Head east on C Street.

Four blocks from the Department of State, you'll reach the **Department of the Interior Museum** *(Mon to Fri 8am to 5pm; guided tours by appointment 2 weeks in advance; 1849 C St.,*

186 Exploring

between 18th and 19th streets NW, Farragut West metro, ☎208-4743), which presents exhibitions of heroic paintings, sketches and historical photographs. Visitors will find a variety of dioramas as well; one shows General Washington's meeting with Lafayette in Morristown in 1780, another a 19th-century Native American trading post and another the fur trade on the Missouri River. The museum also has a room devoted to Native Americans, which contains pottery, baskets, canoes and utensils.

TOUR H: THE BANKS OF THE ANACOSTIA RIVER

The relationship between Capitol Hill and Anacostia is curiously paradoxical. While Capitol Hill is the legislative symbol and the cradle of judicial power of the United States, whose power and glory are represented by the majestic buildings of the Supreme Court and the Capitol, neighbouring South East D.C. is notorious for its high crime rate and poverty. The contrast between these two neighbourhoods is sharp and surprising – it's like seeing the back side of an opulent stage set. Be that as it may, the banks of the Anacostia River are steeped in African American history and boast several interesting museums and sites. Visitors to the area are unlikely to encounter any problems, as long as they take a few basic precautions, such as avoiding deserted areas and above all staying off the streets at night.

Anacostia was named after the Nacotchtank, a Native American tribe that lived at the confluence of the Potomac and Anacostia Rivers. When Captain John Smith explored the region in 1608 and discovered this tribe, their name was soon corrupted into "Anacostia". Shortly thereafter, settlers began taking an interest in this fertile region. Large tobacco plantations were established here in the mid 17th-century, and slaves were brought in to work the land. Thomas Jefferson strongly recommended incorporating the banks of the Anacostia into the district of Washington in 1790, since the area would be of strategic value if the nation's future capital were ever attacked. Jefferson thus made plans for the construction of a navy yard and an arsenal. Like General Washington and architect Pierre L'Enfant, he expected the city to develop essentially along these pleasant shores. Encouraged by these predictions, land speculators snapped up plots of land along the Anacostia in

Tour H: The Banks of the Anacostia River 187

ATTRACTIONS
1. L'Enfant Plaza
2. Marina
3. Fort Lesley J. McNair
4. Navy Yard (Navy Museum, Marine Corps Museum)
5. Marine Barracks and Commandant's House
6. Congressional Cemetery
7. Frederick Douglass National Historic Site
8. Anacostia Museum

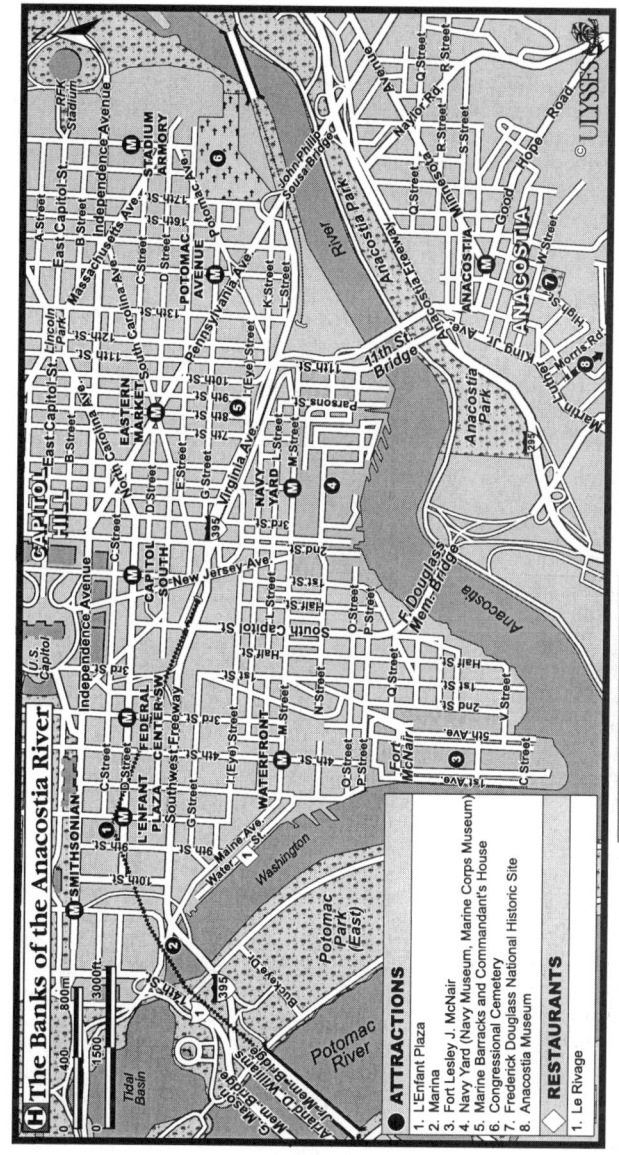

RESTAURANTS
1. Le Rivage

order to resell them at a big profit. But things didn't happen as planned. One of the best-known speculators was John Greenleaf, for whom the point between the Anacostia River and the Washington Channel is named. This ambitious man had accomplished the remarkable feat of making an agreement with Congress that would have been very lucrative had he not gone bankrupt a few years later. The deal allowed him to purchase 3,000 plots of municipal land in exchange for making a loan to the city government. Jefferson eventually chose Greenleaf Point as the site of the city's navy yard.

At the turn of the 19th century, as tobacco plantations gradually exhausted the soil and the tobacco industry plunged into decline, slaves were permitted to purchase their freedom and buy plots of land. This policy, which was very liberal for the time, prompted many freed slaves to settle in the area. However, it wasn't until 1862, in the middle of the Civil War, that Congress passed a law emancipating all slaves in the District and providing for their former masters to be compensated. However, the sale of land along the banks of the Anacostia was halted during the Civil War. To protect the city from advancing Confederate troops, 11 forts were built along the river. Most of these were destroyed after the war.

The construction of new approaches and, in the 1870s, of the 11th Street Bridge, which linked Anacostia to the rest of the city, enabled the area to flourish. In those days, the majority of local residents were white.

Unfortunately, the living conditions in Anacostia quickly began to deteriorate at the beginning of this century. In the wake of the Second World War, the area became the poorest and most rundown part of the District. In the 1950s, in order to improve some of the more dilapidated sections of southeast Washington, the government launched an extensive urban renewal plan, destroying over 6,000 houses and forcing over 15,000 people to move. These demolition sites were replaced by parks and austere modern apartment and office buildings. Only a few houses of known historical significance and a few commercial buildings on the riverbanks escaped the wrecking ball. At the same time, housing projects were built, providing the area with even more decidedly modern architecture. All this prompted a slow exodus of white residents. By 1970, the population of Anacostia was 96% African American.

Tour H: The Banks of the Anacostia River

In the following pages, we will explore a few of the streets along the banks of the Anacostia River. Our itinerary includes the Marina, the Washington Navy Yard, which is safe during daytime thanks to the presence of Navy guards, and the Congressional Cemetery, where members of Congress used to be buried. Next, we'll make our way to the other side of the river to visit the Anacostia Museum and the Frederick Douglass National Historic Site. You can start off the tour at L'Enfant Plaza, a symbol of the urban renewal project of the 1950s and 1960s, or go straight to the Marina or the Washington Navy Yard.

L'Enfant Plaza (1) *(10th and D sts. SW, L'Enfant Plaza metro)* was built in the 1960s. This square, named after the French architect Pierre Charles L'Enfant, who drew up the plans for the city, is surrounded by stern-looking modern buildings. Beneath it lies an immense underground complex that stretches between 9th and 10th streets. Intended as the centerpiece of the new Southeast, it was designed to house offices, a hotel and commercial facilities. Unfortunately, it is one of those severe, gloomy concrete monstrosities that do not do justice to modern architecture.

The **Marina (2)** *(along Water St. SW, Waterfront metro)*, lined with seafood restaurants and little T-shirt stalls, is very popular with Washingtonians, who come here to relax on hot summer days or go for a jog. One of the main attractions is the **Wharf Seafood Market** *(between 9th and 11th sts. SW)*, the oldest outdoor market in the United States, which sells all sorts of fresh fish and seafood.

Just southwest of the marina, along the Washington Channel, lies **Fort Lesley J. McNair (3)** *(4th and P sts. SW, Waterfront metro)*, which is one of the oldest military installations in the country (1794) and is still in use. It was here that Lincoln assassin John Wilkes Booth's companions, among them a woman named Mary Suratt, were imprisoned and hanged.

Take the subway to the **Navy Yard (4)** *(9th and M sts. SE, Navy Yard metro)*. Visitors might be surprised to learn that the capital of the United States, though located inland, has a military port dating back to the early 19th century. Its plans were drawn up by the architect Benjamin H. Latrobe, who also worked on the Capitol. The **Navy Yard Entrance Gate** *(8th and*

M sts. SE), erected in 1804, is one of the features he designed. The Navy Yard stretches along the banks of the Anacostia River, between 1st and 11th streets, in the southeast part of the city. Its construction began around 1800 and continued at a good pace until the British occupied the city in 1814. To prevent the new installations from falling into the hands of the enemy, the Yard's first commandant ordered that they be completely destroyed. After the war, repairs were undertaken and the Navy Yard was once again used for building ships, until it was converted into a naval arms factory in 1886. Weapons were produced here all the way up until 1961. Today, the Navy Yard is one of the Navy's administrative centres.

There are two museums on the compound: the **Navy Museum** *(Mon to Fri 9am to 4pm, Sat and Sun 10am to 5pm; Sicard St., Navy Yard metro, ☎433-4882)* and the **Marine Corps Museum** *(Mon to Sat 10am to 4pm, Sun noon to 5pm; located in the basement of the Marine Corps Historical Center, Parsons Ave., ☎433-3534)*. The Navy Museum, which chronicles the history of the Navy from the American Revolution to the present day, is the more interesting of the two. The exhibition includes several submarines, a fine collection of model ships, a bathyscaphe and various weapons and uniforms. Outside, at Pier 2, you can climb aboard the ***USS Barry***. A uniformed sailor will show you every nook and cranny of the ship and will be happy to tell you all about the seamen's rigorous lifestyle.

The Marine Corps Museum, for its part, traces the history of the U.S. Marines through a wide array of weapons, uniforms and medals.

Upon exiting the Washington Navy Yard, head north on 8th Street to G Street to visit the charming white **Marine Commandant's House (5)** *(801 G St., Navy Yard metro, ☎433-2258)*. Built by George Hadfield in 1805, it has been the home to every Marine Commandant since 1806. For some reason, the British spared this building when they burned the city in 1814. The adjacent barracks are home to the "President's Own", the Marine band, as well as the soldiers who guard Arlington Cemetery and the U.S. President's country residence at Camp David. Unaccompanied visitors are not permitted on the premises, but you can always ask a guard for a private tour or attend the Friday Evening Parade, every Friday evening at

Tour H: The Banks of the Anacostia River 191

8:30pm from mid-May through August *(free; reservations required to reserve seating; information ☎433-6060)*.

The **Congressional Cemetery (6)** *(every day 9am to 5pm, guided tours by appointment; 1801 E St. SE, Potomac Avenue metro, ☎543-0539)*, founded in 1807, was originally reserved for members of Congress, but a few eminent Washingtonian architects, including Thornton, who drew up the original plans for the Capitol, are also interred here. Although many members of Congress opted to be buried in their native state, Congress commissioned Latrobe to design over 80 cenotaphs in their memory. The cemetery is also the final resting place of a number of famous historical figures, including Civil War photographer Matthew Brady, Push-Ma-Ta-Ha, a Choctaw chief who served with Andrew Jackson during the War of 1812, and J. Edgar Hoover, the formidable former Director of the FBI.

Remember that the streets of Anacostia can be dangerous, so it is best to drive or take a taxi to the other side of the river. If you really want to explore the area on foot, do so during the day in a group.

Anacostia has little in the way of tourist attractions, aside from a museum devoted to the history of the African American people and the home of the black abolitionist, Frederick Douglass.

At the **Frederick Douglass National Historic Site ★ (7)** *(one-hour guided tour, every day Apr to Oct 9am to 5pm, Nov to Mar 9am to 4pm; Cedar Hill, 1411 W St. SE; by car, head south on 11th St., drive over the bridge and continue on Martin Luther King Jr. Ave. to W St., then turn left., ☎426-5961)*, you can explore the somewhat unusual Victorian house in which the famous abolitionist spent the last years of his life. You will learn all about Douglass, who was born a humble slave on a Maryland plantation in 1817 and eventually came to occupy a prominent place on the American political scene. At the age of 21, Douglass decided he had had enough of living in misery and fled the plantation where he was supposed to work. He took refuge in new Bedford, Massachusetts, in a Quaker community sympathetic to the abolitionist cause. A born orator, he attracted the attention of a group of militant abolitionists with a memorable speech that he delivered in 1841, in which he presented himself as a "new graduate of the institution of slavery, whose diploma is engraved in the flesh of his back". The speech made a strong impression, enabling Douglass to become one of the best-known and most respected members of the Massachusetts Anti-Slavery Society. His autobiography, *Narrative of the Life of Frederick Douglass, an American Slave*, was published in 1845, enraging that segment of the American establishment still in favour of slavery. Douglass' freedom was seriously threatened by a new law punishing runaway slaves. He promptly fled to England, where he continued vehemently denouncing slavery in the United States and quickly managed to surround himself with English sympathizers, who bought him his freedom in 1846. Officially recognized as a freeman, Douglass returned to the United States in 1847 to continue his battle. He further distinguished himself during the Civil War by actively helping to recruit African American troops, forming the famous 54th and 55th regiments (whose valiance in combat is justly honoured in the film *Glory*, starring Denzel Washington). It was Douglass who persuaded Abraham Lincoln to propose the Emancipation Proclamation. After the war, Douglass continued to play an important role in American politics, becoming the U.S. Ambassador to Haiti. In 1877, he once again flouted the conventions of his time by purchasing a house in Anacostia that ordinarily would only have been sold to a white person. In 1884, two years after the death of his first wife, Douglass stirred up yet another controversy by marrying a white woman named Helen Pitt. This fascinating man died of a heart attack in this house in 1895. In 1900, his widow founded the **Frederick Douglass Memorial Association** and opened up their Cedar Hill home to the public. A tour of the house starts with a short film about this extraordinary man's life. You can then explore the various rooms, decorated with Victorian furniture and bibelots that belonged to the Douglass family.

The **Anacostia Museum (8)** *(every day 10am to 5pm, closed Dec 25; 1901 Fort Pl. SE, by car, take 11th St. south across the bridge, follow Martin Luther King Jr. Ave. to the third light, then turn left on Morris Rd. and continue straight ahead to the museum, ☎357-2700 or 287-3369)* is part of the Smithsonian Institution. Located in a public park near Fort Stanton, this small neighbourhood museum has expanded considerably since it was founded in 1967. Today it not only presents exhibitions on African-American history and culture but also serves as a research facility. It doesn't have a permanent collection but

Charming St. John's Church by Benjamin Latrobe. One of its pews is reserved for the presiding president of the United States. - *L. P.*

Between Lincoln Memorial and the Vietnam Veterans Memorial wall stands a sculptural ensemble called *The Faces of Honour* by Frederick Hart. It consists of three bronze statues of American soldiers in Vietnam.
- *L. P.*

The Arlington National Cemetery, which contains the graves of over 200,000 servicemen and other men and women who have played a significant role in U.S. history.
- *L. P.*

hosts temporary exhibitions such as "Climbing Jacob's Ladder: The Rise of Black Churches in Eastern American Cities, 1740-1877", "The Renaissance: Black Arts of the Twenties", "Mary McLeod Bethune and Roosevelt's Black Cabinet" and "The Frederick Douglass Years: 1817-1895". Call the Smithsonian Information Centre for information on ongoing exhibitions.

TOUR I: ARLINGTON ★★

Located in the State of Virginia, Arlington is a suburb of Washington. The economic ties between the two are clear: the federal capital, short on space, needed Arlington's vast stretches of land for such necessary installations as its airport, as well as the huge national cemetery for military heroes and the enormous Pentagon. In this century, Arlington has become a very desirable area in which to live and is home to a large number of civil servants and affluent individuals who cross the Potomac each day to go to work in Washington.

Captain John Smith discovered these lands along the right bank of the Potomac River in 1608. At the time, the area was inhabited by a peaceful Native tribe. Under a law passed in 1789, the part of Virginia now known as Arlington was ceded to the federal government in order to create the Washington District, and was named the County of Alexandria of the District of Columbia. However, in 1846, the local residents – a small group in those days – elected by referendum to return to the jurisdiction of Virginia. At the dawn of the 20th century, the flourishing local economy attracted more and more people to the area, whose population grew by nearly 60%. The town was now so big that it became necessary to change its name to avoid any confusion with the neighbouring city of Alexandria. In 1920, the County of Alexandria was renamed the County of Arlington, in honour of General Robert E. Lee, whose pretty former home, Arlington House, stands atop a hill overlooking the Potomac and Washington. The town's development was further fostered by World War II, as many of the civil servants who came to Washington to work at the various federal departments chose to set up residence here. Today, Arlington has a population of about 170,000.

Our tour of Arlington's major tourist attractions starts at **Arlington National Cemetery ★★**, which contains the graves of

194 Exploring

over 200,000 servicemen and other men and women who have played a significant role in U.S. history. Next, we'll visit the **Iwo Jima Memorial** ★ and the brand-new **Newseum** ★★, then wind up our itinerary with a tour of the famous **Pentagon**, the nerve centre of the U.S. armed forces.

You'll have to take **Arlington Memorial Bridge** across the Potomac to reach **Arlington National Cemetery** ★★ **(1)** *(every day Apr to Sep 8am to 7pm; in Arlington, VA; drive or walk across Arlington Memorial Bridge, facing the Lincoln Memorial, Arlington Cemetery metro, ☎703-979-4886)*, where many American heroes lie buried on a piece of land once owned by the Custis and Lee families. At the entrance, on the left, there is a small tourist information centre *(Memorial Drive, Arlington Cemetery metro, ☎703-692-0931)*, where you can pick up a map of the cemetery. Anyone who has difficulty walking can take a guided tour on one of the cemetery's Tourmobiles *($4, tickets available at the tourist information centre)*. Passengers board on the other side of Memorial Gate, on the left as you exit the tourist information centre.

Perched atop the hill is **Arlington House** *(guided tour every day Apr to Sep 9:30am to 6pm; Arlington National Cemetery, ☎703-557-0613)*, a large plantation house graced with a portico with Doric columns. Its history is intertwined with that of the families of George Washington and Robert E. Lee. From the house, you can contemplate a **magnificent view** ★★ of Washington – and two centuries of American history stretching at your feet in the form of 200,000 perfectly aligned white tombstones set at regular intervals. Arlington National Cemetery, which now covers 170 hectares, grew outward from this here. The slaves who worked on the plantation built this house for their master, George Washington Parke Custis, President Washington's adopted grandson. It was then was turned over to Robert E. Lee when he married Custis's daughter. General Lee liked to stay at the house and it was here, after declining an offer to head the Union forces, that he wrote his letter of resignation to the U.S. Army on April 20, 1861, thus proclaiming his loyalty to Virginia. A few days later, he left his beloved home to take command of Virginia's army, never to return again. When the State of Virginia joined the Confederate States of America that same year, Lee became President Jefferson Davis's military adviser, then was named Commander in Chief of the Confederate armies. In May 1861, Union forces occupied

Tour I: Arlington 195

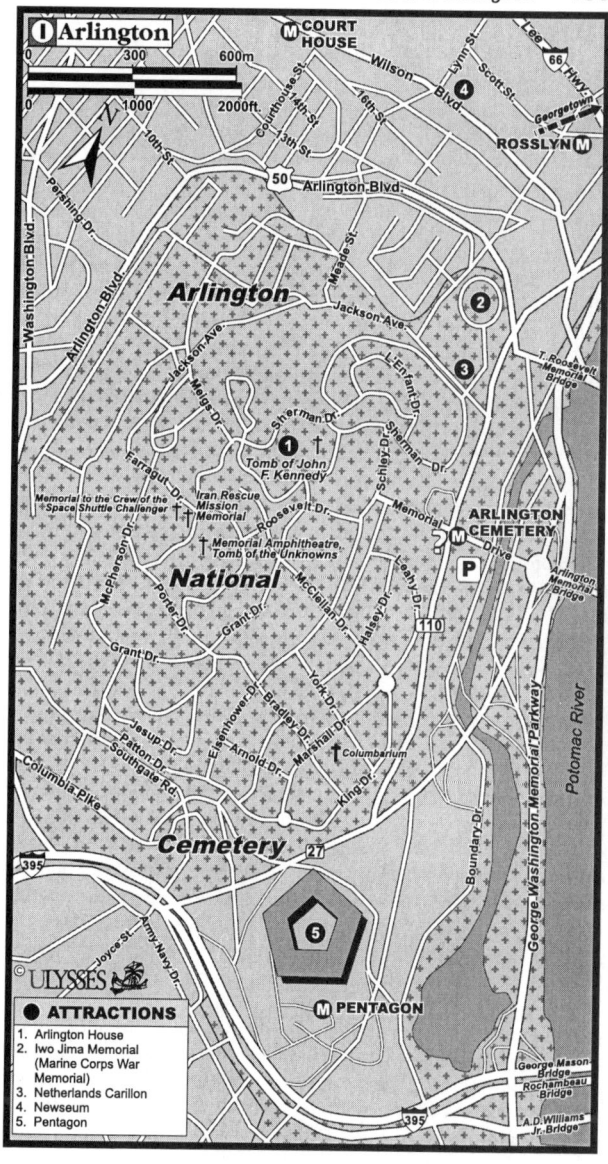

Arlington

ATTRACTIONS
1. Arlington House
2. Iwo Jima Memorial (Marine Corps War Memorial)
3. Netherlands Carillon
4. Newseum
5. Pentagon

The Custis, Washington and Lee Families

The Custis and Lee families, who immigrated from England in the 1600s, both settled in Virginia and became wealthy landowners. The family tree shows the ties between these three great families, who played a major role in U.S. history.

the house because of its strategic location, forcing the rest of the Lee family to flee. In those days, landowners were required to pay real estate taxes in person. Mrs. Custis, who was ill, sent one of her cousins to Washington in her place, and the government used this violation of the law as a pretext to confiscate her property. Thus transformed into a military camp, the estate began to be used as a cemetery. By the end of the Civil War, there were nearly 5,000 graves here, including those of 3,800 fugitive slaves who joined the Union army. General Lee's eldest son sued the U.S. government for so summarily divesting his family of their estate. He won his case and the court ordered the government to give the property back to the family. In 1883, however, Congress offered to buy the estate for $150,000 and the Custis-Lees accepted. It wasn't until 1925 that Congress decided to turn the house into a memorial to General Lee.

The house is now open to the public. Objects once owned by the Lee family are displayed inside, and visitors can see the room where the general wrote his letter of resignation from the Pierre Charles L'Enfant, who drew up the original plans for Washington, D.C., is buried in front of the house. His remains Today, over 200,000 American soldiers are buried in Arlington National Cemetery. The perfectly aligned tombs are simply marked with identical white tombstones, creating a remarkably solemn atmosphere. There are also several monuments to the soldiers who died in the various wars in which the United States has been involved. These are laid out around the Tomb of the Unknown Soldier, a victim of World War I, in front of which an honour guard marches day and night with clockwork precision – a series of 21 steps alternating with 21-second pauses, symbolizing the 21-gun salute. The graves that attract the most visitors are those of President John F. Kennedy and his wife, located side by side. These two tombs are remarkably

Tour I: Arlington 197

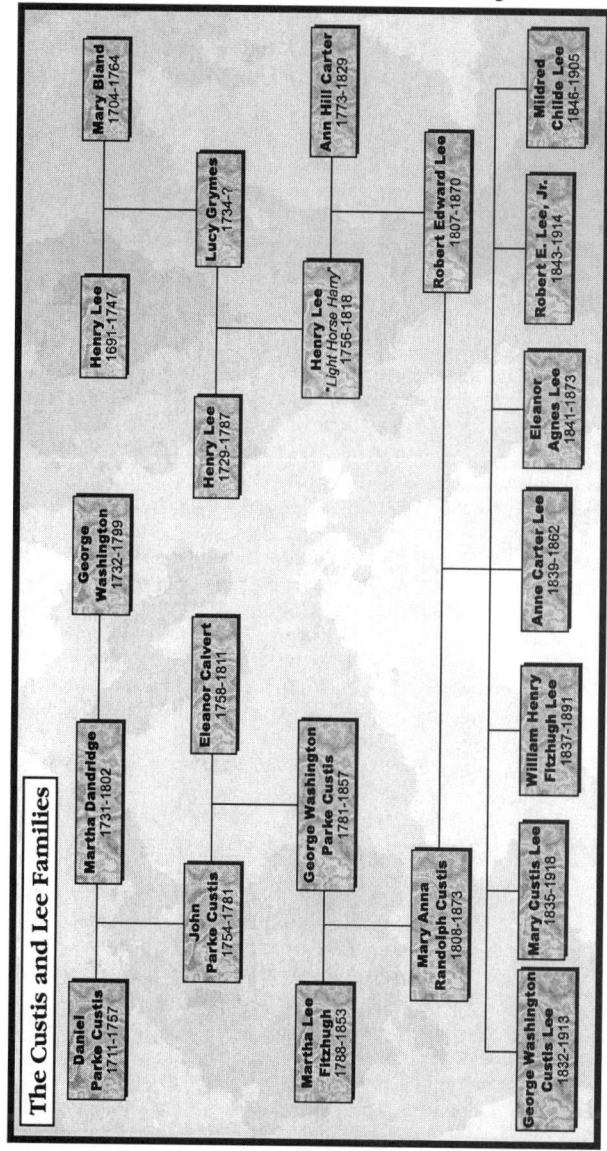

The Custis and Lee Families

- Daniel Parke Custis 1711-1757 — Martha Dandridge 1731-1802 — George Washington 1732-1799
- Henry Lee 1691-1747 — Mary Bland 1704-1764
- John Parke Custis 1754-1781 — Eleanor Calvert 1758-1811
- Henry Lee 1729-1787 — Lucy Grymes 1734-?
- George Washington Parke Custis 1781-1857 — Martha Lee Fitzhugh 1788-1853
- Henry Lee "Light Horse Harry" 1756-1818 — Ann Hill Carter 1773-1829
- Mary Anna Randolph Custis 1808-1873 — Robert Edward Lee 1807-1870

Children:
- George Washington Custis Lee 1832-1913
- Mary Custis Lee 1835-1918
- William Henry Fitzhugh Lee 1837-1891
- Anne Carter Lee 1839-1862
- Eleanor Agnes Lee 1841-1873
- Robert E. Lee, Jr. 1843-1914
- Mildred Childe Lee 1846-1905

EXPLORING

Monuments Commemorating the Space Shuttle Challenger Crew and the Iran Rescue Mission

In 1986, after NASA had enjoyed 19 straight years of success, space exploration might have seemed to some like a routine that man had mastered through modern technology. The tragedy of the Challenger space shuttle, which exploded in mid-flight on January 28 of that year, just a few seconds after liftoff, will be forever etched in the nation's memory. This mission was a very special one, for it was the first time that an ordinary citizen – Christa McAuliffe, a teacher by profession – was joining the astronauts aboard. In some people's minds, it represented the advent of private space travel. McAuliffe was part of the crew, and during her time aboard the shuttle, she was supposed to communicate with all the country's schoolchildren during live teaching sessions. On the day of the tragedy, stirred up by all the publicity surrounding the event, millions of Americans were glued to their TV screens during the live broadcast. Today, everyone still remembers the horrible sight of the shuttle exploding, creating a thick, Y-shaped cloud in the clear blue sky, followed by a shower of debris falling into the Atlantic Ocean. Christa McAuliffe and the six professional astronauts with her perished. In the following weeks, the Coast Guard and Navy combed the bottom of the sea in an effort to retrieve the debris. The few unidentifiable human remains that they found were buried together in a tomb in Arlington National Cemetery. An investigation into the cause of the disaster led to the conclusion that a spark caused by faulty wiring had ignited the pure oxygen in one of the booster rockets.

To the right of the **Challenger Memorial** stands a memorial dedicated to the victims of another air disaster – the eight soldiers who died during an attempt to rescue the hostages held in Iran by Ayatollah Khomeini's Islamic fundamentalist regime. In 1979, the American embassy in Teheran was taken over and 66 Americans were taken prisoner. The fundamentalists agreed to release the women and the African Americans, as well as one ailing white man, but kept the 53 others. The U.S. was unable to reach an agreement with Iranian authorities, and negotiations were eventually halted. At that point, President Jimmy Carter gave the

> go-ahead for a surprise military rescue operation. A
> commando made up of eight helicopters and six transport
> planes was organized. When it arrived in Iran, however, a
> sand storm damaged three of the aircraft and the mission
> had to be aborted. Unfortunately, in the rush to take off
> again, a helicopter collided with one of the transport planes,
> causing both to explode and killing their eight crew
> members. The Iranian government sent the soldiers' remains
> back to the United States after carrying out a macabre
> ceremony during which the bodies were exposed as war
> trophies and publicly desecrated. Taking full responsibility for
> this catastrophe, President Carter arranged for the bodies to
> be buried in Arlington National Cemetery. The failed mission
> prompted Iranian authorities to split up the hostages and
> send them to several different places of confinement to
> thwart any further rescue efforts on the part of the U.S.
> Army. After 444 days of captivity, the 53 hostages were
> finally liberated when Ronald Reagan came into office.

simple – no marble monuments, no epitaphs, just two black tombstones inscribed with their names and a small eternal flame. Other famous people interred in the cemetery include Robert Kennedy, buried near his brother John; Pierre Charles L'Enfant, who drew up the original plans for the capital, and George C. Marshall, the author of the Marshall Plan, an American economic aid program to European nations ravaged by World War II, for which he became the first career soldier to receive a Nobel Peace Prize. The cemetery also contains a memorial to the astronauts who died in the Challenger and Apollo I tragedies. To their right stands another memorial, this one to the eight soldiers who died during the failed mission to rescue the American hostages in Iran.

The **Iwo Jima monument**, or **Marine Corps War Memorial** ★ **(2)** *(in a park next to Arlington Cemetery, between Arlington Blvd. and Ridge Rd.; exit the cemetery through the Weitzel Gate; Arlington Cemetery or Rosslyn metro)*, is one of the most famous sculptures in the United States. Based on a photograph by Joseph Rosenthal, it shows four Marines planting the American flag atop Mt. Suribachi, a decisive moment in the Second World War, marking a turning point in the Pacific campaign. In February 1945, the small Japanese island of Iwo Jima, one of the Bonin Islands, was the scene of savage

200 Exploring

fighting and was defended to the last man by the Japanese, who were trying to drive back the American forces. During the vicious battle, a small detachment of Marines climbed to the top of the mountain to plant the Stars and Stripes there. War photographer Joseph Rosenthal, a native of Washington, witnessed the event and asked the soldiers to pose for a picture. The photograph was quickly circulated all over the United States and earned Rosenthal a Pulitzer Prize that same year. Drawing inspiration from the famous image, sculptor Felix de Weldon cast this statue, which was dedicated on November 10, 1954.

In front of the Iwo Jima monument stands the 38-metre-high **Netherlands Carillon (3)**, a modern steel structure reminiscent of Dutch artist Piet Mondrian's abstract paintings. Made up of 49 bells, it was a gift from the Netherlands to the United States as an expression of thanks for America's help during World War II. A magnificent bed of tulips of all different colours lies at its foot, surrounded by grass.

The city of Arlington boasts a brand-new museum devoted to the world of journalism, the **Newseum ★★ (4)** *(Wed to Sun 10am to 5pm; 1101 Wilson Blvd., Arlington, Rosslyn metro, ☎703-284-3700)*, which opened on April 18, 1997. What could be more appropriate here in the Washington area, where everyone dreams of making the headlines! From Gutenberg to CNN, the museum offers a clear idea of how the media works and the impact it has on society. Interactive simulations enable visitors to take on the role of an editor-in-chief, a television reporter or a radio announcer. Technology envelops you, creating the giddy sensation that you are truly part of the fourth estate.

The **Pentagon (5)** *(Mon to Fri 9:30am to 3:30pm, closed on federal holidays, guided tours only; I-395, Pentagon metro, ☎703-695-1776)*, the headquarters of the Department of Defense, is the largest office building in the world. To give you an idea of its size, each one of its five sides is bigger than the Capitol. Erected in 1941, during World War II, this building, with its shopping centre, two banks, post office, beauty salon, clothing shops, dry cleaner, ophthalmologist's clinic and other businesses serving the 24,000 people who work here, is a veritable city within a city. Visitors can tour the premises, under the close watch of a serviceman, provided they prove that they present no threat. American citizens have to show a photo ID, such as a driver's license; all others, their passport. You'll also have to fill out an exhaustive form, pass through a metal detector and have your bags and personal items X-rayed. If all these security measures don't put you off, you should also be aware that the Pentagon attracts hordes of visitors every year, even though the tour is limited to a few corridors. To avoid waiting in line for hours, we strongly recommend arriving at 9am, half an hour before the first tour starts.

The guided tour starts with a short introductory film on the construction of the Pentagon and how the institution operates. Next, you'll get to explore a few corridors, whose walls are hung with portraits of U.S. presidents and battle scenes, including cartoons sketched by Walt Disney while he was serving his country as an ambulance driver during World War I. The walls of the famous **Hall of Heroes** are inscribed with the names of all recipients of the Congressional Medal of Honor.

TOUR J: OTHER WASHINGTON ATTRACTIONS ★★

Children will love spending an afternoon at the **National Zoological Park** ★★ *(Apr to Oct, every day 8am to 8pm, Nov to Mar, every day 8am to 6pm, closed Dec 25; main entrance 3000 Connecticut Ave., between Cathedral Ave. and Devonshire Pl., other entrances on Beach Dr., in Rock Creek Park, and on Harvard St., at the corner of Adams Mill Rd., Woodley Park-Zoo or Cleveland Park metro, ☎673-4717)*, run by the Smithsonian Institution. The zoo is world-renowned, thanks to both its wide variety of animal species and the Smithsonian's research on animal behaviour and reproduction. As soon as the Smithsonian was founded, it began receiving live animals as gifts. At the time, it had nowhere to put these creatures. Some were sent to zoos outside the city, while others were kept on the Mall and in front of the Castle. When there was no more room for them, Congress created the National Zoological Park in 1889. Today, the facility is much more than your basic zoo, having evolved into a 65-hectare park in the heart of the city, in the steep, picturesque Rock Creek valley. Considered the nation's "official zoo", it receives all sorts of animals from foreign countries, such as the two giant pandas donated by China in 1972 (unfortunately, one of the pair has since died). Other animal residents include kiwis (flightless birds from New Zealand), golden (lion-headed) tamarins from Brazil (adorable little monkeys whose existence is threatened in their natural habitat, due to the massive destruction of the rain forest), Sumatran tigers, elephants, giraffes and a whole slew of invertebrates from all over the world. Over 4,000 animals belonging to nearly 500 different species make their home here in recreated natural settings. The Great Ape House, specially designed for gorillas and orangutans, is one of the most popular exhibits. For those interested in watching the zoo-keepers feed the animals, the pandas are fed around 11am and 3pm. The other animals' meal times vary depending on the season, so it is best to inquire beforehand (the big felines and bears are fed out of public view). It is always best to visit the zoo early in the morning or in the evening, when there are fewer visitors and the animals are more active. Don't miss the Think Tank, an exhibit devoted to animal intelligence; the Invertebrate Exhibit, where you can learn all about the world of invertebrates, from ants to coral to octopuses; the Reptile Discovery Center, and Amazonia, where you can explore a tropical rain forest.

Finally, it should be noted that pets (other than seeing-eye dogs) are not permitted in the zoo and that feeding the animals is strictly forbidden.

The **Kenilworth Aquatic Gardens** *(every day Apr to Sep 7am to 7pm, Oct to Mar 7am to 5pm; Anacostia Ave. and Douglas St., NE, Deanwood metro, ☎426-6905)*, administered by the National Park Service, were founded in 1880. Located on the east bank of the Anacostia River, in northeast Washington, they are home to all sorts of aquatic plants, including water lilies and lotuses. Make sure to see the Victoria Amazonica pond and the East Indian Lotus pond, whose lotuses are grown from seeds that were found in Manchuria and are believed to be between 350 and 600 years old.

The **United States National Arboretum** ★ *(Mon to Fri 8am to 5pm, Sat and Sun 10am to 5pm; 3501 New York Ave. NE, Stadium Armory metro, then take bus 2 to the corner of Bladensburg Rd. and R St. NE, ☎245-4575)* covers nearly 180 hectares, making it one of the largest arboretums in the United States. Though established shortly after the Second World War, it did not open its doors to the public until the 1950s. It boasts the country's largest collection of azaleas, as well as a wide array of other plants, such as roses, hibiscus, rhododendrons, magnolias, dogwoods, boxwoods, holly, etc.

Make sure to visit the magnificent **National Bonsai and Penjing Museum** ★, whose huge collection of bonsai trees were presented to the U.S. by Japan for the American Bicentennial. Some of these twisted little trees are over 300 years old. A wonderfully serene atmosphere pervades the **Japanese Garden**, while the **Herbarium** contains no fewer than 600,000 dried plants. The **Herb Garden**, for its part, is one of the Arboretum's main attractions, with about a hundred different kinds of roses, including some very old varieties, and a reproduction of a 16th-century landscaped garden. Near the rose garden stand 22 columns designed by architect Benjamin Latrobe, which originally adorned the Capitol. They were moved here in the 1950s, during the Capitol's last phase of expansion.

You might be surprised to discover how prominent Catholic institutions are in Washington, D.C. In addition to two universities (Georgetown and Catholic), two hospitals and 34 seminaries, the city is home to the **National Shrine of the Immaculate Conception** *(every day Apr to Oct 7am to 7pm; Nov to Mar 7am to 6pm; 4th St. and Michigan Ave., NE, Brookland-CUA metro, ☎526-8300)*, the largest Roman Catholic church in the United States, with seating for over 3,000. Built in 1920, it is an elegant mixture of Byzantine and Romanesque architecture. On its right side stands the **Knights' Bell Tower**, a gift from the Knights of Columbus, which has a carillon made up of 56 bells cast in Annecy, France. The entire structure is topped with a magnificent gilded dome adorned with red and blue tiles. Dedicated to Mary, who was recognized by the Pope as the patron saint of the United States in 1846, this church boasts an opulent interior featuring stained-glass windows, gilded statuary and a monumental mosaic of Jesus Christ over the main altar. The small chapels that make up the crypt are richly decorated. Among other things, visitors can admire the lovely Mary Altar, made from a block of yellow onyx from Algeria. The concerts given here regularly by the **National Shrine Music Guild** are highly regarded by connoisseurs. Call the information centre for concert dates and times.

The **Washington National Cathedral** ★★ *(Mon to Sat 10am to 4:30pm, Sun 12:30pm to 4:30pm; Massachusetts and Wisconsin avenues, NW, ☎537-7566)*, was built in 14th-century

Anglo-Saxon Gothic style. Its grounds cover 23 hectares, which it shares with three schools, a private college and the offices of the Episcopal Diocese of Washington and the parish of St. Alban. Pierre Charles L'Enfant included a cathedral in his original plans for the city. The idea of building a large national church in the heart of the capital did not, however, elicit a great deal of enthusiasm at the time, since the fledgling nation was preparing to establish the separation of Church and State. It wasn't until 1893 that Congress granted a charter for the creation of the Protestant Episcopal Cathedral Foundation. Henry Yates Satterlee, the first Episcopal bishop of Washington, was the one who decided that the national cathedral should be a cruciform, Gothic structure, believing that style of architecture was most appropriate for exalting the glory of God. Though erected in this century, the cathedral was built with blocks of Indiana limestone according to medieval construction techniques. It has no steel framework; instead, flying buttresses counter the outward thrust of the walls. Officially known as the Cathedral Church of St. Peter and St. Paul, the Washington National Cathedral is both the seat of the Episcopal Bishop of Washington and the presiding bishop of the Episcopal Church of the United States. It took no less than 83 years to build this majestic structure. President Theodore Roosevelt laid the cornerstone in 1907, during a ceremony attended by some 10,000 people. The cathedral's main architect, Philip Hubert Frohman, worked on the project from 1921 until his death in 1972. The nave wasn't consecrated until 1976. Completed in 1990, the Washington National Cathedral is now the sixth largest church in the world, just ahead of Amiens, in France. The top of the Gloria in Excelsis Central Tower, rising 206 metres above sea level, is the highest point in Washington.

Inside the central portal, on the left, is an elevator that takes visitors up to the **Pilgrim Observation Gallery**, which commands a lovely **panoramic view ★** of the entire city.

From the west end of the nave, you can see just how far you are from the altar – 161 metres! This entrance is adorned with one of the cathedral's three rose windows. This magnificent **rose window ★**, made up of 10,500 pieces of glass, focusses on the theme of the Creation, symbolizing the passage from Genesis, "Let there be light". On the left stands a marble statue of George Washington, the first president of the United States, and on the right is a bay devoted to Abraham Lincoln. The floor at the foot of the bronze statue of Lincoln is inlaid with coins bearing his image, while the stained-glass window is an abstract depiction of "The Agony of the Civil War". The central nave is flanked by a series of bays, one of which, on the east side, contains a stained-glass window commemorating the flight of Apollo XI; in its centre you'll see a fragment of lunar rock that the astronauts brought back from that historic voyage. The next bay is dedicated to the 28th president of the United States, Woodrow Wilson, who is interred here. Two adjacent stained-glass windows show scenes from the lives of two great Civil War generals, Robert E. Lee and Stonewall Jackson.

The main altar, showing Christ surrounded by 110 stone-carved figures, is a compositional masterpiece. Above the balcony of the north transept, you can admire the cathedral's oldest rose window, the "Last Judgment", showing a life-sized portrait of Christ. The third rose window, in the south transept, shows the "Triumphant Church". Outside, the archivolt of the south portal is carved with the faces of 44 angels.

Beneath the main altar lies the **crypt**. It was here that the building's first stone was laid, below the altar of the **Bethlehem Chapel**. It was the first part of the cathedral to be fully completed (1929).

The main elements of the Gothic Revival style are harmoniously incorporated into the cathedral's architecture. The west façade is flanked by twin towers, the left dedicated to St. Peter and the right to St. Paul. The hand-carved tympanum over the central portal, representing the Creation, is the work of Frederick Hart. The portal itself is made up of two large bronze choir screens, which are finely decorated with scenes from the lives of Abraham and Moses. The central pillar is a statue of Adam. The numerous gargoyles along the building's exterior serve to drain off rainwater.

The **Bishop's Garden**, a small, enclosed garden south of the cathedral, was designed in accordance with the medieval tradition of planting several little gardens side by side. The entrance is located near the Herb Cottage, a small store on South Road, beneath a replica of a 12th-century porch. As indicated by its name, this used to be the bishop's private garden, and it is very charming. A bronze equestrian statue of

George Washington stands in front of it, marking the starting point of several pleasant paths that wind through the woods.

The **Hillwood Museum** ★ *($10; guided tours by reservation only, Tue to Sat 9am, 10:30am, noon, 1:30pm and 3pm, closed Feb; 4155 Linnean Ave. NW, 30-min walk from the Van Ness-UDC metro station, ☎686-8500)*, a magnificent, 40-room, Georgian house, is the former home of Marjorie Merriweather Post (1887-1973), a businesswoman, philanthropist and major art collector. It now contains an impressive collection of 18th- and 19th-century French furniture and French and Russian decorative art, most notably pieces of Sèvres porcelain, tapestries and treasures from the private collection of the Russian czars. Marjorie Merriweather Post visited the Soviet Union shortly before the Second World War and was one of the last people to be able to purchase items like these, which were confiscated from the imperial family and the Russian aristocracy by the socialist government after the Russian Revolution (1917). The collection thus spans over 200 years of the history of decorative art in Russia, from Peter the Great to the last czar, Nicholas II. The highlight is the Icon Room, which displays a number of exquisite pieces by Carl Fabergé, including two magnificent Fabergé Easter eggs, made for the imperial family. This is the largest collection of Russian decorative art outside Russian territory. The other rooms of this sumptuous house contain portraits of the Romanovs; remarkable, finely worked liturgical objects; gold- and silver-embroidered Orthodox vestments; porcelain owned by Catherine the Great, Empress of Russia; and other precious bibelots. In addition to viewing this impressive exhibition, you can tour the grounds, where you'll find a *dacha* once used as a display space for the decorative art now exhibited in the main house, a charming Japanese garden and a formal garden. A map of the grounds showing the major points of interest is available at the museum entrance.

TOUR K: GEORGETOWN ★★

Georgetown was named after King George II of England – not, as one might think, after George Washington. In fact, this area, formerly known as the Town of George, is much older than Washington itself.

Tour K: Georgetown   207

K Georgetown

● ATTRACTIONS

1. C&O Canal
2. Duval foundry
3. Washington Harbour
4. Grace Church
5. Chesapeake & Ohio Canal Warehouses
6. Georgetown Park
7. Old Stone House
8. Laird Dunlop House
9. Old Houses
10. 3017 N Street
11. Riggs Riley House
12. Foxall House
13. 2812 N Street to 2806 N Street
14. Mount Zion United Methodist Church
15. St. John's Episcopal Church
16. Smith Row
17. 3307 N Street
18. Cox Row
19. Bodisco House
20. Holy Trinity Parish
21. Healy Building
22. Old North Hall
23. Convent of the Visitation
24. Volta Bureau
25. Pomander Walk
26. Tudor Place
27. Dumbarton Oaks
28. Oak Hill Cemetery
29. Dumbarton House

◇ ACCOMMODATIONS

1. Four Seasons Hotel
2. Georgetown Dutch Inn

◇ RESTAURANTS

1. Alamo Grill
2. Café la Ruche
3. Chez-Nous
4. China Regency Restaurant
5. Citronelle
6. La Madeleine
7. Le Séquoia
8. Music City Roadhouse
9. Ristorante Piccolo

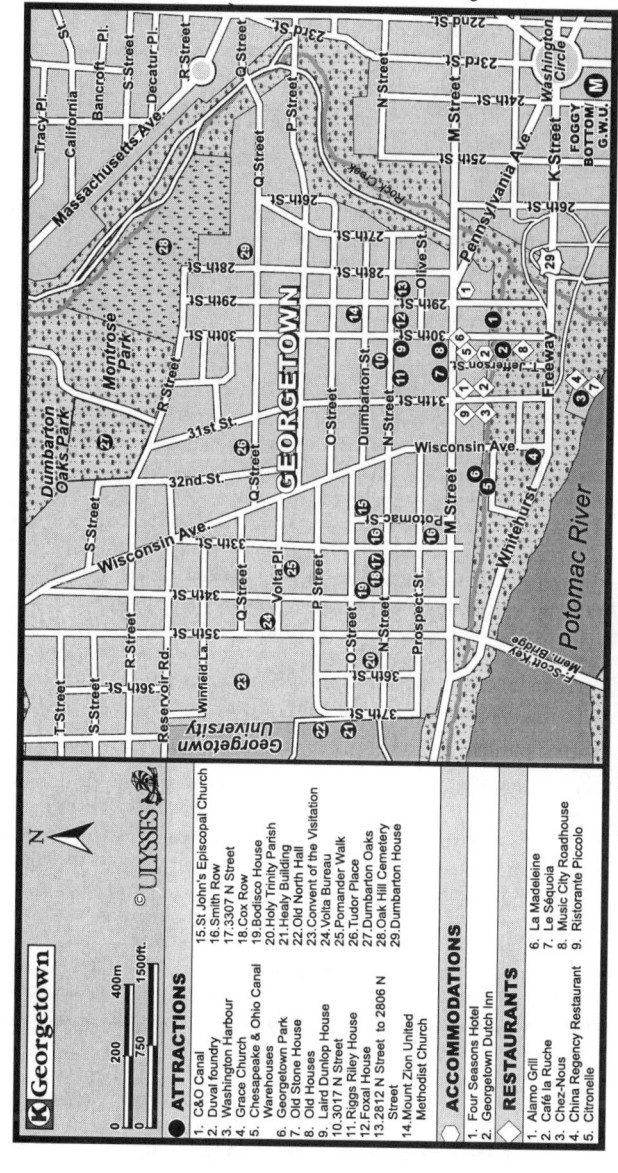

EXPLORING

208   Exploring

Apparently, Captain John Smith was the first person to disembark on the banks of the Potomac where Georgetown is now located (1608). "No place is more convenient for pleasure, profit and man's sustenance", he later wrote. When fur trader Henry Fleet, a fur trader, came here in 1632, he found a small village inhabited by Tohoga Indians. In the early 18th century, the State of Maryland owned the area and granted plots of land here to a few colonists looking for a new place to settle. Two of these individuals played an important role in the history of Georgetown. In 1703, Colonel Ninian Beall, a Scottish immigrant who had fought against Cromwell, was granted over 320 hectares at the mouth of Rock Creek. He named his vast estate after a rock formation near Glasgow, Scotland, the Rock of Dunbarton (later corrupted to "Dumbarton"). The greater part of Georgetown is now located on this land. George Gordon, also of Scottish descent, became the other major local landowner, obtaining a plot of land then known as "Knave's Disappointment". He changed the estate's rather off-putting name to Rock Creek Plantation. Over the years, a small Scottish community settled and flourished on the banks of the Potomac, and in 1751, the local residents asked the State of Maryland to officially authorize the creation of the little Town of George. The Maryland parliament sent six representatives to negotiate with George Gordon and Ninian Beall's son, asking them to return about 20 hectares of land for the new town to be built. The boundary stone that once marked the northeast edge of town can be found in the garden of 1248 30th Street.

The Town of George, advantageously located on the banks of the navigable Potomac, built a transit port for the tobacco trade a few years later. Before long, large warehouses had sprung up along the river, and as the town prospered, elegant homes began to grace its streets. Georgetown College, the first Catholic institution of higher learning in the United States, now Georgetown University, was founded in 1789. The ports of Georgetown and Alexandria became the most important in the region, and Georgetown became leading point of sale for tobacco in Maryland. It was around that time, in 1791, that a decision was made to establish a federal capital for the 13 founding colonies on the banks of the Potomac.

Georgetown did not benefit from Washington's development. Just when its commercial activities started to dwindle, however, the construction of the Chesapeake & Ohio (C&O) Canal breathed some new life into the local economy. This revival was short lived, however. When the canal was on the verge of being completed, the advent of the railroad, and more specifically, the line between Baltimore and Ohio, shattered Georgetown's hopes of becoming a major transportation centre. Faster and more practical than barges, trains quickly won the favour of tradesmen. Furthermore, the advent of the steam ship, which necessitated new port installations on deeper waterways than the Potomac, sounded the death knell for Georgetown's port activities.

Georgetown's decline continued until after the Civil War. In 1871, it was officially incorporated into the District of Columbia and thus joined to Washington. The town became nothing more than a suburb, and many wealthy old families relocated to more fashionable neighbourhoods in Washington, leaving their mansions to crumble. Consequently, many historic buildings were destroyed. The port's Customs House was converted into a post office; even the street names were changed to correspond with the capital's grid pattern.

In the years following the First World War, Georgetown experienced a sort of renaissance. Local residents rediscovered this pleasant area, and Congress passed a law designating Georgetown as an historic district in 1950, prompting a flurry of restoration projects. This law included provisions to protect the area's historic character, requiring all renovations or constructions to be approved by a special committee.

Today, Georgetown is a charming neighbourhood with a faintly colonial atmosphere and scores of art galleries, restaurants and lovely shops. It is home to many high-ranking civil servants and academicians. The following tour will allow you to appreciate the undeniable beauty of this old "town", whose brick sidewalks are still lined with gas lamps and charming little houses.

Unfortunately, there are no metro stations in Georgetown, whose narrow streets and lack of public parking are a motorist's nightmare. It is thus best to explore the area on foot. Seeing as the tour is a bit long, though, you might want to take a bus or taxi to some of the stops on the itinerary.

Take the M Street bridge over Rock Creek. At the **Westin Hotel** (*2800 Pennsylvania Ave., at the corner of M St.*), a modern,

210 Exploring

red-brick building, turn left and walk down 29th Street to the banks of the **C&O Canal ★ (1)**, one of the best-preserved canals in the United States. Begun in 1828, the Chesapeake & Ohio Canal was originally supposed to serve as a navigable waterway between the fertile valleys of the west and those of the east, linking Georgetown directly to Ohio. However, by the time the first 230 kilometres of the canal were dug, as far as Cumberland, a railway line had been laid between Baltimore and Ohio, nipping Georgetown's ambitions of becoming a transportation centre in the bud. Barges simply could not compete with the train. Today, the tow path once used by horses pulling barges is a charming place to take a stroll and look at the locks.

At 30th Street, turn left and cross the canal. The renovated **Duval Foundry (2)** *(1050 30th St. NW)*, on the banks of the canal, occupies an entire block between 30th and Jefferson streets. It was built by William T. Duval between 1856 and 1866. After 1870, the building housed a number of shops and a veterinary hospital for the mules that pulled the barges on the canal.

Head south on Jefferson Street to the banks of the Potomac, where you'll find **Washington Harbour (3)** *(3000-3020 K St. NW)*. This pretty office, condominium and shopping complex, designed by Arthur Cotton Moore, replaced the abandoned industrial buildings of the Georgetown port in 1986. Washington Harbour offers a lovely **view ★** of the Potomac, the John F. Kennedy Center for the Performing Arts and the verdant shores of Theodore Roosevelt Island. Many Washingtonians come here by boat to enjoy an alfresco lunch on the terrace.

Backtrack to the canal and follow it west. Turn left on Wisconsin Avenue. Charming little **Grace Church (4)** *(1401 Wisconsin Ave. NW)*, at the back of a small yard hidden by stately trees, is a Gothic Revival building dating from 1866. It was built as a mission for the boatmen of the C&O Canal.

Continue westward along the banks of the canal. A block farther, you'll come to the **Chesapeake & Ohio Canal Warehouses (5)** *(between Potomac St. and Jefferson Pl.)*, erected back in the port's heyday.

On the other side of the canal, you can visit **Georgetown Park (6)** *(M St., between Wisconsin Ave. and Potomac)*, a large

Old Stone House

and very attractive shopping mall adorned with skylights and wrought-iron ornamentation. The complex is actually a collection of converted garages, shops and hardware stores, among other historic structures, including one of the city's first public markets. One wall of the building is decorated with a trompe-l'œil fresco of an 18th-century Georgetown street.

Head north on M Street, a main artery of Georgetown. You'll pass a number of restaurants and little shops selling all sorts of souvenirs, ranging from your basic T-shirt to antiques, not to mention the paintings displayed in the many local art galleries.

Simple but solid, the **Old Stone House ★ (7)** *(Wed to Sun 9am to 5pm; 3051 M St. NW, ☎426-6851)* may be the oldest extant building in Washington. Erected in 1765 by Christopher Layman, a Pennsylvania cabinetmaker who moved here shortly after the Town of George was founded, it has since been restored and now houses a small museum that shows how an average American family of that era lived. Made entirely of granite and brick, this small house is typical of the homes built by European colonists in the New World. Many of the houses back then had a small store and a kitchen on the ground floor, with the living quarters above. Christopher Layman died in 1767, two years after his house was finally finished.

Continuing up M Street, you'll come to a group of **old houses (8)** *(3001-3009 M St. NW)*, one of which was built by Thomas Sim Lee, a friend of George Washington's and a fervent champion of the patriot cause. While governor of Maryland, Lee developed a taste for real estate and purchased a plot of land, where he built the house at 3001 M Street. In 1910, he decided that he had more space than he needed and sold part of the land to Ross and Getty, who built the neighbouring houses at 3005-3009 M Street. Like all buildings in Georgetown, these were neglected during the area's period of economic decline. However, this group of houses was the first to be restored in the 1950s, launching a crusade to breathe new life into downtown Georgetown.

Turn left on 30th Street. Two blocks north, you'll come to one of the prettiest streets in Georgetown, **N Street** ★. Immediately to the left stands the **Laird-Dunlop House (9)** *(3014 N St. NW)*, built in 1799 for John Laird, a rich tobacco merchant. Opposite, **3017 N Street (10)** is another pretty house built in the 1790s by Thomas Beall, a descendant of wealthy landowner Ninian Beall, who once owned much of the land now occupied by Georgetown. This house once belonged to Jacqueline Bouvier Kennedy, who stayed here in 1963, following the death of her husband, John F. Kennedy. A few houses down, you'll come to the **Riggs-Riley House (11)** *(3038 N St. NW)*, built in 1816 by Romulus Riggs, a Georgetown businessman. The Federal-style architecture of this small house is typical of early 19th-century American buildings. Joseph Riley, a doctor, purchased the house several years later and added a wing to the east side.

Head back to the east part of town. After 30th Street, you'll find the charming little **Foxall House (12)** *(2908 N St. NW)*, named after its owner and architect. Henry Foxall was mayor of Georgetown and owned a successful munitions factory on the west edge of town. From **2812 N Street to 2806 N Street (13)**, there is a series of houses built between 1813 and 1817, whose architecture displays a lovely unity of style. The Federal-style architecture that predominates on N Street can be distinguished from that found in Alexandria by its simple geometric shapes and austere ornamentation.

Head north on 28th Street and turn left on Dumbarton Street. Walk one block to the **Mount Zion United Methodist**

Tour K: Georgetown 213

Church (14) *(1334 29th St. NW, at the corner of Dumbarton)*, built in 1884 by what was probably the first black congregation in the District of Columbia, founded in 1816. The congregation had built a small church on 27th Street, at the corner of P Street, in 1814, but it was destroyed by fire. This red-brick building is a more imposing structure than the old church. Inside, its stamped metal ceiling is quite unique.

Continue west on Dumbarton Street, which becomes O Street after Wisconsin Avenue. **St. John's Episcopal Church (15)** *(3240 O Street NW, at the corner of Potomac and O streets)*, the first Episcopal church in Washington, was built between 1796 and 1804 by architect William Thornton, who also worked on the Capitol (see p 92) and designed the Octagon House (see p 131). Thomas Jefferson helped pay for its construction. Because of financial problems, however, the little church was abandoned in 1931. William Corcoran, the founder of the Corcoran Gallery of Art (see p 132), being the good philanthropist that he was, purchased the building in 1837 and sold it back to the Episcopal Church a few years later.

Walk south down Potomac Street, back to N Street. At the corner, you'll find a remarkable group of buildings known as **Smith Row ★ (16)** *(3255-3263 N Street NW)*, a series of five Federal-style houses erected by brothers Walter and Clement Smith in 1815. Two of their distinguishing features are their dormer windows and their elevated front doors, preceded by a short flight of stairs. John and Jackie Kennedy lived at **3307 N Street (17)** from 1957 to 1961, when they moved into the White House.

A little farther along, you'll find another row of houses typical of 19th-century Georgetown: **Cox Row ★ (18)** *(3327-3339 N St. NW)*. With their recessed panels and vaulted door frames, these houses are among the purest examples of the "Georgetown version" of the Federal style. This harmonious architectural ensemble owes its existence to Colonel Cox, a rich local merchant who served as mayor of Georgetown for 22 years. When the Marquis de La Fayette came here in 1824, Colonel Cox put the house at 3337 N Street at his disposal.

Turn right on 34th Street, then right again on O Street, where you'll find an old brick house that was once a hub of activity for the Georgetown elite. The **Bodisco House (19)** *(3322*

O Street NW; at the corner of 34th St.) was erected in 1815 by a banker named Clement Smith, the same man who built Smith Row on N Street. The Russian legation later purchased it and used it as a residence for the tsar's emissaries, one of whom was named Baron Alexander of Bodisco. In the early part of the century, when he was in his 60s, Bodisco married a 16-year-old girl named Harriett Beall Williams, making tongues wag all over Georgetown. It was here that the newlyweds lived in wedded bliss and threw lavish parties that became legendary.

Go back to N Street. Two blocks to the right, you'll find **Holy Trinity Parish (20)** *(3513 N St. NW)*, which took 75 years to build. The church is made up of three separate structures. The oldest, dating from 1794, was the first Catholic place of worship in the District (it is now the Convent of Mercy). Before the First Amendment of the Constitution recognized freedom of religion for all, Catholic families in the United States had to attend services in small private chapels. Before long, the congregation needed more room, and in 1846 they built a lovely Greco Roman building, to which architect Francis Staunton added a handsome presbytery with a mansard roof, a pure product of post-Civil War architecture (1869).

Farther to the west, N Street ends at the campus of Georgetown University, the oldest Catholic institution of higher learning in the United States, founded in 1789. Facing O Street stands the fortress-like **Healy Building (21)** *(Georgetown University, on the continuation of O Street)*, built in 1879 by Smithmeyer and Pelz, who also designed the Library of Congress. It was named after Patrick Healy, an American Jesuit of African origin who served as prefect of studies of the university in the 19th century. President Washington once delivered a speech to Georgetown students in **Old North Hall (22)**, next to the Healy Building. One of the university's oldest edifices (1792-1793), Old North Hall is an example of one style of Georgian architecture.

The **Convent of the Visitation (23)** *(P and 35 sts. NW)*, adjacent to the Georgetown campus, is the second oldest convent in the United States. French nuns set up residence here in 1799. The complex features three different styles of architecture – Gothic Revival for the chapel, erected in 1825 by architect Joseph Picot de Corivière; Federal for the convent itself, a much more austere building dating from 1857, and Victorian for the

Academy Building (1874), which is graced with a mansard roof and arched windows.

The other attractions on our itinerary are farther to the north, alongside Dumbarton Oaks Park and Montrose Park. You might want to take a taxi or a bus, though it is possible to get there on foot, if you don't mind a long (but very pleasant) walk. If you choose to walk can see two other points of interest, both on Volta Place. To do so, take 35th Street north to Volta Place, then turn right. You'll find a big building that looks like a temple, with two large Corinthian columns supporting its entryway. This is the **Volta Bureau (24)** *(1537 35th St. NW)*, erected in 1893. The French government awarded Alexander Graham Bell the *Prix Volta* for inventing the telephone. The prize included $10,000 in cash, which Bell used to found the American Association to Promote the Teaching of Speech to the Deaf, whose headquarters are now at this yellow brick building.

A little farther along on Volta Place, you'll find **Pomander Walk (25)** *(on Volta Place, between 33rd and 34th sts. NW)*, a charming little lane lined with recently renovated houses. These 10 adorable little homes were built in the late 19th century. An oasis of tranquility with a truly enchanting atmosphere.

At Wisconsin Avenue, turn left, walk one block, then turn right on Q Street. Continue to 31st Street, and turn left. You'll find yourself in front of **Tudor Place ★ (26)** *($5 suggested contribution; guided tours, reservations required; Tue to Fri 10am, 11:30am, 1pm and 2:30pm; Sat 10am to 3pm, no reservations required; 1644 31st St. NW, ☎965-0400)*, a magnificent Georgian house designed by the celebrated architect William Thornton, who also worked on the Capitol (see p 92). The house belonged to Martha Custis Peter, who was George Washington's wife Martha's granddaughter. When her grandmother died, Martha Custis Peter inherited $8,000, enabling her to purchase this plot of land, which overlooked Georgetown and offered a view of the Potomac in the distance. The person who owned the land previously had built what are now the wings of the house. The building was not grand enough for Martha Custis Peter's taste, so she asked William Thornton to remodel it. The work dragged on a bit, but Tudor Place was finally finished in 1816. To lend this stuccoed brick house an air of prestige, Thornton added the central portion, which he adorned with a semicircular, columned front porch reminiscent of a small temple. Upon Martha Peter's death, the property went to the youngest of her three daughters, Britannia Wellington Peter Kennon. Though a fervent supporter of the Confederate cause and a relative of General Robert E. Lee's, Britannia welcomed the officers of the Union army into her home. The Marquis de La Fayette was also a guest in this magnificent house, which remained in the Peter family until 1983, when it was given to the Tudor Place Foundation. In 1988, a small museum exhibiting various objects related to the Peter family history opened its doors to the public. A good portion of the furniture on display comes from Mount Vernon, George Washington's home.

Walk north on 31st Street to R Street, where you'll find **Dumbarton Oaks** ★★ **(27)** *(Tue to Sun 2pm to 5pm; 1703 32nd St. NW, between R and S sts., ☎342-3200)*, a splendid house once owned by Mr. and Mrs. Robert Woods Bliss. It now contains a remarkable museum, where the couple's private collection of Byzantine and pre-Columbian art is displayed. There are actually several buildings on the estate, erected by different owners. The original Federal-style house was built by Senator William Hammond Dorsey in 1801, in the middle of about 9 hectares of land that he had purchased from Thomas Beall, a descendant of Ninian Beall. After being bought and sold numerous times, the lovely house was finally purchased by Edward Linthicum, who began modifying it in 1860 to give it a more Victorian look, adding wings to the main building. Mr. and Mrs. Bliss, who had inherited a large fortune, bought Dumbarton Oaks in 1920, along with 21 hectares of surrounding woodland. They expanded and modernized the house and hired a landscape architect by the name of Beatrix Farrand to design the splendid, terraced **gardens** ★★ *($2; Apr to Oct every day 2pm to 6pm, Nov to Mar every day 2pm to 5pm; 31st and R streets, ☎338-8278)*, considered a veritable masterpiece of landscape architecture in the United States. Depending on the season, cherry blossoms, forsythia, azaleas, dogwoods, magnolias, clematis, fuchsia, gardenias, chrysanthemums, lilies and numerous varieties of rose bloom here in a brilliantly orchestrated symphony of colour and fragrance. The Blisses wanted the grounds to remain relatively wild, however, and thus left 11 hectares north of the house in their natural state. These 11 hectares of woodland now form Dumbarton

Oaks Park. Various gardens were laid out around the house on the remaining land.

In the course of their frequent travels, Robert Bliss, a diplomat, and his wife began collecting rare pieces of Byzantine art, which are now on display at Dumbarton Oaks. The **Byzantine Collection** ★★ is made up of nearly 1,500 works from the eastern Mediterranean regions and dating from the 4th to the 15th century. Some 12,000 Byzantine coins, forming one of the finest coin collections in the world, are also exhibited here.

In 1929, the Blisses hired the architect Lawrence White to build the **Music Room** ★, a lavishly decorated auditorium where some of the greatest musicians of our time, including Igor Stravinsky and Nadia Boulanger, have performed. The coffered wooden ceiling is a replica of the 17th-century one that adorns the Château de Cheverny in France's Loire Valley, while the mantelpiece, dating from the 17th century, is from the Château de Thébon, near Bordeaux, France. The frescoes are by Allyn Cox.

Dumbarton Oaks also boasts a **Pre-Columbian Museum** ★, which displays another of the Blisses' collections. Architect Philip Johnson was commissioned to build the eight circular pavilions that now house this museum in 1963. Each section displays art from different pre-Columbian civilizations.

When Mr. and Mrs. Bliss left Dumbarton Oaks in 1940 and moved to Montecito, California, they donated their Byzantine and pre-Columbian collections, their library of more than 14,000 volumes, and several buildings on the estate to Harvard University, on condition that the school establish a museum and research centre here. The 11 hectares of woodlands were given to the National Park Service for the public's enjoyment.

Walk east down R Street to the entrance of **Oak Hill Cemetery (28)** *(Mon to Fri 10am to 4pm; 3001 R St. NW, at the corner of R and 30th streets, ☎337-2835)*, which covers over 10 hectares along the west bank of Rock Creek. William Corcoran, the founder of the Corcoran Gallery of Art (see p 132), donated the first six hectares of land and is buried here. Two of the cemetery's more noteworthy monuments are the Gothic Revival-style Oak Hill Chapel, built by architect James Renwick (who also designed the Smithsonian Castle and

218 Exploring

the original Corcoran Gallery of Art, now the Renwick Gallery) in 1850 and the Van Ness Mausoleum, built in 1833 by George Hadfield, who modelled if after the Temple of Vesta in Rome.

Continue east on R Street, then turn right on 28th Street and left on Q Street. **Dumbarton House (29)** *(guided tours only, Tue to Sat 10am to 1pm; 2715 Q St. NW, ☎337-2288)*, built around 1798 and formerly known as Bellevue (nice view), because of its location, is probably the oldest of the great houses in upper Georgetown. It was designed and built by its first owner, Samuel Johnson. In 1805, Joseph Nourse purchased the house and decided to remodel it. He hired the architect of the day, Benjamin Latrobe, who worked on such high-profile projects as the Capitol.

Earlier in the 20th century, several minor modifications were made to the façade, including the addition of a balustrade. In 1915, when Q Street was extended, the lovely building seemed to be slated for destruction. In the end, however, the entire structure was moved nearly 100 metres north to save it from the wrecking ball. In 1928, the National Society of the Colonial Dames of America, an organization devoted to education and the preservation of historic buildings, purchased the house to use it as their headquarters. They also opened a small museum containing furniture, china and a few lovely paintings.

★ TOUR L: THE OUTSKIRTS OF WASHINGTON

This section proposes two excursions just a few kilometres outside the Washington area. The first is to the small city of **Alexandria**. The architecture of its historic neighbourhoods confers on it undeniable colonial charm. The second outing leads further south, to the famous plantation home of George Washington at **Mount Vernon**.

Alexandria ★★

Alexandria is set on the west bank of the Potomac, fewer than 10 kilometres from Washington. Visitors can reach it easily by taking the blue and yellow metro lines to King Street station. To reach Alexandria by car from downtown Washington, take 14th Street south and cross the bridge that spans the Potomac.

Tour L: The Outskirts of Washington 219

At exit 11A, take George Washington Memorial Parkway in the direction of National Airport. Parking is very limited in downtown Alexandria so it is advisable to obtain a parking permit from the **Ramsay House Visitors Center** *(221 King St., at the corner of Fairfax St.).*

Founded in 1748, three years after neighbouring Georgetown, the little town of Alexandria was similarly a flourishing tobacco trading port. The town was named in honour of the Alexander family, who formerly owned the land on which the new agglomeration was built. Alexandria quickly became the centre of commercial and social life for the region's plantations, including Mount Vernon, and soon was equipped with warehouses, shipyards, inns, and little houses standing side by side with rich Georgian residences. (If Georgetown is characterized by its Federal architecture, then Alexandria's trademark is its Georgian style.) In 1775, during the American Revolution, Alexandria became a refuge for patriots, including notably George Washington, who owned a small house in town in addition to his beautiful plantation at Mount Vernon. The beginning of the 19th century marked a turning point in Alexandria's economy. Despite the town's official incorporation into the district of Washington by the American Congress in 1801, a congressional edict prohibited the construction of any federal administrative buildings here, stymying economic development which was already suffering from stiff competition from the ports of Georgetown and Baltimore. Crippled by debt and unable to turn any profit from its association with the federal capital, Alexandria was finally returned to Virginia in 1846, thanks to the unrelenting pressure applied by its residents. During the years of the Civil War, federal troops occupied the city from 1861 on. Its main buildings were then converted into military hospitals and a fort was constructed on Shooter's Hill, the present-day site of the George Washington Masonic National Memorial.

Today, Alexandria is an elegant city that has taken full advantage of the economic activity generated by the proximity of the federal capital. The 1960s were marked by the rediscovery of architectural treasures in the older sections of the city, attracting a well-off stratum to the area, and the old Georgian houses that are clustered along the cobbled street of historic Alexandria were bought up and restored.

220 Exploring

The best place to start off a tour of Alexandria is **Ramsay House Visitors Center** *(every day 9am to 5pm, closed Dec 25 and Jan 1; 221 King St., corner of Fairfax St., ☎703-838-4200)*, located in the city's oldest building (1749-1751), where visitors can pick up maps of Alexandria's historic area. From March to November, guided walking tours of the city's older neighbourhoods are also offered for the modest sum of $3.

One of the most beautiful sections of Alexandria can be seen on Prince Street between the Waterfront and Fairfax Street. It consists of two blocks of houses bordering a cobbled street that slopes down to the river. The first, **Captain's Row ★** *(Prince St., between Union St. and Lee St.)*, is a group of modest, but charmingly alluring homes. The second block, **Gentry Row ★** *(200-299 Prince St., between Lee St. and Fairfax St.)*, presents some superb examples of Georgian architecture.

A few houses north on Fairfax Street, there is a very pretty Georgian manor called **Carlyle House ★** *($3; guided tours every half hour, Tue to Sat 10am to 4:30pm, Sun noon to 4:30pm, closed Dec 24, Dec 25 and Jan 1; 121 N. Fairfax St., ☎703-549-2997)*. This house was built in 1752 by Scottish entrepreneur John Carlyle, a friend of George Washington's. In April 1755 it became the headquarters of English General Edward Braddock and served as the meeting place of the English general and five colonial governors appointed by the king during which they organized a campaign against the French and the Native Americans. On this occasion, the general proposed to a young George Washington that he serve under his orders. When John Carlyle died in 1780, the manor was passed on to his daughter Sarah. Since 1970, the Northern Virginia Regional Park Authority has owned the property. After six years of major restoration work, this magnificent two-story Georgian residence is now open to the public, who can admire its interior completely decorated in green and blue and furnished in a style typical of its era.

Just next door on Fairfax Street, on the edge of **Market Square**, which was the heart of local economic activity in the days when tobacco planters brought their crops here to be sold, visitors can see the oldest bank in Virginia: the **Bank of Alexandria** *(133 N. Fairfax St.)*, built in 1807.

Gadsby Tavern Museum ★ *($3; guided tours only; Apr to Sep, Tue to Sat 10am to 5pm, Sun 1pm to 5pm; Oct to Mar, Tue to Sat 11am to 4pm, Sun 1pm to 5pm; 134 N. Royal St., ☎703-838-4242)*, which was built in two stages in 1752 and 1792, stands northwest of Market Square. This house was George Washington's headquarters in 1754, when he was a lieutenant-colonel in the Virginia militia. (In that period, Washington lived nearby, at 508 Cameron Street). Today there is a restaurant on the ground floor, while the rest of the building serves as a small museum recreating the ambience of a tavern from the days of John Gadsby, its former owner and namesake. The **Ballroom**, which takes up most of the second story, was the setting of elegant evenings that assembled the upper crust of Alexandria society. The original woodwork that decorated the walls of this room is now preserved at the Metropolitan Museum of Art in New York.

The **Boyhood Home of Robert E. Lee** *($3; guided tours only; Feb to Dec, Mon to Fri 10am to 3:30pm, Sun 1pm to 3:30pm; 607 Oronoco St., ☎703-548-8454)* is an old Georgian house that was built in 1795 by John Potts, a local businessman. Robert E. Lee's father, who served as governor of Virginia from 1792 to 1795, moved his family to Alexandria in 1810, to this beautiful estate that has now been turned into a museum, and where General Lee (see Arlington House, p 194) spent his childhood years.

Another house built in 1785 by Philip Richard Fendall has been converted into a small museum that presents furniture and personal objects that belonged to the Lee family. **Lee-Fendall House** *($3; Tue to Sat 10am to 4pm, Sun noon to 4pm; 614 Oronoco St., corner of Washington St., ☎703-548-1789)* is located across the street from the Boyhood Home of Robert E. Lee.

The **Lyceum** *(Mon to Sat 10am to 5pm; 201 S. Washington St., ☎703-838-4994)* is a museum dedicated to the history of the city of Alexandria. Housed in a neoclassical building modelled after a Greek temple, it presents exhibitions of antique prints, photographs, ceramics, and Civil War paraphernalia.

Christ Episcopal Church ★ *(Mon to Fri 9am to 4pm, Sat 9am to noon, Sun 2pm to 4:30pm; corner of N. Washington St. and*

The George Washington Masonic National Memorial

Cameron St., ☎703-549-1450) is the most interesting of the city's many old churches. John Carlyle was responsible for bringing the construction of the church, which spanned the years from 1767 to 1773, to completion. In addition to hand-painted mural tablets on which the faithful can read the *Apostle's Creed* and *Our Father*, visitors can see the pews reserved for George Washington (no. 60) and Robert E. Lee (no. 46). Several Confederate soldiers rest in a small cemetery outside the church.

Like many great political men of the young American Republic, George Washington was a Freemason. In fact, he was the first Master of the Alexandria Lodge, which was founded in 1788. Today, the **George Washington Masonic National Memorial** *(every day 9am to 5pm, closed Dec 25; 101 Callahan Dr., King Street metro, ☎703-683-2007)* stands on a hill that was once proposed as a potential site for the Capitol. The memorial was financed by over three million Masons from all over the United States and was inaugurated in 1932, before work on the structure was even completed (it's construction lasted from 1923 to 1960). It houses objects commemorating George Washington in a building designed to evoke the Pharos (lighthouse) of Alexandria in Egypt, one of the Seven Wonders of the World. The Alexandria Lodge that Washington ran assembled a hoard of objects that either belonged to him or were related to his life. Unfortunately, part of this treasury was destroyed in 1871 in a fire at the building that housed the old lodge on Market Square. What remains of the collection is now exhibited in this memorial, including such items as the high-backed armchair from which the Grand Master officiated, a letter written in his hand, and the clock from his bedroom in Mount Vernon, which was stopped at the time of his death, 10:20am, December 14, 1799.

From the top of the tower, which rises 122 metres above Alexandria, there is a superb **panoramic view** ★★ of the city and its surroundings.

Mount Vernon ★★★

For visitors to Virginia and Washington D.C., the estate at **Mount Vernon** *($7; every day, Apr to Aug 8am to 5pm, Nov to Feb 9am to 4pm, rest of the year 9am to 5pm; 25 km south of Washington DC on the George Washington Memorial Pkwy., ☎703-780-2000)* is an inevitable destination, an absolute must that annually ranks as the second-most-visited historic residence in the United States after the White House.

To reach Mount Vernon by car from downtown Washington D.C., take 14th Street south over the bridge that spans the Potomac. Then take exit 11A and travel along George Washington Memorial Parkway in the direction of National Airport. By public transit, take the yellow Metro line to Huntington station. From there, take bus number 11P to the estate.

The Mount Vernon plantation is set on a rise that provides a splendid view of the west bank of the Potomac River. The property of the Washington family, which originally covered over one thousand hectares, was granted to John Washington by Lord Culpeper in 1674. In 1735, George Washington's father settled his family here for a few years before he decided give it to Lawrence Washington, George's older half-brother, who named the estate Vernon in honour of his former commander, Admiral Edward Vernon of the British Navy. George was only 11 years old when his father died, and he became very close to Lawrence, whom he visited often on the plantation. When the latter died in 1752, George Washington took possession of the estate and rented it to his sister-in-law. In 1759, Washington returned from campaigns against the French and the Native Americans, wed Martha Custis, mother of two children from a previous marriage and, naturally, settled his new family at Mount Vernon. In this era, Washington began work to enlarge the main house. The estate was practically self-sufficient: wheat and corn were cultivated, cotton and silk were spun, butter was churned, wine grapes were harvested, flour was milled, fish was salted, and so-on. There was even a cobbler on the premises. The full operation of the estate required no fewer than 200 slaves, who were owned by George Washington. According to his last wishes, these slaves were enfranchised after the death of his wife, Martha Custis Washington.

Washington enjoyed retreating to this beautiful Mount Vernon house. He was particularly fond of the agricultural aspect of the place, which in his words constituted "the most delicious of occupations". He lived here from 1752 to 1774, when he was elected to the First Continental Congress in Philadelphia. His political years, and then the American Revolution, kept him far from Mount Vernon, but against the hopes of some he chose to leave his position as Commander in Chief of the Army at the end of the war against the English and return to Mount Vernon. During the six years that followed, Washington lived in his Virginia home and had it enlarged once again. However, anarchy and dissension among the founding colonies put the young Republic in peril, so the Constitutional Convention of Philadelphia was created in 1787 to draw up a new constitution. The hero of the Revolution was asked to preside over this convention, which took him away from Mount Vernon yet again. Once the American Constitution was enacted by the 13 original states, the electoral college selected George Washington as the first American President. After eight years as head

Tour L: The Outskirts of Washington

of the nation, Washington declined the offer of a third term as president and retired from public life in March 1797 to while away quiet days at his cherished Virginia plantation. His retirement was cut short two years later, when the President died of quinsy on December 14, 1799, at the age of 67 years. His remains were interred on the grounds in the family vault overlooking the Potomac. His wife Martha died two years later and was lain to rest at his side. After their deaths, the house remained in the Washington family for several years, but gradually it was abandoned. A woman from North Carolina named Ann Pamela Cunningham undertook to save the estate from ruin. To that end she founded the Mount Vernon Ladies Association and launched a fundraising campaign to amass the $200,000 necessary to acquire the plantation. Since 1858, the former home of George Washington has been the property of the Mount Vernon Ladies Association, which has restored the estate buildings in its aim of showing visitors the quality of the President's daily life before he ascended to the highest office in the land.

In the two-story main house, which still contains its original furniture, it is possible to visit the **Large Dining Room** in which Washington enjoyed entertaining crowds of guests. This is the very room in which he received news of his election as the first American president, on April 14, 1789. The **Study Room** served as his office, where he occupied himself with plantation business and meetings with his managers. The room houses many objects that belonged to Washington, as well as the leather armchair that he used during the eight years of his presidency. On the upper floor, the bedrooms may be visited, including the **Master Bedroom**, in which Washington died December 14, 1799.

The **tomb of George and Martha Washington** is set in a shady corner outside. Behind a simple, cast-iron gate, under a vault, rest the two marble coffins, each engraved with a simple inscription – one reads "Washington", and the other reads, "Martha, Consort of Washington".

OUTDOORS

Pierre Charles L'Enfant, architect of the city of Washington, had envisioned a new capital of expansive green spaces crisscrossed by large open avenues. Although he was dismissed by President Washington, the main thrust of his project was pursued and Washington became a majestic capital embellished by urban parks such as the Mall and large areas left wild, like Rock Creek Park, Theodore Roosevelt Island and Montrose Park. All of these wide open spaces are perfect for relaxing or participating in a variety of sporting activities. Washington is also a riverside city, and sailors and river-cruise fans will want to visit some of the interesting spots near the city's marina.

PARKS

Rock Creek Park ★★ *(3545 Williamsburg Lane NW, DC 20008, ☎282-1063)* is one of the largest urban parks in the United States. Spread out over 710 hectares, from the mouth of Rock Creek to the border of the District of the Columbia, it offers visitors many trails for walking, horseback riding and bicycling. In addition, **Pierce Mill** *(☎426-6908)*, which is open to the public; the **Nature Center** *(5200 Glover Rd. NW, ☎426-6829)*, which houses a planetarium and offers various educational programs aimed at children and adults of all ages; and the vestiges of **Fort Stevens**, which was erected during the Civil War and was the site of the only battle of that conflict to have taken place in the District, are all located withing the park limits. With tennis courts, two nine-hole golf courses, playgrounds and more than 30 picnic areas, Rock Creek Park is a favourite destination of Washingtonians for weekend family outings. Camping is not permitted in the park.

For a list of activities in Rock Creek Park contact:
Superintendent, Rock Creek Park, 3545 Williamsburg Lane NW, Washington, DC 20008-1207, ☎282-1063.

Theodore Roosevelt Island H *(cross the Theodore Roosevelt Bridge, turn right on George Washington Memorial Pkwy., then take the Theodore Roosevelt Island exit, ☎703-285-2598)* is a little island right in the middle of the Potomac River between Georgetown and Arlington that has been left in its natural state. It is crisscrossed by a few walking trails and is home to the **Roosevelt Memorial**, a large statue of former American President Theodore Roosevelt. The island's park wardens will organize guided walking tours with seven days advance notice; contact the telephone number above. This small island is basically made up of marshland and woods, and shelters very interesting flora and fauna. If you look closely, you can spot muskrats, wild rabbits and turtles, as well as a number of bird species including starlings.

OUTDOOR ACTIVITIES

Hiking

Hiking is an activity that almost everybody can take part in and there are many places in Washington and its surrounding area to do just that. Here is a list of fun walks:

The **George Washington Carver Nature Trail** *(Anacostia Museum, 1901 Fort Pl. SE, Washington, DC 20020, ☎357-2700)* is a enjoyable trail that extends over almost 12 kilometres. The departure point is at Anacostia Museum.

The **Mount Vernon Trail** *(Turkey Run Park, McLean, VA 22101, ☎703-285-2598)* runs almost 30 kilometres along the shore of the Potomac between Theodore Roosevelt Island and George Washington's ancestral home in Mount Vernon, Virginia. It is a very pretty path that offers magnificent views of the Potomac, the city of Washington and the old city of Alexandria.

Rock Creek Park *(3545 Williamsburg Lane NW, Washington, DC 20008, ☎282-1063)* offers walkers a selection of several equally lovely hikes. This magnificent, 710-hectare urban park overlooking Rock Creek is crisscrossed by a gamut of trails, including a 2.5-kilometre-long "getting-back-in-shape" trail that starts near Calvert Street and Connecticut Avenue. Maps of the park trails are available from the superintendent's office, at the address mentioned above. Guided tours of the park are also organized. For more information, contact the park superintendent (see p 228).

Theodore Roosevelt Island *(Washington, DC, ☎703-285-2598)* is a small, serene island in the middle of the Potomac between the cities of Georgetown and Arlington. Although it has been left to grow wild, walking excursions are possible on a little, three-kilometre path laid out for this very purpose. Visitors can admire the protected flora and fauna of this ecosystem in complete tranquillity because bicycles and automobiles are not permitted on the island.

People can also take a stroll along the C & O Canal and admire the many locks that were built here to make the river navigable. The **Chesapeake & Ohio Canal** stretches over 195 kilometres between the cities of Georgetown and Cumberland, Maryland, and is bordered on either side by narrow towpaths that nowadays are overrun by walkers and cyclists. For more information on the types of excursions that are possible here, contact:

C & O National Historic Park, P.O. Box 4, Sharpsburg, MD 21782, ☎301-739-4200, ≠301-413-2600.

Great Falls Park *(parking $4; Visitor Center every day 10am to 5pm; 9200 Old Dominion Dr., Great Falls, VA 22066, ☎703-285-2965, ≠703-285-2223)* is located on the outskirts of Washington and is lined with a total of about 26 kilometres of pretty walking trails.

Biking

Washington and its surrounding area offer great possibilities for two-wheelers. Whether on the paths of Rock Creek Park or on the banks of the Potomac, cyclists can enjoy a variety of beautiful outings. It is also possible to pedal all the way to Mount Vernon along the **Mount Vernon Trail**, which runs along the Potomac and offers spectacular views of Washington and Alexandria.

A number of companies rent bicycles and also organize guided cycling tours of the major tourist attractions in the capital region, including the following:

Big Wheel Bikes, 1034 33rd St. NW, Washington, DC 20007, ☎337-0254, ≈333-7035.

Bike the Sites, 3417 Quesada St. NW, Washington, DC 20015, ☎/≈966-8662, bikesites@aol.com.

Bikes may also be rented from:

Thompson Boat Center, 2900 Virginia Ave. NW, Washington, DC 20037, ☎333-9543.

Washington Sailing Marina, 1 Marina Dr., Alexandria, VA 22314, ☎(703) 548-9027.

Horseback Riding

Rock Creek Park is home to a large network of over 23 kilometres of bridle paths. To tour the park on horseback contact:

Rock Creek Park Horse Center, 5100 Glover Rd. NW, Washington, DC 20015, ☎362-0117.

Outdoor Activities 231

Golf

The federal capital of the United States is blessed with several beautiful golf courses, some right in the heart of the city and others on its outskirts. Here is a list of the main courses:

East Potomac Park Golf Course, Ohio Dr. at Hains Point, Washington, DC, ☎488-8087.

Langstone Golf Course, corner of 26th St. and Benning Rd. NE, Washington, DC 20018, ☎397-8638.

Rock Creek Golf Course, Rock Creek Park, corner of 16th St. and Rittenhouse St. NW, Washington, DC 20015, ☎882-7332.

Miniature Golf

East Potomac Park Golf Course, Ohio Dr. at Hains Point, Washington, DC, ☎488-8087.

Tennis

Washington offers a few public courts that are open to Washingtonians and visitors alike. Courts must be reserved in person in advance at the Rock Creek Park service centre.

Rock Creek Park, corner of 16th St. and Kennedy St. NW, Washington, DC, ☎722-5949.

There are also courts at:

East Potomac Park, 1090 Ohio Dr. SW, Washington, DC, ☎554-5962.

Skating

Every winter, when the water in the **Reflecting Pool** in front of Lincoln Memorial freezes, Washingtonians don their skates and

232 Outdoors

enjoy the free feeling of gliding about in the majestic setting of the Mall.

At the same time of year it is possible to skate along the **C&O Canal** in Georgetown. Check on ice conditions ahead of time, though, by contacting the **Visitor Center**.

Swimming

Although many hotels have swimming pools available to guests, it is also possible to have a dip at one of Washington's public pools. A list of these is available from the **Department of Recreation and Parks**, Aquatics Branch, ☎576-6436.

Water Sports

Washington is a true water town – at one time it was an important river port. Today, a number of companies organize cruises on the Potomac, sailing trips, and simple canoe and pedal-boat outings on the artificial lake called the Tidal Basin.

Cruises

The following companies organize short guided cruises on the Potomac, allowing for a whole other way to discover the capital.

Capitol River Cruises *(1301 Parkvale Rd., Rockville, MD 20853, ☎301-460-7447)* offers 50-minute guided tours of the capital that leave daily from the port in Georgetown.

The **Dandy Restaurant Cruise Ship** *(Zero Prince St., Alexandria, VA 22314, ☎703-683-6076, ≈301-683-7442)* organizes outings on the Potomac that combine cruising and dining. A perfectly romantic atmosphere is guaranteed in its magnificent marble and mahogany interior dining room, as the ship meanders the river, navigating under the bridges of the capital and serving up beautiful views of Washington to accompany passengers' meals.

DC Ducks: The Boats on Wheels *(every day 10am to 4pm; 2640 Reed St. NE, Washington, DC 20018, ☎832-9800, ⇝832-9040)* proposes guided tours of the city in an "amphibious" vehicle. Departures are from Union Station.

Odyssey Cruises *(Gangplank Marina, 600 Water St. SW, Washington, DC 20024, ☎488-6010, ⇝488-6011)* and **Spirit Cruises** *(Pier 4, corner of 6th St. and Water St. SW, Washington, DC 20024, ☎554-8000, ⇝488-1330)* both offer dinner cruises on the Potomac.

The **Potomac Riverboat Co.** *(205 The Strand, Alexandria, VA 22314, ☎703-684-0580, ⇝703-548-9001)* possesses a magnificent boat from which passengers can admire some of Washington's biggest tourist attractions, including the Lincoln Memorial, the Jefferson Memorial, the Washington Monument and the Kennedy Center for the Performing Arts. The duration of the tour is about 90 minutes.

For a more rustic experience, visitors can relive the journey of the old boatmen of the C & O Canal by travelling this once busy commercial waterway on a horse-drawn barge. To take part in this unique experience contact **C & O Canal Barge Rides** *(Apr to Oct; P.O. Box 4, Sharpsburg, MD 21782, ☎301-739-4200)*. Departures are from Georgetown. While on board, a park service guard in period costume explains the history of the construction of this amazing canal.

Canoeing, Kayaking and Pedal Boating

All sorts of boats may be rented from **Thompson Boat Center** *(Apr to Oct, every day 6am to 8pm; 2900 Virginia Ave. NW, Washington, DC 20037, ☎333-9543)*, so visitors can participate in their favourite water sports. Courses for beginners are also offered.

To take a little pedal-boat tour of the Tidal Basin, located in the heart of Washington, head to **Tidal Basin Pedal Boats** *($7 an hour, $1.75 for an additional fifteen minutes; Mar to Sep, every day 10am to 6pm; Ohio Dr. NW at the Tidal Basin, Washington, DC 20242, ☎484-0206)*.

234　Outdoors

Sailing and Windsurfing

Windsurfing buffs will be pleasantly surprised to discover that it is possible to take part in this sport on the Potomac just a few yards from downtown. Small sailboats and windsurfers can be rented at the **Washington Sailing Marina** *(Apr to Oct, every day 9am to 8pm; 1 Marina Dr., Alexandria, VA 22314, ☎703-548-9027)*. For those who are interested, courses are also available.

ACCOMMODATIONS

This chapter offers a wide selection of hotels, listed by district and in order of price, from the least to the most expensive. The prices mentioned were in effect at press time and apply to a double-occupancy room in the high season. However, Washington's numerous hotels offer different discounts depending on the time of year and the length of the stay. Several hotels also offer discounts to corporate employees or members of automobile clubs. Hotels with vacancies sometimes grant guests certain little advantages, such as a room with a better view for the regular price or again, a reduced rate. Do not hesitate to inquire about these kinds of specials upon making your reservations. Also, before you leave, make sure to reserve your accommodations according to the district in which you wish to stay, and be sure to compare the prices and the discounts. Finally, note that you must add the 13% hotel tax plus to a $1.50 occupancy fee per night to the price of the room.

Washington hotels are generally of high quality. Rooms are, for the most part, spacious, modern and air conditioned. Many hotels also have very well-equipped fitness centres and swimming pools. Since a lot of business people visit Washing-

> ## Ulysses' Favourites
>
> **Accommodations**
>
> For luxury:
> Carlton (p 243) and Willard Inter-Continental Washington (p 244).
>
> For business people:
> Washington Marriott (p 248), Renaissance Mayflower Hotel (p 249) and Loews L'Enfant Plaza (p 239).
>
> For charming little hotels:
> Georgetown Dutch Inn (p 255) and George Washington University Inn (p 250).
>
> Rooms with a view:
> Watergate Hotel (p 253), Hotel Washington (p 242), Hay-Adams Hotel (p 243) and Loews L'Enfant Plaza (p 239).
>
> Excellent value for your money:
> Red Roof Inn (p 240) and Georgetown Dutch Inn (p 255).

ton, a good number of hotels are marvellously well situated close to downtown and to the major tourist attractions.

Bed-and-breakfasts are also popular in Washington. These entail staying in the room of a private home; however, you might have to share a bathroom. This kind of accommodation offers the advantage of partaking in a more family-type ambiance. Breakfast is always included in the price of the room.

To obtain a complete list of bed and breakfasts, you can apply to one or the other of the following associations, which can also make reservations for you.

The Hotel-Rate Merry-Go-Round

Since most visitors to Washington are businesspeople and civil servants, hotel prices are generally higher during the week and during the school year than during school breaks, in summer and on weekends. Before you leave, make sure to inquire about major discounts that may apply during your stay. Above all, do not hesitate to shop around, since Washington's biggest hotels offer up to 50% discounts, sometimes more, in summer. Therefore you can stay at a luxury hotel, with all its added bonuses, for about the same price you'd pay for a lesser-quality hotel or some inns. This is why you should compare rates and not think twice about calling the establishments you thought might have been too pricey.

Bed & Breakfast Accommodations, P O Box 12011, Washington, DC 20005, ☎328-3510, ≈332-3885.

Bed & Breakfast League/ Sweet Dreams & Toast, P O Box 9490, Washington, DC 20016-9490, ☎363-7767, ≈363-8396.

Those on limited budgets can stay at a **youth hostel**. The Washington International AYH-Hostel (see p 240) is conveniently located near the downtown area and the Washington Convention Center.

Staying at **universities** is not always easy because of the numerous restrictions that apply to this type of accommodation, only available in summer, namely during school holidays. Moreover, reservations must be made long in advance. Nevertheless, this is a more economical option that can prove appealing. Those with an international student card (which should be procured prior to departure) can expect to pay between $20 and $35, plus taxes. Prices are slightly higher for those without this card. Note that breakfast is not included in the price, though there are cafeterias on the premises where you can eat for little money. In Washington, **Howard University** and the **Catholic University of America** welcome visitors during certain periods of the year. Unfortunately, George Washington University does not offer any accommodations to tourists, though it might prove interesting to students, as it is well situated near major tourist attractions and the pleasant Dupont Circle district. Only students planning on an extended stay in the capital (at least a month) can get a room here. The other universities are a little off the beaten path and hard to reach, but may be worth your while nonetheless. Their addresses are listed below:

Howard University *($20; Shaw-Howard U. metro)*, Rev. James Coleman, Resident Life Office, 2401 4th Street NW, Washington, DC 20059, ☎806-5661 or 806-5653.

Catholic University *($22; Brookland-CUA metro)*, Office of Conferences and Summer Programs, 108 St. Bonaventure Hall, Washington, DC 20064, ☎319-5277.

Georgetown University *($20; Farragut North or Farragut West metro)*, G. U. Office of Housing and Conferences Services, Washington, DC 20057, ☎687-4560.

If you prefer to book a room in or around Washington through a hotel reservation service, contact one of the following agencies:

Capitol Reservations Tour & Travel Services, 1730 Rhode Island Avenue NW, Suite 1114, Washington, DC 20036, ☎452-1270 or 1-800-VISIT-DC, ≈452-0537.

Accommodations Express, 801 Asbury Avenue, 6th Floor, Ocean City, NJ 08226-3625, ☎(609) 391-2100 or 1-800-974-7666, ≈(609) 525-0111.

Hotel Reservation Network, 8140 Walnut Hill Lane, Suite 203, Dallas, TX 75231, ☎(214) 361-7311 or 1-800-964-6835, ≈(214) 361-7299.

CAPITOL HILL AREA

Because it is lined with government offices and prestigious buildings such as the Library of Congress, this district is rather limited in choice of accommodations. Furthermore, venturing too far into the South East is not advised. We have therefore tried to give you a wider choice by including an establishment

Capitol Hill Area

south of the Mall, on L'Enfant Plaza, even though it isn't part of the Capitol Hill area.

The **Capitol Hill Guest House** *($65 sb and bkfst incl., $90 pb and bkfst incl.; 101 5th St. NE, Capitol South metro, ☎547-1050 or 1-800-261-2768)* is a three-story home that has been converted into a hotel and offers rooms that are clean and well-kept, though a bit lifeless. Some rooms have private bathrooms. Warm and friendly welcome. Reservations required in advance. Smoking not allowed.

Located in a heavily administrative part of town, at the gates of the Mall and Capitol Hill, the **Loews L'Enfant Plaza Hotel** *($210; ≡, ☉, ≈, ℛ, pb; 480 L'Enfant Plaza SW, 20024, L'Enfant Plaza metro, ☎484-1000, ≠646-4456)* is a luxury hotel whose every room is equipped with a small balcony affording splendid views over the city and the Potomac. These elegantly furnished rooms have been designed to ensure great comfort and provide all necessary services to businesspeople. The large bathrooms even put a radio and a television set at your disposal. The hotel also houses several restaurants and bars where you can enjoy a delicious meal or snack on the terrace. Moreover, the establishment boasts a magnificent rooftop swimming pool, open all year round. Ideally situated behind the impressive Smithsonian Institution, only a stone's throw from Washington's other most beautiful museums, the hotel also offers guests direct access to the L'Enfant Plaza metro via its elevator. Though sure to satisfy those seeking opulent surroundings, the place is regrettably located in the very heart of the L'Enfant Plaza complex, an unfortunate example of tasteless architectural modernism.

DOWNTOWN

Though the area surrounding the White House is also part of downtown, we thought it best to incorporate the hotels of the latter area in the following section in order to respect the division set out in the "Exploring" chapter. The hotels presented below are thus located within a perimetre stretching from Union Station to the east, the White House to the west, the Mall to the south and K Street to the north.

240 Accommodations

Washington's youth hostel, the **Washington International AYH-Hostel** *($19 for members, $22 for non-members; ≡, sb; 1009 11th St. NW, Metro Center metro, ☎737-2333)*, is located one block north of the Convention Center, in a relatively safe neighbourhood near the downtown area. This well-kept hostel contains 250 beds distributed throughout small, 8- to 18-bed dormitories, with separate quarters for women and men. An equipped kitchen, lockers for personal effects or luggage and a laundromat are also at guests' disposal. Moreover, the very affable staff organizes group activities such as city tours, movies and theatre outings. It is best to reserve by telephone at least 24 hours in advance. If you wish to mail-in your reservation, you should do so two weeks before leaving.

The **Hotel Harrington** *($75; ≡, pb, ℜ; at 11th St. and E St. NW, 20004-1398, Metro Center or Federal Triangle metro, ☎628-8140 or 1-800-424-8532)* hardly distinguishes itself from other hotels for the beauty of its rooms. Indeed, they are rather timeworn, gloomily decorated and somewhat noisy. The bathrooms are very small, but clean. The establishment's main asset is indisputably its location in the very heart of downtown, a stone's throw from the Old Post Office and the gates of the National Theater, Warner Theater and Ford's Theater. Guests can park at the hotel for $6.50 a day. The hotel also boasts a small laundromat on the third floor near the elevators; tokens are available at the front desk.

In the very heart of the small Chinatown stands a relatively modern red-brick building that houses the **Red Roof Inn** *($89; ≡, ⊘, parking; 500 H St. NW, 20001, Gallery Place metro, ☎289-5959 or 1-800-THE-ROOF, ≈682-9152)*, a very worthwhile choice for the location, rates and the quality of its rooms. The hotel's 197 rooms are fairly spacious, simply yet attractively decorated and equipped with two double beds. The bathrooms are also large, completely redone and very clean. Guests here also have access to a laundromat. A very respectable place, located near the main attractions of the Mall and downtown.

The Best Western hotel chain boasts an establishment in Chinatown: the **Best Western Downtown Capitol Hill** *($115 bkfst incl.; ≡, ℜ; 724 3rd St. NW, 20001, Union Station metro, ☎842-4466 or 1-800-242-4831, ≈842-4831)*. The fairly sizeable rooms offer two double beds or a queen-size bed. The hotel also houses a restaurant where you will be served a continental-style breakfast. Free parking for guests.

The **Days Inn Premier Convention Center Hotel** *($115; ≡, ⊘, ≈, ℜ; 1201 K St. NW, 20005, McPherson Square metro, ☎842-1020 or 1-800-562-3350, ⇝898-0100)* has large pleasant rooms decorated in warm tones and with modern-style furnishings. The good-size bathrooms are equipped with hair dryers. At the entrance of each room are a closet with an ironing board, an iron and an in-room safe. The establishment also boasts a fitness centre and a relaxing swimming pool. Moreover, the place is well situated, only a minute from the Convention Center and near both McPherson Square and Franklin Square.

The **Crowne Plaza Washington DC** *($225; ≡, ⊘, ℜ, ≈; at 14th St. and K St. NW, 20005, McPherson Square metro, ☎682-0111, ⇝682-9525)* is a very beautiful Beaux-Arts-style hotel with very reasonable rates in the low season and on weekends. You can get a lovely room here for as little as $69 during these periods. The very lovely lobby, whose archway is adorned with finely decorated coffers, is indicative of the comfort and refinement of the rooms. Indeed, the entirely renovated rooms are both cosy and elegantly furnished. Each of them is graced with a king-size bed or two double beds and a small closet with a safe in which you can keep your valuables. All rooms also boast an iron and ironing board as well as cable television. Admirably situated, a few blocks from the White House and by Franklin Square, this hotel is also in proximity of the Mall's main museums as well as the Dupont Circle district, for your restaurant outings.

The **Madison Hotel** *($225; ≡, pb, ⊘, parking, ℜ; at 15th St. and M St. NW, 20005, McPherson Square metro, ☎862-1600 or 1-800-424-8577, ⇝785-1255)* is one of the most beautiful hotels in the American capital. Its exceedingly refined interior is decorated with Louis XVI-style antique furnishings. Need we mention that the rooms are equally luxurious and very comfortable? The establishment is also renowned for the cuisine served in its restaurant, Le Montpellier.

The interior design of the **Grand Hyatt Washington** *($230; pb, ≡, ⊘, ≈, ℜ, parking; opposite the Washington Convention*

Center, 1000 H St. NW, 20001, Metro Center metro, ☎582-1234 or 1-800-233-1234, ≈637-4781) is very impressive, with its large atrium topped by a glass roof allowing an abundance of natural light to pass through it. In this stunning interior garden, guests can have coffee or a meal by an artificial pond in the middle of which stands a white grand piano on a small "promontory". A wonderfully quiet and relaxing spot. Two glass-wall elevators go up to the rooms, giving guests a lovely bird's-eye view of this elegant central garden, with its lagoon, waterfalls and lush plants. The 900 fair-sized rooms are also furnished and designed for maximum comfort. The only quibble here is that for an establishment of this category, one would expect greater attentiveness and amiability from the staff.

Conveniently located in the American capital's business district, the **Westin Washington, D.C. City Center Hotel** ($229; ≡, pb, ℛ, bar, parking, ⊘; 1400 M St. NW, 20005, McPherson Square metro, ☎429-1700 or 1-800-WESTIN-1, ≈785-0786) offers sure value. The hotel boasts large, attractive and very comfortable rooms, in the tradition of this luxury hotel chain.

NEAR THE WHITE HOUSE

The establishments mentioned below are located in one of Washington's most high-class districts, which means they are rather expensive. The advantage is that these prestigious places are close to all the tourist attractions. Business travellers will also enjoy certain privileges such as luxury, refinement and the proximity of downtown. Nightlife and restaurant options are rather limited in this area, though.

Conveniently located on Pennsylvania Avenue, on the edge of downtown, is the **Hotel Washington** ($185; ≡, pb, ℛ, ⊘; at 15th St. and Pennsylvania Ave. NW, 20004, Metro Center metro, ☎638-5900 or 1-800-424-9540, ≈638-1595), from which you can get a good view of the White House, the presidential residence. The establishment boasts 350 large and spacious rooms offering great comfort as well as a pleasant rooftop terrace, whence you can enjoy the view over the city. The hotel's current specials include a $99 family package with lodging and breakfast for four people.

Near the White House

The austere exterior of the **JW Marriott Hotel** *($200; ≈, parking, ☉, ≈, ℜ; 1331 Pennsylvania Ave. NW, 20004, Metro Center metro, ☎393-2000, ⇌626-6991)* is deceiving. Despite its dull architecture, this huge establishment with close to 800 rooms is an excellent choice, successfully combining comfort and refinement in a contemporary setting. Moreover, the hotel is linked to an adjacent shopping arcade where you will find such stores as a florist, a souvenir shop and a hairdressing salon, among others.

The Capital Hilton *($250; ≈, pb, ☉, ℜ, bar, parking; at 16th St. and K St. NW, 20036, McPherson Square metro, ☎393-1000 or 1-800-HILTONS, ⇌639-5784)* is a luxury hotel located only a stone's throw from the White House. You might just rub shoulders with a few of the celebrities visiting Washington who stay here.

Situated on Lafayette Square, opposite the White House, the **Hay-Adams Hotel** *($265; ≈, pb, ☉, ℜ; 1 Lafayette Sq., corner of 16th St. and H St. NW, 20006, Farragut West metro, ☎638-6600 or 1-800-424-5054, ⇌638-2716)* was named after two men, President Lincoln's private secretary, John Hay, and Henry Adams, President Adams' grandson, both of whom built their homes on a piece of land across from the White House in 1884. Their private mansions soon became the meccas of high society, attracting politicians, writers, artists and other notables. In 1927, a property developer had the two villas razed to have this magnificent hotel, which was named the Hay-Adams House, built in their stead. Designed according to an Italian Renaissance-inspired model, the structure was later adorned with a combination of styles, blending a somewhat Tudor or Elizabethan, somewhat Italian interior with Doric, Ionic and Corinthian columns. The establishment remains a marvellous combination of luxury, elegance and grand comfort. Its restaurant, Le Lafayette, is one of the most prized in the city.

If you have a taste for luxury, **The Carlton** *($320; ≈, pb, ℜ, ☉; 923 16th St., at K St. NW, 20006, ☎638-2626 or 1-800-562-5661)* is a real gem. The Italian Renaissance-style interior exudes both elegance and refinement. You will first notice the grand lobby's magnificent, opulent coffered ceiling, from which impressive crystal chandeliers hang. This prestige establishment, which frequently welcomes heads of state, opened its doors in 1929 and has since been listed as an historic monument. Furnished with beautiful antiques and flooded with natural light pouring in through large picture windows, this hotel is without a doubt one of the most beautiful in the city. The magnificent rooms are spacious and each equipped with a large marble bathroom, a bar, a fax machine and an in-room safe. The hotel also boasts a renowned restaurant, the Lespinasse, where guests can enjoy gourmet French cuisine. The Library Lounge, whose walls are adorned with mahogany woodwork and old portraits, is a relaxing place to have a drink in a cosy ambiance.

The jewel of the capital's hotels, the **Willard Inter-Continental Washington** *($365; ≡, ⊘, pb, ℜ; 1401 Pennsylvania Ave. NW, 20004, Federal Triangle or Metro Center metro, ☎628-9100 or 1-800-327-0200, ⇥637-7326)* is a luxury hotel set up in a Beaux-Arts-style building with a sloping roof. The establishment prides itself on having played host to a good many American presidents and crowned heads from the world over in its particularly elegant, antique-furnished lounges. The lobby, for its part, boasts finely decorated high-coffered ceilings enhanced by sparkling crystal chandeliers. The large and spacious rooms are carefully arranged down to the smallest detail. Recently renovated and graced with stylish furnishings, the establishment offers 340 luxurious rooms equipped with a mini bar and fax machine, and over 35 superb suites. Located a stone's throw from the White House, on distinguished Pennsylvania Avenue, the Willard is Washington's most prestigious hotel. This is the place where Reverend Martin Luther King Jr. wrote his legendary speech, *I Have a Dream*...

DUPONT CIRCLE AND ADAMS MORGAN

This section lists the high-quality establishments in the Dupont Circle district and its surrounding area. Also included are a few hotels in Adams Morgan, located a little farther north of Dupont Circle, another charming neighbourhood on account of its shops and ethnic restaurants.

You can enjoy budget accommodation at the **Washington International Student Center** *($17 bkfst incl.; sb, tv; 2451 18th St. NW, 20009, Woodley Park-Zoo metro, ☎667-7681 or 1-800-567-4150)*, which offers six- to eight-bed dormitories.

Dupont Circle and Adams Morgan 245

The place also boasts two kitchens where you can prepare your own meals and a common room in which guests like to chat or watch TV. In the pleasant Adams Morgan district, near scores of ethnic restaurants, this hostel has a very warm and relaxed ambiance.

On a small and very quiet residential street right in the centre of Adams Morgan stands a red-brick house, three floors of which harbour a bed-and-breakfast, the **Adams Inn** *($55 bkfst incl. and sb, $70 ≡, pb and bkfst incl.; tv; 1744 Lanier Pl. NW, 20009, Woodley Park-Zoo metro, ☎745-3600 or 1-800-578-6807, ⇝319-7958)*, run by charming owners. The rooms are simple but clean, and some are equipped with a double bed and a private or shared bathroom. Reservations and deposit required. Major credit cards accepted. A limited number of parking spaces are available for $7 a night. Note that smoking is forbidden in both the rooms and common spaces. No animals allowed.

You will be very warmly received at the **Windsor Inn** *($69 bkfst incl.; ≡, pb, ℝ; 1842 16th St. NW, 20009, Dupont Circle metro, ☎667-0300 or 1-800-423-9111, ⇝234-3309)*, a small hotel comprising two separate but adjacent buildings. Though the rooms are a little old-fashioned and simply decorated, they are nevertheless relatively large and very comfortable. Moreover, in a city where hotel room prices quickly reach astronomical sums, this place offers guests excellent value for the money. The bathrooms, however, are somewhat small and only equipped with a tiny shower. The establishment also boasts two suites, at $150 for the large and $130 for the smaller one, both located in the main building. The former suite is very pleasant and boasts a cosily furnished living room with a sofa bed, fireplace and television set, as well as a large bedroom equipped with a king-size bed and another television. The suite also overlooks a small courtyard. Certain rooms are reserved for smokers, but these rooms tend to reek of cigarette fumes; it is more advisable to opt for a non-smoking room or light-up outside. The other building has been attractively renovated inside, which confers on it a considerably more pleasant and warmer ambiance than the main building. Try to get a room in this annex instead.

Run by the same owners as the Windsor Inn, the **Embassy Inn** *($69 bkfst incl.; ≡, pb; 1627 16th St. NW, 20009, Dupont*

Circle metro, ☎234-7800 or 1-800-423-9111, ≈234-3309) is a small establishment located in the very heart of Dupont Circle, near scores of small restaurants, cafés and bars. Though the rooms are rather small, their decor somewhat outdated and the bathroom showers of some slightly overused, they will do nonetheless. The charming staff will be delighted to greet you every night with cocktails and petits fours, offered to all clients free of charge. This will give you the opportunity to meet your fellow guests over drinks. A 24-hour fax service is available to hotel customers. Tickets for guided tours of the city as well as subway passes are sold at the hotel's reservation desk.

A charming eight-room boarding house, **The Brenton** ($75 bkfst incl.; pb; 1708 16th St. NW, 20009, Dupont Circle metro, ☎332-5550 or 1-800-673-9042) is popular with gay and lesbian visitors. Conveniently located in an old Victorian-style city house near the gay village in Dupont Circle, this is a good and affordable establishment. Reservations are strongly recommended.

The rooms at the **Holiday Inn Central Washington, DC** ($79; ≡, pb, ℜ, ⊘, ≈; 1501 Rhode Island Ave. NW, 20005, McPherson Square metro, ☎483-2000 or 1-800-248-0016, ≈797-1708) are somewhat lacking in character, but offer quite decent comfort. Brightened up by vivid-coloured patterned curtains and wall-to-wall carpets, these rooms are equipped with modern varnished-wood furniture, color televisions and coffee makers. The bathrooms are stocked with a hair dryer. In warm weather, guests here can relax by the rooftop pool and admire the view of the cityscape.

Somewhat out of the Dupont Circle area, a large, modern red-brick building in proximity of Logan Circle houses the **Travelodge Hotel** ($89 bkfst incl.; ≡, pb, parking, ⊘; 1201 13th St. NW, 20005, McPherson Square metro, ☎1-800-458-2817 or 1-800-578-7878, ≈871-9624). Though the establishment's hallways are not especially cheerful-looking, the fairly small rooms have been entirely renovated and offer good comfort. They are equipped with television sets, queen-size beds or two double beds, small work tables, chests of drawers and small coffee-makers. The bathrooms are surprisingly large and all are pleasantly decorated in maroon and beige. This is one of the chain's more upscale establishments. All rooms are non-smoking.

Dupont Circle and Adams Morgan 247

A block away from the small Dupont Circle, the entirely renovated but slightly dreary **The Hampshire Hotel** *($99; ≡, pb, R, K, ℜ; 1310 New Hampshire Ave. NW, 20036, Dupont Circle metro, ☎296-7600 or 1-800-368-5691, ≈293-2476)* offers 82 large identical rooms equipped with slightly old-looking 19th-century imitation furniture. They are nevertheless clean and offer either king-size beds or two double beds, as well as an iron and ironing board in the cupboard. The bathrooms are relatively small, but fully equipped. You can get a copy of the *Washington Post* delivered free of charge to your door. Business people can also use the fax service.

The rooms and suites at the **Governor's House Hotel** *($110; ≡, pb, ℜ, ⊘, =, K; 1615 Rhode Island Ave. NW, 20036, Farragut North or Dupont Circle metro, ☎296-2100 or 1-800-821-4367, ≈331-0227)* are of excellent value for your money. The cosy, fully-renovated and relatively large rooms are modernly and comfortably furnished. Some also have kitchenettes. The hotel is conveniently located near Scott circle, between the Dupont Circle area and downtown. Guests can also dine on the premises at Herb's Restaurant.

The 76 rooms of the **Best Western New Hampshire Suites** *($149; ≡, pb, K, ℜ; 1121 New Hampshire Ave. NW, 20037, Farragut North metro, ☎457-0565 or 1-800-762-3777, ≈331-9421)* live up to this hotel chain's standards: spacious, modern and comfortable. Reproductions of abstract paintings adorn the blue-and beige-hued walls of the rooms. Each room is also equipped with a kitchenette and a refrigerator, a coffee maker and microwave oven, as well as a small living room. An iron and ironing board are also provided in every room as is a hair dryer in the bathroom. A basement room has been converted into a laundromat at guests' disposal.

The **Doubletree Hotel Park Terrace** *($155; ≡, pb; 1515 Rhode Island Ave. NW, 20005, Dupont Circle or Farragut North metro, ☎232-7000, ≈332-8436)* offers simple but comfortable and well-illuminated rooms. The bathrooms are equipped with a shower/bath and a hair dryer. Also provided in the rooms are a mini bar, a coffee maker, an iron and ironing board as well as a large closet.

The staff at the **Quality Hotel Downtown** *($160; ≡, pb, K, ℜ, ⊘, ≈; 1315 16th St. NW, 20036, Farragut North metro,*

☎232-8000 or 1-800-368-5689, ≈667-9827) seem to be constantly overworked. The hotel itself must have seen better days. The establishment's hallways give you a first glimpse of things to come in the rooms, namely a somewhat dreary and badly preserved interior. Though the rooms are sizeable, they are charmless and could use some renovations: the faded walls need a paint job and the stained wall-to-wall carpeting needs to be changed. The bathrooms, for their part, are rather small and not always sparklingly clean. The management doesn't seem to want to do anything about the sad state of the rooms. Parking is available at extra charge. The hotel houses a laundromat, for which you will need a good handful of quarters. Unfortunately, the fitness centre and swimming pool are located outside the hotel itself.

The **Embassy Square, A Summerfield Suites Hotel** *($179 bkfst incl.; ≡, pb, ≈, ℜ, ⊘; 2000 N St. NW, 20036, Dupont Circle metro, ☎659-9000 or 1-800-424-2999, ≈429-9546)* has nothing but different-sized suites, making it an ideal place for families or for extended stays. The simply decorated but tasteful rooms are pleasing. The one-bedroom suites comprise a bedroom with a small bathroom, a walk-in closet, a double bed and a living room with sofa bed to accommodate an extra person, as well as a desk. They also boast a fully equipped kitchen, with dishwasher, refrigerator, coffee maker, stove and microwave oven. Also on the premises is an outdoor pool surrounded by deckchairs and parasols where you can relax after a long day out on the town. The establishment also has a laundromat. Conveniently located near Dupont Circle and its restaurants, the place can be a real deal for families with its discounts packages.

The **Washington Marriott** *($179; ≡, pb, ℜ, ⊘, ≈, parking; 1221 22nd St. NW, 20037, Dupont Circle metro, ☎872-1500, ≈466-5714)* boasts a huge lobby with green-and-white marble floors, covered with large, richly coloured carpets, as well as emerald-green-striped crimson sofas and armchairs. The establishment has 418 rooms on nine floors, which are relatively large and attractively decorated with wallpaper enhanced by a frieze whose colours match the lobby's. The walls are adorned with a large mirror as well as paintings depicting Asian scenes. The bathrooms are decent and fully equipped. You will also find an iron and ironing board in the closet.

Built around a large open area pompously decorated with Greek columns, lush plants and waterfalls that surround the tables of a small café, the suites of the **Embassy Suites Hotel Downtown** *($189; ≡, pb, ℝ, ℛ, ☉, ≈; 1250 22nd St. NW, 20037, Dupont Circle metro, ☎857-3388 or 1-800-EMBASSY, ⇸293-3173)* consist of a room that functions as both a living room and dining room. Each of them boasts a sofa bed for two, a small kitchen equipped with a refrigerator, a microwave oven and a coffee maker, as well as a large and cosy bedroom. Fully renovated and well-kept, the Embassy is an excellent choice. There is also a small souvenir shop on the main floor.

We've had warmer welcomes than at the **Dupont Plaza Hotel** *($200; ≡, pb, ℝ, ℛ; 1500 New Hampshire Ave. NW, 20036, Dupont Circle metro, ☎483-6000 or 1-800-841-0003, ⇸328-3265)*, a 314-room hotel located right on the Dupont Circle roundabout. The rooms are somewhat lacking in charm, though they are spacious, relatively comfortable and boast large picture windows that provide plenty of natural light. Decorated with modern-style varnished-wood furnishings from the seventies, they could have offered a little more refinement for the price. On the plus side, the hotel is ideally situated in the very heart of a neighbourhood with plenty of restaurants for all tastes and budgets.

Travellers have come to expect elegance from Hilton-chain hotels. And the **Embassy Row Hilton Hotel** *($240; ≡, pb, ☉, ≈, ℛ, bar; 2015 Massachusetts Ave. NW, 20036, Dupont Circle metro, ☎265-1600 or 1-800-HILTONS, ⇸328-7526)* does not disappoint with its attractive, spacious, elegantly decorated and super-comfortable rooms. This 193-room establishment was recently entirely and tastefully renovated. The large and fully equipped bathrooms are all in marble. Fax services, parking and daily delivery of the *Washington Post* are available upon request. The rooftop swimming pool is only open in summer.

Among the hotels that have marked the history of Washington is the **Renaissance Mayflower Hotel** *($280; ≡, pb, ℛ, ☉, parking, mini bar; 1127 Connecticut Ave. NW, 20036, Farragut North metro, ☎347-3000 or 1-800-HOTELS-1, ⇸466-9082)*, a magnificent four-star establishment steeped in luxury. Its large lobby is paved in Italian marble, has elegant crystal chandeliers, a mahogany reception desk and stylish furnishings. The rooms measure up to the refinement and comfort you would expect from this type of establishment. Spacious and adequately furnished, they are graced with lovely, fully equipped marbled bathrooms. The suites have the added advantage of opening out onto a small private terrace. Nicknamed "The Promenade", the long hallway leading to the Grand Ball Room, where presidential inauguration balls have been held for over 60 years, is like a hall of mirrors enhanced by gilt furnishings, candelabra and magnificent bouquets of flowers. The Café Promenade, with fresco-adorned walls and large crystal chandelier hanging beneath a cupola, recreates a most pleasant Mediterranean ambiance. You can have lunch here while being serenaded by a harpist or guitarist from atop a small balcony. Finally, you can admire the superb proportions and frescoed ceiling of the Chinese Room. Just for the record, Franklin D. Roosevelt resided here for some time after being elected president of the United States. Lyndon B. Johnson, John F. Kennedy and J. Edgar Hoover, for their part, were among the regular clients of this grand Washington hotel, now listed as an historical monument.

FOGGY BOTTOM

The Foggy Bottom district is mid-point between Georgetown and downtown. For the last few years, this area, which essentially used to attract the student population and the African-American community, has become very prized by the middle-classes and civil servants. Though the George Washington University has its headquarters here, the place is hardly a nightlife mecca. There are a few good places in which to stay, however, some of which have acquired worldwide fame, including the Watergate hotel.

Students enrolled in courses at the university any time between May and August can rent a room in one of its residence halls through **George Washington University Housing** *($22 to $35; ≡, K; 2121 I St. NW, 20052, Foggy Bottom metro, ☎994-6688)*. Write to Ms. McNath, Residential Life. Spaces are limited, so make arrangements long in advance.

One of the best places in the district for those seeking affordable accommodation is unquestionably **The George Washington University Inn** *($89; ≡, pb, K, ℝ, ℜ; 824 New*

Hampshire Ave. NW, 20037, Foggy Bottom metro, ☎337-6620 or 1-800-426-4455, ⇝298-7499), a charming little hotel whose very inconspicuous entrance is marked by a small wrought-iron portal. This establishment rents out pleasant, fully renovated suites comprising a bedroom with old drawings of the city of Washington hanging on its walls, a large and very clean bathroom, a living room with television and sofa bed, as well as a small kitchen with a table and chairs in the middle. Particular attention has been paid to the decor, giving the rooms a warm and pleasant ambiance. Moreover, guests are offered a free pass to the university's nearby pool and fitness centre. Simple, perfectly well-kept and located in one of Foggy Bottom's quiet neighbourhoods all make the place a real must.

The history of the **Howard Johnson** *($100; ≡, pb, ℜ, ℝ, ⊘, ≈; 2601 Virginia Ave. NW, 20037, Foggy Bottom metro, ☎965-2700 or 1-800-964-2000, ⇝337-5417)* is tied in with the Watergate scandal, as Gordon Liddy, one of the instigators of the break-in at the Democratic Party headquarters in the Watergate complex, led the entire operation from one of the rooms here. The recently renovated units, some of which have small balconies, are standard to this hotel chain. The establishment also boasts a rooftop swimming pool as well as a sun deck.

Near Washington Circle and the university, the **Doubletree Guest Suites** *($129; ≡, pb, K, ℝ, ≈; 801 New Hampshire Ave. NW, 20037, Foggy Bottom metro, ☎785-2000 or 1-800-222-TREE, ⇝785-9485)* is a hotel that boasts 95 one-room and six two-room suites. The establishment's brown-brick exterior is rather bland, but the suites are altogether modestly and comfortably decorated with simple furniture, but somewhat outdated. The rooms have one or two beds, a large closet, a living room and dining room in one, with a sofa bed that sleeps two, a fully equipped kitchen with dishwasher, stove, microwave oven and refrigerator. The good-size bathrooms are supplied with hair dryers. Guests here also have access to a rooftop swimming pool.

If you want to stay at a suite while you're in the capital, **One Washington Circle** *($150; ≡, pb, K, ℝ, ℜ, ⊘, ≈; 1 Washington Circle NW, 20037, Foggy Bottom metro, ☎872-1680 or 1-800-424-9671, ⇝887-4989)* is a very good choice. The lobby's lacquered-wood walls, as well as the hallway in different shades of blue give a nice touch to the place. You can choose between five suites of various sizes, all of which open out onto a private balcony. The smallest suite, known as the Guest Suite, consists of one room that functions as a bedroom, living room and dining room at once. It boasts a king-size bed, a sofa bed, a small table and television set, a fairly large kitchen equipped with a microwave oven, stove and refrigerator, an attractive and very clean bathroom and a large closet with an iron and ironing board. Guests also benefit from a fitness centre and an outdoor swimming pool. Take note of the establishment's worthwhile weekend discounts.

It goes without saying **St. James Suites** *($185 bkfst incl.; =, pb, K, R, ⊘, ≈; 950 24th St. NW 20037, Foggy Bottom metro, ☎457-0500 or 1-800-852-8512, ⇥659-4492)* is a good hotel, with 195 very lovely suites and a few studios. All are tastefully decorated so that guests feel like they're in an apartment and not in a hotel room. All the units are uniformly divided and furnished with the utmost care for detail. The hotel's marbled lobby creates a harmonious effect by blending contemporary and older furniture. The good-size rooms comprise a television set, a queen-size bed and two double beds. The fully equipped kitchen is both large and functional, boasting the indispensable refrigerator and stove as well as a dishwasher. The living and dining room, with its crimson wall-to-wall carpet and green sofa with earth-coloured stripes, is very tastefully and meticulously decorated. The walls of the white-marbled bathrooms are outlined with a fine flowered pattern. Everything has been done to make guests feel comfortable and at home. The establishment also boasts a fitness centre and a beautiful outdoor swimming pool surrounded by deckchairs.

The **Sheraton City Center** *($195; =, pb, R, ⊘; 1143 New Hampshire Ave. NW, 20037, Foggy Bottom metro, ☎775-0800 or 1-800-526-7495, ⇥775-6950)* is not exactly located on the most attractive stretch of New Hampshire Avenue – it is also right across the street from a gas station! Moreover, we have come to expect a better-kept interior from Sheraton-chain establishments. Indeed, the rooms' furnishings are somewhat decrepit and the stained wall-to-wall carpet could certainly use a change. Decorated in shades of beige and brown, the whole also lacks a little vibrancy. The bathrooms, however, are clean and equipped with hair dryers. For the price, we advise you to consider this place as a last resort!

The Watergate complex is world-famous for the unfortunate events that led to the downfall of President Nixon, but you might forget what happened within its architecturally unique buildings when you see one of the most opulent hotels in Washington: the **Watergate Hotel** *($295; ≡, pb, ℝ, ℛ, ⊙, ≈, parking; 2650 Virginia Ave. NW, 20037, Foggy Bottom metro, ☎965-2300, 1-800-424-2736 or 1-800-225-5843, ≈337-7915)*. Modernism and elegance await you at this establishment, which is right by the Potomac and near the Kennedy Center for the Performing Arts. Recognizable by its modern spiral architecture, the hotel surrounds a small garden. It comes as no surprise that this place offers the highest quality rooms and suites. The establishment also boasts a delightful restaurant, L'Aquarelle, which its French chef strives to keep among the best restaurants in the city. To better cater to its guests, the hotel has a remarkable fitness centre, saunas and an olympic-size swimming pool, as well as a professional in-house masseur. The hotel's huge black-and-white marbled lobby houses luxury boutiques, a hairdressing salon and a few souvenir shops. All in all, a truly superb hotel!

EMBASSY ROW AND KALORAMA

Few hotels line elegant Massachusetts Avenue, nicknamed "Embassy Row", northeast of Sheridan Circle. This stretch is lined more with the sumptuous private mansions built by the 19th-century American plutocracy, much to the delight of present-day visitors. We have therefore supplemented this section with places located in the vicinity, in a posh residential district known as "Kalorama".

Located in a townhouse in the heart of a pleasant neighbourhood, the **Connecticut-Woodley Guest House** *($55; ≡, pb/sb; 2647 Woodley Rd. NW, 20008, Woodley Park-Zoo metro, ☎667-0218, ≈232-0082)* offers spartan rooms with private or shared bathrooms. The biggest rooms are equipped with television sets. Free parking for clients.

You'll be very warmly welcomed at the **Kalorama Guest House** *($60 to $85 bkfst incl.; sb, pb, ≡; 1854 Mintwood Pl. NW, 20009, Woodley Park-Zoo metro, ☎667-6369, ≈319-1262)*, after finding this hard-to-come-by budget hotel. All the rooms in this Victorian house are non-smoking. The telephone and television are in the common room. The place also boasts laundry facilities. Come nightfall, you can enjoy a glass of lemonade or sherry on the patio with your fellow boarders. Parking fee.

At the northwest boundary of the district stands the **Days Inn Uptown on Connecticut Avenue** *($79; ≡, pb, ℝ; 4400 Connecticut Ave. NW, 20008, Van Ness-UDC metro, ☎244-5600 or 1-800-DAYS-INN, ≈244-6794)*, an establishment whose gloomy rooms conform to the norms of the Days Inn chain. A $5 per night fee is charged if you want to park your car on the premises.

You might get lost in the maze of corridors of the **Sheraton Washington** *($150; ≡, pb, ℝ, ~, ℜ; 2660 Woodley Rd. NW, 20008, Woodley Park-Zoo metro, ☎328-2000 or 1-800-325-3535, ≈387-5436)*, a large, cross-shaped hotel with 1,505 luxurious rooms. The busy lobby may explain why the welcome here is short but sweet. The large rooms are elegantly decorated with old pictures on the walls. The bathrooms, however, are slightly less luxurious than the rooms themselves. Each room also has a closet in which you will find an iron and ironing board. Conveniently located in a pleasant neighbourhood and near small restaurants, the Sheraton is a good choice if you don't mind the lack of personality of this type of establishment.

GEORGETOWN

Georgetown is quite possibly the most charming place to stay in Washington, due to its narrow streets, its art galleries and restaurants, as well as the architecture of its little brick houses surrounded by small flower gardens. However, as it is a rather residential district offering little space to big hotels, only very few such places are to be found here. We have nevertheless included two establishments that struck us as the most interesting.

The **Georgetown Dutch Inn** *($110 bkfst incl.; ≡, pb, K, ℝ; 1075 Thomas Jefferson St. NW, 20007, Foggy Bottom metro, ☎337-0900 or 1-800-388-2410, ⇝333-6526)* is a charming little colonial-style inn located in the very heart of Georgetown, near the C&O Canal. Because the subway does not serve Georgetown, the closest metro is Foggy Bottom. Then it's a good fifteen minutes to reach this hotel. Housed in a brick building typical of the district, this cosy establishment is graced with stylish antique furniture, wallpaper, old pictures and gilt-framed mirrors, giving the place the utmost charm. The inn boasts 47 good-sized one-room suites as well as seven other two-room duplexes. The kitchens are fully equipped with a refrigerator, oven and dishwasher. Not only is the hotel undeniably charming, but the staff is most affable.

On the way into Georgetown, near Rock Creek, stands the modern, red-brick building housing the **Four Seasons Hotel** *($345; ≡, pb, ℝ, ⊙, ≈, parking, ℜ; 2800 Pennsylvania Ave. NW, 20007, Foggy Bottom metro, ☎342-0444 or 1-800-268-6282, ⇝944-2076)*, a magnificent place that combines elegance with comfort in an enchanting setting. Guests here can have breakfast in a lovely ding room with picture windows looking out onto a beautiful verdant garden. The rooms are spacious and elegantly decorated with cosy furnishings. Facilities include a fitness centre and a swimming pool as well as the professional massage services.

The pretty red-brick exterior of the Crestar Bank.
The round bell-clock tower and terracotta designs
enhance this building's look. - *L. P.*

A Miró sculpture: one of the works gracing the East Building garden. - *L. P.*

RESTAURANTS

Whether you like French, Indian, Chinese or Italian cuisine, Washington is chock-full of dining options that will tantalize your tastebuds. It would be impossible to include all of the little restaurants that line the streets of the capital, so this chapter simply presents those that have the most to offer.

The restaurants located in the major neighbourhoods of the city are described in this chapter in order of price, from the least to the most expensive. Prices mentioned in this guide, unless otherwise indicated, apply to a meal for one person, excluding tip, taxes and drinks.

$	under $10
$$	$10 to $20
$$$	$20 to $30
$$$$	over $30

The chapter also includes an index of restaurants according to type of cuisine, so you can easily find the establishments that interest you the most.

Ulysses' Favourites

Restaurants

For the terrasse:
    La Tomate (p 271)
    Le Séquoia (p 281)

For the ambiance:
    Marrakech (p 266)
    Raku (p 272)
    Felix (p 276)
    Café Lautrec (p 277)

For fine dining:
    Jin-Ga Restaurant (p 274)
    L'Aquarelle (p 275)
    La Citronelle (p 282)
    La Fourchette (p 278)

For good beer with your meal:
    John Harvard's Brew House (p 264)
    Brasserie Les Halles (p 264)

Washington Restaurants by Type of Cuisine

Steak Houses
Annie's Paramount Steak House (p 272)
Morton's of Chicago Steakhouse (p 274)
Prime Rib Restaurant (p 275)

Californian
Citronelle (p 282)
Le Séquoia (p 281)

African - Caribbean
Maracas Bay Café (p 270)

Asian
Jin-Ga Restaurant (p 274)
Raku (p 272)

Chinese
China Regency Restaurant (p 281)
Hunan Gallery (p 279)
Hunan Chinatown (p 266)

French
Brasserie Les Halles (p 264)
Café Lautrec (p 277)
Café Promenade (p 266)
Café La Ruche (p 280)
Chez Nous (p 282)
Citronelle (p 282)
L'Aquarelle (p 275)
La Fourchette (p 278)
Le Rivage (p 279)
Porter's (p 267)
Tout Va Bien (p 272)

Italian
Anna Maria's (p 269)
Bertolini's (p 264)
Coco Pazzo (p 265)
Gusti's (p 270)
Il Radicchio (p 270)
Isola Verde (p 277)
La Tomate (p 271)
Pizzeria Uno Chicago Bar & Grill (p 265)
Ristorante Piccolo (p 281)

Japanese
Raku (p 272)

Lebanese
Kalorama Café (p 277)
Skewers (p 271)

Mexican
Alamo Grill (p 280)
Cactus Cantina (p 279)
Peyote Café (p 276)
Red Sage (p 266)
Sol (p 272)

Moroccan
Marrakech Restaurant (p 266)

Thai
Bua Restaurant & Bar (p 269)
Star of Siam (Adams Morgan) (p 277)
Star Of Siam (Foggy Bottom) (p 273)

Restaurants with terraces
Annie's Paramount Steak House (p 272)
Café Deluxe (p 279)
Cup'a Cup'a Expresso Bar and Coffee (p 273)
Gusti's (p 270)
Java House (p 268)
Kramerbooks Café & Grill (p 268)
La Tomate (p 271)
Le Séquoia (p 281)
Mudd House (p 269)

Restaurants with terraces (ctd...)
Raku (p 272)
Sol (p 272)

For Breakfast
Au Bon Pain (p 262, 273)
Cup'a Cup'a Expresso Bar and Coffee (p 273)
Firehook Bakery (p 267)
Firehook (p 268)
Franklyn's (p 276)
Java House (p 268)
Kramerbooks Café & Grill (p 268)
Starbucks Coffee (p 268, 269)
The Mudd House (p 269)
Timothy's World Coffee (p 264)

Near the Mall and the Museums
Bertolini's (p 264)
Café des Artistes (p 268)
Manhattan Deli (p 262)
National Air and Space Museum Restaurants (p 263)
Restaurant 701 (p 267)

Sandwiches, Salads and Hamburgers
Au Bon Pain (p 262, 273)
Café Luna (p 268)
Capitol City Brewing Company (p 265)
Foster Brothers Coffee (p 279)
Franklyn's (p 276)
Friday's (p 265)
Harry's Restaurant and Saloon (p 262)
John Harvard's Brew House (p 264)
La Baguette (p 273)
La Madeleine (p 280)
Manhattan Deli (p 262)
Music City Roadhouse (p 280)

262 Restaurants

Sandwiches, Salads and Hamburgers
National Air and Space Museum Restaurants (p 263)
Planet Hollywood (p 265)
Restaurant 701 (p 267)
Samantha's (p 273)
Sign of the Whale (p 269)
Trumpets Restaurant & Lounge (p 271)

Take note that a tip of 15% (calculated on the total bill, excluding tax) is the standard gratuity for service and it is not included in the bill, but rather must be left by the client for the waiter or waitress. In North America, service and tip are one and the same.

DOWNTOWN AND THE MALL

The bakery chain **Au Bon Pain** *($; every day 8am to 7pm; Union Station, Union Station metro, ☎898-0299)* prepares excellent sandwiches that are perfect for a quick bite. It is also a good place to pick up French bread and pastries. This outlet is on the ground floor of the Union Station shopping mall.

For hamburgers, salads and sandwiches, **Harry's Restaurant and Saloon** *($; 436 11th St. NW, ☎624-0053)* is a name to keep in mind. There is a bar on the premises where you can relax with a refreshing beer at the end of a day of sightseeing.

Manhattan Deli *($; 801 Pennsylvania Ave. NW, near the National Archives, ☎737-2211)* is a good spot for a quick breakfast to start off a day of museum visiting on the Mall. It is a cafeteria-style establishment that offers breakfasts and simple, economical meals for lunch and dinner. Pancakes, pizzas, roast chicken, sandwiches and hamburgers all figure on the menu. With its location just in front of Navy Memorial, this is a good place to keep in mind during outings on the Mall.

The Starbucks Craze

The trend toward little coffee shops offering coffee-lovers brews from the four corners of the world, which was launched a few years ago in Seattle, has taken North America by storm. The Starbucks concept was conceived in that very same northwestern city and became the model on which all those to follow were based. Usually these restaurants serve muffins, pastries and sandwiches in addition to coffee, making them great places for breakfast or a light lunch. There are about thirty Starbucks shops in the Washington area. Here are a few addresses:

800 7th Street NW (☎289-1576)
700 14th Street NW (☎783-3048)
1730 Pennsylvania Avenue NW (☎393-1811)
1734 L Street NW (☎293-9180)
801 18th Street NW (☎785-2024)
3122 M Street NW (☎625-6706)
1501 Connecticut Avenue NW (☎588-1280)
1700 Connecticut Avenue NW (☎232-6765)
1301 Connecticut Avenue NW (☎785-4728)
1810 Wisconsin Avenue, Georgetown (☎298-6822)
1401 New York Avenue NW (☎637-9555)
3125 Lee Highway, Arlington (☎703-527-6506)
532 King, Alexandria (☎703-836-2236)

is a cafeteria-style establishment that offers breakfasts and simple, economical meals for lunch and dinner. Pancakes, pizzas, roast chicken, sandwiches and hamburgers all figure on the menu. With its location just in front of Navy Memorial, this is a good place to keep in mind during outings on the Mall.

The **National Air and Space Museum Restaurants** *($; every day 10am to 5pm; corner of Independence Ave. and 4th St. SW, in the National Air and Space Museum, ☎371-8750)* offer museum-goers a quick fill in the form of sandwiches and salads in two separate establishments, **Flight Line** and **Wright Place**. Flight Line is a large cafeteria on the ground floor of the museum, while Wright Place is on the upper floor and serves grilled steaks and pizzas in addition to sandwiches. The latter is brightly illuminated by large bay windows overlooking the

Mall and the Capitol and is decorated with flowers and green plants. It turns out to be a very pleasant, if somewhat noisy, place to eat.

Timothy's World Coffee *($; 700 11th St. NW, corner of 12th St. and G St., ☎639-0381)* is an excellent choice for breakfast or a quick lunch. Set on a small square adorned with modern sculptures and water gardens, this café is a very relaxing spot to take a break where patrons can enjoy warm drinks, muffins, cakes, bagels and salads. One wall of the café has been converted into a sort of newsstand that displays a huge selection of papers.

Despite its basement location, **John Harvard's Brew House** *($-$$; 1299 Pennsylvania Ave. NW, corner of 13th St. and E St., ☎783-2739)* will surprise with a beautiful brasserie-designed interior. Windows have been installed in the dining room to give customers a peek at the pub's impressive copper mash tuns. The resolutely modern interior decor is accentuated by high-backed leather booths, copper and steel-coloured walls and an undulating ceiling. Although the establishment is slightly on the noisy side, as pubs often are, it is a very pleasant spot to enjoy a reasonably priced meal. The menu includes a few pizzas, sandwiches and some simple dishes such as roast chicken, nachos and the perennial steak. Of course, the brews are the real draw for the establishment's regular clientele.

For Italian cuisine, head to **Bertolini's** *($$; 801 Pennsylvania Ave. NW, ☎638-2140)*, a charming little restaurant with a terrace overlooking the Navy Memorial. Pleasantly decorated with brightly coloured frescoes, this establishment offers pizzas, *antipasti* and *paste e risottto* at reasonable prices. It is ideally situated near the Mall and is a great choice for a light meal after a day of museum visiting.

Brasserie Les Halles *($$; every day 11:30am to midnight; 1201 Pennsylvania Ave NW, ☎347-6848)* is an absolute must for a taste of very high calibre French cuisine. With its large terrace on Pennsylvania Avenue, this is an excellent spot for a late supper after an evening at the theatre. The French brasserie cuisine includes such noteworthy dishes as a delicious cassoulet (Toulouse style, of course), chicken wings stuffed with chanterelle mushrooms, and pig's feet worthy of the purest Alsatian culinary tradition. The service is very friendly and attentive.

The **Capitol City Brewing Company** *($$; 1100 New York Ave. NW, ☎628-2222)* offers up simple cuisine essentially comprised of salads, pasta, hamburgers and sandwiches in an interesting decor of frescoes depicting workers toiling in a pub. The excellent beers on the menu perfectly complement a meal here and are highly recommended.

Coco Pazzo *($$; Union Station, Union Station metro)* is a very enjoyable Tuscan restaurant that offers quick sandwiches, pizzas, gnocchi and fresh pasta. The filet of salmon with red onions, cucumbers and capers is excellent as is the rabbit with sage and prosciutto. Although it is spread over two floors in the Union Station shopping mall, this restaurant has managed to maintain a charming atmosphere and its prices are very reasonable.

The cuisine at **Friday's** *($$; 1201 Pennsylvania Ave. NW, ☎628-8443)* is quick and simple. The restaurant offers a variety of sandwiches, hamburgers and salads in a dining room that is warmly accented with Tiffany lamps. However, the staff seems overwhelmed by the crowds of diners at this popular spot and the service is a bit slow and impersonal.

Experiencing slight hunger pains in the middle of a shopping spree or while waiting to see a movie? **Pizzeria Uno Chicago Bar & Grill** *($$; Mon to Sat 11am to midnight, Sun noon to midnight; Union Station, Union Station metro, ☎842-0438)*, on the upper floor of the city's main train station comes highly recommended. The menu offers a wide selection of pizzas to satisfy every predilection at prices that remain affordable.

The **Planet Hollywood** *($$; 1101 Pennsylvania Ave NW, ☎783-7827)* chain of restaurants needs no introduction. Almost every major city on the planet is home to one of these miniature Hollywood movie museums where patrons dine surrounded by such memorabilia as mannequins of Arnold Shwartzenegger (in his *Terminator* costume) and Robin Williams (in *Fisher King* garb) and costumes and accessories worn by the biggest stars of American film, like Beetlejuice's mask, Freddy's hand, Darth Vader's mask, and the Magnum 357 that belonged to agent Clarice Starling (played by Jodie Foster) in *The Silence of the*

Lambs. Pizzas, salads, pasta, hamburgers and sandwiches are the fare on the menu.

Hunan Chinatown *($$-$$$; 624 H St. NW, ☎783-5858)* offers excellent traditional Hunan cuisine in the heart of Chinatown. The dining room is decorated in brown tones accentuated by mirrors on one wall that make the place seem larger. Two of the restaurant's specialties are absolute musts: the duck smoked with tea leaves and the dumplings are both excellent. The service is expert and very friendly.

It's not every day that you see a restaurant that has put as much emphasis on and brought as much attention to the design and decoration of its interior as has **Red Sage** *($$-$$$$; 605 14th St. NW, ☎638-4444)*. The establishment actually comprises a restaurant-bar, called the Chili Bar and, in the basement, a number of private dining rooms reserved for groups and the Fine Dining Restaurant. Despite its exuberant decor, the Chili Bar is a very friendly spot that serves hearty chilli, of course, as well as fajitas and tacos at very affordable prices. The Fine Dining Restaurant is a whole other story, with prices that are just incredibly exaggerated.

The Renaissance Mayflower Hotel is home to a small restaurant called **Café Promenade** *($$$; 1127 Connecticut Ave. NW, ☎347-2233)* that also serves as a tea room in the afternoon. Its decor and menu both evoke the ambience of the Mediterranean. Frescoes on the walls, colonnades and statues adorn its cosy interior. The service is courteous and impeccable. In the evening, diners are serenaded as they leisurely savour their meals by the musical accompaniment of a harpist or a guitarist seated in a small balcony. The duck conserve and the Mediterranean crab cakes are excellent, and the restaurant's famous bouillabaisse will please even the most demanding connoisseurs.

The **Marrakech Restaurant** *($$$; 617 New York Ave. NW, ☎393-9393)* is a real change of scenery. It is difficult to imagine that just behind this building's bare façade, adorned only with an inscription in Arabic, there is a magnificent Moroccan restaurant. But a knock is answered by a person dressed in Arab garb who pulls open the door of this very unique house. Inside, hidden behind a heavy, embroidered curtain is a dining room richly decorated with carpets, booths, embroidered cushions and Moroccan crafts. Although the dining area is air conditioned, ceiling fans serve as reminders of the hot Moroccan climate and emphasize the North African atmosphere. Diners are treated to a belly dance in the middle of the evening at about 9:30pm. As for the cuisine, the restaurant proposes an interesting and unique set menu of five different dishes that will satisfy even the most ravenous appetites. The meal is composed of *pastiya* (a chicken patty with honey, almonds and scrambled eggs, dusted with cinnamon and sugar), chicken with lemon and olives, beef or lamb couscous, and a basket of fresh fruit. Mint tea and baklava top it all off. Marrakech Restaurant is a true find and highly recommended for fans of Moroccan cuisine and, considering the services offered, the prices here are very reasonable.

Porter's *($$$; corner of 14th St. and K St. NW, ☎682-0111)*, in the Crowne Plaza Hotel, is one of Washington's fine dining establishments, but the atmosphere here is a bit on the snooty side.

Restaurant 701 *($$$; 701 Pennsylvania Ave. NW, ☎393-0701)* is a stylish establishment that maintains a dress code. Its location near the Mall is undoubtedly an advantage for visitors to the capital, but the slight pretentiousness of the service is surprising considering the type of cuisine in question. The restaurant's terrace overlooking Navy Memorial proves to be very pleasant, though, and makes up for that minor annoyance. Inside, tables covered in white cloths are set in a semicircle around a long bar. The restaurant serves pasta and sandwiches as well as delicious, well-prepared fish dishes. The filet of tuna accompanied by pasta with herbs and beans, and the trout in Shenandoah sauce Chardonnay are both worth sampling.

AROUND THE WHITE HOUSE

The **Firehook Bakery** *($; 912 17th St. NW, ☎429-2253)* offers a selection of teas and coffees that you can scoff down with muffins, cookies and cakes for a quick breakfast. There are a few tables in a small room at the back of the shop, which is renowned for its excellent bread. At noon, sandwiches and salads are served here.

The **Starbucks Coffee** *($; 1730 Pennsylvania Ave. NW, ☎393-1811)* that is two steps from the White House presents a wide selection of coffees, as well as muffins, pastries and a few sandwiches to satisfy peckish noon-time appetites.

Café des Artistes *($$; Wed to Mon 11am to 3pm; corner of 17th St. and New York Ave. NW, ☎638-1439)* is a restaurant located in the large colonnaded hall on the ground floor of the Corcoran Gallery, which offers elegantly presented sandwiches and salads, including a smoked fish platter. Every Sunday from 9am to 2pm the restaurant hosts a jazz and gospel music brunch.

DUPONT CIRCLE

The best muffins in the city are to be found at **Firehook** *($; 1909 Q St. NW, corner of Connecticut Ave., ☎588-9296)*, a tiny establishment that offers but a cramped counter for breakfast. No patio, no tables, and unfortunately no chairs figure here. A nice alternative to the counter is to order a snack to take out and enjoy it leisurely on a bench in Dupont Circle.

The coffee at **Java House** *($; 1645 Q St. NW, corner of 17th St., ☎387-6622)*, which is roasted on the premises, will doubtlessly please aficionados of the brown nectar. The restaurant has a large, pretty, flower-decorated terrace that is very sunny and proves to be a wonderful spot for breakfast. The decor of the indoor dining room on the other hand is rather cold.

Kramerbooks Café & Grill *($; 1517 Connecticut Ave. NW, ☎387-3825)* is another good spot for breakfast and it boasts a pretty patio laid out with tables and parasols. A few sandwiches are served at lunch for those who prefer quick inexpensive fare.

Diners can also savour breakfast on the small patio of **Café Luna** *($; 1633 P St. NW, ☎387-4005)*, just downstairs from the Lebanese restaurant Skewers. Brunches are offered on the weekend. Although the restaurant is a bit tucked away and does not benefit from much sunshine, it is an unpretentious establishment that is perfectly appropriate for quick, simple fare.

For a quick breakfast in the Dupont Circle neighbourhood head to **The Mudd House** *($; 1724 M St. NW, ☎822-8455)*, a little, decent spot that offers a comfortable, relaxed atmosphere and serves coffees, teas, muffins, pastries and cakes.

The **Starbucks Coffee** *($; 1700 Connecticut Ave. NW, ☎232-6765)* craze has spread across the United States like wildfire. It must be said that coffee lovers will appreciate the breadth of varieties offered in these shops, which make them ideal for breakfast and a quick lunch. In addition to muffins and pastries, a few sandwiches are served here. Two other Starbucks Coffee outlets are located on Connecticut Avenue, at 1501 Connecticut Avenue NW at the corner of N Street, ☎588-1280, and at 1301 Connecticut Avenue NW, ☎785-4728, on the border of the Foggy Bottom district.

Sign of the Whale *($-$$; Mon to Thu 11:30am to 2am, Fri and Sat 11am to 3am, Sun 11am to 2am; 1825 M St. NW, ☎785-1110)*, located in an old house, does double duty as a small restaurant and a pub. Its interior decor, completely done in varnished wood, is reminiscent of an Irish pub. A superb old sculpted-stone chimney leans against one of the exposed brick walls. The dining area is in the back of the room, through the pub and past the long bar where beer flows freely. Budweiser is the brew of choice here, but there is also a good selection of other brands listed on a blackboard. This establishment is famous for its weekend brunches and for the crab festival that takes place every Sunday evening. During the rest of the week, salads, hamburgers and other sandwiches are the mainstays.

The Dupont circle area is decidedly rich in culinary flavour. Almost all of the world's cuisines are represented here. The **Bua Restaurant & Bar** *($$; every day 11:30am to 2:30pm and 6pm to 11pm; 1635 P St. NW, ☎265-0828)*, a small establishment that really does not look like much from the outside, serves excellent Thai cuisine. Its interior decor is not very sophisticated and the dining room is actually a bit sombre, but these drawbacks should not dissuade potential patrons, because although the surroundings lack sparkle, the food here is very good and reasonably priced and the hospitality is tremendous. The restaurant also offers a small terrace.

Anna Maria's *($$; Mon to Thu 11am to 1am, Fri 11am to 3am, Sat 5pm to 3am, Sun 5pm to 1am; 1137 Connecticut Ave.*

NW, ☎667-1444 or 667-7461) houses a dining room that has a rather cosy atmosphere created by exposed wooden ceiling beams, wooden chairs upholstered in green leather, tables lit by little candles and small wall alcoves adorned with plants, decorative plates and paintings. In the entrance way there are the perennial photographs of Hollywood celebrity patrons, including Eddy Murphy and Peter Graves (one of the stars of the television series *Mission Impossible*), and at the end of the room there is a bar. Although it is a bit dark, the ambiance is warm and the service is efficient and quick. Italian specialties figure on the menu, including spaghetti with all sorts of sauces; veal marsala with prosciutto, onions and mushrooms; veal Parmigiana covered in tomato sauce and cheese; and chicken breasts *à la* Milanese.

Gusti's *($$; 1837 M St. NW, corner of 19th St., ☎331-9444)*, an Italian restaurant established in 1949, is located in an old, stylish corner house. The interior is made up of two small dining rooms painted in warm colours. The first is decorated in orange-yellow tones, with little Greek colonnades and woodwork painted in greyish blue, and is furnished with leather-padded wooden chairs. The second room is brighter, with its orange colour scheme and woodwork covered in green. In addition, there is a large, very pleasant terrace on 19th Street decorated with flowers and parasols. For a very reasonable price, diners here enjoy very good, classic Italian cuisine composed of *antipasti*, pizzas and all sorts of pasta. On the whole this restaurant offers excellent value.

The **Maracas Bay Cafe** *($$; Tue and Sun 11am to 10pm, Wed 11am to 11pm, Fri and Sat 11am to midnight; 1636 R St. NW, corner of 17th St., ☎588-5886)* specializes in Caribbean and African cuisine. Chicken, either curried or in a sauce, a variety of salads and a few seafood dishes are proposed. This establishment also offers free home delivery.

Il Radicchio *($$; Mon to Sat from 11:30am, Sun from 5pm; 1509 17th St. NW, ☎986-2627)* is a small, charming Italian restaurant the walls of which are covered in frescoes depicting animals. Wood-oven baked pizzas, pasta and carpaccio are featured on the menu, and the fare is simple but excellent.

Have a craving for couscous or tabouli? **Skewers** *($$; 1633 P St. NW, ☎387-7400)* is the place to go! This restaurant offers delicious Lebanese and Tunisian cuisine. Some evenings spotlight couscous, but these vary from week to week, so diners should call ahead to find out when that special is offered. The interior of the establishment is prettily decorated in an Oriental style with embroidered cushions, engraved copper crafts and sparkling colours. There is also a tiny terrace. Reservations are advised for those who wish to dine outdoors. In addition to the excellent cuisine, the service is very friendly and attentive.

Reservations are recommended to get a good table at the Italian restaurant **La Tomate** *($$; 1701 Connecticut Ave. NW, corner of R St., ☎667-5505)*. This charming little restaurant, completely done in shades of green and white, boasts a very pretty, long terrace sheltered from the street traffic by a row of small trees and flower pots. There is even a tiny pergola laid out with a few tables. The charm of this establishment combined with its very good selection of pasta dishes makes it one of the best choices in Dupont Circle. Diners can sample excellent *Farfalle Salmone Affuminato e Vodka*, a delicious dish of farfalle pasta with smoked salmon, peppers, vodka and cream, or *Tagliatelle Verdi all'Adriatico*, a generous portion of spinach pasta with clams, scallops and shrimp in a basil tomato sauce. To accompany meals, a small selection of white and red wines is available by the glass or by the bottle at very reasonable prices.

The **Trio Restaurant** *($$; corner of 17th St. and Q St. NW, ☎232-6305)* is the perfect spot for a drink and a bite with friends on a charming terrace. The kitchen here cooks up a real bargain: an excellent filet mignon for about $10! Therefore, this place has a solid reputation in the neighbourhood and diners who want a table on the patio must arrive early.

Trumpets Restaurant & Lounge *($$; 1603 17th St. NW, ☎232-4141)* is well-known in Washington's lesbian and gay communities. Wednesday evenings are reserved for women only. In the basement of a modern, 17th-Street building, the establishment reveals an original interior design, decorated with large sofas, paintings and television screens. In addition to a variety of sandwiches, American nouvelle cuisine figures on the menu. Diners can savour such original dishes as the excellent artichokes stuffed with pine nuts and herbed goat cheese accompanied by a couscous salad.

The specialty of **Annie's Paramount Steak House** *($$-$$$; 1609 17th St. NW, ☎232-0395)* is no mystery. It is beef, of course, and it is always perfectly prepared despite the fact that it is served in a dining room that stands out for its lack of atmosphere. As at any self-respecting American steak house, it is available here in a variety of cuts that defies both the imagination and bovine morphology.

The restaurant **Raku** *($$-$$$; 1900 Q St. NW, ☎265-7258)* is a favourite in the Dupont Circle area. It proposes an original menu that draws on the aromas of Japanese, Thai, Malaysian, and Indian cuisines. This very natural and delicious fare is served in a sober and bare interior, the decoration of which consists of bamboo plants in the windows and colourful parasols hanging from the ceiling that create a very attractive lighting scheme. There are a few tables along the sidewalk, but it is sometimes hard to get an outdoor spot because this restaurant is so popular with Washingtonians.

The two beautiful terraces of the restaurant **Sol** *($$$; 1639 R St. NW, ☎232-6965)*, at the corner of R Street and 17th Street, make it a very pleasant establishment. Give in to temptation and start off by sipping a refreshing margarita under a shady parasol. For the next course, enchiladas, gazpacho and tacos are featured on the menu. This is a charming spot and the staff here is friendly, so this an especially enjoyable place to have a simple meal on a sunny day. On the other hand, the prices are a bit inflated.

The French restaurant **Tout Va Bien** *($$$; 1839 M St. NW, ☎965-1212)*, established in an interior that is reminiscent of a house in Provence, is a veritable little gem. The dining room is laid out against a large, orange-toned stone wall adorned with frescoes painted around a small, round chimney. The floor and ceiling are also decorated with frescoes and woodwork. The menu presents very well-prepared French specialties such as Breton-style salmon steak, veal escalope with morels, Provençale mussels, and escargots in garlic butter. All of it is prettily presented and served by a friendly, attentive staff. The only drawback here is the lack of originality on the dessert list.

FOGGY BOTTOM

In the same vein as La Baguette, **Au Bon Pain** *($; corner of 19th St. and M St., ☎466-2764)* is a French bakery that serves breakfasts of muffins, croissants and *pains au chocolat*, as well as a selection of salads and sandwiches for lunch. Outdoor tables are also available.

La Baguette *($; 2001 M St. NW, ☎293-3265)* is a little, quick-service French café that offers breakfasts and sandwiches at lunchtime. If the interior seems a bit cold and austere, diners can always opt for one of the outdoor tables.

The **Cup'a Cup'a Expresso Bar and Coffee** *($; 600 New Hampshire Ave. NW, ☎466-3677)*, located between the Watergate Hotel and the Kennedy Center for the Performing Arts, is a very pleasant little café that serves a breakfast of muffins and pastries, as well as sandwiches and salads for lunch. The interior is simple but cosy thanks to very pretty framed photographs. The room is lit by modern-style, small blue halogen lamps. A beautiful terrace furnished with wrought-iron tables and chairs provides a view of trees, flowers and greenery and of the Potomac off in the distance. Plainly put, this is just a wonderful spot for breakfast.

For a meal on the run, head to the **Art Gallery Grille** *($-$$; 1712 I St., ☎298-6658)*, where salads and few more sophisticated dishes are served on a street-side terrace. The ambiance is informal and the service is quick.

English pub atmosphere reigns at **Samantha's** *($-$$; 1823 L St. NW, ☎223-1823)*, a small restaurant-café that posts a menu of salads, hamburgers, pizzas and pasta. The woodwork on the exposed brick walls and the stained-glass windows at the entrance create a very cosy atmosphere. A small patio on the street has been furnished with chairs and tables.

Star of Siam *($$; Mon to Sat 11am to 3pm and 5pm to 11pm; Sun 5pm to 11pm; 1136 19th St. NW, between L St.*

and M St., ☎785-2839) is probably one of the best Thai restaurants in the city. The establishment consists of a relatively small, modestly decorated dining room in an old house. Its curry cuisine is famous in Washington now, but despite high praise, prices here remain very affordable. The service is courteous and friendly. This is unquestionably one of the best bets in the capital.

In an elegant, sober, sparse interior, **Jin-Ga Restaurant** *($$$; every day 1:30pm to 10:30pm; 1250 24th St. NW, between M St. and N St., ☎785-0720)* offers excellent Korean fare that will ravish the most demanding aficionados of Asian cuisine. The restaurant's dining room is in the semi-basement of a modern building that stands behind the preserved façade of another older building. Between these two outer walls there is a delightful little garden with a fountain, which contributes to the peaceful atmosphere that permeates this establishment. For those who have never sampled Korean cuisine, it is considered to be one of the best Asian national cooking styles alongside Japanese cuisine. The friendly staff is dedicated and happy to assist diners in choosing items from the menu.

Vidalia *($$$; 1990 M St. NW, ☎659-1990)* prepares relatively good fare that is somewhat expensive. Vidalia onions, a chief ingredient in the cuisine here, are displayed in a crate at the entrance to the restaurant's basement dining room. Although the presentation of the dishes is quite harmonious and refined, it does nothing to disguise the paucity of the portions, which may very well fail to satisfy diners with big appetites.

Morton's of Chicago Steakhouse *($$$-$$$$; Washington Sq., 1050 Connecticut Ave. NW, ☎955-5997)* is another restaurant where beef is king. Although it's just as expensive as its competitor, the Prime Rib Restaurant, it has the advantages of being less stuffy and having a completely charming staff that provides patrons with a warm welcome and very attentive service. The restaurant's simply decorated dining room has a pleasant, cosy atmosphere thanks to low-key lighting, white walls accented with red brick, baskets of flowers and fruit, and imposing bottles of red wine. As for the presentation of the menu, it lacks nothing in originality: diners order from a display of various cuts of raw beef. Although the house specialty is steak, excellent lamb dishes and Maine lobster are also served. If you have any room left after the meal, do not hesitate to order the delicious New York cheesecake or the Godiva chocolate cake, both of which are excellent.

Aficionados of French gastronomy will love the very stylish restaurant of the Watergate Hotel, **L'Aquarelle** *($$$$; 2650 Virginia Ave. NW, ☎298-4455)*, the windows of which deliver a very lovely view of the Potomac. The head chef, Robert Wiedmaier, has put in the necessary effort to maintain this establishment as one of the best in the city. Foie gras, pheasant, squab, salmon and lobster are among the classics on the menu, all of which may be accompanied, of course, by a delicious bottle of wine. A well-tended appearance is the norm at this restaurant.

Who would think you would have to dress up to eat a steak? This is exactly what's required at the **Prime Rib Restaurant** *($$$$; 2020 K St. NW, ☎466-8811)*, a favourite haunt of Washington's jet set. People seem to frequent this place more to be seen than to savour the delicious steak that is served to the accompaniment of a live pianist, so the ambience is rather cold and starchy. Just to be admitted to this deluxe steak house, customers must exude elegance and men are required to wear suit jackets and ties. The exterior of the building is not at all impressive, but inside the restaurant is beautifully decorated with black lacquer walls accented by a fine, gold border and stuffed leather armchairs that create the allure of a private men's club. Reservations are strongly recommended, and even then the restaurant is so crowded that you may have to wait quite a while, or opt for cocktails at the bar, before being seated. Prime rib is the highlight of the menu, and although it is absolutely delicious and as juicy as it could possibly be, the portions served are so gargantuan that they could easily satisfy two or three people. It is obvious why every diner leaves with a doggy bag. The accompanying vegetables are remarkable for their lack of inspiration and are not included in the excessive price of the prime rib, which seems completely aberrant. As for the service, suffice it to say that it is below the norm for a fine dining establishment.

ADAMS MORGAN

Franklyn's *($; 2000 18th St. NW, corner of Vernon St., ☎319-1800)*, on the edge of Adams Morgan, brews one of the best cappuccinos in the city. This appealing little café is run by its similarly pleasant owners and constitutes an excellent choice for a breakfast of English muffins, toast, cinnamon rolls or scones. Very good sandwiches are also served for lunch, which can be accompanied by freshly made juices. The two owners, who are real cat lovers, have made the feline the omnipresent theme of the decor: statuettes, decorative plates, cat tracks printed on the menu and on chair backs, and little porcelain kitties ornament the interior of this establishment.

For a simple light meal or a drink on a charming terrace, head to **Roxane** *($-$$; 2319 18th St. NW, ☎462-8330)*, a small, rooftop restaurant that serves Mexican cuisine. Its patio is set around a large bar where margaritas are mixed up and an incredible selection of tequilas may be sampled, creating the atmosphere of a seaside resort. As for the food, the menu lists fajitas, Mexican-style shrimp and scallops, tortillas, guacamole, salads and a variety of sandwiches.

Another Tex-Mex restaurant is located just downstairs from Roxane. The **Peyote Café** *($-$$; 2319 18th St. NW, ☎462-8330)* is deliciously decorated with cacti, lizards and coyotes in a very accomplished western theme. In addition to fajitas, nachos, *burritos* and tacos, the Texan and Mexican grill dishes are very highly recommended. On weekends, an excellent brunch of New-Orleans-style French toast is served here. The friendly and very welcoming owners have made this establishment a pleasant, inexpensive spot.

The restaurant **Felix** *($$; 2406 18th St. NW, ☎483-3549)* presents an original, stylish two-story interior, one wall of which bears frescoes and sculptures depicting the skyscrapers of a modern city. This is a very busy spot in the evening when there is a live jazz band on hand and patrons come to enjoy the music along with drinks and meals. The menu features a very tasty paella, rainbow trout, *moules marinières* (mussels cooked in their own broth with onions) and simple steaks. While the fare here is perfectly respectable and the prices affordable, the main draw is the atmosphere.

The Italian restaurant **Isola Verde** *($$; 2327 18th St. NW, ☎332-8899)*, with its interior of black and white striped booths and little, individually painted wooden tables, offers a jazz pianist on some evenings in addition to a tasty classic Italian menu of pizzas, pasta and *antipasti*. For a simple meal or a refreshing drink, this is an excellent choice.

The **Kalorama Cafe** *($$; 2228 18th St. NW, ☎667-1022)* is another option for Lebanese cuisine. The atmosphere is rather impersonal, but the main courses of *shish kebab* and *shish taouk* are very tasty, as are the tabouleh and *fattoush* salads, and the hummus, *baba ghannouge* and falafel plate appetizers. The service is very slow but friendly.

The **Little Fountain Café** *($$; 2339 18th St. NW, ☎462-8100 or 462-8411)* is a tiny, completely charming restaurant located in a semi-basement. A small fountain is affixed to one wall of the dining room. There is but one table, for two, on the minuscule terrace, which could make diners feel a bit claustrophobic were it not for the flowers and green plants that make the spot so appealing. Respectable, traditional cuisine is served here at affordable prices.

Despite the rave reviews showered on the **Star of Siam** *($$; Mon to Sat 11am to 3pm and 5pm to 11pm, Sun 5pm to 11pm; 2446 18th St. NW, ☎986-4133)* by various critics, this restaurant has maintained its very reasonably priced menu. The praise proves to be well earned – this is one of the best Thai restaurants in the city and its delicious curry cuisine justly holds a well-established reputation in Washington. Although the dining room is modest and soberly decorated, it is an excellent place to spend an evening and the service staff is affable and smiling. The *Tom Kar Gai*, a lightly spiced soup of chicken and coconut milk, and the curried chicken with basil are two of the excellent dishes available.

Café Lautrec *($$-$$$; Mon to Thu 5am to 2am, Fri and Sat 5am to 3am, Sun 5am to 2am; 2431 18th St. NW, ☎265-6436)* has become an Adams Morgan institution easily recognized by its façade which features a mural reproduction of *Aristide Bruant*, one of the famous paintings by the artist from Albi who is the restaurant's namesake. The interior decor is also completely devoted to Toulouse Lautrec, with posters of his works as well as paintings imitating his style adorning the walls. Give in to temptation by sampling the excellent onion soup with Porto and the zucchini fritters. Salads, lamb brochettes, Provençale shrimp and scallops, and the chef's specialty, Lautrec chicken, are also served. Coffee lovers will definitely appreciate the vast selection offered here, which includes Café Modigliani (with Amaretto), Cezanne (anisette), Dali (cognac and coffee liqueur), Degas (Curacao and cognac), Renoir (hazelnut liqueur), Gauguin (rum) and Matisse (scotch and coffee liqueur). All in all, this is truly an enjoyable place for an evening meal or a drink. Saturday nights feature a live pianist.

An interesting mix of American and Japanese cuisines is presented at the rooftop restaurant **Perry's** *($$-$$$; 1811 Columbia Rd. NW, ☎234-6218)*. The place does not look like much from the outside and the service is no-fuss, but the food is completely original and delicious. Excellent, fresh sushi and spaghetti in a tomato basil sauce may be sampled from the same menu. As for the unique atmosphere, be your own judge!

Among Washington's gastronomical options, the French restaurant **La Fourchette** *($$$; Mon to Fri 11:30am to 10:30pm, Sat 4pm to 11pm, Sun 4pm to 10pm; 2429 18th St. NW, ☎332-3077)* is the one that earned our love at first sight. This charming little restaurant, located in the heart of Adams Morgan, resembles a small Parisian café. It presents a rather rustic interior with slightly hard booths and wooden chairs and tables. The decor is limited to one brick wall hung with a few beautiful laminated photographs and adorned with a mural fresco. In the summertime, it offers but a few outdoor tables. Nonetheless, this sparse atmosphere is the setting for one of the best culinary experiences to be had in Washington, and the prices here remain affordable. The restaurant's bouillabaisse, served in generous portions, has contributed in part to its reputation. The Provençale mussels, prepared in garlic butter, are absolutely delicious. Whether its the *carré d'agneau forestière* accompanied by julienne zucchini, carrots, fresh mushrooms and potatoes; the calf sweetbread in cream; or the calf's tongue with mustard; the subtle flavours concocted here are simply enchanting as they delicately mingle on the palate. For dessert, even if you are amply sated, treat yourself to the special pleasure of orange quarters in Grand Marnier accompanied by sugar-coated, caramelized zest: a completely delicious and refreshing sensation!

AROUND THE CATHEDRAL

For a light lunch on the go, head to **Foster Brothers Coffee** *($; 3238 Wisconsin Ave. NW, ☎237-2202)*, a small, informal establishment that serves a few sandwiches and pastries... and coffee, of course!

Patrons of the restaurant **Cactus Cantina** *($$; 3300 Wisconsin Ave. NW, ☎686-7222)* are surprised as they enter by a small "museum" displaying an exhibition of Native American and cowboy clothing and crafts. The interior of this establishment is decorated in a western theme with saloon-style wood tables and chairs, but its pleasant terrace bordering Wisconsin Avenue and Macomb Street is the best spot for enjoying a Mexican meal of tacos, *ceviche*, chili, enchiladas or fajitas.

Café Deluxe *($$; 3228 Wisconsin Ave. NW, corner of Macomb St., ☎686-2233)* is in many ways reminiscent of a Parisian bistro with its minimalist decor and waiters dressed in long white aprons. The cuisine here is rather simple and perfectly adequate for a light lunch. Various salads, sandwiches and Mexican dishes are offered. In nice weather, it is very pleasant to sit on the patio.

The decor of **Hunan Gallery** *($$; 3308 Wisconsin Ave. NW, corner of Macomb St., ☎362-6645)* is in the same spirit as that of most Chinese restaurants. For a very modest price, this restaurant serves respectable Chinese and Szechwan cuisine, including Peking duck and Hunan-style lamb. There is also free delivery service.

WATERFRONT RIVERSIDE

The French restaurant **Le Rivage** *($$$; 1000 Water St. SW, ☎488-8111)*, located on the second floor of a rather ugly building near the seafood market and the marina, doesn't look like much from the outside. However, it is in fact a delicious restaurant with a very cosy interior furnished with plush booths that has made a reputation for itself by offering its clientele high-quality, seafood-based cuisine. Excellent fish soup, Maryland soft-shell blue crab, lobster, and queen scallops, as well as some meat dishes, may be savoured here. In addition, the windows of the dining room afford a very beautiful view of the Potomac.

GEORGETOWN

For a quick meal in Georgetown head to **La Madeleine** *($; 3000 M St. NW, ☎337-6975)*, a restaurant with a very rustic interior decorated with exposed wood ceiling beams and red brick walls. Simple but decent fare is served here, essentially comprising all sorts of sandwiches, soups, pasta and salads.

The **Music City Roadhouse** *($; 1050 30th St. NW, ☎337-4444)* is located on the C & O Canal, near the second lock. Very simple cuisine, adequate for a lunch or a quick supper with friends, is served in its upper-floor restaurant. The western-style establishment also houses a bar with a few pool tables.

If you're in the mood for Mexican fare, head to the **Alamo Grill** *($$; 1063 31st St. NW, ☎342-2000)*, a friendly establishment with a Far West and mainly wooden decor. The Mexican music that is played at top volume creates a relaxing, convivial atmosphere. The cuisine is in the most traditional Tex-Mex vein, but will perfectly do nonetheless. Chili con carne, guacamole, fajitas and tacos are among the specialties of the house.

Café La Ruche *($$; 1039 31st St. NW, ☎965-2684)* is a small typically French restaurant. Its friendly owner, who is originally from France, does the cooking, and he must have been homesick when he decided to decorate his modest restaurant with a multitude of little tricoloured flags and French street signs. In any case, it makes for a friendly, genuine family atmosphere. For very reasonable prices, patrons are graciously served traditional dishes of French cuisine such as trout *meunière*, mussels *marinière* and an excellent duck *à l'orange*. For more modest appetites there is a selection of salads, sandwiches, quiches and *croque-monsieur* on the menu as well. Save a bit of room for dessert though, because the pastries are excellent.

Washington Harbour is a very enjoyable place to dine while benefitting from a beautiful view that extends over the Potomac, the Kennedy Center and the skyscrapers of Arlington. Among the options here, the **China Regency Restaurant** *($$; 3000 K St. NW, ☎944-4266)* offers quality cuisine in a pretty dining room decorated with antique Chinese furniture. The traditional Chinese cuisine is excellent and is served by a friendly, attentive staff. This establishment also offers free delivery.

A beautiful, charming and romantic interior can be found at **Ristorante Piccolo** *($$; Mon to Thu 11:30am to 11pm, Fri and Sat 11:30am to 2am, Sun brunch 11:30am to 2:30pm; 1068 31st St. NW, ☎342-7414)*, whose amber-coloured walls exude the warmth of Italy. As the name of the establishment hints, the flavours of Italian cuisine, with olive oil reigning supreme, are concocted here. Very good home-made pastas such as the *Ravioli Verde* and *Vittello alla Piccolo* and delicious grilled seafood are among the items on the menu. The romantic atmosphere is sometimes overdone on weekends when a strolling violinist takes over the dining room (for shower crooners of *O Sole Mio* only!).

The large terrace planted with tall trees, flowers and greenery at **Le Séquoia** *($$-$$$; 3000 K St. NW, ☎944-4200)* is unquestionably the prettiest in Washington, so it is not surprising to see so many Washington families dining here during the day. Admirably situated on the edge of the Potomac, this restaurant offers a superb view of it and a holiday-like atmosphere. It is ideal for a meal or even just a drink in the afternoon. For evening meals, there is also an indoor dining room with a modern, stylish decor reminiscent of a Frank Lloyd Wright interior. The theme of the room is water and navigation. At the entrance, there is a large mural depicting young competitive rowers, and the balustrade of the bar is of the sort found on steamboats. Large bay windows completely surround the dining room, maximizing its exceptional location and its magnificent view of the river. The menu features both simple dishes, such as hamburgers, sandwiches, pizzas and pasta, as

11:30am to 2:30pm and 7:30 to 2am, Sun brunch 11:30am to 3pm; 1066 31st St. NW, ☎333-2134). This charming, often jam-packed little bistro offers a very interesting, albeit expensive menu. In addition to the classic pepper steak and steak *tartare*, diners can savour a delicious *filet mignon Tour d'Argent au Château-neuf-du-Pape* (not that there is anything pretentious about its name!). For starters, why not give in to Jacques Brel mussels or a cheese fondue? Warm and friendly, this establishment is very popular with Georgetown residents, so it is preferable to reserve a table ahead of time.

Aficionados of French and Californian nouvelle cuisine will without doubt appreciate the excellent, refined and admirably presented fare at the restaurant of the Latham Hotel, **Citronelle** *($$$-$$$$; 3000 M St. NW, ☎625-2150)*. The great French chef Michel Richard, now established in Los Angeles, is credited with the creation of the Citrus chain of restaurants that includes this establishment, and although the master rarely makes an appearance here, his well-schooled team carries the ball. The large oak-floored, stone-walled dining room is very attractive thanks to floral arrangements and foliage plants, and diners can appreciate a view of the incessant bustle in the kitchens from their tables. The menu changes frequently, but among the classics that can be sampled are fried foie gras with *shiitake* mushrooms, *Kataifi* shrimp (shrimp rolled in pastry crust and deep fried) and a duck conserve with figs and Porto. As for the desserts, their flavours are in every detail equal to the beauty of their presentation!

ENTERTAINMENT

Washington has become a mecca of cultural life over the years, due to its incredible collection of museums, of course, but also thanks to the vitality of the J.F. Kennedy Center for the Performing Arts, its stage productions, numerous improv theatres, comedy shows for all tastes and concerts. Music, dance, theatre, musicals, satire... there as many artistic productions as there are stages in the city. Indeed, Washington boasts no less than some twenty theatres, including four at the J.F. Kennedy Center. The capital, once considered the "testing ground" of productions intended for New York audiences, has thus become an essential stopping-place for the country's big stage productions.

This chapter offers a sampling of the night-time cultural activities that await you in Washington. To obtain detailed information about shows currently playing, the best source is the arts-and-entertainment section of the city's biggest daily paper, the *Washington Post*, as well as that of the *Washington Times*. Other newspapers also publish the time table of the various cultural activities taking place in Washington; among these are the *Washington Magazine*, *Where Magazine* and the *City Paper*. You can also enquire at the **Washington, DC Convention and Visitors Association (WCVA)** *(1212 New York*

Ave. NW, Washington, DC 20005, ☎789-7000) to obtain the Calendar of Events Brochure.

How To Obtain Half-Price Show Tickets

An organization known as **TICKETplace** *(Tue to Fri noon to 4pm, Sat 11am to 5pm; 730 21st St., at H St. NW, in the Lisner Auditorium at George Washington University, Foggy Bottom metro, ☎842-5387)* offers half-price tickets for a limited number of available seats, valid for the day of purchase. Take note that tickets for Sunday shows are sold by this organization on Saturdays.

In addition to stage productions, musicals and improv troups, this chapter includes a list of Washington's cinema complexes as well as a whole section on the most prominent bars and dance clubs in the city.

This chapter also features a whole section catering to the gay and lesbian community. Those who wish to obtain more information should consult *MW (Metro Weekly) Magazine* *(☎588-5220)*, a free local newspaper available at most bookshops and cafés throughout the city, or the *Washington Blade* *(☎797-7000)*, another free publication. The latter is available in various cafés and restaurants in Dupont Circle as well as in all good bookshops in that area.

THE CIRCUS

The famous **Ringling Brothers and Barnum and Bailey Circus** *(8607 Westwood Center Dr., Vienna, VA 22182, ☎703-448-4000 or 1-800-424-3709)* has produced world-renowned shows such as the *Walt Disney World on Ice Show*. Call the number above for more information about current productions. Though located outside Washington, the circus is easily reached by taking the MARC train from Union Station.

DANCE

Washington is not to be outdone when it comes to dance, boasting its own ballet company, which performs at the J.F. Kennedy Center for the Performing Arts as well as at the Warner Theater. This is the **Washington Ballet** *(3515 Wisconsin Ave. NW, ☎362-3606)*, a dance troupe whose repertoire includes everything from contemporary dance shows to more classical productions such as Tchaikovski's famous Christmas classic, *The Nutcracker*. Tickets are sold at the J.F. Kennedy Center. Or, you can get more information about current productions on the Internet at: *home.worldweb.net/wa*.

OPERA AND CLASSICAL MUSIC

Though opera is much prized by Washingtonians, judging by the number of sold-out productions, you may still be able to purchase tickets for the **Washington Opera** *(J.F. Kennedy Center for the Performing Arts, ☎416-7851 or 1-800-876-7372)*, provided you reserve your seats long in advance.

A host of classical music concerts are given at the **J.F. Kennedy Center for the Performing Arts** *(2700 F St. NW, Washington, DC 20566, ☎467-4600 or 1-800-444-1324, ≈416-8421)*, which you can contact to receive the calendar of events held at the Concert Hall or the Terrace Theater. The Kennedy Center also frequently presents small free concerts at the Theater Lab. Performances are also given by children's choirs as well as chamber music ensembles here.

You can also attend classical music concerts given by the **Washington Civic Symphony**, which performs at **Constitution Hall** *(at 18th St. and D St. NW, Farragut West metro, ☎638-2661)*.

THEATRE

The **Arena Stage** *(at 6th St. and Main Ave. SW, Waterfront metro, ☎488-3300, ≈488-4056)* has acquired a solid reputation

286   Entertainment

in the performing arts in the United States. Presented on a rotating basis in the three halls are a medley of classic plays and comedies, vaudeville shows and musicals.

The newly renovated main hall of the **DAR Constitution Hall** *(1776 D St. NW, Farragut West metro, ☎628-4780, ⇝628-2570)* can accommodate over 3,700 people. In addition to staging a variety of shows every year, including classical music concerts, ballets and plays, the DAR hosts prestigious awards ceremonies and conferences.

The **Discovery Theater** *(Arts and Industries Pavilion, 900 Jefferson Dr.SW, Smithsonian metro, ☎357-1500)* is a small venue where plays as well as musical events and puppet shows for children are presented. Internet surfers can find out more by checking out the *www.si.edu* web site.

All Americans have heard of **Ford's Theater and Lincoln Museum** *(511 10th St. NW, Metro Center metro, ☎347-4833 or 1-800-899-2367, ⇝638-1001)* at least once in their American history classes. It is, of course, the place where President Abraham Lincoln was assassinated while attending a play. After being closed for years following the event, Ford's Theater has since reopened its doors and presents dramatic plays as well as musicals.

For many years, plans to live up to Washington's cultural aspirations by building a big arts centre remained at the centre of debate. In fact, the idea of building a cultural centre dates back to 1958, on President Eisenhower's instigation. J.F. Kennedy also supported the project, but it was not until the events of November 1963 in Dallas that U.S. Congress allotted a sum of 23 million dollars for the construction of the centre, which was named after the late lamented President Kennedy, who was assassinated by Lee Harvey Oswald. Today, the **J.F. Kennedy Center for the Performing Arts** *(2700 F St. NW, Foggy Bottom metro, ☎467-4600 or 1-800-444-1324, ⇝416-8421)* presents an extraordinary selection of dramatic and comic plays, classical ballet and contemporary dance, symphony orchestras, operas and even films. You can get more information on the Net at: *www.kennedy-center.org*.

Built in 1921, the **Lincoln Theater** *(1215 U St. NW, U Street-Cardozo metro, ☎328-9177, ⇝328-9245)* once played host to the greatest African-American musicians and comics. The very beautiful theatre can now accommodate close to 1,200 people. Presented here are everything from live music and dance performances to young stand-up comics.

The biggest Broadway plays and musicals have often been presented at the **National Theater** *(1321 E St. NW, Metro Center metro, ☎628-6161 or 1-800-447-7400, ≠638-4830)*, the oldest theatre still in operation in the United States. Broadway's new creations were once tested here, their opening nights held before a Washingtonian audience. Though the federal capital is no longer used as a testing ground, big plays are still presented here before hitting Broadway or other major American stages.

Murder-mystery buffs are sure to enjoy **Shear Madness** *(Tue to Thu 8pm, Fri 9pm, Sat 6pm and 9pm, Sun 3:30pm and 7pm; Kennedy Center Theater Lab, 2700 F St. NW, Foggy Bottom-GWU metro, ☎416-8290 or 1-800-444-1324, ≠416-8295)*, a hilarious production in which the audience participates and helps solve the mystery.

With such a beautiful library in the city devoted exclusively to William Shakespeare and his work, it comes as little surprise that a professional theatre company stages the famous English playwright's best pieces here. And an excellent troupe of actors performs this author's classic repertoire at the small, 450-seat **Shakespeare Theater** *(450 7th St. NW, Archives-Navy Memorial metro, ☎547-3230, ≠547-0226)*.

One of the most beautiful theatres in the city, with its stunning marbled entrance, gilding, ceilings and beautiful large concert hall, is unquestionably the **Warner Theater** *(1299 Pennsylvania Ave. NW, Metro Center metro, ☎628-1818, ≠783-0204)*, a veritable showbusiness institution in Washington. Opened in 1924, the fully restored theatre positively glitters; its interior design alone is worth seeing. Broadway productions, comedies, concerts as well as both classical and modern ballets are presented here.

The initiatives of the **Wooly Mammoth Theater** *(1401 Church St. NW, Dupont Circle metro, ☎393-3939, ≠667-0904)* are also noteworthy. Indeed, this theatre greatly encourages the production of new plays written by young local playwrights.

Those feeling confident enough can even submit their own script, maybe even getting the chance that one of their plays will be staged here, if their potential is ever recognized!

Though located outside the capital, the **Wolf Trap Farm for the Performing Arts** *(1624 Trap Rd., Vienna, VA 22182, ☎703-255-1900, ≈703-255-1918)* is worth a trip, should the opportunity arise. The huge outdoor stage welcomes scores of rock bands and singers as well as classical music concerts, ballets and film screenings. No matter which show you attend, the Wolf Trap Farm generally hardly lacks in ambiance.

The **Carter Barron Amphitheater** *(Rock Creek Park, at 16th St. and Colorado Ave. NW, ☎619-7222 or 426-6837)* is another outdoor arena. Up to 4,000 people can gather here to attend summer jazz concerts, among others.

Finally, the **RFK Stadium** *(East Capitol St., between 19th St. and 20th St. SE, ☎547-9077 or 546-3337)* also hosts a few rock concerts, though only in summer.

Dinner Theatres

One of the best-renowned dinner theatres around Washington may well be the **Burn Brae Dinner Theater** *(Tue to Sun 7pm, Wed and Sun brunch; P.O. Box 180, Burtonsville, MD 20866, ☎301-384-5800 or 1-800-777-BBDT, ≈301-421-1027)*, a charming place where, after stocking up on the buffet, you can enjoy a performance put on by professional actors. Advance reservations required.

As its name indicates, the **Mystery On The Menu Theater** *($40; 1728 Wisconsin Ave. NW, Suite 154, ☎333-6875)* offers patrons a few murder mysteries to solve. Interactive evening guaranteed. Performances on certain nights only. Call ahead for schedule.

The **West End Dinner Theater** *(4615 Duke St., Alexandria, VA 22304, ☎703-370-2500, ≈703-370-2328)* often presents very good matinée or evening comedies. Advance reservations required.

IMPROV AND COMEDY

The American political scene provides plenty of fodder for all kinds of fierce but hilarious satire, and American comics rarely miss such golden opportunities. You can attend a few good shows at the following places. Note, however, that it is best to reserve your seats in advance.

For several years now, **Capitol Steps Political Satire** *(Fri and Sat nights; 1505 King St., Alexandria, VA, ☎703-683-8330, ≈703-683-5912)* has been presenting a comedy troupe who have periodically appeared on major American television networks. The theme: politics in all its forms!

Humour also awaits you at the **Comedy Café** *(1520 K St. NW, McPherson Square or Farragut North metro, ☎638-5653 or 638-JOKE, ≈347-8487)*, a place where young comic talent has often been discovered. The place is very popular, so remember to reserve in advance.

The troupe that performs at **Gross National Product** *(1602 South Springwood Drive, Silver Spring, MD, ☎301-587-4291, ≈301-587-4688)* deservingly caught the attention of PBS and has been featured on its airwaves several times. Skits, impersonations, improv and political satire are put on here.

Political satire is also very popular at **Mrs. Foggybottom and Friends** *($25; Sat 8pm; 2853 Ontario Rd. NW, ☎332-1796 or 1-800-470-3380, ≈332-1110)*, a veritable comedy institution in Washington.

Are you the next Sherlock Holmes? If you think solving murder mysteries is a piece of cake, why not get to the bottom of it and check out **Shear Madness** *(Tue to Thu 8pm, Fri 9pm, Sat 6pm and 9pm, Sun 3:30pm and 7pm; Kennedy Center Theater Lab, 2700 F St. NW, Foggy Bottom-GWU metro, ☎416-8290 or 1-800-444-1324, ≈416-8295)*, where your participation is needed to help solve the case presented to you.

MOVIE THEATRES

The following movie theatres present the latest Hollywood movies:

AMC Union Station 9, 50 Massachusetts Avenue NW, Washington, DC, ☎703-998-4262.

Cineplex Odeon, 4000 Wisconsin Avenue NW, Washington, DC, ☎333-FILM, ext. 789.

Cineplex Odeon West-End, at 23rd Street and L Street NW, Washington, DC, ☎333-FILM, ext. 794.

Cineplex Odeon Mazza Gallerie 3, 5300 Wisconsin Avenue NW, Washington, DC, ☎333-FILM, ext. 826.

Cineplex Odeon Avalon, 5612 Connecticut Avenue NW, Washington, DC, ☎333-FILM, ext. 787.

Cineplex Odeon Cinema, 5100 Wisconsin Avenue NW, Washington, DC, ☎333-FILM, ext. 788.

Cineplex Odeon Embassy, at Connecticut Avenue and Florida Avenue NW, Washington, DC, ☎333-FILM, ext. 800.

Cineplex Odeon Dupont Circle 5, 1350 19th Street NW, Washington, DC, ☎333-FILM, ext. 792.

Cineplex Odeon Foundry, 1055 Thomas Jefferson Street NW, Washington, DC, ☎333-FILM, ext. 827.

Cineplex Odeon Janus 3, 1660 Connecticut Avenue NW, Washington, DC, ☎333-FILM, ext. 793.

Cineplex Odeon Outer Circle, 4849 Wisconsin Avenue NW, Washington, DC, ☎333-FILM, ext. 790.
Foreign films are featured here fairly regularly.

Cineplex Odeon Tenley, 4200 Wisconsin Avenue NW, Washington, DC, ☎333-FILM, ext. 791.

Movie Theatres 291

Cineplex Odeon Uptown, 3426 Connecticut Avenue NW, Washington, DC, ☎333-FILM, ext. 799.

Key, 1222 Wisconsin Avenue, Georgetown, ☎333-5100. Original French films with English subtitles are frequently featured here.

Film buffs and repertory-film regulars will be delighted with the **American Film Institute** *(J.F. Kennedy Center for the Performing Arts, 2700 F St. NW, ☎828-4000)*, which presents classic American and foreign films as well as avant-garde cinematic works.

SPECTATOR SPORTS

Washington's professional hockey team, the **Washington Capitals,** plays its home games at **MCI Center** *(601 F St. NW, Washington DC 20004, ☎301-336-2277)*. The National Hockey League season is from October to April. The **Georgetown Hoyas Basketball** team also plays in this stadium *(ticket reservations ☎800-664-5056 or 301-985-6250, Tickets@greatseats.com)*, from November to April, as does the city's professional basketball team, the **Washington Wizards** *(ticket reservations ☎202-661-5065)*. Game times and ticket prices vary.

Since the United States hosted the second-to-last World Cup of football, or soccer as its called in North America, this sport has gained a number of fans and enthusiasts and a few professional teams have sprouted up, even if the majority of Americans are still not crazy about it. For information about the matches of the **Washington Warthogs,** contact the **USAir Arena** *(1 Harry S. Truman Dr., Landover, MD 20785, ☎301-499-3000, ⇌301-499-3329)*.

Another team, **DC United Soccer** *(13832 Redskin Dr., Herndon, VA 20171, ☎703-478-6600, ⇌703-736-9451)*, plays at RFK Stadium, Washington's 56,000-seat sports arena.

If you want to see an American football game featuring the famous **Washington Redskins** *(Jack Kent Cooke Stadium, 1600 Raljon Road, Raljon, MD 20785-4236, ☎301-276-6060)*. The football season is from September to December. It is very difficult to get seats to a Redskins game, though, because the

BARS AND NIGHTCLUBS

Three Washington districts have become synonymous with nightlife, namely Georgetown, Dupont Circle and Adams Morgan. Night owls should find plenty to do in the capital. Indeed, whether you are among those bent solely on dancing or, rather, enjoying a relaxing drink with friends, or again, looking for places in which to meet someone, enjoy a good cigar, laugh or listen to rock, jazz or blues, Washington has a lot to offer. This section presents you with a number of suggestions for your nights out that should hopefully meet every taste and budget.

Generally speaking, the evening doesn't really kick off until 9pm in Washington, and things don't truly heat up until the stroke of midnight. Bars usually close at around 3am on Fridays and Saturdays, and around 2am on week nights.

Note that certain establishments have cover charges, notably when a show is presented, while others do not. Moreover, the legal drinking age here is 21. Bars and dance clubs are required by law to check your age, so be sure to bring along I.D. with your birthdate even if you are over thirty, because carding is sometimes routine.

Places to Dance

Dupont Circle

Located on the third floor of a Victorian house, the **Childe Harold's Step Childe** bar *(Fri and Sat; 1610 20th St. NW, Dupont Circle metro, ☎483-6700)* turns into a nightclub on weekends, when a large crowd gathers to dance to loud eighties' music.

Planet Fred *(1221 Connecticut Ave. NW, Dupont Circle metro, ☎331-3733)* is another well-known place in the Dupont Circle district. The clientele here is rather young and unconventional, which gives the place an original and very enjoyable ambiance. On weekends, the dance floor is swamped with dancers who get down and dirty to a mean beat.

The theme decors and menus change constantly at **Cities** *(2424 18th St. NW, Dupont Circle metro, ☎328-7194)*, a bar-restaurant where bands perform on the small stage on certain nights, or you can dance to nineties' music.

Those looking for a nightclub with an eclectic decor and pumped-up music should appreciate **Ozone Le Club Industriel** *(1214 18 St. NW, Dupont Circle metro, ☎293-0303)*, a very trendy dance club with giant-screen televisions on its walls.

Downtown

In the heart of downtown Washington is the chic **Coco Loco** club *(810 7th St. NW, Gallery Place-Chinatown metro, ☎289-2626)*, a Brazilian restaurant that turns into a nightclub on Fridays and Saturdays where you can dance to Latin rhythms such as *salsa*, *merengue* and *samba*. Dress code.

Right nearby, the **Ritz** *(919 E St. NW, between 8th and 9th Sts., Gallery Place-Chinatown metro, ☎638-2582)* may well catch your attention with its five dance floors, each playing a different kind of music. Reggae, jazz, blues — something for everyone! Proper attire compulsory.

The great decade of John Travolta movie-musicals is still going strong at **Polly Esther's** *(605 12th St., NW, Metro Center metro, ☎737-1970)*, where fans of the Bee-Gees and seventies disco music will have a blast. The decor of this *Saturday Night Fever* den, with its dance floor and strobe lights, recalls this decade's somewhat gaudy fashion in every way.

Club Zei *(Zei Alley, a little north of I Street NW, between 14th and 15th Sts., McPherson Square metro, ☎842-2445)* boasts a very high-tech interior. Spread over several floors, the establishment offers some sections ideal for dancing, others more secluded for sipping a drink. The Zei clientele mostly consists of students and ambitious young executives dressed in the latest fashions. Need we say that you should be dressed in your best to get into this nightclub?

Foggy Bottom

There are curiously few nightclubs in this district despite the fact that it is swarming with George Washington University students. If you really want to stay in this part of town, you will have to make do with **Deja Vu** *(1217 22nd St. NW, Foggy Bottom-GWU metro, ☎333-1100)*, an establishment where a clientele mainly made up of young people dance to rock and nineties' music every night.

The South East

We've mentioned before in this guide South East district should be avoided come nightfall. We therefore advise you, once again, to take a taxi to your destination there, unless you have the opportunity to go in a group to **Tracks 2000** *(1111 First St. SE, Navy Yard metro, ☎488-3320)*, the biggest dance club in and around Washington. The place boasts three dance floors, including one outside, several bars, a patio, pool tables and a whole series of video games. The music played here is relatively varied, but mainly consists of disco and techno. The place is, for the most part, frequented by a gay clientele (particularly on Saturday nights), though anyone can be admitted, provided they are gay-positive.

Georgetown

Winston's *(3295 M St. NW, near 33rd St., Foggy Bottom-GWU metro, then a good 20 min. walk, ☎333-3150)* is an enjoyable and lively place that mainly attracts a large contingent of students who come here every night of the week for a good time and to dance to the latest music.

Adams Morgan

In the heart of the Adams Morgan district is **Heaven and Hell** *(2327 18th St. NW, ☎667-4355)*, a two-floor establishment featuring alternative music. On the main floor, Hell is equipped with a bar and tables where you can have a drink in the midst of a seemingly devilish decor, while on the floor above, Heaven offers a more peaceful and mellow ambiance, with comfortable sofas and television screens.

Sports Bars

Located near the White House, **Fanatic's** *(1520 K St. NW, Farragut North or McPherson Square metro, ☎638-6800)* is equipped with satellite dishes and about thirty television screens broadcasting sports of all kinds. The place also boasts pool tables and dart boards. Patrons here can also enjoy very simple fare such as sandwiches, chicken wings or shrimp. Karaoke enthusiasts can let loose here, as well.

The decor at the **Senators All American Sports Café** *(Holiday Inn on the Hill, 415 New Jersey Ave. NW, Union Station or Judiciary Square metro, ☎638-1616 or 1-800-638-1116)* is primarily devoted to sports in all its forms. The place is also popular as a dancing venue at night. If you wish to eat here, you should reserve a table in advance.

The **Rock Sports Bar and Restaurant** *(717 6th St. NW, Gallery Place metro, ☎842-ROCK)* is Washington's biggest sports bar. The establishment boasts numerous television screens distributed over its three floors, as well as pool tables and a dance floor. Moreover, the rooftop terrace is equipped with another bar, known as the **Tiki Bar**.

Ardent supporters of the American football team the Washington Redskins will appreciate the **Grand Slam** *(Grand Hyatt Washington, 1000 H St. NW, Metro Center metro, ☎582-1234)*, a bar where you can sometimes meet the team's players. Matches are shown on three giant screens and there are pool tables and interactive video games here, as well. The Grand Slam also serves lunch and dinner.

Finally, if you're passing through the city of Arlington, you can check out the **Teams Sports Bar** *(Crystal Gateway Marriott, 1700 Jefferson Davis Hwy., Arlington, Crystal City metro, ☎920-3230)*, where the decor and particularly the conversation focus on sports. Open every day, the place is pleasant if a little noisy.

Jazz and Blues Bars

Small jazz bands often play at **B. Smith's** *(Union Station, 50 Massachusetts Ave. NE, Union Station metro, ☎289-6188)*, a pleasant and very popular bar with local residents. Calling ahead for show schedules is advised.

Jazz luminaries such as Charlie Byrd, Wynton Marsalis and Sarah Vaughn have graced the stage at the **Blues Alley** *(1073 Rear Wisconsin Ave. NW, Georgetown, ☎337-4141)*, one of the oldest jazz clubs in the city. The place, which also serves good Creole cooking, has a stellar reputation in the capital; it is therefore best to make your reservations in advance. The cover charge varies according to the concert offered, but is generally rather steep. Call ahead to inquire about schedules and listings.

Not far from the White House is another establishment, namely **Georgia Brown's** *(950 15th St. NW, McPherson Square metro, ☎393-4499)*, where you can listen to local musicians play jazz tunes during Sunday brunch.

Madame's Organ *(2003 18 St. NW, ☎667-5370)* is an establishment located, as its name indicates (in a clever play on words where the letter *M* is transposed), in the charming Adams Morgan district. The nightclub's interior is very oddly decorated in shades of pink, but it is one of the most delightful places to spend an evening listening to great blues.

Though located in a rather unappealing part of Dupont Circle come nightfall, the **Vegas Lounge** *(1415 P St. NW, Dupont Circle metro, ☎483-3971)* is a charming blues bar run by an equally charming blues devotee.

Easily identifiable by its façade adorned with a fresco of Toulouse-Lautrec, **Café Lautrec** *(2431 18th St. NW, ☎265-6436)* hosts small jazz concerts every night. A great reason to continue your evening here after enjoying an excellent meal (see p 277).

Almost directly across the street from Café Lautrec is **Cities** *(2424 18th St. NW, ☎328-7194)*, a very pleasant bar-restaurant decorated with frescoes and sculptures of skyscrapers. Jazz bands frequently perform here. Very good ambiance.

In a small town house converted into a café-restaurant, **City Blues** *(2657 Connecticut Ave. NW, Woodley Park-Zoo metro, ☎232-2300)* is a place where you can enjoy small and relatively simple meals, followed by an evening of listening to local bands playing blues or jazz.

Bars

The **Dubliner Pub** *(Phoenix Park Hotel, 520 North Capitol St. NW, Union Station metro, ☎737-3773 or 1-800-824-5419)* is a very popular Irish pub in Washington. Ordering a *Guinness* here is therefore only right and proper, of course! The place serves small meals, but regulars cherish it most for the ambiance, the beer and the nightly performances.

If you're in search of a bar for a quick meal or a good beer in a warm and pleasant ambiance, head to the **District Chophouse and Brewery** *(509 7th St. NW, Gallery Place metro, ☎347-3434)*, which boasts a whole variety of home-brewed beers. Cigar aficionados will be glad to know that they can light a stogie here.

The ambiance at **Kinkead's** *(2000 Pennsylvania Ave. NW, ☎296-7700)* is altogether different. Though not as laid-back and mostly frequented by go-getting executives, the place has considerable charm. A pianist tickles the ivories here six nights a week.

If you like the delightful ambiance of piano bars should head to **Mr. Smith's of Georgetown** *(3104 M St. NW, ☎333-3104)*, a great place where a very good pianist plays soft melodies every night. The place also hosts small bands every Friday and Saturday night.

There are two Murphy's establishments in the region, one in Washington, **Murphy's** *(2609 24th St. NW, Woodley Park-Zoo metro, ☎462-7171)*, and the other in Alexandria, aptly named **Murphy's of Alexandria** *(713 King St., Alexandria, VA, ☎703-548-1717)*, where you can listen to small bands play very good Irish tunes. True to this people's *joie de vivre*, a warm ambiance here is assured every night.

Housed in a former Oldsmobile showroom, the peculiar microbrewery **Bardo Rodeo** *(2000 Wilson Blvd., Arlington, Court House metro, ☎527-1852)* is decorated with various car models and frescoed murals. The place, where beer reigns supreme, offers an impressive selection of wonderful home-made brews. Moreover, pool sharks are sure to appreciate the 25-odd pool tables available to them.

Billy Martin's Tavern *(1264 Wisconsin Ave. NW, ☎333-7370)* has become a virtual institution in Georgetown. Open since 1933, this establishment offers a menu featuring fairly simple American cooking and a warm ambiance reminiscent of that of old pubs.

The interior decor of **Shelly's Back Room** *(1331 F St. NW, Metro Center metro, ☎737-3003)* is rather original. Indeed, part of the barroom is furnished and decorated in such a way as to give customers the impression of being in a log cabin in the country. Decorating touches thus include false windows adorned with rustic curtains, on the walls. You can sit in large and comfortable armchairs or seats set out around small coffee tables, while having a drink and a light meal followed by a good cigar. Indeed, Shelly's Back Room carries a whole selection of them, from famous Cuban to Dominican cigars. The bar counter is situated at the back of the room and has one of the friendliest atmospheres. Truly one of our favourite places.

Havana smokers may very greatly appreciate **Buttlers, The Cigar Bar** *(Grand Hyatt Washington, at 10th and H Streets NW, Metro Center metro, ☎637-4765)*, a fashionable establishment where they can enjoy a cocktail and a fine cigar while listening to a jazz band. Cigars are sold on the premises. Proper dress compulsory.

The **Capitol City Brewing Co.** *(1100 New York Ave. NW, Metro Center metro, ☎628-2222)* is one of Washington's leading microbreweries, and you can savour their home-brewed beers right on the premises.

In the same vein, the **District Chophouse and Brewery** *(509 7th St. NW, Gallery Place metro, ☎347-3434)* serves home-made beer as well as meals. The place also boasts pool tables.

The **Hard Rock Café** *(999 E St. NW, Gallery Place metro, ☎737-7625)* has a friendly, rather young ambiance. Rock bands play here at night.

Those with a yen for sushi or a *margarita* can drop by **Perry's** *(1811 Columbia Rd. NW, ☎234-6218)*, a delightful if always jam-packed bar with a superb terrace, in the Adams Morgan district.

The Washington Hotel, located in the very heart of downtown, is home to the **Sky Terrace Lounge** *(Washington Hotel, at 15th St. and Pennsylvania Ave. NW, Metro Center metro, ☎638-5900)*, where visitors can have a drink or a cocktail while enjoying the stunning view of the main monuments of the Mall and the White House.

The Gay and Lesbian Scene

Washington's gay and lesbian community mostly gathers in and around the Dupont Circle district, which boasts the most establishments catering to this particular clientele. The main ones are listed below.

Dupont Circle

The **Badlands-Annex** *(1413 22nd St. NW, Dupont Circle metro, ☎296-0505)* is essentially a dance club. The place has a number of video screens as well as pool tables. Karaoke on certain nights. Friday nights attract the biggest crowds, which can sometimes seem a little claustrophobic given the tininess of the place. All drinks are on special Tuesday nights, which also draws hordes of people. Primarily frequented by men, this establishment features drag queens belting out songs on certain nights.

The Circle Tavern, Terrace, and Underground *(1629 Connecticut Ave. NW, Dupont Circle metro, ☎462-5575)* is a three-floor establishment that caters to the gay clientele. The main floor, known as the **Underground**, is equipped with a dance floor. The floor above houses a tavern with two bars, as well as tables and chairs. The top floor, for its part, boasts yet another bar, leading out onto a lovely, often jam-packed terrace, whence you can admire the view over Connecticut Avenue. Wednesdays at the Underground are lesbian nights. Certain theme nights are organized here; it is best to call ahead to inquire about scheduled events.

A very fashionable crowd frequents **JR's** *(1519 17th St. NW, Dupont Circle metro, ☎328-0090)*, a somewhat clichéd bar, but one that welcomes a large clientele of dynamic young executives known in America as guppies (gay urban professionals).

Newly opened, the **Cobalt** *(at 17th and R Streets NW, Dupont Circle metro, ☎232-6969)* is a pleasant bar with a resolutely modern decor where you can also listen to good music.

A good place to meet people, the **Fireplace** bar *(at 22nd and P Sts. NW, Dupont Circle metro, ☎293 1293)* is spread over two floors. The music played here is generally pretty good.

Dupont Windows *(1635 17th St. at R St. NW, Dupont Circle metro, ☎328-0100)* is located above the Dupont Italian Kitchen restaurant. Its large windows and cosy interior make it a delightful place to have a drink and chat with friends.

Those in search of a Latino gay bar should head to **Escandalo** *(2122 P St. NW, Dupont Circle metro, ☎822-8909)*, an establishment frequented by the Latin-American gay and lesbian community. The place is ideal for those who wish to dance to sensual *salsa* beats and meet very friendly people.

Located in a two-story building, **Omega DC** *(2122 P St. NW, Dupont Circle metro, ☎223-4917)* boasts two bars and a dance floor on the main floor and two more bars as well as pool tables upstairs. The music here is generally fairly up-beat. The club is mainly frequented by a fairly young clientele made up of African Americans and whites.

Trumpets *(1603 17th St. NW, Dupont Circle metro, ☎232-4141)* is both a restaurant and a bar. Gay and lesbian patrons come here to enjoy a light meal or a drink, and chat with friends in the midst of a somewhat new-age decor. Wednesdays are lesbian nights.

Outside Dupont Circle

The **Bachelor's Mill** *(1104 8th St. SE, Navy Yard metro, ☎544-1931)* clientele is mostly made up of African-American men. It is advised that you take a taxi here, because the place is located in a rather rough neighbourhood.

DC Eagle *(639 New York Ave. NW, Mount Vernon Square metro, ☎347-6025)* is a leather bar for men only. This several-floor establishment boasts a bar, pool tables and pinball machines on its main floor. The second floor is equipped with another bar as well as a terrace. Caution is also advised to those heading here; taking a taxi is strongly recommended.

Saturday nights are very popular at the **Delta Elite** *(3734 10th St., at Michigan Ave NE, Brookland metro, ☎822-8909)*, a very pleasant bar where you can dance the night away. The clientele is essentially composed of African-American men.

The Edge-Wet *(56 L St. SE, Navy Yard metro, ☎488-1200)* is a trendy gay nightclub. Friday and Saturday nights mostly attract the gay African-American community, while Wednesday nights are devoted a the lesbian clientele. The place boasts several bars and two dance floors. Nude dancers.

Women will undoubtedly appreciate the **Hung Jury** *(1819 H St. NW, Farragut North metro, ☎279-3212)*, one of the few lesbian bars in the city. A few meals are served here during the day, while the place turns into a dance club come nightfall. The music is generally good, if relatively commercial. Men are allowed in, provided they are accompanied by a woman.

Yes indeed, Washington has its very own country-style gay bar! The bar in question is **Remington's** *(639 Pennsylvania Ave. SE, Eastern Market metro, ☎543-3113)*, an establishment fit with a large dance floor where you can try your hand (or feet) at country & western dancing! Those not familiar with the intricacies of the dance steps involved need not worry, for a charitable soul is sure to teach you the basics! This establishment is very popular with Washington's gay community, so expect to wait your turn on the dance floor or at the bar.

Tracks 2000 *(1111 First St. SE, Navy Yard metro, ☎488-3320)* is the most popular gay dance club in town, notably on Saturday nights. The place has three dance floors, including one outside, and a considerable number of bars. Moreover, those who wish to have a little something to eat can have a quick meal at the snack bar. Techno music is often featured, though some nights are devoted to disco. Getting here by taxi is strongly recommended, for the neighbourhood is certainly not the safest.

SHOPPING

Washington is sure to satisfy ardent window-browsers. Indeed, the city has plenty of shops and shopping centres where you might find a few bargains at the clothing stores, secondhand bookshops or jeweller's along the streets and mall corridors. Washington is also highly recognized for its numerous art galleries in Dupont Circle and Georgetown, where professional and amateur collectors alike do their shopping. The Smithsonian Institution also sells small souvenirs, as do several art boutiques set up in the city's main museums, where you will be able to unearth a thousand and one finds.

ART GALLERIES IN DUPONT CIRCLE AND GEORGETOWN

Washington has become a veritable Mecca for art collectors and therefore a paradise for local artists, who can sell their work. A brochure called *Galleries Magazine* is published monthly. It profiles the various exhibitions held in Washington and Baltimore art galleries. You can obtain it at one of the city's art galleries or by writing directly to the publisher at the following address:

304 Shopping

Galleries Magazine
PO Box 3705, Washington, DC 20007, ☎301-270-0180, ☎301-270-0561.

Because the exhibitions at the following Washington art galleries are temporary, we haved provided you with their addresses without, however, a description of their contents:

Addison/Ripley Gallery
9 Hillyer Court NW, Washington, DC 20008, ☎328-2332.

Affrica
2010-1/2 R Street NW, Washington, DC 20008, ☎745-7272.

America, Oh Yes!
2020 R Street NW, Washington, DC 20009, ☎483-9644.

Anton Gallery
2108 R Street NW, Washington, DC 20008, ☎328-0828.

Burdick Gallery
2114 R Street NW, Washington, DC 20008, ☎986-5682.

Burton Marinkovich Fine Art
1506 21st Street NW, Washington, DC 20036, ☎296-6563.

Chao Phraya Gallery
2009 Columbia Road NW, Washington, DC 20009, ☎745-1111.

Foundry Gallery
9 Hillyer Court NW, Washington, DC 20008, ☎387-0203.

Gallery 10
1519 Connecticut Avenu, NW, Washington, DC 20036, ☎232-3326.

Gallery K
2010 R Street NW, Washington, DC 20009, ☎234-0339.

Geoffrey Diner Gallery
1730 21st Street NW, Washington, DC 20009, ☎483-5005.

Art Galleries in Dupont Circle and Georgetown 305

Kathleen Ewing Gallery
1609 Connecticut Avenue NW, Washington, DC 20009, ☎328-0955.

Marsha Mateyka
2010 R Street NW, Washington, DC 20009 , ☎328-0088.

Pensler Galleries
2029 Q Street NW, Washington, DC 20009, ☎328-9190.

Robert Brown Gallery Dupont Circle
2030 R Street NW, Washington, DC 20009, ☎483-4383.

Studio Design Inc.
1508 19th Street NW, Washington, DC 20036, ☎667-6133.

Studio Gallery
2108 R Street NW, Washington, DC 20008, ☎232-8734.

The Tartt Gallery
2017 Q Street NW, Washington, DC 20009, ☎332-5652.

Troyer Fitzpatrick Lassman
1710 Connecticut Avenue NW, Washington, DC 20009, ☎328-7189.

Venable Neslage Galleries
1803 Connecticut Avenue NW, Washington, DC 20009, ☎462-1800.

Very Special Arts Gallery
1300 Connecticut Avenue NW, Washington, DC 20036, ☎628-0800 or1-800-933-8721, ≈737-0725.

Washington Printmakers Gallery
2106-1/2 R Street NW, Washington, DC 20008, ☎332-7757.

Elizabeth Guarisco Gallery
2828 Pennsylvania Avenue NW, Washington, DC 20007, ☎333-8533, ≈625-0834 (Georgetown).

Shopping

The Dunham Gallery
3075 Canal Towpath NW, Washington, DC 20007, ☎337-7860 (Georgetown).

Classic Design Galleries
1214 31st Street NW, Washington, DC 20007, ☎342-2116 (Georgetown).

THE MAIN SHOPPING CENTRES

The Connecticut Connection *(1101 Connecticut Ave. NW #802, Washington, DC 20036, Farragut North metro, ☎833-9415, ≈833-9420)* is a shopping complex located in the very heart of Washington.

Who would have thought you could find a host of different shops at the Pentagon? This is indeed the case, as the place boasts a large shopping centre, the **Fashion Center at Pentagon City** *(1100 South Hayes St., #M100, Arlington, VA 22202, Pentagon City metro, ☎703-415-2400, ≈703-415-2175)*. The complex houses more than 160 shops, including big-name retail stores like Macy's, a Disney shop, restaurants and a multiplex cinema.

Georgetown boasts a brand-new shopping centre whose architecture is a real acievement. It is **Georgetown Park** *(3222 M St., NW, #140, Washington, DC 20007, ☎342-8190, ≈342-1458)*, a magnificent four-story block that has managed to preserve some of its Victorian architecture. The place boasts hundreds of enterprises, including restaurants, the wonderful FAO Schwarz toy store, perfume shops and a Dean & Deluca outlet, among others.

The **Mazza Gallerie** *(5300 Wisconsin Ave. NW, Washington, DC 20015, Friendship Heights metro, ☎966-6114, ≈362-0471)* is a shopping centre with close to 50 shops, on the border of the federal District of Columbia, near Bethesda.

Located in the same area, the **Montgomery Mall** *(7101 Democracy Blvd., Bethesda, MD 20817, Bethesda metro, ☎301-469-6000, ≈301-469-7612)* is a large shopping centre housing close to 200 shops, a multiplex and restaurants.

The **White Flint Mall** *(11301 Rockville Pike, North Bethesda, MD 20895-1021, White Flint metro, ☎301-468-5777, ≈301-984-3509)* harbours many young clothing designer's boutiques. There is a free shuttle service between the subway station and the mall.

As its name indicates, **The Old Post Office Pavilion** shopping centre *(1100 Pennsylvania Ave. NW, Washington, DC 20004, Federal Triangle metro, ☎289-4224, ≈898-0653)* is set up in the former post office pavilion, in the heart of downtown Washington. Numerous small stands where merchants and artists sell their wares, as well as restaurants and shops of all kinds can be found here. Be sure to climb to the top of the former post office's tower, whence you can take in the magnificent view over downtown Washington.

The **Shop at National Place** *(529 14th St. NW, Washington, DC 20045, Metro Center metro, ☎783-9090, ≈737-2379)* is a three-floor shopping centre. The place contains about one hundred shops and restaurants, and is directly linked to the JW Marriott Hotel (see p 243).

Over the last few years, the **Union Station** *(40 Massachusetts Ave. NE, Washington, DC 20002, Union Station metro, ☎289-1908, ≈289-6263)* train station has undergone a major facelift. A beautiful shopping centre has been set up inside this Beaux-Arts-style building, to the delight of both travellers and local residents. The centre boasts 125 shops and restaurants as well as a nine-cinema multiplex.

TRAVEL ACCESSORIES

If you wish to purchase travel goods such as bags, suitcases, voltage adaptors, etc, you can do so at **Lane's Luggage** *(1146 Connecticut Ave. NW, Washington, DC 20036, ☎452-1146 or 1-800-249-8456)*, a good shop located on one of the city's most prestigious avenues.

Located on the second floor of the Georgetown Park shopping centre (see p 306), the **Voyageur Travel with Style** *(3222 M St. NW, Washington, DC 20007, ☎342-5488)* shop carries a fine selection of *Samsonite* travel bags and suitcases as well as a host of other American big brand-name luggage. European travellers can also pick up adaptors and converters here. The shop also has a small section catering to backpackers. You should have no problem finding virtually everything you need to travel in style.

Washington also boasts two **The Complement** shops, where various travel goods are sold. One is located at 1016 20th Street NW (☎331-1200), and the other at 17th Street and I Street NW (☎785-9111).

BOOKSHOPS

Located in the Dupont Circle district, **Barnes & Noble Booksellers** (3040 M St. NW, Washington, DC, ☎965-9880) carries a very good selection of general books.

The **Politics and Prose Bookstore-Coffee House** (5015 Connecticut Ave. NW, Washington, DC 20008, ☎364-1919, ≈966-7532) may satisfy politics booklovers.

As its name indicates, **Cheshire Cat Children's Book Store** (5512 Connecticut Ave. NW, Washington, DC, ☎244-3956, ≈244-1860) specializes children's books and has an excellent selection of them.

Stopping by a bookshop that doubles as a café is always a pleasant experience. **Kramerbooks and Afterwords Café** (1517 Connecticut Ave. NW, Washington, DC 20036, ☎387-1462, ≈232-6777) is one of these and offers customers coffee while they shop for the latest best-selling novels.

Lambda Rising (1625 Connecticut Ave. NW, Washington, DC 20009-1013, ☎462-6969) caters to the gay and lesbian community, offering a very good selection of works relating to homosexuality. You can also pick up all the gay-oriented papers published in the capital here.

Backstage, The Theater Book Store (2101 P St. NW, Washington, DC, ☎775-1488) is sure to please those who enjoy reading film scripts and plays.

If you're looking for road maps, head to **The Map Store** (1636 Eye St. NW, Washington, DC 20006, Farragut Square *metro, ☎628-2608 or 1-800-544-2659, ≈628-2610)*, which clearly specializes in such wares. The place also stocks a few travel guides.

The **International Language Center** *(1753 Connecticut Ave. NW, Washington, DC, ☎332-2894)* is a special bookshop that offers a good choice of foreign-language books and newspapers (other than English).

Businesspeople and computer buffs should find everything they are looking for at the **Computer Literacy Bookshop** *(Vienna, Tysons Corner, VA, ☎1-800-258-9390, ≈703-734-7773)*. Though not located in Washington itself, this bookshop is surely the best of its kind near the capital.

Travel Books and Language Center *(4437 Wisconsin Ave. NW, Washington, DC 20016, ☎202-237-1322, ≈202-237-6022)* is the best travel bookshop in Washington and perhaps even one of the best in the United States, offering an incredible choice of guidebooks, maps and all levels of language-learning material.

CLOTHING STORES

Washington boasts one of the highly reputed **Burberry's** clothing stores *(1155 Connecticut Ave. NW, Washington, DC 20036, ☎463-3000, ≈293-3763)*, which offers chic and classic clothing.

The Chanel house of haute couture has a shop in Washington, the **Chanel Boutique at the Willard Collection** *(1455 Pennsylvania Ave. NW, Washington, DC 20004, ☎638-5055, ≈638-1652)*, a lovely establishment where fans of haute couture will find the latest collections from the celebrated Parisian fashion house.

Lerner New York has four outlets in the Washington area. One boutique is housed at the **Montgomery Mall** *(Bethesda, MD, ☎301-469-7118)*, another at **Tysons Corner Center** *(McLean, VA, ☎703-893-9887)*, a third at the **Landmark Center** *(Alexandria, VA, ☎703-256-4640)* and a fourth at the **Ballston Commons** *(Arlington, VA, ☎703-527-4429)*.

Shopping

Children's Stores

For comic strips, toys and everything for children's delight, head to **Another Universe** *(3060 M St. NW, Washington, DC 20007, ☎333-8651)*. A great place for those looking for that special gift.

Return to your childhood and let yourself be enchanted by the treasures galore at **FAO Schwarz** *(3222 M St. NW, Washington, DC, ☎965-7000)*. Young and old alike will appreciate the incredible variety of stuffed animals, educational games and gadgets offered here. The window displays, for their part, are often magical.

You will find scores of very original limited-edition wares at **Planet Hollywood** and **Warner Bros.** *(1101 Pennsylvania Ave. NW, Washington, DC 20004, Federal Triangle metro, ☎783-7827 or 783-0582, ≈347-1552)*. In addition to the endless variety of official Warner Bros. film-studio T-shirts featuring major cartoon characters such as Bugs Bunny and the Road Runner, these shops stock sweaters, watches, sunglasses and so much more. A real treasure trove for star-struck kids of all ages!

The shop **Bashi Bazouks** *(1627 Connecticut Ave. NW, Washington, DC 20009, Dupont Circle metro, ☎518-4000, ≈518-2303)* boasts a host of items imported from Brussels bearing the effigy of characters from the Tintin comic strip. Statuettes, china, T-shirts, watches and neckties for fans of Tintin, Snowy, Captain Haddock, Professor Calculus and detectives Thomson and Thompson.

PHOTO EQUIPMENT

If you're in need of a photographer's professional services, whether for I.D.-card photos or simply to have rolls of film developed, check out **DeKun Photoservices** *(3708 Macomb St. NW, Washington, DC 20016, ☎966-3220)*, located near the National Cathedral.

Purchasing photographic equipment in the United States can sometimes be a bargain for European travellers, provided, of course, they take the time to shop around and compare prices in Washington. The **Embassy Camera Center** *(1735 Connecticut Ave. NW, Washington, DC, Dupont Circle metro, ☎483-7448)* may interest them with an assortment of several big brand-name items such as Pentax, Nikon and Canon.

You will find a few good brands of cameras at **Roncom** *(1451 L St. NW, Washington, DC, ☎722-8317)*, a pleasant place where you can also get your rolls of film developed. Of note, for that matter, is that the cost of developing film is lower in the United States than it is in Europe.

Penn Camera boasts two outlets in Washington. One is located at 1015 18th Street, between K Street and L Street *(☎785-7366)*, and the other at 915 E Street NW, Metro Center subway station *(☎347-5777)*. Both shops carry the major brand-name cameras as well as bags, lenses, filters and various practical accessories for photographers.

To have your rolls of film developed with the utmost speed, you can entrust your memories to **Woodley 1 Hour Photo** *(2627 Connecticut Ave. NW, Woodley Park-Zoo metro, ☎265-0223)*, which, as its name indicates, will rush to process them in an hour's time. Though this kind of service is fast and convenient, the prints provided are not of the highest quality!

MUSIC

The **HMV Record Stores** *(1229 Wisconsin Ave. NW, Washington, DC 20007, ☎333-9292)* are known to offer the widest selection of CDs, in a great variety of musical styles and at the best prices. You are sure to find whatever you're looking for at this Georgetown branch, or order that rare recording you simply cannot find anywhere in town.

Located barely 5 minutes from the Dupont Circle subway station, the **Melody Record Shop** *(1623 Connecticut Ave. NW, between K and R Streets, Washington, DC, ☎232-4002)* carries a good selection of CDs of various musicals styles, including rock, jazz, classical music and reggae, as well as Latin American recordings.

312 Shopping

Closer to the downtown area, the **Sam K Record Shop** *(1839 7th St. NW, Washington, DC, ☎234-6540)* also boasts a fine selection of CDs of all kinds.

FLORISTS

Say it with flowers! And do so by heading to **Caruso Florists** *(1717 M St. NW, Washington, DC, ☎223-3816)*, located near Connecticut Avenue.

A lovely shop in Georgetown, **Dove Florist** *(2300 Wisconsin Ave. NW, Washington, DC, ☎333-3366)* also boasts interesting flower arrangements.

Georgetown Parkside Florist *(2611 P St. NW, Washington, DC, ☎342-9402)* offers a great selection of cut flowers and house plants, as well.

Whether you wish to buy lovely flower arrangements or have a bouquet of your favourite flowers delivered outside the city, **Allan Woods Flowers & Gifts** *(2645 Connecticut Ave. NW, Washington, DC, ☎332-3334)*, a small florist located near the National Zoological Park and Rock Creek Park, is a good choice.

Arlington Florist *(6035-A Wilson Blvd., Arlington, VA, ☎703-534-7210)* is conveniently located for those who wish to pick up a spray or a bouquet of flowers to lay on the grave of a loved one buried at Arlington National Cemetery.

WINE AND SPIRITS

For Europeans used to finding wine and spirits in any large food store, it is sometimes surprising to discover that this is not the case in North America. We have thus listed a few places that may prove of interest to amateur wine conoisseurs:

Addy Bassin's MacArthur Beverages *(4877 MacArthur Blvd. NW, Washington, DC, ☎338-1433)*;

Cairo *(at 17th St. and Corcoran St. NW, Washington, DC, ☎387-1500)*;

Wine and Spirits 313

Burka's *(3500 Wisconsin Ave., at Idaho St. NW, Washington, DC, ☎966-7676)*;

Martin's Wine & Spirits *(1919 Florida Ave. NW, opposite the Hilton Hotel, Washington, DC 20009, ☎986-1700)*.

CANDY AND CHOCOLATES

Chocolate lovers will be in seventh heaven at **Chocolate Chocolate** *(1050 Connecticut Ave. NW, Washington, DC, ☎466-2190)*, which clearly specializes in such decadent treats.

Fans of Belgian pralines, which are not as sweet as and contain more cocoa than North American chocolate, will be licking their chops after visiting **Prestige Belgian Chocolate** *(5345 Wisconsin Ave. NW, Washington, DC, ☎364-5353)*.

The **Godiva Chocolatier** outlets have long since acquired a solid reputation in the North American chocolate-shop business with their great selection of fine chocolates. Washington boasts two of these shops, one at 3222 M St. NW, Washington, DC, ☎342-2232, and the other at the Union Station shopping centre *(Union Station NW, Washington, DC, ☎289-3662)*.

Now here's place that will make children green with envy and dentists rejoice! **La Bonbonnière** *(1724 H St. NW, Washington, DC, ☎333-6425)* offers a dazzling variety of sweets in every colour of the rainbow.

JEWELLERY

Is Cartier's really still in need of an introduction? This famous Parisian jeweller's, synonymous with luxury and good taste, is, of course, known throughout the world for the beauty and quality of its creations. Devotees will find a **Cartier** outlet in Washington *(5468 Wisconsin Ave., Chevy Chase, ☎301-654-5858)*, where rings, jewels, bracelets and other gem-encrusted jewellery go for a fortune, to say the least.

As the song goes, *Diamonds are a girl's best friend*… To this, Marilyn Monroe added, not without mischief, "*The French are glad to die for Love... but I prefer a man who lives and gives... expensive Jewels!"* If the romantic lover in you fully subscribes to this dictum, which is not altogether devoid of common sense, **C de Carat** *(1127 Connecticut Ave. NW, in the Mayflower Hotel, Washington, DC, ☎887-5888)* is sure to have something for your great generosity, which will certainly delight your beloved.

J & A Jewelers *(Union Station, 50 Massachusetts Ave. NW, Washington, DC, ☎289-8880)* also offers, though at more affordable prices, beautiful jewellery to highlight that special occasion.

If you're looking for vintage creations, head to **Justine Mehlman Antiques** *(2824 Pennsylvania Ave. NW, Georgetown, ☎337-0613)*.

Located in Georgetown, **Solovey** *(3222 M St. NW, Georgetown Park, ☎333-1188)* offers a variety of interesting gold, silver and platinum jewellery.

Low-priced imitation classic jewellery and original designs can be purchased at **Impostors** *(Union Station, Washington, DC, ☎842-4462)*, a jeweller's located in Union Station shopping centre. They have another location in Washington *(3270 M St. NW, Washington, DC, Tel. 625-2363)*.

SPORTING GOODS

Shoes, walking boots, tennis and squash racquets as well as a variety of other sporting goods are available at **Racquet & Jog** *(915 19th St. NW, Washington, DC, ☎861-6939)*.

A shop specializing in general sporting goods, **Sports Zone** *(1501 K St. NW, Washington, DC, ☎371-8810)* offers quality garments and all kinds of accessories for both budding sports buffs and the finest athletes.

A delightful shop located in the heart of Georgetown, **Patagonia** *(1048 Wisconsin Ave. NW, Washington, DC, ☎333-1776)* is one of the best of its kind, boasting a host of items such as hiking boots, tents, sleeping bags and warm fleece garments for lovers of the great outdoors.

Whether you are a die-hard downhill skiing fan or prefer long cross-country skiing treks, the **Ski Center** *(at Massachusetts Ave. and 49th St. NW, Washington, DC, ☎966-4474)* should provide you with the necessary equipment for your winter outings as well as the latest fashionable ski-suits.

INDEX

Accommodations	235
Adams Inn	245
Adams Morgan	244
Best Western Downtown Capitol Hill	240
Best Western New Hampshire Suites	247
Brenton	246
Capital Hilton	243
Capitol Hill Area	238
Capitol Hill Guest House	239
Carlton	243
Connecticut-Woodley Guest House	253
Crowne Plaza Washington DC	241
Days Inn Premier Convention Center Hotel	241
Days Inn Uptown on Connecticut Avenue	254
Doubletree Guest Suites	251
Doubletree Hotel Park Terrace	247
Downtown	239
Dupont Circle	244
Dupont Plaza Hotel	249
Embassy Inn	245
Embassy Row	253
Embassy Row Hilton Hotel	249
Embassy Square, A Summerfield Suites Hotel	248
Embassy Suites Hotel Downtown	249
Foggy Bottom	250
Four Seasons Hotel	255
George Washington University Housing	250
George Washington University Inn	250
Georgetown	254
Georgetown Dutch Inn	255
Governor's House Hotel	247
Grand Hyatt Washington	241
Hampshire Hotel	247
Hay-Adams Hotel	243
Holiday Inn Central Washington, DC	246
Hotel Harrington	240
Hotel Washington	242
Howard Johnson	251
JW Marriott Hotel	243
Kalorama	253
Kalorama Guest House	254

Index 317

Accomodations (Cont'd)
  Loews L'Enfant Plaza Hotel 239
  Madison Hotel 241
  Near the White House 242
  One Washington Circle 251
  Quality Hotel Downtown 247
  Red Roof Inn 240
  Renaissance Mayflower Hotel 249
  Sheraton City Center 252
  Sheraton Washington 254
  St. James Suites 252
  Travelodge Hotel 246
  Washington International AYH-Hostel 240
  Washington International Student Center 244
  Washington Marriott 248
  Watergate Hotel 253
  Westin Washington, D.C. City Center Hotel 242
  Willard Inter-Continental Washington 244
  Windsor Inn 245
Airports
  Baltimore-Washington International Airport 65
  Washington National Airport 64
Alexandria 218
American National Red Cross (Around the White House) 136
Anacostia Museum (Banks of the Anacostia River) 192
Antoine-Louis Barye (Around the White House) 135
Architecture 54
Arlington House (Arlington) 194
Arlington Memorial Bridge (Arlington) 194
Arlington National Cemetery (Arlington) 194
Arthur M. Sackler Gallery (The Mall) 150
Arts and Industries Building (The Mall) 147
Baltimore-Washington International Airport 65
Bank of Alexandria (Alexandria) 220
Banks 77
Bars and Nightclubs
  B. Smith's 296
  Bachelor's Mill 301
  Badlands-Annex 299
  Bardo Rodeo 298
  Billy Martin's Tavern 298
  Blues Alley 296
  Buttlers, The Cigar Bar 298

318 Index

Bars and Nightclubs (Cont'd)
- Café Lautrec 296
- Capitol City Brewing Co. 298
- Childe Harold's Step Childe 292
- Circle Tavern, Terrace, and Underground 299
- Cities 293, 296
- City Blues 297
- Club Zei 293
- Cobalt 300
- Coco Loco 293
- DC Eagle 301
- Deja Vu 294
- Delta Elite 301
- District Chophouse and Brewery 297, 299
- Dubliner Pub 297
- Dupont Windows 300
- Edge-Wet 301
- Escandalo 300
- Fanatic's 295
- Fireplace 300
- Georgia Brown's 296
- Grand Slam 295
- Hard Rock Café 299
- Heaven and Hell 294
- Hung Jury 301
- JR's 300
- Kinkead's 297
- Madame's Organ 296
- Mr. Smith's of Georgetown 297
- Murphy's 297
- Murphy's of Alexandria 297
- Omega DC 300
- Ozone Le Club Industriel 293
- Perry's 299
- Planet Fred 292
- Polly Esther's 293
- Remington's 301
- Ritz 293
- Rock Sports Bar and Restaurant 295
- Senators All American Sports Café 295
- Shelly's Back Room 298
- Sky Terrace Lounge 299
- Teams Sports Bar 295
- Tiki Bar 295

Index

Bars and Nightclubs (Cont'd)
- Tracks 2000 .... 294, 302
- Trumpets 300
- Vegas Lounge 296
- Winston's 294

Bartholdi Fountain (Capitol Hill) 101
Belmont House (Dupont Circle) 174
Biking 230
Blaine Mansion (Dupont Circle) 174
Bodisco House (Georgetown) 213
Boyhood Home of Robert E. Lee (Alexandria) 221
British Embassy (Embassy Row and Kalorama) 180
Bureau of Engraving and Printing (The Mall) 153
Bus 68
Business Hours 76
Byzantine Collection (Georgetown) 217
C&O Canal (Georgetown) 210
Cairo (Dupont Circle) 173
Canadian Embassy (Downtown) 116
Canoeing 233
Capital Children's Museum (Capitol Hill) 107
Capitol (Capitol Hill) 95
Captain's Row (Alexandria) 220
Car 68
Car Rentals 71
Carlyle House (Alexandria) 220
Castle (The Mall) 147
Central Library (Downtown) 123
Chesapeake & Ohio Canal Warehouses (Georgetown) . 210
Children 84
Chinatown Gateway (Downtown) 112
Christ Episcopal Church (Alexandria) 221
Christ Episcopal Church (Capitol Hill) 104
Church of the Epiphany (Downtown) 122
Climate 12, 80
Clothing 80
Colorado Building (Downtown) 121
Columbus Doors (Capitol Hill) 99
Congress 42
Congress Bells (Downtown) 118
Congressional Cemetary (Banks of the Anacostia River) . 191
Constitution Gardens (The Mall) 159
Constitution Hall and the DAR Museum (Around the White House) 136

Index

Consulates	60
Convent of the Visitation (Georgetown)	214
Corcoran Gallery of Art (Around the White House)	132
Courthouse of the District of Columbia (Downtown)	116
Cox Row (Georgetown)	213
Crestar Bank (Downtown)	122
Cruises	232
Crypt (Capitol Hill)	100
Cultural Life	51
Customs	59
Decatur House (Around the White House)	129
Department of Commerce (Downtown)	118
Department of State (Foggy Bottom)	185
Department of the Interior Museum (Foggy Bottom)	185
Department of the Treasury (Downtown)	118
Diplomatic Reception Rooms (Foggy Bottom)	185
District Building (Downtown)	120
Drugs	85
Dumbarton House (Georgetown)	218
Dumbarton Oaks (Georgetown)	216
Dupont Circle (Dupont Circle)	172
Duval Foundry (Georgetown)	210
East Building (The Mall)	164
Eastern Market (Capitol Hill)	103
Economy	49
Electricity	85
Embassies and Consulates	60
Embassy of Finland (Embassy Row and Kalorama)	181
Embassy of Haiti (Embassy Row and Kalorama)	178
Embassy of Pakistan (Embassy Row and Kalorama)	178
Embassy of the Republic of Cameroon (Embassy Row and Kalorama)	179
Emergencies	82
Entertainment	283
Bars and Nightclubs	292
Cinema	290
Circus	284
Classical Music	285
Comedy	289
Dance	285
Gay and Lesbian Scene	291, 299
Improv	289
Opera	285
Theatre	285

Index 321

Entrance Formalities 59
Exchanging Money 77
Exploring 89
  Tour A: Capitol Hill 92
  Tour B: Downtown 108
  Tour C: Around the White House 123
  Tour D: The Mall 139
  Tour E: Dupont Circle 169
  Tour F: Embassy Row and Kalorama 176
  Tour G: Foggy Bottom 181
  Tour H: The Banks of the Anacostia River 186
  Tour I: Arlington 193
  Tour J: Other Washington Attractions 201
  Tour K: Georgetown 206
  Tour L: The Outskirts of Washington 218
Faces of Honour (The Mall) 158
Federal Triangle (Downtown) 116
Folger Building and Playhouse Theater (Downtown) ... 122
Folger Shakespeare Library (Capitol Hill) 102
Ford's Theater (Downtown) 113
Fort Lesley J. McNair (Banks of the Anacostia River) ... 189
Foxal House (Georgetown) 212
Franklin Delano Roosevelt Memorial (The Mall) 156
Frederick Douglass National Historic Site (Banks of the
  Anacosti 191
Freedom Plaza (Downtown) 119
Freer Gallery of Art (The Mall) 151
Future Center (Capitol Hill) 107
Gadsby Tavern Museum (Alexandria) 221
Gentry Row (Alexandria) 220
Geography 10
George Washington Masonic National Memorial
  (Alexandria) 219, 222
Georgetown 206
Georgetown Park (Georgetown) 210
Golf 231
Grace Church (Georgetown) 210
Grant Memorial (Capitol Hill) 94
Great Hall (Capitol Hill) 102
Guided tours 63
Hall of Heroes (Arlington) 201
Handicapped Travellers 84
Health 81
Healy Building (Georgetown) 214

Index

Hiking	228
Hillwood Museum (Other Washington Attractions)	206
Hirshhorn Museum and Sculpture Garden (The Mall)	146
Historical Society of Washington DC (Dupont Circle)	172
History	13
Abolitionism and Civil War	25
Birth of the USA and Choice of a capital	17
Capital Becomes a City	23
Colonial Era	14
From One War to the Next	30
Off to War and Back Again	32
Towards American Hegemony	35
Holidays	76
Holy Trinity Parish Church (Georgetown)	214
Horseback Riding	230
Hotel Washington (Downtown)	121
Indonesian Embassy (Dupont Circle)	174
Insurance	80
Internal Revenue Service (Downtown)	118
Interstate Commerce Commission (Downtown)	118
Islamic Center (Embassy Row and Kalorama)	180
Iwo Jima Memorial (Arlington)	199
J. Edgar Hoover Building (Downtown)	114
James Garfield Memorial (Capitol Hill)	95
Jefferson Memorial (The Mall)	154
John F. Center for the Performing Arts (Foggy Bottom)	182
Judiciary Square (Downtown)	110
Justice Department (Downtown)	118
Kayaking	233
Kenilworth Aquatic Gardens (Other Washington Attractions)	202
Korean War Memorial (The Mall)	156
Lafayette Square (Around the White House)	129
Lair-Dunlop House (Georgetown)	212
Laundromats	85
Lee-Fendall House (Alexandria)	221
Library of Congress (Capitol Hill)	101
Lincoln Memorial (The Mall)	157
Lincoln Park (Capitol Hill)	104
Lock Keeper's House (Around the White House)	139
Lyceum (Alexandria)	221
L'Enfant Plaza (Banks of the Anacostia River)	189
Marina (Banks of the Anacostia River)	189

Index

Marine Commandant's House (Banks of the
  Anacostia River) 190
Marine Corps Museum (Banks of the Anacostia River) .. 190
Marine Corps War Memorial (Arlington) 199
Market Square (Alexandria) 220
Market Square (Downtown) 115
Measures 84
Miniature Golf 231
Money 76
Mount Vernon 223
Mount Vernon Square (Downtown) 123
Mount Zion United Methodist Church (Georgetown) ... 212
Movie Theatres 85
Museum of Natural History (The Mall) 161
Museums 85
Music Room (Georgetown) 217
National Air and Space Museum (The Mall) 144
National Aquarium (Downtown) 119
National Archives and Records Administration
  (Downtown) 117
National Bonsai and Penjing Museum (Other
  Washington Attractions 203
National Building Museum (Downtown) 110
National Gallery of Art (The Mall) 164
National Jewish Museum (Dupont Circle) 173
National Museum of African Art (The Mall) 150
National Museum of American History (The Mall) ... 159
National Museum of Women in the Arts (Downtown) .. 122
National Portrait Gallery and National Museum
  of American Art 112
National Postal Museum (Capitol Hill) 107
National Shrine of the Immaculate Conception
  (Other Washington Attractions) 203
National Statuary Hall (Capitol Hill) 100
National Zoological Park (Other Washington
  Attractions) 201
Navy Memorial (Downtown) 114
Navy Museum (Banks of the Anacostia River) 190
Navy Yard (Banks of the Anacostia River) 189
Navy Yard Entrance Gate (Banks of the
  Anacostia River) 189
Netherlands Carillon (Arlington) 200
Newseum (Arlington) 200
Oak Hill Cemetery (Georgetown) 217

324 Index

Octagon House (Around the White House) 131
Old Executive Office Building (Around the
  White House) 131
Old Houses (Georgetown) 212
Old North Hall (Georgetown) 214
Old Post Office Pavilion (Downtown) 118
Old Senate Chamber (Capitol Hill) 100
Old Stone House (Georgetown) 211
Old Supreme Court Chamber (Capitol Hill) 100
Organization of American States Building (Around the
  White House 138
Outdoor Activities 228
Outdoors 227
Outskirts of Washington 218
Parks 227
Passport 60
Peace Monument (Capitol Hill) 95
Pedal Boating 233
Pentagon (Arlington) 200
Pershing Park (Downtown) 120
Petersen House (Downtown) 113
Pharmacies 85
Philadelphia Row (Capitol Hill) 104
Phillips Collection (Dupont Circle) 175
Plane 64
Politics 40
  Citizens Who Don't Vote 48
  Congress 42
  Democracy in the Capital of the Democracy 46
  Making of a Law 44
  President 43
  Progress or Decay? 48
  Scissors, Paper, Rock 41
  Supreme Court 46
Pomander Walk (Georgetown) 215
Population 50
Portrait 9
Post Offices 78
Practical Information 59
  Weights and Measures 84
Pre-Columbian Museum (Georgetown) 217
President 43
Public Holidays 76
Public Transportation 74

Index

- Quadrangle (The Mall) 148
- Ramsay House Visitors Center (Alexandria) 219, 220
- Reflecting Pool (The Mall) 158
- Religion 86
- Renwick Gallery of the National Museum of American Art 130
- Restaurants 257
  - Adams Morgan 276
  - Alamo Grill 280
  - Anna Maria's 269
  - Annie's Paramount Steak House 272
  - Around the Cathedral 279
  - Around the White House 267
  - Art Gallery Grille 273
  - Au Bon Pain 262, 273
  - Bertolini's 264
  - Brasserie Les Halles 264
  - Bua Restaurant & Bar 269
  - Cactus Cantina 279
  - Café Deluxe 279
  - Café des Artistes 268
  - Café La Ruche 280
  - Café Lautrec 277
  - Café Luna 268
  - Café Promenade 266
  - Capitol City Brewing Company 265
  - Chez Nous 282
  - China Regency Restaurant 281
  - Citronelle 282
  - Coco Pazzo 265
  - Cup'a Cup'a Expresso Bar and Coffee 273
  - Downton and the Mall 262
  - Dupont Circle 268
  - Felix 276
  - Firehook 268
  - Firehook Bakery 267
  - Flight Line 263
  - Foggy Bottom 273
  - Foster Brothers Coffee 279
  - Franklyn's 276
  - Friday's 265
  - Georgetown 280
  - Gusti's 270
  - Harry's Restaurant and Saloon 262

Index

Restaurants (Cont'd)
- Hunan Chinatown 266
- Hunan Gallery 279
- Il Radicchio 270
- Isola Verde 277
- Java House 268
- Jin-Ga Restaurant 274
- John Harvard's Brew House 264
- Kalorama Cafe 277
- Kramerbooks Café & Grill 268
- La Baguette 273
- La Fourchette 278
- La Madeleine 280
- La Tomate 271
- Le Rivage 279
- Le Séquoia 281
- Little Fountain Café 277
- L'Aquarelle 275
- Manhattan Deli 262
- Maracas Bay Cafe 270
- Marrakech Restaurant 266
- Morton's of Chicago Steakhouse 274
- Mudd House 269
- Music City Roadhouse 280
- National Air and Space Museum Restaurants 263
- Perry's 278
- Peyote Café 276
- Pizzeria Uno Chicago Bar & Grill 265
- Planet Hollywood 265
- Porter's 267
- Prime Rib Restaurant 275
- Raku 272
- Red Sage 266
- Restaurant 701 267
- Ristorante Piccolo 281
- Roxane 276
- Samantha's 273
- Sign of the Whale 269
- Skewers 271
- Sol 272
- Star of Siam 273, 277
- Starbucks Coffee 268, 269
- Timothy's World Coffee 264
- Tout Va Bien 272

Index

Restaurants (Cont'd)
- Trio Restaurant 271
- Trumpets Restaurant & Lounge 271
- Vidalia 274
- Waterfront Riverside 279
- Wright Place 263

Restrooms 86
Riggs-Riley House (Georgetown) 212
Rotunda (Capitol Hill) 99
Rotunda (Downtown) 117
Safety 83
Sailing 234
Saint Mark's Episcopal Church (Capitol Hill) 103
Salon Doré (Around the White House) 134
Sewall-Belmont House (Capitol Hill) 105
Sheridan Circle (Embassy Row and Kalorama) 176
Shopping 82, 303
- Art Galleries in Dupont Circle and Georgetown .. 303
- Bookshops 308
- Candy and Chocolates 313
- Clothing Stores 309
- Florists 312
- Jewellery 313
- Main Shopping Centres 306
- Music 311
- Photo Equipment 310
- Sporting Goods 314
- Travel Accessories 307
- Wine and Spirits 312

Signers Memorial (The Mall) 159
Skating 231
Small Senate Rotunda (Capitol Hill) 100
Smith Row (Georgetown) 213
Smithsonian Institution 53
Smokers 83
Society of Cincinnati (Dupont Circle) 175
Spectator Sports 291
St. John's Church (Around the White House) 129
St. John's Episcopal Church (Georgetown) 213
St. Mary's Episcopal Church (Foggy Bottom) 185
Stained-glass Window from the Soissons Cathedral
  (Around the White House) 135
Subway 75
Superior Court of the District of Columbia (Downtown) . 116

Index

Supreme Court	46
Supreme Court (Capitol Hill)	104
Swimming	232
Taxes	82
Taxi	72
Telecommunications	78
Telephone	79
Temperance Fountain (Downtown)	115
Temperatures	13
Tennis	231
Textile Museum (Embassy Row and Kalorama)	180
Time Difference	75
Tipping	82
Tomb of George and Martha Washington (Mount Vernon)	225
Tourist Information	62
Train	67
Treasury Building (Around the White House)	127
Tudor Place (Georgetown)	215
Turkish Embassy (Embassy Row and Kalorama)	178
Union Station and Plaza (Capitol Hill)	106
United States Botanic Gardens (Capitol Hill)	101
United States Holocaust Memorial Museum (The Mall)	152
United States National Arboretum (Other Washington Attractions)	202
Vietnam Veterans Memorial (The Mall)	158
Vietnam Women's Memorial (The Mall)	158
Volta Bureau (Georgetown)	215
Washington Club (Dupont Circle)	173
Washington Harbour (Georgetown)	210
Washington Monument (The Mall)	156
Washington National Airport	64
Washington National Cathedral (Other Washington Attractions	)203
Washington, George	21
Water Sports	232
Watergate (Foggy Bottom)	185
Weights	84, 86
Weights and Measures	84
West Building (The Mall)	165
Westin Hotel (Georgetown)	209
Wharf Seafood Market (Banks of the Anacostia River)	189
White House (Around the White House)	124
White House Visitor Center (Around the White House)	128

Willard Hotel (Downtown)	121
Windsurfing	234
Woodrow Wilson House (Embassy Row and Kalorama)	179

OTHER ULYSSES GUIDES

EUROPE

Cycling in France
Cycling the picturesque back roads of France — everyone has dreamed of doing it, and now Ulysses makes it possible. Burgundy, the Loire Valley, the Vaucluse and other splendid regions are revealed thanks to numerous suggested tours. All of this is complemented by information on preparing your journey and the services available along the way.
Carole Saint-Laurent
212 pages, 20 maps
$22.95 CAN $16.95 US   £9.99
2-89464-008-0

French for Better Travel
Thousands of words and expressions to make your next trip *à la française* a success. Colour illustrations, phonetic pronunciation and two-way index help you get your message across.
192 pages, 6 double pages of colour illustrations
$9.95 CAN $6.95 US   £4.50
ISBN 2-89464-181-8

Lisbon
Once the departure point of explorers and now the guardian of a glorious past, Lisbon will host the century's last World Exposition in 1998. What better time to introduce the only complete practical guide for Lisbon. Besides cultural and practical details, the guide also covers the extension of the subway system, the new bridge over the Tage and the many restoration and renovation projects underway throughout the city.
Marc Rigole, Claude-Victor Langlois
272 pages, 15 maps
8 pages of colour photos
$18.95 CAN $13.95 US   £8.99
2-89464-155-9

Portugal, 2nd edition
A new edition of the most practical guide covering every region in Portugal. *Pousadas*, *quintas*, medieval chateaux, museums, festivals, Algarve beaches... it's all in there! The riches of Porto are also revealed as is Lisbon, host-city of the 1998 World Exposition.
Marc Rigole, Claude-Victor Langlois
384 pages, 32 maps
8 pages of colour photos
$24.95 CAN $17.95 US   £12.99
2-89464-080-3

Provence-Côte d'Azur, 2nd edition
Once again Ulysses offers both these magnificent French regions in one book. Monaco, Nice, Marseille and Avignon are just some of the legendary sites covered. Spend some time by the seaside, in the casinos or explore hillside villages on the Vaucluse plateau and in the Luberon.
Hans Jörg Mettler, Benoit Éthier, Howard Rombough
368 pages, 38 maps
8 pages of colour photos
$29.95 CAN $21.95 US   £14.99
2-89464-112-5

CANADA

Affordable B&B in Québec 98-99
Four types of accommodations are described to help discover the intimate side of Québec: rooms in private homes with breakfast included, small country inns, farm-stays, and country houses which can be rented for longer stays. All the information for making reservations is included.
300 pages, 19 maps
Fédération des Agricotours
14 pages of colour photos
$12.95 CAN $9.95 US   £6.50
2-89464-096-X

Atlantic Canada, 2nd edition
This second edition sees the province of Newfoundland and Labrador added to the those of New Brunswick, Nova Scotia and Prince Edward Island. Picturesque fishing villages, the famous Cabot Trail, national parks, beaches and, of course, the brand new Confederation Bridge linking Prince Edward Island to the mainland, it's all in there!
Benoit Prieur
304 pages, 25 maps
8 pages of colour photos
$24.95 CAN $17.95 US   £12.99
2-89464-113-3

Calgary
Set between the Rocky Mountains and vast ranchlands and prairies, Calgary is one of the fastest growing cities in North America. This Ulysses Guide reveals the best of this dynamic Western city: museums, parks, gardens, Olympic installations and of course the famous Stampede, the "greatest show on earth"!
Jennifer McMorran
192 pages, 12 maps
$17.95 CAN $12.95 US   £8.99
2-89464-168-0

Canada
Finally a Ulysses Guide on this vast country. Every province and territory, right up to the Arctic Circle and beyond, has been covered with a fine-tooth comb in order to produce the most complete travel guide. The major cities like Vancouver, Toronto and Montreal, the smallest hamlets, exhilarating outdoor adventures from sea to sea!
Collective
544 pages, 100 maps   8 pages of colour photos
$29.95 CAN $21.95 US   £14.99
2-89464-159-12

Hiking in Québec, 2nd edition
The only hiking guide devoted exclusively to all regions of Québec! This guide presents descriptions of close to 100 hikes in every corner of Québec, classified according to their level of difficulty. Tables with distances and altitude changes for each hike are also included.
Yves Séguin
270 pages, 15 maps
$22.95 CAN $16.95 US   £11.50
2-89464-013-7

Montréal
Revised every year, this guide reveals more than 300 sights in this Québec metropolis along 20 walking, bicycling and driving tours. There are detailed maps for each tour, plans of the galleries of the Museum of Fine Arts and maps of the underground city. Hundreds of practical addresses for every budget.
François Rémillard et al.
416 pages, 26 maps
8 pages of colour photos
$19.95 CAN $14.95 US   £9.99
2-89464-111-7

Ontario, 2nd edition
This guide covers Canada's richest and most populous province thoroughly, with sections on Niagara Falls, the Thousand Islands, Ottawa, Toronto, and even Northern Ontario.
Pascale Couture
336 pages, 26 maps
$24.95 CAN $14.95 US   £11.50
2-89464-011-0

Ontario & Québec with Via
Travel the rails between Canada's two most populous provinces. Tour exciting and fascinating cities like Montréal, Québec City, Toronto and Ottawa and take a break in peaceful hamlets throughout the province. This guide is the perfect complement to your next train journey.
Collective
128 pages, 10 maps
$9.95 CAN $7.95 US   £5.99
2-89464-158-3

Ottawa
Here is the first complete practical and cultural guide on the Canadian capital. Visitors will be lead through the city's fine museums and across Parliament Hill, shown to the best tables and given the inside track on the festivals that liven the streets in the summer and the Rideau Canal in the winter.
Pascale Couture
192 pages, 12 maps
$17.95 CAN $12.95 US   £8.99
2-89464-170-2

Toronto
Discover another side of Canada's biggest metropolis, from the hustle of downtown Yonge Street to the picturesque shores of Lake Ontario, to the shops and theatres. Walking tours through its multicultural neighbourhoods and city streets; restaurants and bars for all tastes and budgets.
Jennifer McMorran, Alain Rondeau
260 pages, 16 maps
$18.95 CAN $13.95 US   £9.99
2-89464-015-3

Québec, 2nd edition
The long-awaited 2nd edition of the Bible on *la belle province* is here! Still more sights and thousands of practical addresses for every region. Travellers will also find an augmented outdoor activities section, more maps, brilliant colour photos and illustrations.
François Rémillard et al.
608 pages, 85 maps
32 pages of colour photos
$29.95 CAN $21.95 US   £14.99
2-921444-78-X

Vancouver, 2nd edition
Completely updated, revised and augmented, this new edition reveals the best of this young and vibrant metropolis. Coverage of its multi-ethnic neighbourhoods, magnificent parks and great restaurants is joined by a rich cultural perspective. Practical addresses for every budget and taste.
Collective
200 pages, 15 maps
$17.95 CAN $12.95 US   £8.99
2-89464-120-6

Western Canada, 2nd edition
A new edition for the only travel guide to cover both Alberta and British Columbia. The mighty Rocky Mountains, superb skiing resorts, national and provincial parks: they're all in here! And so is the western metropolis of Vancouver, the burgeoning city of Calgary and Victoria, for a spot of tea!
Collective
464 pages, 51 maps
8 pages of colour photos
$29.95 CAN $21.95 US   £14.99
2-89464-086-2

ORDER FORM

ULYSSES TRAVEL GUIDES

☐ Affordable B&Bs in Québec	$12.95 CAN $9.95 US	☐ Lisbon	$18.95 CAN $13.95 US
☐ Atlantic Canada	$24.95 CAN $17.95 US	☐ Louisiana	$29.95 CAN $21.95 US
☐ Beaches of Maine	$12.95 CAN $9.95 US	☐ Martinique	$24.95 CAN $17.95 US
☐ Bahamas	$24.95 CAN $17.95 US	☐ Montréal	$19.95 CAN $14.95 US
☐ Belize	$16.95 CAN $12.95 US	☐ New Orleans	$17.95 CAN $12.95 US
☐ Calgary	$17.95 CAN $12.95 US	☐ New York City	$19.95 CAN $14.95 US
☐ Canada	$29.95 CAN $21.95 US	☐ Nicaragua	$24.95 CAN $16.95 US
☐ Chicago	$19.95 CAN $14.95 US	☐ Ontario	$24.95 CAN $14.95 US
☐ Chile	$27.95 CAN $17.95 US	☐ Ottawa	$17.95 CAN $12.95 US
☐ Costa Rica	$27.95 CAN $19.95 US	☐ Panamá	$24.95 CAN $16.95 US
☐ Cuba	$24.95 CAN $17.95 US	☐ Portugal	$24.95 CAN $16.95 US
☐ Dominican Republic	$24.95 CAN $17.95 US	☐ Provence - Côte d'Azur	$29.95 CAN $21.95 US
☐ Ecuador	$24.95 CAN $17.95 US	☐ Québec	$29.95 CAN $21.95 US
☐ El Salvador	$22.95 CAN $14.95 US	☐ Québec & Ontario with Via	$9.95 CAN $7.95 US
☐ Guadeloupe	$24.95 CAN $17.95 US	☐ Toronto	$18.95 CAN $13.95 US
☐ Guatemala	$24.95 CAN $17.95 US	☐ Vancouver	$17.95 CAN $12.95 US
☐ Honduras	$24.95 CAN $17.95 US	☐ Washington D.C.	$18.95 CAN $13.95 US
☐ Jamaica	$24.95 CAN $17.95 US	☐ Western Canada	$29.95 CAN $21.95 US

ULYSSES DUE SOUTH

☐ Acapulco	$14.95 CAN $9.95 US	☐ Cancun Cozumel	$17.95 CAN $12.95 US
☐ Belize	$16.95 CAN $12.95 US	☐ Puerto Vallarta	$14.95 CAN $9.95 US
☐ Cartagena (Colombia)	$12.95 CAN $9.95 US	☐ St. Martin and St. Barts	$16.95 CAN $12.95 US

ULYSSES TRAVEL JOURNAL

☐ Ulysses Travel Journal .... $9.95 CAN
(Blue, Red, Green, Yellow, Sextant) $7.95 US

ULYSSES GREEN ESCAPES

☐ Cycling in France $22.95 CAN ☐ Hiking in Québec $19.95 CAN
$16.95 US $13.95 US
☐ Hiking in the .. $19.95 CAN
Northeastern U.S. $13.95 US

TITLE	QUANTITY	PRICE	TOTAL

Name _____

Address _____

_____

_____

Payment : ☐ Money Order ☐ Visa ☐ MasterCard

Card Number _____

Signature _____

Sub-total	
Postage & Handling	$8.00*
Sub-total	
G.S.T. in Canada 7%	
TOTAL	

ULYSSES TRAVEL PUBLICATIONS
4176 St-Denis,
Montréal, Québec, H2W 2M5
(514) 843-9447 fax (514) 843-9448
www.ulysses.ca
*$15 for overseas orders

U.S. ORDERS: **GLOBE PEQUOT PRESS**
P.O. Box 833, 6 Business Park Road,
Old Saybrook, CT 06475-0833
1-800-243-0495 fax 1-800-820-2329
www.globe-pequot.com